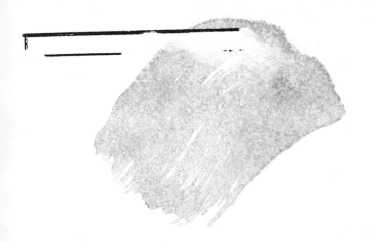

Counterpoint:

Debates about Debate

Arthur N. Kruger

Professor of Speech
C.W. Post College

The Scarecrow Press, Inc.
Metuchen, N. J.   1968

Books by Arthur N. Kruger

Modern Debate: Its Logic and Strategy

Championship Debating
I. 1949-1960
II. 1961-1966
(with Russel R. Windes)

A Classified Bibliography of Argumentation and Debate

Essentials of Logic
(with Peter T. Manicas)

Essential Logic Workbook
(with Peter T. Manicas)

Counterpoint: Debates about Debate

To my own debaters, in appreciation for
what they have taught me about debate

"...in the absence of debate, unrestricted
utterance leads to the degradation of opinion."

Walter Lippmann

Preface

As might be expected, many teachers of debate are fairly good debaters themselves. Not only have they debated social, political, and economic questions as undergraduates, but as teachers of debate they have debated the many issues inherent in the theory of debate, the teaching of debate, and the conduct of debate programs. As a party to many such debates, including one that is still in progress, I conceived the idea of this book--the idea that in teaching debate, just as in other areas, the truth has the best chance of emerging from a vigorous clash of opinion. As John Stuart Mill wrote, "There is always hope when people are forced to listen to both sides: it is when they attend only to one that errors harden into prejudices, and truth itself ceases to have the effect of truth, by being exaggerated into falsehood...." This, then, is the underlying premise of Counterpoint.

The book consists of eleven sections and contains debates on twenty-six issues, which cover most aspects of the theory, teaching, and practice of academic debate. Although a few issues overlap and some repetition occurs, the nature of the subject makes this unavoidable. On the whole the essays are written with spirit and conviction, which is not surprising since most of them are rejoiners to opposing views. Unfortunately, polemical writing is sometimes marred by a desire to vent a grudge, by an obstinate refusal to deal fairly with the other side, or by hasty composition. But such flaws are minor when weighed against the insights that emerge from a vigorous clash of opinion. As Aristotle put it, "The ability to raise searching difficulties on both sides of a subject will make us detect more easily the truth and error about the several points which arise."

Counterpoint is designed as a supplementary reader for argumentation and debate courses and as a reference book for all seri-

ous students of debate. As such, it is intended to provide a fruitful source of subjects for written reports, term papers, and classroom discussions. Since it is a book of controversies, perhaps it
will in turn generate a few and add even more zest to the teaching
of what is already a lively subject.

A. N. K.

Table of Contents

7

I. Aims and Values

Issue A: Is Academic Debate Contrary to the Principles of Sound
           Scholarship?

    Arguing affirmatively, Alzada Comstock, in her article
"The Cost of Debating," advances three reasons for her
position: (1) The subjects chosen for academic debate
require many years of study and hence are beyond the
capacity of college students. Since students dabble care-
lessly and confidently "in fields where diplomats and
bankers step warily," academic debating develops dilett-
antes and "mental toddlers." (2) College debaters dis-
tort and misapply evidence in order to win. (3) The
"code of debating" requires a refutation of every point
advanced by the other side.

    In rebuttal, William Norwood Brigance, in his article
"The Debate as Training for Citizenship," argues, from
examples and personal experience, that intercollegiate debaters "are perfectly capable of comprehending the questions they discuss"; that dishonest practices in the use of
evidence are self-defeating and thus not conducive to winning; that teachers can and usually do discourage dishonesty; and that no code of debating requires a refutation
of every point but rather a clash on the issues, which is
a different matter.

1. The Cost of Debating
Alzada Comstock

    The sport of intercollegiate debating is approaching football and
hockey in popularity. Teams from men's and women's colleges debate in their own triangular or hexagonal leagues; cross the lines of
the sexes and meet each other; and make transatlantic voyages for
Anglo-American matches.

    The conventional comments on this phenomenon of the educa-

tional world are of two types. Some of them are to the effect that
it is a fine thing to see an intellectual sport divide interest with the
great college games. According to the others it is encouraging to
find that the students are interested in such serious matters as the
nationalization of coal mines and the recognition of Russia.

One who has watched the development of intercollegiate debating through the last decade wonders whether it is in fact encouraging; whether, instead, it has not injured the spirit of inquiry and
the standards of scholarship in the colleges in which it has a strong
hold. These careless and confident dabblings in fields where diplomats and bankers step warily, are they, after all, so commendable?

The most obvious sin against that common sense which is the
foundation of intellectual achievement is committed in choosing the
subjects. When in the course of the educational process our American undergraduates are faced with unfamiliar scientific or philosophical questions, they show a commendable caution which European students of the same age could profitably emulate. But let a debate
appear on the horizon, and discretion is abandoned. Abandoned in
one direction only, to be sure, but that an important one; for economics, politics, and law make the playground in which they almost
invariably gambol.

The results are vastly amusing at first thought, but not at
second. For they are alert and thoughtful young men and women,
those who entertain us in this wise. They can write as good a son-
net as the best of us who listen, and comment as wisely upon the
effect of required work on the sophomoric mind. They would refuse
with an amused wariness to discuss the structure of the atom or the
theory of mutation if they had no background for it other than a few
courses in Latin and French. And yet under the debating system
which flourishes in our colleges they plunge, strangely blind to their
own inadequacy, into a group of subjects which require quite as
many years of familiarity as these. Unprotesting, we watch them
cast off their intellectual dignity and stumble, grotesque and foolish,
over the unfamiliar ground.

Behind these debaters lie unexplored fields of which they could
speak with authority and intelligence. The organization of the schools

through which they have passed and are passing; the habits of the
society in which they are the "younger generation"; the various
types of censorship, aesthetic and moral, to which they are subjected: to their arguments over these the rest of us would be forced
to listen respectfully, held by an intimacy of contact and often by a
suppleness of mind which we could not match.   Instead we have encouraged the building up of a system under which they toss about
malapropisms concerning international law and the economic life of
nations.

An old saying, which characterizes the mental equipment of
various types of humanity, has a most uncomplimentary description
of that one who "knows not, but knows not that he knows not." If
debating is producing an inability to distinguish that which one knows
from that of which one is ignorant, it is time for us in the colleges
to take thought as to whether it should keep its place in the world
of education.

If the first requisite of intellectual control is the ability to
distinguish the points on which one can speak with authority, the
second is honesty.   "I understand that my figures are distorted, but
I think the other side won't know it," is heard in some form or
other wherever preparations for intercollegiate debates are being
made.   These are the people who at this very moment should be
learning to scorn to alter a laboratory drawing or to misapply a
quotation in a history paper.   But the belief that fairness and judgment should be sacrificed to the matching and checking of points is
ingrained in the debating system.   How far the tendency spreads in
the academic world it is difficult to say.   Certainly it cannot fail
to have influenced the academic code of the debaters themselves.

A third offense against the spirit of scholarship which we are
striving to keep alive in our colleges lies in that code of debating
which apparently requires a complete and devastating refutation of
every point adduced by the opposing side.   Reason and fact are cast
to the winds.   One by one the items are ticked off the list, and the
ticker retires, flushed and victorious.

It is said to be the habit of youth to believe that all phenomena
are divided into black and white, sinful and pure, false and true.

But does our experience bear this out? Is it not the attitude of the
provincial and small-minded, whether in youth or age, and does not
educated youth veer away as naturally from the black-white code in
economic and political life as it does from dogma in religion and
the arts?

At any rate, if we are trying to develop the power to weigh
and balance evidence on one side and the other, to sift the chaff
from the wheat, to recognize both the faults and the excellencies of
a given piece of scientific or literary work, why have we allowed a
system to grow up which penalizes deliberate and reasoned argument?
The alternative would have been less easy but so much more satisfying! To sift the arguments for and against a resolution; to yield
the obvious, recognizing that for every step in progress some in-
jury is done; to sacrifice the lesser for the great; to hammer home
a main contention in the fervor of the belief that it transcends others
which run against it and others which support it--this is a true intellectual achievement. In its place we have chosen to encourage a
mechanical, monotonous, and undiscriminating formalism.

In the American women's colleges of the East an organization
has grown up which intensifies and perpetuates these defects. Bibliography committees keep the debaters from direct contact with the
field in which the subject lies and so from the opportunity to learn
methods of selection. Coaching committees freeze into stiff forms
the resulting fragments of fact and argument. Under this regime
selective power, flexibility of mind, and grace of diction are lost.
The product of the cramming system is strained and humorless and
her speeches are formless and unwieldy.

In these respects, at least, the debating system of our colleges is at odds with the otherwise improving traditions of American
undergraduate scholarship. When these intellectually elect among
the students can distinguish between the subjects in which they are
mental toddlers and those in which they stand in the company of
adults; when honesty and discrimination are allowed their place in
the handling of the material; and when the speakers are permitted
individuality of thought and flexibility of expression, debating will
perhaps assist the process of education rather than impede it.

Reprinted from Educational Review, 70:24-25, June, 1925. At the
time of writing, Alzada Comstock was an associate professor of
economics at Mount Holyoke College.

2. The Debate As Training for Citizenship
William N. Brigance

"I do not know the method of drawing an indictment against a
whole people, " once said that great statesman, Edmund Burke, but
Miss Comstock in her article upon "The Cost of Debating" in the
Educational Review seems to have discovered the method. With a
single gesture she indicted the whole system of intercollegiate debating and all who engage in it. Nowhere in the article can one
find a hint that debating, like wives or apple pies, might be of various kinds and so might be good or bad according to the kind. Instead she drew her indictment against the whole tribe of debaters,
adhering to the grand old philosophy that "the only good Indian is a
dead Indian. "

"It is said to be a habit of youth, " writes this author, "to believe that all phenomena are divided into black and white, sinful and
pure, false and true. " One is wont to wonder if it is "this habit of
youth" that leads her to indict all debating as black, sinful, and
false.

Now I do not defend intercollegiate debating in all of its forms
--some is good, some poor--but it is only fair to ask for a judicious discrimination between the good and the poor and for a further
inquiry as to whether all debating, good and poor, should be con-
demned to die.

There were three articles of indictment offered by Miss Comstock: first, that subjects chosen for debates were those in which
students were "mental toddlers"; second, that debaters resorted to
dishonest practices in order to win; and third, that the "code of debating apparently requires a complete and devastating refutation to
every point adduced by the opposing side, " which practice is an offense against the spirit of scholarship.

     At the risk of being guilty of this third indictment let us ex-
amine these contentions singly. As to the first--that the subjects
debated are those in which students are but "mental toddlers" and
therefore unable to comprehend fully--this is but a new version of
that age-old fault-finding with youth. I believe the opponents of the
younger Pitt once said that he should be spanked and sent back to
school, but their opposition did not prevent him from becoming
their master as prime minister of the British Empire when scarcely older than the average intercollegiate debater of today, nor from
maintaining control of that government for more than nine years.
We are supposed in college to be giving our youth an intellectual
background for citizenship, yet we are told that these earnest,
straight-thinking youths who come to us for this training should not
be allowed contact with the vital public questions of today. It was
of such an argument that Macaulay said it was "worthy of the fool
in the old story who resolved not to go into the water until he had
learned to swim. " Among the outstanding questions of the last few
years, declared to be above the mental grasp of our college youth,
are:

          The Allied Debts

          Japanese Immigration

          Child Labor

          Unemployment Insurance.

     All of these questions have been prominently before the public
eye. They are questions that every citizen should be informed upon
and about which every political quack in the country has passed
judgment upon in print. They are questions of which the fundamental principles are taught in every college in the land and which
all college students are supposed to be capable of understanding so
long as they sit in the lecture room armed with a notebook and pencil. Yet when the most brilliant of these same students (from which
debaters are universally chosen) essay to make a prolonged and intensive study of this same question with a view to holding a contest
with a friendly rival, they are, chameleon-like, declared to have
turned into "mental toddlers" unable to comprehend such a question.
Upon this same ground we might rule out the classroom theses and

term papers now required of their students by so many teachers of
economics, history, and politics. I deny the inference. My personal experience with intercollegiate debaters leads me to the conclusion that they are perfectly capable of comprehending the questions they discuss. Four years ago I trained a team debating the
question of the Allied Debts. The members of that team studied
that question from Bastable to Herbert Hoover, came to the independent conclusion--and planned their case upon this conclusion--
that although as a matter of precedent cancellation would be unwise,
yet in the case of certain Allied Powers, as Belgium, France, and
Italy, full payment with normal interest was absolutely impossible.
It was a view which no politician of that time had dared support.
Yet the recent funding of the Belgian debt recognized this very principle and in all probability the funding of the French debt will also
recognize it! Again, at the close of the Wabash-Notre Dame debate
last year upon the Wisconsin Plan of Unemployment Insurance, Dean
Thomas J. Konop of the Notre Dame College of Law, who served
as chairman, said, "I was a member of the Wisconsin state industrial commission when this bill was debated for the first time in the
Wisconsin legislature. I can truly say that for a thorough grasp of
the economic principles underlying unemployment insurance and for
a clear and forceful exposition of the case, nothing that I heard in
that legislature equalled what I have heard here tonight from these
college debaters." "Mental toddlers" indeed! These instances are
not offered as an encomium upon the college with which I happen to
be associated, for the fact that its debating teams have met with defeats as well as victories would indicate that the quality of its teams
is not far different from that of most others in the Middle West.

The second article of indictment against debating was that
"wherever preparations for intercollegiate debates are being made"
contestants resort to some form of dishonesty, such as distorting
figures, in order to win. Now of course we have the unsocial
among us always. Levying taxes incites people to falsify tax returns and prohibition produces its bootleggers, yet most of us adhere to the belief that it is best to retain tax levies and prohibition
in spite of these evils. To make a blanket charge of dishonesty

against all debaters, however, is simply and obviously a misstatement of fact. Personally, I have heard of such practices, but in my experience with debaters as a coach I have never heard such a thing even suggested, nor have I ever had reason to suspect such a thing from any opposing team, nor have I found it in any debate I ever judged--although in most such debates I have had the evidence of the case at my finger tips from my study of the same question with my own debaters and could have detected any important juggling of evidence. Aside from the moral deterrent to such practices there is also one of expediency. A debater, like a lawyer, who distorts figures or misquotes does so upon the supposition that his opponents know less of the case than he does. This is a dangerous supposition for there is no easier way in all the world for a team to lose a debate than to be caught distorting evidence, and a well informed opponent is not easily so imposed upon. I believe that honesty among the teachers who supervise this sport can almost entirely prevent such dishonest practices, for such a teacher, by his very attitude, invites or repels even the suggestion of such practices; and in my relations with my fellow teachers I have ever found them highly honorable. If our athletic teams can play the game according to rules, certainly our debaters, in this higher form of contest, also can.

We now come to the third article of indictment against debating. With anti-climactic grandeur we are told that the code of debating "requires a complete and devastating refutation of every point adduced by the opposing side." Verily "the mountain was in labor and brought forth a mouse." Let us assume, however, that the argument is invested with dignity. It is still ambiguous, for in the language of argumentation there is no such thing as a "point." The materials of proof are (1) issues, (2) argument, and (3) evidence. Patently this indictment did not mean that the code of debating required "complete and devastating" refutation of all argument and evidence produced by the other side. Such a statement would at the same time be ridiculous and self-evidently untrue for it would take far more time to refute each argument and piece of evidence than it would take to offer them in the first place. Obviously what was

meant was that the code of debating required refutation of every issue adduced by the other side.   Interpreted in this manner the statement is not an untruth but it is half of a truth.   Issues are the "ultimate irreducible, essential matters of fact or upon which the conclusion of the question hinges."   There are always, then, two sides
to any actual issue of debate, otherwise the question is not a debatable one.   To illustrate: on the question of the tariff one very
prominent issue of recent years has been, "Does the tariff aid the
farmer?"   The proponents of a high tariff answer "yes" and of a
low tariff, "no."   Each believes his answer the right one.   So with
the issues of contest debating.   An issue, by definition, has two
sides and to accuse debaters of trying to refute all issues of the opposing side is but another way of complimenting them upon their effort in debate.

But let us take the case to higher ground.   Debating in our
colleges and universities is a protest against our unbalanced curriculum.   Our youths in college for four years act as mental tankards
for knowledge.   By textbook and lecture we pour into them highly
concentrated extracts of facts, figures, and principles, hoping, too
often, that the process of fermentation will be delayed until after
graduation.   But the result often is not fermentation but stagnation.
Few indeed are the counterbalancing courses that stimulate our college students into using their knowledge, into creative thinking, into expressing ideas upon any subject.   Whenever there arises an
educator who leads his students into this neglected field, like Professor George Baker late of Harvard and now of Yale, the results
are both astonishing and enlightening.   Debating is one of the few
opportunities offered for that much needed creative thinking and for
that reason it attracts to its ranks students of the highest mental
caliber.   At Wabash College for years half of our Phi Beta Kappa
students have been debaters and part of the other half have been unsuccessful contestants for debating honors.

"By their fruits ye shall know them," it has been written, and
despite all critics the college debater has profited in afterlife by
his training.   Willis John Abbott, writing almost thirty years ago
in the Review of Reviews [August, 1896] pays this tribute to such

training: "In proportion to their attendance they [the small western colleges] seem to have produced a greater number of graduates intelligently interested in public affairs and able clearly and convincingly to express their views before an audience. . . . Oratorical contests awaken the enthusiasm which at some more famous eastern institutions of learning is aroused only by victory on the football field.   The debating society is an arena in which victory is more eagerly sought than on the athletic field. "

Unfortunately no complete record has been kept of the success generally of intercollegiate debaters throughout the country but only by individual institutions here and there. There is a record, however, of the winners of the famous Interstate Oratorical Contest-- which offers the same advantages of training and in which exist to the same degree the alleged evils of debating--and this record covering the years 1874 to 1902 reveals that there are now listed in Who's Who in America twenty of the fifty-eight winners of first and second place--over one third! They include one author, one governor, one bishop and two other clergymen, two United States senators, two United States representatives, three lawyers, and eight educators including five college presidents! A brilliant record indeed for men who, in their college days, had been injured by "careless and confident dabbling in fields where diplomats and bankers step warily"!

We are still a nation of speech makers and so long as we continue as a republic we shall in all probability remain one. We demand of our public citizens that they be effective speakers. Let us then not cast aside this valuable training for citizenship.

Reprinted from Educational Review, 72:222-225, Nov., 1926. At the time of writing, the author was a member of the department of public speaking at Wabash College, Indiana.

Issue B: Does Academic Debate Promote a Respect for the Truth?

In other words, does academic debate effectively train students to understand, develop, and value the truth-seeking process? In "The Academic Debate--Its Aim and Method," William Wetzel contends that it does not and raises the following issues:

(1) Does it state the problem in such a way as to find the truth?
(2) Does it put the student in the attitude of wanting to know the truth?
(3) Does it put him in a situation where he is most likely to find the truth?
(4) Does it give him the kind of moral training that would lead him to advocate the truth?

In his essay of the same title, Clarence S. Dike considers these issues from the opposite point of view.

3. The Academic Debate--Its Aim and Method
William A. Wetzel

This is a time when psychology and pedagogy are applying the acid test to many of our educational practices. One after another of our idols, which we have imagined to be pure gold, are discovered to be made of much baser metal. Some educators are becoming suspicious of the genuine worth of the debate as organized in academic circles. It is a fact that "an educated man should know not only that other people are in the wrong, but why they are in the wrong. And to do this it is necessary to study with all possible patience the brief of the devil's advocate."[1]

All this is equivalent to saying that the only effective answer to error is truth. The debate, therefore, must be judged from this point of view:

1. Does it state the problem in such a way as to find the truth?

2. Does it put the student in the attitude of wanting to

know the truth?

3. Does it put him in a situation where he is most likely to find the truth?
4. Does it give him the kind of moral training that
   would lead him to advocate the truth?

The state of New Jersey has recently required of all its high
schools that they offer a course in "Problems in Democracy." It
must be that the educational leaders of the state have come to see
the importance of giving our secondary school pupils training in the
art of thinking straight on public questions. This is just the kind
of training that the academic debate was supposed to give.

Sound thinking presupposes a problem. The debate falls down
in its effort to state a problem. It frequently confines mental activity as narrowly as the question put to the innocent witness, "Have
you ceased beating your wife?" The statement of the question is
frequently such as to lead to disputatious hair-splitting without advancing the truth. It leads to trying to unhorse one's opponent without riding one's own steed. The debate offers only one solution to
any question. The negative needs simply to prove the impracticability of the affirmative side of the question. To do this it may offer
a counter proposition, but it need not do so. Is there not a better
way to state a civic problem for the purpose of a debate?

The immigration problem is before the American people today.
The question is debated in Congress, but not in the usual academic
fashion. The debater has first bounded his problem. Then he has
thought out the solution to the problem, and finally, he has come
before his fellow congressmen to persuade them to apply his remedy.
The question, "Resolved, that immigration should be prohibited for
the next two years," has recently been submitted for debate in academic circles. This is too narrow a statement for a fair-minded
and thorough study of the problem. The first question is: Is any
kind of action necessary, and if so, why? If action shall be taken,
shall it take the form of admitting no one for a period of time, or
shall it take the form of selected immigration, prohibiting indefinite-
ly certain undesirables? If the remedy shall take the form of prohibiting all immigration for a time, how long shall the prohibition

continue? In other words, the finding of the best remedy necessarily implies a consideration of the whole problem. And it implies
the consideration of the whole problem by every one who attempts
to draw the final conclusion. The partition of the problem among
debaters, as usually found, is most artificial and corresponds to no
real situation in life. It seems, therefore, that the debate is not
adapted to stating a question in such a way as to bring out the
truth.

Secondly, does the academic debate put the student in the attitude of wanting to know the truth? The quality of open-mindedness
is none too common in society at large. We are guided too much
by our prejudices. We hang the man first, then try him. The experience of the writer is that high school seniors show a strong in-
clination toward coming to conclusions too soon. What is the effect
of assigning a student on one side or the other of a debate? He is
no longer a student, he instantly becomes an advocate, a partisan.
He goes to the library, not to learn something, but to prove something. The difference is the difference between the poles--and it is
this difference that gives character to the whole exercise. It becomes a contest, and more and more the elements of the football
game, cheering section and school songs and the like, are introduced. The success of the "contest" is gauged by the amount of
"school spirit" that it engendered. There is little of the spirit of
open-mindedness in this exercise. Therefore, the conclusion must
be that the academic debate does not put the student in the attitude
of wanting to know the truth.

In the third place, does the academic debate put the student in
a situation where he is most likely to learn the truth? This question is already answered in the second. His investigation is like an
ex parte hearing. It brings out only one side. And the performance at the final contest is frequently laughable. At times there is
neither co-ordination nor conflict of ideas until the rebuttal. It re-
sembles a football contest, in which the two teams run through their
signals during the bigger part of the game, and the captains meet
in personal combat at the end. The essence of any plan is that it
produce what it is designed to produce. Preparation for an academ-

ic debate means to gather evidence to prove one's side. Therefore,
the debate does not naturally place the student in a situation where
he is most likely to learn the truth.

Finally, does the academic debate give the student the kind of
moral training that would lead him to advocate the truth? Under
what circumstances is a man the more likely to become skilled in
finding the truth, and desirous of expounding the truth? Is it when
he is trained first to define the problem which he considers vital,
then search out the significant facts, and from these facts without
fear or prejudice draw his conclusions; or when he arbitrarily assumes a position and then searches out such facts only as substantiate this position? One could almost say that the strength of the
student's moral training would vary in inverse ratio with his skill
in this latter respect.

The final conclusion, therefore, is, that the academic debate
does not give the student exercise in the kind of moral training that
would lead him to advocate the truth. The whole argument of this
paper is based on the assumption that the debate is an educational
exercise, designed not simply to make fluent speakers or disputatious advocates, but that it is designed to furnish a legitimate and
much needed training in citizenship. Therefore, the kind of debate
that should be encouraged in our schools is the kind typified by the
Lincoln-Douglas debates, or the Webster-Hayne debates. It would
still be possible to have interscholastic debates. But it would be
necessary to score each debater independently for the thoroughness
of his study, the logic of his conclusions, and the clarity of his exposition. In such a debate there might be as many conclusions
drawn as there are contestants. But each contestant would arrive
at his conclusions sincerely, according to the light which he had received. It seems, therefore, that the kind of training in debating
that will be valuable to our young people is that which offers exercise in the analysis of a vital problem, skill in digging out significant facts, ability in combining these facts so as to draw a logical
conclusion, and finally, power to convince others of the validity of
the argument.

Reprinted from Education, 42 (September 1921), 39-42, by permission of The Bobbs-Merrill Company, Inc., Indianapolis, Indiana.
At the time this article was written, Dr. Wetzel was Principal of
the High School, Trenton, N.J.

Notes

1. Preston Slosson, "The Devil's Advocate," Independent, January
    22, 1921, p. 89.

4. The Academic Debate--Its Aims and Method
Clarence S. Dike

Dr. William A. Wetzel, Principal of the Trenton High School,
had an article in Education for September, in which, under the
above title, he questioned the value of the academic debate. He contended that the only answer to error is truth, and maintained that
the debate failed to advance the truth, inasmuch as (1) it does not
state the problem in such a way as to find the truth; (2) it does not
put the student in the attitude of wanting to know the truth; (3) it
does not put him in a situation where he is most likely to find the
truth; and (4) it does not give him the kind of moral training that
would lead him to advocate the truth. The article calls attention to
several undesirable tendencies in connection with the methods of conducting academic debates. But the author, to give emphasis to his
article, speaks of these tendencies in the light of actualities necessarily ever-existent.

That there is a tendency for debating in high school and college to present a partisan attitude toward absolute truth, there can
be no doubt. That it actually always does so is questionable. All
methods and practices, whether educational, political, economic, or
religious, are more or less subject to the same criticism. The
world is searching for absolute truth; but it has to compromise with
evil, because of the inconsistencies of our civilization. For instance, our modern system of court procedure has been criticized.
One lawyer argues that black is white; another lawyer, equally vera-

cious and honorable, argues that white is black. It is assumed
that somehow, between the conflicting contentions, justice will appear. It is true that too often she is a gray compromise rather
than an ideal; but should we abolish our court practice because it
does not always relate itself to the absolute truth? Merely because
a particular practice is subject to criticism, should it be cast out
as unfit? Until it can be proved that the evil in the practice ex-
ceeds the good, or until something better is evolved, it is common
sense to continue the practice.

Let us take up the four points upon which the article bases its
indictment. First, does the debate state the problem in such a way
as to find the truth? Granting that some few questions are poorly
stated, in that they allow for quibbling as to the meaning of terms,
most questions are very carefully worded so as to bring about a
real clash of ideas, balancing as nearly as possible the conflicting
opinions on the subject. The question: "Resolved, that immigration should be prohibited for the next two years," was objected to,
on the ground that it was narrow, and did not involve a careful
study of the whole problem of immigration. Is it to be expected
that high school students should understand all the history and politics involved in any broad subject like immigration? Time was
when such broad topics as "Education," "Virtue," "Adversity," and
the like, were assigned as themes for English composition; but we
have grown sensible in our understanding of what the adolescent
mind is capable of. We now narrow a subject for the sake of unity
and definiteness. So it is with the question for debate. A specific
problem is stated which calls for specific treatment as part of the
truth. Isn't it better to have a definite, concrete conception of part
of the truth than to have a general, abstract, indefinite idea of the
whole truth? By apprehending such pieces of truth from time to
time, a pattern of the whole truth may, by a process of induction,
be constructed.

Secondly, does the debate put the student in the attitude of
wanting to know the truth? There is no doubt a tendency on the
part of the individual student who argues for a thing to become prejudiced in favor of the trend of his argument. The good debating

coach, however, knows that both sides of the argument must be
clearly understood. Where both sides are studied, even though, for
the purposes of argument, one champions a side, he is very likely
to form definite opinions on the subject; and the writer's experience
has been that instances are very numerous of debaters who confess,
after the debating season is over, that their sympathies are with
the opposite side. And in extenuation of the tendency toward a
biased opinion on the part of some students, doesn't one form his
opinions on what he hears and reads anyway? Suppose those same
pupils had been one-sided in their reading and conversation on the
subject, would they be any less prejudiced? The debating training
certainly has the advantage of presenting both sides.

In the third place, does the academic debate put the student in
a situation where he is most likely to learn the truth? This question is already answered in the second. Preparation for an academic debate means to gather evidence to prove one's side. And to
prove one's side, one must understand the side of the opponent.
Both sides are weighed and carefully studied. One's opinion is
formed in the process, irrespective of the demands of the question.
If the question had not made a demand, the opinion would not have
been formed.

Finally, does the academic debate give the student the kind of
moral training that would lead him to advocate the truth? The answer to this question is so involved in the philosophy of education
and the conduct of life that it would probably take a sage to answer
it. Dr. Wetzel claims that arguing for what one does not sincerely
believe is immoral at all times and under every circumstance.
Would he criticize dramatics because the actor says and does things
contrary to his own personality? The debate is a game, a contest,
in which the contestants are playing a part. The more spirit of
rivalry there is in the event, the more does one feel the spirit of
the contest. To eliminate the spirit of make-believe as immoral is
to deprive the world of its greatest bouyancy and its highest imagination.

The final conclusion, therefore, is that although debating, like
anything else in life, is not perfect, still until something better is

evolved it is one of the best devices for motivating oral expression
and for teaching some of the essential problems of citizenship.

Dr. Wetzel's article offers a substitute for debating as it is
now conducted. He says: "The kind of debate that should be encouraged in our schools is the kind typified by the Lincoln-Douglas
debate, or the Webster-Hayne debates. It would be necessary to
score each debater independently for the thoroughness of his study,
the logic of his conclusions, and the clarity of his exposition." To
assume that such a public speaking contest will ever displace the
game of debating is to assume that throwing the medicine ball will
displace the game of football.

It must be conceded, however, that some of the debaters in
high school and college are likely to become convinced of the validity of their own arguments, and so form their opinions on current
problems a little hastily. The cause of this tendency is inherent in
the debate itself. To remove the cause entirely would tend to render the debate a mere speaking contest, such as Dr. Wetzel suggests as a substitute, devoid of the incentive of rivalry, the motivating principle of the debate. Since the tendency cannot be removed
without killing the contest, the question arises: Should the operation be performed, or should the patient be allowed to live in the
hope that the effects of the malady--which are greatly exaggerated,
anyway--may be checked and in a measure prevented?

And how can this tendency be lessened? First, all candidates
for places on the contest should be allowed to speak on either side
of the question. Second, those who make places on the team should
be drilled in speaking on both sides of the question. Third, the debating coach should guard the speakers against forming their opinions hastily. Fourth, two contests might be held wherever practic-
able, the debaters changing sides in the second contest.

Such a prescription ought to prove quite efficacious in checking
an undesirable element in academic debating, an element the effects
of which Dr. Wetzel so greatly dreads.

Reprinted from Education, 42:339-342, February, 1922, by permission of The Bobbs-Merrill Company, Inc., Indianapolis, Indiana.

Aims and Values   31

At the time this article was written Mr. Dike was a member of the
English Department of Atlantic City High School, Atlantic City, N.J.

Suggestions for Further Reading

Abernathy, Elton. "Things I Dislike in Debate," Southern Speech
     Journal, 15:216-218, March, 1950.
Ballantine, Arthur, and Clyde R. Miller. "Are We Really?"
     Gavel, 13:17-18, November, 1930.
"Collegiate Debating," New Republic, 79:221, July 11, 1934.
"Collegiate Debating and Writing," Nation, 90:452-3, May 5, 1910.
Graham, John. "Dangers in Debate," Journal of the American For-
     ensic Association, 2:94-103, Sept., 1965.
_____. "Usefulness of Debate in a Public Speaking Course,"
     Speech Teacher, 14:136-39, March, 1966.
Haiman, Franklyn S. "A Critical View of the Game of Forensics,"
     Journal of the American Forensic Association, 1:62-66,
     May, 1964.
Green, Clarence. "Debating at School," Nation, 90:627, June 23,
     1910.
Kruger, Arthur N. "Nature, Aims, Values, and Criticisms," Section
     IV, A Classified Bibliography of Argumentation and Debate.
     Metuchen, N.J, Scarecrow Press, 1964. Pp. 46-78.
Shepard, David W. "An Indictment of Debate," Speaker and Gavel,
     2:18-21, November, 1964.
Wagner, Russell H. "Collegiate Debating Today; Reply to Collegi-
     ate Debating," New Republic, 80:313, October 24, 1934.

Issue C: <u>Is Debate Primarily a Means of Truth-Seeking or Persuasion</u>?

Although the alternatives contained in this issue are not mutually exclusive, Hugo E. Hellman, in responding to Wayne N. Thompson's article "Discussion and Debate: A Re-Examination," apparently felt that Thompson preferred discussion to debate and that, like certain other writers, Thompson was suggesting that discussion should replace debate in the curriculum. In response to this view, Hellman, in "Debating Is Debating--And Should Be," argues that both discussion and debate are part of the deliberative process and that in a democracy there must be room for debate when discussion fails to achieve the desired accords.

The first three parts of Thompson's article have been omitted since they deal with the nature and teaching of discussion. Reprinted here is what Thompson calls a "new philosophy of debate," to which Hellman objects. Specifically, he disagrees with Thompson's contentions that debating is not a "game," a "contest," or an "exercise in sophistry," and that it is "not properly a form of persuasion." Hellman concludes that to accept such a philosophy "would be to sound the death knell of debating as we have always understood it."

5. Discussion and Debate: A Re-Examination
Wayne N. Thompson

Loose thinking and loose talking about the objectives of discussion and debate endanger both the value and the prestige of courses offered in these techniques. Comments at the 1943 War Problems Conference, and elsewhere, indicate that some teachers have become infatuated with certain secondary results to a degree that they no longer appreciate the distinctive contribution that discussion and debate can make to the education of young men and women. The action of the Army Specialized Training Program directors in elimi-

32

nating "formal public speaking" from that curriculum, in part because of unfortunate practices and statements by a few teachers, indicates the necessity for re-evaluating other speech activities to determine their fundamental purposes.

This article, therefore, aims to expose secondary objectives
and erroneous objectives for what they are, and to show the significance of the primary purposes. It further proposes to develop a
new philosophy of debate to guide the classroom teacher and to challenge the validity of many of the aspects of the older debate theory.
To conserve space, we will say little about the implications of these
techniques for a democratic society or about the oral nature that is
usually characteristic of both. . . .

IV

McBurney and Hance[7] in speaking of the background of discussion say in part:

> Out of this impatience with the authoritarianism of the
> past came what we today know as scientific method.
> The advances which this method has brought in the phy-
> sical sciences during the last two centuries are a com-
> monplace. And yet, through it all, the equally (if not
> more) important problems of policy in the realm of prac-
> tical affairs have been left very largely to methods
> grounded in force, creed, and dogma. "The essential
> need [today] is the improvement of the methods and con-
> ditions of debate, discussion, and persuasion." "That,"
> says Professor Dewey,[8] "is the need of the public."

McBurney and Hance, and other authors, have developed the
discussion technique as an instrument for problem solving, but no
real modernization of debate philosophy has occurred in response to
John Dewey's call. This article, therefore, will attempt to point
out some of the false purposes of debate, to develop a new philosophy for debate instructions, and to indicate some of the implications
of that new philosophy.

Debating is not a game. To almost all laymen, and to some
teachers, debating is little more than a game in which teams, two
against two, sit crouched behind wooden file-boxes and sheaves of
newspaper clippings, and watch a timekeeper flip printed cards.
The outward form--the placing of the speakers, the orderly division

of the event into speeches of specified lengths occurring in a prear-
ranged order--should not be confused with the real purpose of the
activity. Students may go through such formality yet never actually
debate. "I do not believe that debating is a game, " says Lester
Thonssen. [9]

Debating is not a contest. This misconception, which results
in more instances of malpractice than does any other, probably
arises from the competitive trappings that often surround college
and school debates and from the fact that the speakers develop two
antagonistic cases. The presentation of both sides, however, is not
proof of the existence of a contest but is simply a step necessary
for the accomplishment of the real purpose of debate--the finding of
truth. Without both cases, no judge could find the truth. The debater should realize that his function is to build the strongest possible case for his side and that his "opponents" are rendering a social service by presenting the other side.

Debating is not an exercise in sophistry. Many who shudder
at the term sophistry, practice it. Even those who know better,
and whose ideals are of the highest, are likely to be so steeped in
the thinking and the practice of the contest coach that they cannot
resist the temptation to teach their classes how to defeat opponents.
Asking a series of questions propounding a dilemma, leading the opponent into a damaging admission, placing false emphasis upon certain aspects of the proposition so that others will be overlooked,
avoiding the main issue, and many other devices may be useful in
defeating an opponent but they are not helpful in arriving at truth.
Every debate instructor should condemn such sophistry, for the
function of debate is to make one's case look as good as it is, but
not better; to make the opposing case look as bad as it is, but not
worse.

Debating is not properly a form of persuasion. As usually
practiced, we admit, debate is a form of persuasion, but current
practice is not necessarily correct. [10] The thesis that debate is
properly a form of persuasion rests upon the premise that ideas
should be imposed upon the public, whereas the concept that debate
should be a form of investigating and testing a proposed solution

rests upon the premise that both sides should be presented and that the listeners should make the decision. We are not denying that certain circumstances justify and even necessitate the practice of persuasion, but we are submitting that the second philosophy is the correct one for the classroom teacher of discussion and debate. Four reasons support this conclusion:

1. Teaching students to investigate both sides of a proposition and to compare and contrast them before making a decision is more desirable educationally than teaching them how to convince others to accept their point of view. A citizenry of men and women who weigh both sides forms a stronger basis for a working democracy than does a citizenry of men and women trained in the art of persuasion. Moreover, students who can evaluate both sides are better equipped to solve their individual problems than are those who are persuaders.

2. Even the persuader should master debating as an investigative technique. Otherwise, he has no sound ratiocinative method of deciding which side to advocate.

3. The idea that debate is a form of persuasion is more likely to lead the student into tricky practices than is the idea that debate is a form of investigation.

4. Even if persuasion should be used, debate is the wrong form for it to take.

The idea that debate should be a division of persuasion rather than a division of investigation is inconsistent with the form of debate. Whereas the purpose of persuasion is to move opinion in a predetermined direction, the form of debate is designed to permit both sides to be heard. Thus, every persuasive plea can be immediately countered, and the effectiveness of the advocate reduced. The debate situation, on the other hand, is well adapted to the careful testing of a proposition and to the suspension of judgment until both sides have been heard. Debate, therefore, is useful in a democratic society because it is not a form of persuasion and because it makes difficult the practice of demagoguery and authoritarianism.

Debating is more than an exercise in public speaking. Although debaters improve very much in delivery, skill in presenta-

tion is always a means and not an end. Several types of speech
activity may result in better speaking; the distinctive value of debate lies elsewhere.

Debating is more than an excuse for stimulating research.
Learning to make a bibliography and to take notes for a specific
purpose constitutes a valuable contribution to the education of the
student-debater. Likewise, accumulating information on a significant problem and becoming more aware of the contemporary political and social issues are desirable outcomes. Yet, these values
are secondary, accruing to the student as he tries to achieve the
primary purpose, which now we shall develop in a positive manner.

V

Debate is a technique for testing the wisdom of a specific solution. Three aspects of the definition are of special significance.

First, debate is a technique to be taught and to be mastered.
Classroom debates should be regarded not as ends in themselves,
but as laboratory periods for the mastery of a method. The better
the student understands that his real purpose in studying debate is
to master a technique for dealing with problems the better is the
chance that he will profit from the course.

Debate as a technique differs from discussion in two basic respects, the first of which is that it is more highly organized. In
formal debate, both sides have an equal amount of time; and in legislative and forensic debating, there are rules to make sure that
both sides will have a fair opportunity for presenting their arguments.
The obviousness of the organizational feature is unfortunate, because
many people are so impressed by it that they fail to see the more
significant characteristics.

The real importance of the organizational feature is the equality of opportunity.[11] Here is something basic to democracy--both
sides have the right to be heard, and the decision is in abeyance
until both cases have been given. This right, like most rights, entails a responsibility: Both sides must be competently presented.

Moreover, debate is bilateral, while discussion is multilateral.[12] Being multilateral, the second is discursive, exploring the

problem area, finding all possible solutions, considering each, and balancing the various solutions, the one against each of the others. Debate, on the other hand, deals with a more sharply defined area, requiring the student to contrast the advantages and the disadvantages of only one solution. This distinction indicates both a limitation of debate and its distinctive power: it is limited to the consideration of one solution at a time; it is strong in that the reduction of the number of factors permits greater clarity and thoroughness. The instructor should insist that his students take full advantage of the bilaterality of debate, beginning with the careful wording of the proposition.

Second, debate should be a device for investigating and testing rather than one for persuasion. This point of view we have already considered at some length; its importance as a factor in the philosophy of both the instructor and the student can hardly be overestimated.

Third, debate deals with a specific solution, perhaps arbitrarily chosen, perhaps not the best, but the one to be studied at a particular time. Students should learn to appreciate the value of concentrating their efforts upon a single solution until its development is complete.

VI

Now, we will seek to discover ways in which this concept of debate affects some of the conventional beliefs.

1. Winning (defining winning as the overcoming of an opponent) is not the proper objective of debating. To win an argument when one is on the wrong side is worse,[13] socially speaking, than to lose. The blame, however, should be placed not upon him who wins, if he is ethical, but upon him who fails in his responsibility of presenting his argument with all possible skill. The ideal debater, the one with the greatest social utility, is the one who develops his case to its true degree of power. The one who develops his case so that it appears better than it is is as harmful socially as the one who presents a weak case when weakness is unjustified. If judges adopted this point of view, the spirit in which debaters approach a prob-

lem would be more conducive to reflective thought.   Current methods of debate judging penalize only the weak, but is not he who
overdevelops his arguments just as dangerous?

2. Debaters should be considered as co-workers and not as
antagonists.   Although they present opposing points of view, they
are cooperating in the process of subjecting a proposition to a rigorous test, and the affected population, which usually includes the
participants, gains when truth is found.   Previous authors have assumed that debate is competitive and discussion cooperative, but
such a distinction is based upon practice rather than upon the inherent nature of the techniques.   The argument that debate should
be competitive because it has been competitive is obviously unsound.

Here we are presenting a new philosophy to guide debate instructors: the speakers are cooperating in the desirable enterprise
of finding truth.[14]   They cooperate best when they present the
strongest true case possible and at the same time apply principles
of evidence and of reasoning to expose weaknesses in the opposing
case.   We submit that the successful teaching of the philosophy of
cooperation will eliminate many of the malpractices that have promoted criticism of debate.   In short, the student should learn that
he is debating upon a proposition and not against an opponent.

3. Debaters should be considered as investigators and not as
persuaders.   This point, which has been developed previously, is
consistent with the paragraph immediately above.   The application of
this concept, which we feel is likewise an advance over the old,
should do much both (a) to assist students in developing the power
of thinking upon a proposition independently and clearly and (b) to
strengthen democracy through making each individual an investigator
and decision-maker rather than a pawn of rival persuasive forces.
The philosophy that the debater is helping himself, his opponent, and
his listeners think to a decision is more consistent with our ideals
of democracy than is the old philosophy that the debater is trying to
make others agree with him.

4. Debating both sides of a proposition is neither morally
wrong nor hypocritical.   Some writers have charged that debating
both sides results in various evils, such as insincerity, shallowness,

and the presentation of arguments known to be poorly founded or
fallacious. These malpractices, which also occur among speakers
who debate only one side, are the result of other causes--weak-
nesses in the character of the offender or a misunderstanding of the
proper function of debate.

On the contrary, the instructor should encourage his students
to debate both sides or at least to brief them. Two reasons support this statement: (1) By debating both sides, he is more likely
to realize that propositions are bilateral. It is those who fail to
recognize this fact who become intolerant, dogmatic, and bigoted.
(2) Outside the classroom, debating both sides is a more significant
and practical activity than debating one side. In testing the proposition "Resolved that I should attend graduate school, " the individual,
although he may secure opinions, ultimately must develop both sides
himself. In arriving at an opinion, which may be the basis for action, upon such a proposition as "Resolved, that I should vote Republican, " the individual (if his debate course taught him to think
for himself) sorts out arguments from all that he hears and mental-
ly constructs both cases before deciding whether the proposition
should be affirmed or denied. Even the persuader (again, if he
thinks his way to decisions) debates both sides with himself before
determining which side to support. [15]

5. Using a counterplan is not a legitimate negative technique,
for it makes the situation multilateral. The objection, however,
does not rest alone upon definition and theory. On the contrary, the
use of a counterplan destroys a very practical sort of value, the
thoroughness that the testing of a single solution permits. Thoroughness may be lost in three ways: first, the necessity for juggling
four factors (for and against the solution expressed in the proposition; for and against the counterplan) may cause confusion; next, the
consideration of a second solution may reduce the amount of time
available for testing the original; finally, the negative in relying
upon a counter proposition may fail to present the arguments against
the specified solution. Developing the virtues of a second plan is
not the same as showing the weaknesses of the first. [16]

Space limitations prevent the further development of the implications of bilaterality as a fundamental feature of debate. Without comment, we suggest that if one accepts the premise that debate is bilateral, he also must accept the following:

a. Propositions should be so worded that they are clearly bilateral. Wordings requiring the affirmative to attack the status quo create multilaterality.

b. The stock issue of necessity is not legitimate, hinging as it does upon the good and the bad aspects of the status quo rather than upon the merit of the solution.

c. Defense of the status quo, with or without repairs, is not a valid negative position. The negative, however, need not confine itself to the direct refutation of the points advanced by the affirmative; in addition, it should present arguments on issues which the affirmative has overlooked.

6. The commonly held idea that debate should follow discussion is illogical. If the thinking in the discussion group is accurate, debating the adopted solution is futile, merely confirming the previous decision. If the thinking is inaccurate, it is more efficient to improve the discussion than to nullify the conclusion. Time can be saved and confusion avoided if debate, meaning the careful study of the strong and the weak points of a particular solution, is carried on concurrently with discussion. If this plan is followed, the group, after defining and analyzing the problem, will carry on a series of debates, each studying thoroughly a particular solution. After weighing the arguments concerning each solution, the group will be ready to make the best possible decision.

7. Debate and discussion are not antithetical. Most authors have assumed that the differences between discussion and debate are great and that the two are even in conflict. Nichols, for example, says, "Discussion emphasizes the search for truth; debate seeks to persuade others to accept the truth. Discussion purposes the discovery of the best solution to the problem; debate advocates the adoption of the solution discovered."[17] Discussion and debate, of course, are not identical, but the points of likeness are more significant than the points of difference. Both are concerned with the solving of problems and the finding of truth; both are methods rather

than ends; both are characteristically oral and are usually group techniques; both are methodologies upon which the democratic state as a whole and the individuals composing it must depend. The two should be considered, therefore, not as antagonistic, but as complementary; the chief point of difference is in scope, the one serving as the tool for dealing with multilateral situations, for studying the problem area and finding a solution; the other serving as the tool for affirming or denying specific solutions, for testing carefully upon a bilateral basis.

Two quotations from a well-known contemporary textbook will serve to epitomize this section: "The duty of the affirmative speakers is to make the strongest possible case for the adoption of the motion; the negative should present the strongest arguments against it. Democracy is based on the assumption that when this is done, the listeners can be trusted to make a wise decision. "[18] This idea should serve as the foundation for a philosophy of debate--a philosophy that has been previously stated but not carried to its logical conclusion either in theory or in practice. We disagree, however, when the same authors say, "As far as the debater is concerned, the public debate is admittedly not a search for truth. He thinks he has found it and is presenting the reasons and the evidence which support his belief. "[19]

Here in the philosophy of the debater as a person with a closed mind, of the debater as an advocate, is the germ for most of the evils charged against debating--dogmatism, overzealousness resulting in sharp practices, and insincerity. We are not objecting to the truth of the picture of what now is; we are objecting to the use of this philosophy as the basis for the teaching of debate in the future.

Although legislative and other forms of debate in which antagonists, friendly or otherwise, seek to gain victory through the swaying of the undecided members of the group often serve a useful purpose, the same values can be achieved under this new philosophy of the debaters as investigators and co-workers. The good in the usual type of debate lies not in the antagonism but in the development of both cases so that the listeners can better arrive at a decision. The new philosophy not only retains this feature but also makes it central.

VII

Some may fear that the application of this new philosophy will result in a deterioration in quality, because the competitive element will be removed. To this, we reply:

1. The spirit of competition need not be eliminated, for those who wish can still judge debates and give decisions. The change is in the basis for the decision, which becomes "Which team developed its case the more completely and accurately?" rather than "Which team overcame its opponent?"

2. The validity of the argument rests upon the definition of quality. What will be eliminated as a result of the change in the nature of competition is the attempt to maneuver an opponent into an embarrassing position; the use of evidence known to be false or weak; the omission of issues unfavorable to a given side; the use of long lists of questions and tricky plans and counterplans; the withholding of important arguments and evidence until late in the debate; and the substitution of rhetorical virtuosity, emotional appeal, and oratorical flamboyancy for ideas. The new type of debate, like discussion, need not be devitalized and anemic, nor should it be. Instructors should continue to teach good delivery and effective rhetoric, factors which continue to be virtues unless they obscure ideas or serve as substitutes for ideas.

Discussion and debate, then, are complementary, both providing methodologies for dealing with our problems of living. The student who masters them and who is able to solve problems more wisely than he would otherwise, is the student who has gained the most from his study. The instructor who has taught his students to face problems systematically has served the greatest purpose. There are, of course, other values, but those must not be permitted to obscure the primary ones.

Discussion is a technique for group action in studying and solving problems. Debate is a technique for testing the wisdom of a specific solution. The instructor would do well to be guided by these concepts as he builds his course and teaches it.

Reprinted from the Quarterly Journal of Speech, 30:288-299, October, 1944. Dr. Thompson is Professor of Speech at the University of Texas.

Notes

7. Ibid., pp. 17-18.
8. John Dewey, The Public and Its Problems (1927), p. 208.
9. "The Social Values of Discussion and Debate," Quarterly Journal of Speech, 25:116, 1939.
10. "But because the outside world is not undistinguished for sharp practice gives us no reason for encouraging that sort of thing in educational circles. . . . Discussion and debate, to be consistent with liberal educational ideals, should not foster a sort of predatory attitude--an attitude based upon a driving desire to beat the other fellow. Unfortunately that attitude is being developed in some quarters. As long as it exists, one phase of our subject will not be above suspicion."--Lester Thonssen, op. cit., pp. 116-117.
11. In analyzing the nature of debate, Ewbank and Auer give equality of opportunity as one of the four characteristics. Their other three are bilaterality, persuasive purpose, and decision by majority vote after the debate.--Op. cit., p. 394.
12. A. Craig Baird points out this distinction in his Public Discussion and Debate (1937), p. 358.
13. The extent of the disaster that results from winning in such a case depends upon the circumstances. The baseball pitcher who "wins" the argument and throws a high fast ball, which the batsman knocks out of the park, may lose a game. The cabinet member who wins when he is wrong may lose a war.
14. "Debate should be an honest effort to discover truth. It should promote tolerance. During the preparation for debate and during the contest, the debater should bear in mind his own liability to error. Far from resenting the fact that others disagree with him, he should welcome opposition. If he believes in his own side, opposition is opportunity. 'He that wrestles with us,' as Burke well said, 'strengthens our nerves and sharpens our skill. Our antagonist is our helper.' Adversaries in debate should have at least one common purpose--the search after truth."--William T. Foster, Argumentation and Debating (1932), pp. 270-271.
15. "We recognize the importance of the trained advocate in a democratic society; but we also recognize the fact that the social justification of persuasion and advocacy will be much clearer when we know that the advocate has reached his conclusion reflectively."--McBurney and Hance, op. cit., p. 332. Although McBurney and Hance are speaking here of discussion, the point would seem to hold for debate of the type we are advocating.
16. These comments should not be construed as indicating that we

believe that all problems should be considered upon a bilateral basis. Rather, the purpose is to show how debate
should be used. Discussion, which includes a series of debates, each finishing a proposition before proceeding to the
next, is the proper method for handling many problem situations.

17. Alan Nichols, Discussion and Debate (1941), p. 4. Similar pas-
    sages can be found in other books and articles. Symptoma-
    tic is Halbert Gulley's title "Debate Versus Discussion,"
    Quarterly Journal of Speech, XXVIII (1942), 305-307.
18. Ewbank and Auer, op. cit., p. 405.
19. Ibid., p. 406.

6. Debating Is Debating--And Should Be
Hugo E. Hellman

This article has a purpose and a thesis. Its purpose is two-
fold: (1) to take issue specifically with the "new philosophy of debate" advocated by Professor Wayne Thompson in the Quarterly
Journal of October, 1944; and (2) to take issue generally with the
current group of enthusiasts for group discussion who conceive of it
as something basic among speech activities and before which debate
must bow respectfully and retire to a seat in the back row or bow
out entirely. Among the group discussion enthusiasts I include
those teachers of speech who make group discussion the fundamental
training technique by which the arts of public speaking are to be
taught. Among them I also include those writers who turn out college textbooks on discussion and debate in which four of the five
parts (400 of 500 pages) are devoted to discussion, e.g., Ewbank
and Auer's Discussion and Debate. And among the enthusiasts I also include those who would arrogate to discussion the primary place
on the ground that it is "the special technique of democracy" or
"the essence of democracy," e.g., McBurney and Hance's The Principles and Methods of Discussion.

The thesis here is that debating is debating, and is not "a
fourth type of discussion . . . that can be employed only after a
great deal of preliminary discussion has taken place,"[1] and it is not
"bilateral discussion" as Professor Thompson insists in the article
referred to above.

I

Let us turn first to this "new philosophy of debate"--this "challenge to the validity of many of the aspects of the old debate theory"--this "attempt to point out some of the false purposes of debate. " Professor Thompson begins with certain pronouncements, including (1) "Debating is not a game"; (2) "Debating is not a contest"; (3) "Debating is not an exercise in sophistry"; (4) "Debating is not properly a form of persuasion"; (5) "Debating should be classed as a division of investigation"; (6) "Debate is more than an exercise in public speaking"; and (7) "Debating is more than an excuse for stimulating research. "

Let us first be sure of our terms, and then proceed to examine these dicta. By "debating" here is meant formal debating, intercollegiate and interscholastic debating, because the Professor refers to teams, judges, time limits--all elements that distinguish this type of debate from other forms. In defining further, it should be noted that he is stating a question of fact--he says debating is this and it is not so and so. He is not talking here of what might be or should be, but of what is--about the debating your boys did in that tournament last week, about what debaters have been doing in debates since your undergraduate days on a team. His definition, therefore, should fit objective reality, not his own notions of what debate might be. With these definitions in mind, let us examine his premises.

First, Thompson declares that debating is not a game, and second that it is not a contest. Since these terms are not defined, we assume that the dictionary definition is intended here. Webster says a contest is "an earnest struggle for superiority" and that a game is "a contest according to a set of rules. " In the face of these, who can deny that our formal debates are games and contests? No one contends that they are the same as football, basketball, tennis, or tiddly-winks, but they are a type of contest if they involve "an earnest struggle for superiority"--and they do; and they are a game if they proceed "according to a set of rules"--and they do. Wherever debaters argue and refute with the objective of maintaining their views over opposing ones, and whenever they follow

certain rules for timing and speaking order, they are indulging in
a game or a contest by definition. To quote Lester Thonssen (as
Professor Thompson does) as saying that "I do not believe debating
is a game" does not alter the fact.

The third premise is that debate is not an exercise in sophistry. Here I am tempted to agree until the definition of sophistry
emerges. It is defined by example, and includes (1) "asking a
series of questions propounding a dilemma, " (2) "leading the opponent into a damaging admission, " (3) "placing false emphasis upon
certain aspects of the proposition so that others will be overlooked, "
and (4) "many other devices useful in defeating an opponent . . .
but not helpful in arriving at truth. " If these be sophistry, and if
the use of them makes a debate an exercise in sophistry, it is difficult to understand how anyone who has listened to college debaters
can say that collegiate debating, as it is presently practiced, is not
an exercise in sophistry. I question whether there has ever been a
good collegiate debate in which these things have not played a major
part. They are an essential of debating as it is in fact practiced;
and it is in the realm of what is and not of what should be that we
are speaking.

Although he does not say so, perhaps Professor Thompson
means that debating should not include these things, because he
does add later that these are "not helpful in arriving at the truth. "
But here again, I fear, the facts contradict the philosopher. These
things--this "sophistry"--can be tremendously helpful in arriving at
truth, and if Professor Thompson doubts it let him ask any good
successful practicing lawyer. The barrister will tell him that he is
succeeding in a tradition (2000 years old) for using questions and
dilemmas as techniques for leading the guilty into damaging admis-
sions and as a means of arriving at the truth.

The fourth pronouncement is that "debating is not properly a
form of persuasion, " and to this is added the strange observation:
"As usually practiced, debate is a form of persuasion, but current
practice is not necessarily correct. " This is equivalent to saying
that something is not what it usually is in practice, and is therefore a simple contradiction. But I would hasten to add that no one

holding the "old" philosophy of debate ever thought of debate as a
form of persuasion. No one, within my knowledge, ever thought of
a contest debate as a propaganda device (like a campaign speech or
a sermon). Each of the speeches, however, taken singly, is a
form of persuasion, and so for each of the debaters the debate is
an exercise in persuasion and persuasive speaking. This the "old"
philosophy held, I believe, quite logically.

Having reached the conclusion that debating is an exercise in
persuasion, little need be said of Professor Thompson's fifth contention that debating should be classed as a division of investigation
rather than as a division of persuasion. Why teach debating, which
is for the debaters and therefore also for us as their teachers, under the heading that calls it something else?

The last two dicta are that "debating is more than an exercise in public speaking" and "more than an excuse for stimulating
research." No one questions these. Any proponent of old-fashioned debate would be quick to agree with both, but since he finds
them so stated as a part of the doxology of a "new philosophy of debate," he might justly resent the implication that he has ever held
otherwise.

Our conclusion is that debating is most certainly not what
Professor Thompson believes (or at least says) it is. But, you
may say, perhaps he is speaking of debate ideally--as he thinks it
should be. If so, the obvious rejoinder is that he should say so--
as he does in the second part of the piece where he gets down to
the serious business of setting forth this "new philosophy." Here,
in another series of dicta, we are told that "winning is not the proper objective of debating," that "debaters should be considered as co-
workers and not as antagonists," and that "debaters should be considered as investigators and not as persuaders." The implication
of all of this is obvious. The use of these terms "investigator" and
"co-worker" (right out of the jargon of discussion) indicates that he
would have the debater adopt (to use another term from the jargon)
"the attitude of the discussant." In other words, he would have the
debater cease to be a debater and become a discusser; and of course
when he does, debating ceases to be debating and becomes discus-

sion. Professor Thompson would call it "bilateral discussion," but
whatever you call it, it is not debate. And so the simple fact finally and somewhat deviously emerges that under this new philosophy, debate is "out"; it is gone, it is done. Only discussion remains.

II

The crux of the matter, then, is: Should we adopt this new
philosophy of "debate"? To adopt it, I believe, would be to sound
the death knell of debating as we have always understood it--debat-
ing in which the debater tries to win, debating in which the opposition is an antagonist, and debating in which the debater does his
level best to be a persuader. Your answer will depend largely
upon your philosophy of education, your concept of your job as a
teacher of speech and your own beliefs concerning the relative
merits of discussion and debate as exercises for developing skill in
speaking.

Personally, my own experience has forced me to the conclusion that participation in debate is far better speech training than
participation in discussion. Let us, however, meet the champions
of discussion on their own ground. Let us meet them not on the
field of the immediate objectives of speech training (which, I assume, are to teach people to speak well--including persuasively),
but over in that byway on which they move so glibly among such
milestones as "the search for truth" and "social utility" and "the
special techniques of democracy" and "the essence of democracy."
Let us forget for a moment that we have some simple fundamental
objectives of teaching young men and women to stand up on their
hind legs and say things effectively, and go philosophizing on such
long-range objectives as contributing to the survival of democracy
by teaching "techniques for arriving at the truth in face-to-face or
co-acting groups," i.e., teaching this "essence of democracy." In
other words, let us assume that it is the peculiar province of the
teacher of speech to see to the survival of our democratic way of
life; and having made the assumption, ask ourselves whether "old-
fashioned" debate still has anything to contribute to that survival.

As the first step toward the answer, I would submit that the proponent of discussion who insists that his technique is the "essence" of the function of the citizens of these United States is guilty of some rather inaccurate observations of our American democracy. It may be possible that in some pure democracy, some ideal democracy, this may be the essence of the process, but in our American brand (which is not "pure," but "republican") the essence is something else. For what is discussion? In the language of a good authority it is defined as "the cooperative deliberation of problems by persons thinking and conversing together in face-to-face or co-acting groups" [J.H. McBurney and Kenneth G. Hance, The Principles and Methods of Discussion (1939) p. 10] with the objective of finding solutions. It is a group process of "solution finding."

On the other hand, debate (not the game now, but the real thing) is a process for achieving decisions, a technique for securing the adoption and action upon a proposal. It is a device for decision making. And what are we as citizens? What is the essence of our job as participants in democracy? Are we not called upon to function ten times as "decision makers" to once as "solution finders?" Consider for a moment any half-dozen of our problems of recent years. Do they come to us as questions for discussion (in the form of neat little fairy tales these writers use in the first chapters of their textbooks to introduce us to discussion)? Or do they come to us as propositions for debate? Were we asked a few years ago: "What are we going to do about England? About Russia? About China?" Or was it a question of lend-lease vs. status quo? Were we asked a few months ago: "How are we going to get an occupant for the White House for the next four years?" Or was it "Roosevelt vs. Dewey?" And right now is it going to be: "How shall we solve the problems of achieving a peaceful world?" Or are we faced with the proposition: "Should we support Dumbarton Oaks?" The answers, I believe, are obvious. They come to us as propositions for debate. Our job as citizens was not one of solution finding or problem solving, but of decision making. And does this not suggest that if we must label something the "essence of democracy," debate might bear the title as logically as discussion?

This is not to suggest that citizens may not be faced with
"discussion problems," but it is to insist that in matters of public
policy the problems we face are more often of the nature: "Should
we or shouldn't we?"--at least at that point where they come to the
attention of the average voter. In their theorizing about discussion,
its proponents also theorized about democracy, and so wandered
from reality concerning both. They lost sight of the fact that we
the people do not "rule" in this republic, but rather only decide between alternative courses of action--or more accurately (and even
more simply) we decide to accept a proposed course or reject it
and do nothing (i.e., stand by the status quo). In this there is
very little of the "problem, hypothesis, deduction," etc. and "the
essential phases of the scientific method of John Dewey" with which
the discussion theorists would have us and our students preoccupied.
But there is in it everything of the debate process, the "old-fashioned" debating process, including antagonists and protagonists, persuaders, a good stiff contest, and usually good wholesome hunks of
sophistry on both sides! Such is democracy as it is.

Here again, of course, the proponent of discussion may argue
that he is speaking of the ideal situation, and contend that what I
have described is not democracy as it should be. He may insist
that ours is a very imperfect democracy and that in his ideal democracy things are going to be quite different. In it, questions of
policy are going to be approached by the scientific method and all
of our citizens, when faced with a problem, will sit down together
"in a face-to-face or co-acting group" with the pure and open minds
characteristic of "the discussion attitude" to solve that problem.
That, I agree, is going to be wonderful. As a matter of fact, it
will probably be Utopia.

But what in the meantime? As I write these lines, a class of
twenty young men and women await my coming in a classroom down
the hall, to be led a step further along in my course, Discussion
and Debate. Should I prepare them for a life in Utopia, for a
world peopled with pure and open minds and "discussion attitudes?"
Should I teach them an art of speaking in which the struggle, the
contest, the antagonism, the striving to win, are foreign--an art in

which the speaker is preoccupied with finding the truth, and preoccupied with the notion that he must state his case only to "the true
degree of its power?" For that, says Professor Thompson, is the
debater "with the greatest social utility." I suggest that if I do, I
am a victim of the same sort of mental processes that afflicted the
Utopian pacifist. To teach young men not to "debate" in a world
in which there will be men who will is like teaching young men not
to fight in a world in which there will be men who will take up the
sword.

My students, I greatly fear, are not going out into a Utopian
society in which every member will always state his case "to the
true degree of its power." Their personal worlds, I fear, will include life-insurance salesmen and Fuller brush men, editorial writers and bigots. And in their public lives, I fear, they are going
to find Hitlers and Mussolinis, New Dealers and Old Guard Republi-
cans, anti-Britishers and anti-Russians, Chicago Tribunes, Silver
Shirts, Walter Winchells, Huey Longs, and Cecil Browns, some of
whom it has been rumored do not always stick to the "discussion
attitude" and sometimes do not state their cases "to the true degree
of their power." These people are debaters, and just as you must
match the sword against the sword in the field of battle, so must
you match a debater against a debater in the field of argument. I
shall continue to insist that debating is debating--and should be.

Reprinted from the Quarterly Journal of Speech, 31:295-300, October, 1945. At the time of writing, Hugo Hellman taught at Mar-
quette University.

Notes

1. A.T. Weaver, Gladys Borchers, C.H. Woolbert, The New Better Speech (1937), p. 81.

Suggestions for Further Reading

Auer, J. Jeffrey. "Discussion and Debate," Gavel, 21:48-49, Jan-
    uary, 1939.
Beckman, Vernon E. "Let Debate Go On," Debaters Magazine, 3:
    195-96, December, 1947.
Dunbar, Willis F. "Let's Not Debate; Pupils Should Learn the
    Techniques of Settlement, Not Argument, in Our Schools,"
    Clearing House, 21:67-71, October, 1946.
Ehninger, Douglas. "Discussion and Debate: Another Analysis,"
    Gavel, 21:62-63, May, 1939.
Lahman, Carroll P. "Debate and Discussion--Rivals or Allies?"
    Debaters Magazine, 3:3-5, 27, May, 1947.
Moses, Elbert R., Jr. "Debate Vs. Discussion; Reply to F. B.
    Riggs," School and Society, 64:84-85, August 3, 1946.
Musgrave, George M. "A Challenging Point of View," Debaters
    Magazine, 1:22-23, October-December, 1945.
Nichols, Alan. "The Discussion-Debate Duality," Southern Speech
    Journal, 7:100-102, March, 1942.
Nichols, Egbert R. "Editorially Speaking," Debaters Magazine, 1:
    104-106, October-December, 1945.
Riggs, Francis B. "School Debates," School and Society, 63:155,
    March 2, 1946.

II. The Debate Proposition

Issue D: Is the Traditional Classification of Debate Propositions Satisfactory?

A thoroughgoing exposition of the classification of propositions would require a book, since it would involve logical and epistemological considerations that have vexed philosophers for centuries. The most commonly used classification of debate propositions is that of fact, value, and policy; and although various writers, including this one, have tried to improve on this classification, it is still used by most debaters and teachers of debate.

In his article "The Classification of the Argumentative Proposition," Walter F. Terris proposes a two-fold classification: "propositions of judgment" (which would include the propositions now called "fact" and "value") and "propositions of policy." On the other hand, Gary Cronkhite, in his article "Propositions of Past and Future Fact and Value: A Proposed Classification," proposes a four-fold classification: (1) propositions of fact, which he would subdivide into (a) propositions of past or present fact and (b) propositions of future fact (predictions); and (2) propositions of value, which he would subdivide into (a) propositions of past or present value (now referred to as "value") and (b) propositions of future value (now referred to as "policy").

7. The Classification of the Argumentative Proposition
Walter F. Terris

Classification, as used in this article, is the step in analysis which determines what type of proposition an advocate is analyzing. Thus the advocate would classify (in most modern systems) the proposition "The United States should adopt a system of socialized medicine," as a proposition of policy and the proposition "The Russian

53

military base in Cuba constitutes a threat to the security of the
Western Hemisphere, " as a proposition of fact or value. A system
of classification usually leads the advocate into a system of stock
issues or at least a standard procedure for further analysis.

Probably the first reason for classifying propositions is that
it is always done. But stronger grounds ought to exist for so ven-
erable a practice. The process of classification seems to imply
that propositions are indeed different and being different they are,
or at least ought to be, handled in different ways. Classification is
therefore the first step in the analysis of a proposition. After we
have classified a proposition we ought to be able to predict what
sort of treatment will best develop its argumentative potential.

If one is familiar, however, with recent treatises on argumentation and particularly with the variant schemes of classification
used in them, he might conclude that classification is an innocuous
and pointless exercise. The idea that classifying a proposition determines what stock issues an advocate shall use is of very recent
origin and is not universally accepted. Assuming that writers could
agree that a particular classification gives rise to a particular form
of debate case, even then probably few writers could agree what the
precise content of that case should be. In fact, one of the most
widely used argumentation texts implies only the vaguest connection
between the classification of the argumentative proposition and the
construction of a case. In that text the only direct use of such a
classification is to aid in the selection and wording of a proposition
for debate. Thus classification seems unnecessary so long as the
proposition is well-worded, has a proper sentence structure, and is
clearly intelligible.[1] Of what real use then is classification? If it
is not directly necessary to the process of analysis, ought we to be
rid of it?

I believe the process of classification is, or can be, important to the analysis of argumentative propositions. If the classifications are conceived clearly, they can serve to point the advocate to
the basic issues upon which the acceptance of a proposition rests,
and to insure that the advocate has considered all the possible areas
of dispute surrounding his proposition. In order to clarify the pro-

cess of classification, I will attempt to trace the development of the
theory of classification in modern writing on the subject, to examine the present status of the theory, and to suggest specific
changes that will render it clearer and more useful.

The first American book on argumentation based the classification of debate propositions on distinctions between conviction and
persuasion. George Pierce Baker in 1895[2] and Baker with Henry
Barrett Huntington in 1905[3] distinguished two types of argument.
Argument to convince, they say, "aims only to produce agreement
between writer and reader. . . ."; whereas argument to persuade,
although depending on and growing out of conviction,

> aims to prepare the way for the process of conviction or
> to produce action as the result of conviction. In pure
> conviction one appeals only to the intellect of a reader
> by clear and cogent reasoning. In persuasion one may
> produce desired action either by arousing emotion in re-
> gard to the ideas set forth or by adapting the presenta-
> tion of one's case as a whole or in part to special in-
> terests, prejudices, or idiosyncrasies of a reader.[4]

The idea that conviction and persuasion, or logic and emotion,
could be rigorously separated dominated the field for many years.
The duality constituted the basis for the classification until late in
the 1920's. In 1928 Victor A. Ketcham[5] used the duality for his
scheme of classification but with a result that was decidedly original.
Ketcham did not rigidly affirm the absolute separability of emotions
and logic. For Ketcham the two became mutually dependent and the
one was seen as automatically implying the other. His basic premise was that all argument was directed toward some action desired
from the audience. The nature of the action, in turn, depended upon
the nature of the matter in dispute. Thus he ignored classification
since propositions, though differing in wording and directness, all
seek action.

Ketcham himself went no further than the bald assertion that
conviction implied persuasion. But in his support of this assertion
he pointed the way to a new basis for classification. Up to this
point classification was based on the motives of the speaker, for to
judge whether a proposition was aimed at conviction or persuasion
was ultimately a judgment of the intent of the advocate. When

Ketcham declared that all argument sought action and the particular
action intended was determined by the nature of the matter in dispute, he implied a new way to classify an argumentative proposition. Rather than judging his motives and intent, the advocate
might analyze the issue which occasioned the dispute.

The nature of the material in dispute became the basis for
further development of the theory of classification. In the early
1930's the new edition of Argumentation and Debating by William
Trufant Foster altered its approach to the classification of propositions. [6] The alteration was carried into the edition of 1945, in
which Foster asserted:

> There are propositions of fact and propositions of pol-
> icy or principle. "Germany is unable to pay the repara-
> tions" is a proposition of fact. On the other hand, "All
> the war debts should be cancelled" is a proposition of
> policy or principle. [7]

Foster made no distinction between policy and principle. The important thing about his scheme was that it no longer depended upon
the motives of the speaker. On the contrary, it depended upon the
very nature of the material in dispute. Classification, therefore,
became a matter of objective analysis. The proposition of fact was
a statement recognizing the existence of certain conditions or relationships in the environment. The proposition of policy was the
statement of a policy or principle designed to affect conditions in
the environment. This objective scheme opened up the possibility
of a direct application of Bishop Richard Whately's concept of presumption. [8] Since a proposition of policy or principle sought always
to change conditions, then it could be assumed that the presumption
was on the side of him who would resist that change.

Moreover, the classification of propositions according to the
nature of the matter in dispute gave rise to stock patterns for analyzing virtually any argumentative proposition. The proposition of
fact, because it was structurally similar to the argumentative propositions used in legal pleadings, was ripe for the application of
Quintilian's doctrine of status. [9]

Probably by analogy with the proposition of fact, the proposition of policy was linked with a system of stock issues. There

seemed no possibility of using Quintilian's pattern of three standard
statuses (the conjectural, the definitive, and the qualitative) for the
analysis of propositions of policy or principle.   However Foster developed an analogous system of five stock issues which attempted to
do for policy what status did for fact.   The stock issues were:

> (1) Do present conditions demand a change?   (2) If any
> change is to be made, is the proposed change the best
> one?   (3) Is it practical?   (4) Is it theoretically sound?
> (5) Would the disadvantages of the proposed change more
> than offset the advantages?[10]

But the generalized division into fact and policy soon appeared
inadequate.   The category of policy seemed further divisible.   For
instance, one could advocate a world government simply as a desirable Utopian system, and one could advocate the city-manager
form of government for Sioux City, Iowa as a practical mode of action.   The reasoning here is that an advocate may argue a policy
on purely theoretical or ideal grounds without considering practical
weaknesses.   An advocate can restrict his argument, for instance,
to the relative theoretical economic advantages of a centrally con-
trolled economy as opposed to a market-controlled economy.   Of
course, when he came to the point of advocating its immediate adoption or its adoption at a specific date, matters of expediency and
practicability would be involved and he himself might reject what
theoretically he had favored.   Thus there developed a distinction between theoretic policy and practical policy.

The question of fact also began to seem less simple than once
it had.   Application of the doctrine of status introduced a scheme
for dividing the question of fact.   An advocate might argue that
Roosevelt had actually tried to increase the number of justices on
the Supreme Court.   He might also try to argue that Roosevelt's
plan was not an attempt to destroy the power of the Court but rather an attempt to improve its function.   Finally, he might argue that
the action, however one might define it, was justified by the Court's
past irresponsible action.   The first would be a relatively factual
judgment based on historical evidence.   The second would be a matter of definition and, although involving judgments about a man's intent, might be inferred on the grounds of relatively objective histor-

ical fact. The third, however, was something totally different. To say that an action was justifiable was to place a value on that action; it was to make a moral judgment; it was to apply principles which were not open to objective observation.

Now let us see how these two further distinctions between theoretic policy and practical policy on the one hand and objective fact and evaluational fact on the other were carried into the writing on classification.

A. Craig Baird in 1928[11] attempted to distinguish these two forms of policy proposition. He divided all propositions into three forms: (1) those of fact, (2) those dealing with proposals advocated as theoretically sound, and (3) those dealing with matters of practical policy. Readers of his Public Discussion and Debate, although admitting the theoretical possibility of distinguishing two forms of policy proposition, found in practice that the two were often indistinguishable. The distinction was dropped entirely in the edition of 1950,[12] and Baird returned to the twofold division of fact and policy.

Russell H. Wagner made the most lasting division in the question of fact.[13] He too had three forms of proposition. His three categories were fact, value, and policy. Propositions of fact were those statements which asserted existence or causal relations of things and events. Propositions of value were those statements which assigned a value to some thing or event. The primary distinction between fact and value was that the latter asserted that to be true which could never be accepted as fact since value dealt with the intangibles of tastes and morals. Propositions of policy, routinely, were those propositions which called for action.

Wagner's scheme of classification, although the first to use the word "value" for one type of proposition, was not the first to attempt the division of the proposition of fact into objective and evaluative types. Two years before, Nichols and Baccus made a similar distinction but used the name "theory" for the new type of proposition. Though this form of proposition had a name that might indicate that Nichols and Baccus were dividing the proposition of policy, two other factors make it clear that it was a division of

fact. The form of the theory proposition was similar to the simple
assertion of fact. Also the tests they would apply to a proposition
to establish its classification revealed that the key to the classification of a proposition of theory was the validity of the evaluation implied in the proposition.[14]

Though similar, the later classification of Wagner had a greater sophistication of definition, and the choice of the term "value" in
place of "theory" was happier.

The tripartite scheme of classification of fact, value, and policy has held stable though not unchallenged for the last twenty-five
years. McBurney, O'Neill, and Mills use the same classification
with essentially the same justification.[15] Freeley sanctions the
classification.[16] Ehninger and Brockriede concur.[17] Kruger also
agrees that there are propositions distinguishable as fact, value,
and policy, but insists that the original proposition of fact must be
further divided. Whereas previous writers had included within the
proposition of fact both the recognition of conditions and of the
causes of conditions, Kruger feels impelled to tease these apart.
The proposition of fact, he says, "pertains to events that have happened, are happening, or will happen. . . ." A proposition of explanation affirms "a reason why something has happened, is happening, or will happen. . . ." Value and policy follow routinely.[18]
Kruger's subdivision seems to grow from a questionable analogy between classifications of propositions and arguments of sign and
cause. For this reason, and for another that will appear later, it
seems likely that the subdivision will have to be abandoned sooner
or later.

As the fact-value-policy scheme has grown and developed,
writers have become increasingly aware of the relationship between
the system of classification one chooses and the method of analysis
one uses. McBurney, O'Neill, and Mills, though denying that any
proposition can be fully analyzed by any system of stock issues,
agree that stock issues do give a handy and effective method for the
preliminary analysis of a proposition. They agree further that the
nature of the analysis of a proposition will depend on the class in
which one places it. They imply that the issues derived from any

proposition will bear a general form which depends on the class into which the proposition falls.[19]

Freeley asserts what McBurney, O'Neill, and Mills merely
imply. Accepting without argument stock-issue analysis of the proposition of policy (need-plan-benefit), Freeley goes on to argue that
if a debater is to affirm a proposition of fact, he must ask and answer two questions. The first question asks for criteria by which
the alleged fact may be judged as true, the second asks whether
the alleged fact fulfills the criteria. The stock issues for the proposition of value follow the same criteria-application pattern. The
first question asks for standards of judging whether a thing is good,
virtuous, or is otherwise of value, the second asks whether the subject matter of the proposition fulfills these criteria.[20]

Just as Ketcham in 1928 shifted the emphasis from the purpose of the speaker to the nature of the material in dispute, Freeley seemed to be moving in another direction. He indicated that
there might be an inadequacy in the tripartite classification of propositions as fact, value, or policy. If the method for handling the
material of one proposition were the same as that for handling the
material of another, then was there justification for calling them by
different names or distinguishing each of them from a proposition
of policy? According to Freeley's treatment of the stock issues of
the propositions of fact and value, the issues had the same general
form in each case. In both types he asked for a set of criteria to
judge the truth of an assertion, and in both cases he asked that
those criteria be applied to the assertion. Both the proposition of
fact, then, and the proposition of value may be analyzed by the criteria-application stock issues.[21]

But does the similarity of handling constitute sufficient reason
for abandoning or altering a system of classification which has gained great currency over the last quarter-century? Lee Hultzén has
given us a pair of criteria for such distinctions as we are trying to
make here. In erecting his particular structure of stock issues in
a proposition of policy, he cites two criteria for judging whether
such a structure is valid. It is valid, he says, "if students of the
art find that the divisions subtend operations differing one from an-

other. " The second criterion is that the system be exhaustive, that is that it cover all possible cases in its particular category and that, when used in analyzing a proposition, it leaves out nothing that is important to the dispute. [22]

According to Freeley, both propositions of fact and propositions of value may be completely analyzed by applying the criteria-application stock issues. [23] If Hultzén's criteria are valid then, the distinction between a proposition of fact and a proposition of value is invalid.

Before we can condemn the hoary scheme of the trifurcated classification, we must ask whether Hultzén's criteria are reasonable. It seems to me that they are admirably reasonable, for what is the purpose of categorizing propositions? Is it not to aid the advocate in discovering the issues inherent in the proposition? Is classification not an attempt to isolate the questions an advocate must ask of his proposition in order to reveal its issues? There probably is no other valid reason for its existence. If we distinguish two categories of proposition of which we ask the same questions, [24] or whose issues fall into the same general form, then it appears there is little or no reason for distinguishing them in the first place. Thus one is led to conclude that there is no significant difference between propositions of fact and propositions of value since both are open to analysis by the same methods.

If the distinction between fact and value is invalid, must one then return to the single distinction between an undifferentiated proposition of fact and the proposition of policy? This single distinction has been acceptable to Baird and other writers already mentioned. To answer the question we must examine this distinction also to see whether we can arrive at a better one.

The use of the term "fact" to describe a type of proposition is unfortunate. In contexts other than the classification of propositions we tend to use the term as distinct from "inference." That is, we say that we ought to be able to distinguish between fact and inference. Yet in this context of classification we call what is obviously an inference a proposition of fact.

To be precise, a fact is that which is directly and immediately

verifiable by any qualified observer. Logicians go even further in
distinguishing between fact and inference. The fact is the Ding an
sich; the statement of a direct and immediate observation of that
fact is what the logician would call an immediate inference; and the
term mediate inference is used to designate any statement or assertion based on one or more immediate inferences or another mediate
inference. [25] In this framework none of our argumentative propositions is a fact, and none is even an immediate inference, for both
facts and immediate inferences are invariably undebatable. One cannot debate the immediate inference that a bar of metal is 477.21
mm $\pm$ .01mm long. Much less can one debate the fact upon which
this inference is based. One might be able to debate the mediate
inference that the bar is too long for a particular use, but only if
there is no immediate way of measuring. At best our debatable
propositions are mediate inferences many times removed from facts.

We might still be able to use the term "fact" without confusion in a rhetorical sense if we limited it to a proposition which
needs no further substantiation than its own statement. But even
this is a slippery use of the term. Perhaps in the bare report
where there is not the slightest tincture of judgment or evaluation,
not the least attempt to persuade, we might employ "proposition of
fact" as an apt designation (though it seems doubtful that a human
mind could deliver such a report). The moment doubt or dispute
arises in the audience the proposition of fact becomes something
else. The speaker would at that point muster argument to back his
bare assertion, and the proposition would be recognized not as a
fact but rather as a judgment of the speaker.

Thus, the first change I should advocate is one of terminology.
If the term "proposition of fact" must be used, let it be used only
for the subject matter of report where argument does not enter--if
such a report can be found. The propositions we defend through
argument are not facts at all; they are judgments.

A proposition of policy is a proposed action we advocate as
the result of a judgment, or a series of judgments leading to a mode
of action. We judge that a condition is bad, that a certain policy
would eliminate the bad condition, and that the policy is one that we

can afford, and we conclude from all these simple judgments that
we should adopt the policy. The proposition of policy, then, is a
complex judgment concerning a course of action. For this complex
judgment let us arbitrarily retain the name "proposition of policy. "

The issues of a proposition of policy are in themselves simple
judgments. To the simple judgments which comprise the issues of
a proposition of policy or to those simple judgments which before
we have called propositions of fact or value let us assign the name
"proposition of judgment. "

But now what of those distinctions that seemed so evident to
Wagner and his followers? Are the differences between fact and
value only chimerical? It seems necessary from our previous discussion to rule these categories out at least as major classes equal
to the proposition of policy. We have shown that the proposition of
policy and the proposition of judgment may be distinguished on two
grounds: the difference in the operations used to analyze them, and
their comparative complexity. It should be noted in particular that
this does not rule the fact-value distinction out of sub-categories of
the proposition of judgment. The distinction has no bearing on the
analysis of a proposition of judgment (that is, the stock issues that
may be applied to it), but it does affect the material subsumed in
the analysis. There are indeed factual and value judgments. Their
structures are not dissimilar, but the materials from which proof
is drawn to argue them are different.

The judgment that the Copernican theory of the structure of
the solar system was better than the Ptolemaic theory is one based,
today at least, on factual data open to qualified observers. The
evidence used to prove the judgment would be factual in nature.
However, when Copernicus first enunciated his theory he had not
one shred of factual evidence to support it. Galileo's subsequent
acceptance of the judgment had two reasons: the theory contradicted
Aristotle--and Galileo distrusted Aristotle--and it was simpler than
the Ptolemaic theory because it reduced the number of epicycles
necessary to explain all phenomena. Galileo's first reason was emotional, the second might be termed esthetic: both of them clearly
classifiable as values. The structure of the argument was the same

in both cases, for indeed both of them had the same proposition. The evidence only was of a different nature. The fact-value distinction depends, therefore, not on the wording or form of the proposition but rather on the type of evidence that must be used to prove it.

Such a distinction, then, may be useful in pointing the advocate to the type of evidence he must discover and to indicate to him what test he must apply to the evidence to determine its soundness.

There are thus two general forms of argumentative propositions: those of judgment and those of policy. These two types subtend two different operations of analysis. The proposition of policy is a complex judgment to act based upon a series of simple judgments. The proposition of judgment is in itself a simple judgment.

The proposition of judgment may be either a factual judgment or a value (or moral) judgment. If a factual judgment, then the evidence used to support the issues will be factual in nature. If a value or moral judgment, the evidence used to support the issues will be based on some value system or moral principle. In any given proposition of judgment there may be a mixture of both factual and moral evidence, ranging from the purely factual by infinite gradations to the purely moral.

This change in the theory of classification has several advantages. It eliminates the idea that propositions differ absolutely in kind. One sees, on the contrary, that the proposition of policy is merely a complex judgment comprised of a series of propositions of judgment. The change also eliminates the confusions in the distinction between fact and value and the resultant futile attempts to distinguish their analysis. The change should result in a clearer understanding of the relation between classification and analysis and should clarify the work of the advocate in dealing with propositions.

Reprinted from the Quarterly Journal of Speech, 49:266-273, October, 1963. Mr. Terris is Assistant Professor of Speech at the University of Denver.

Notes

1. James H. McBurney, James M. O'Neill, and Glen E. Mills, Argumentation and Debate. New York, 1959, pp. 37-39.
2. George Pierce Baker, The Principles of Argumentation. Boston, 1895.
3. George Pierce Baker and Henry Barrett Huntington, The Principles of Argumentation. Boston, 1905.
4. Ibid., p. 7.
5. Victor A. Ketcham, Argumentation and Debate. New York, 1928, p. 5.
6. William Trufant Foster, Argumentation and Debating. Boston, 1932, pp. 13-14. (First published in 1917.) This is not to say that Foster had deserted the conviction-persuasion duality because patently he had not, but he did not use the duality as the sole basis for classifying propositions.
7. William Trufant Foster, Argumentation and Debating, 2nd rev. ed. Boston, 1945, p. 13. The sections under discussion here are identical in both the 1932 and 1945 editions.
8. Richard Whately, Elements of Rhetoric, 7th ed. London, 1846, p. 112.
9. The Institutio Oratoria of Quintilian, trans. H. E. Butler, iii. vi, 1-104, passim. Cf. Otto Alvin Loeb Dieter, "Stasis," Speech Monographs, XVII, November 1950, pp. 345-369.
10. Foster, 1945, p. 14.
11. A. Craig Baird, Public Discussion and Debate. Boston, 1928, pp. 41, 42.
12. A. Craig Baird, Argumentation, Discussion and Debate. New York, 1950, pp. 22, 23.
13. Russell H. Wagner, Handbook of Argumentation. New York, 1938, pp. 15-16.
14. Egbert Ray Nichols and Joseph H. Baccus, Modern Debating. New York, 1936, p. 103.
15. McBurney, O'Neill, and Mills, pp. 22-24.
16. Austin J. Freeley, Argumentation and Debate. San Francisco, 1961, pp. 22-23.
17. Douglas Ehninger and Wayne Brockriede, Decision by Debate. New York, 1963, pp. 217-228. These authors, however, add a fourth type of proposition, the proposition of definition, which appears to be an alternative form of the proposition of fact.
18. Arthur N. Kruger, Modern Debate. New York, 1960, pp. 15-16.
19. McBurney, O'Neill, and Mills, pp. 33-36.
20. Freeley, pp. 34-35.
21. Both the propositions of fact and value are also analyzable by means of the classical status. This can best be seen by applying status to two propositions, one clearly a proposition of fact, the other a proposition of value. "Separate school facilities are inherently unequal" would be a proposition of fact. "The separate but equal doctrine is harmful to our educational system" would be a proposition of value. (Both of these are paraphrases of propositions found in Ehninger and Brockriede, pp. 218-219.) The conjectural status

is determined by the answer to the question "What is the
fact in question: did it occur, what is its nature?" In the
first case it would be answered by a description of the separate facilities, in the second by a description of the influence of the doctrine on the educational system.   The definitive status is determined by the answer to the question
"How may this fact be defined?" In the first case it would
be answered by an attempt to show that the definition of unequal would fit the description, in the second by a definition
of the doctrine's influence as harmful.   The qualitative status would be determined by the answer to the question "Is
the fact qualified or justified?" The application of this status is obvious.

22. Lee Hultzén, "Status in Deliberative Analysis," in The Rhetori-
    cal Idiom, ed. Donald C. Bryant. Ithaca, N. Y., 1958, p.
    103.

23. And also by the classical doctrine of status (above, no. 21).

24. It might be argued here that though the questions are of a simi-
    lar form they are not identical when you come to ask speci-
    fic questions of specific propositions. This is true and a
    discussion of this dissimilarity appears later in this article.

25. See Ernst Cassirer, Substance and Function and Einstein's
    Theory of Relativity. [Chicago], 1953, pp. 143-148 for this
    sense of the word fact. See also James Edwin Creighton
    and Harold R. Smart, An Introductory Logic, New York,
    1953, pp. 117 ff. for one of innumerable treatments of me-
    diate and immediate inference.

8. Propositions of Past and Future Fact and Value:
A Proposed Classification
Gary Cronkhite

One of the most difficult skills for the beginning speech student to master is the ruthless narrowing of his general topic to a
specific thesis which he can handle in a limited time. Methods for
narrowing the expository topic are difficult enough to find, but they
eventually appear. However, the dimensions upon which an argumentative speech may be narrowed are often more elusive. The argumentative proposition of a given type has often been considered to
contain a given number of issues, each of which is inviolate, with
a vast gulf fixed between the types of propositions, preventing one
from being transformed into the other. The purpose of the present
paper is to propose a scheme for the classification of propositions
which seems to allow more freedom in moving from one type of

proposition to another, and seems to yield at least two dimensions
on which propositions may be narrowed.

Wagner, to whom is attributed the classification of propositions into categories of fact, value, and policy,[1] specified propositions of fact as those asserting existence or relationships of objects
or events, while propositions of value were to be those assigning a
value label to an object or event.[2] Terris rejected this distinction
between fact and value as major types of propositions on the ground
that the same scheme of analysis is used in both: one first establishes the criteria by which an assertion may be judged true and
then applies the criteria to the assertion. He proposed that propositions of fact and value be subsumed under "propositions of judgment," retaining "propositions of policy" as a second classification.
He wrote, "The proposition of policy is a complex judgment to act
based upon a series of simple judgments. The proposition of judgment is in itself a simple judgment."[3] Further, "The fact-value
distinction depends . . . not on the wording or form of the proposition but rather on the type of evidence that must be used to prove
it."[4] More specifically:

> The proposition of judgment may be either a factual or a
> value (moral) judgment. If a factual judgment, then the
> evidence used to support the issue will be factual in na-
> ture. If a value or moral judgment, the evidence used
> to support the issues will be based on some value sys-
> tem or moral principle. In any given proposition of
> judgment there may be a mixture of both factual and
> moral evidence ranging from the purely factual by infinite
> gradations to the purely moral.[5]

Terris is not clear whether he means to specify that propositions which involve judgments of fact "should" be supported by factual evidence, or that audiences typically make "factual judgments" on
the basis of "factual evidence." If he means to suggest that audiences actually make controversial factual judgments solely on the
basis of factual evidence, then his speculation does not fit the facts.
The literature of social psychology is saturated with evidence that
individuals tend to misperceive and to forget information which conflicts with their predispositions, attitudes, and values. Hasdorf and
Cantril, for example, demonstrated that students viewing a film of a

game between two schools counted more rule infractions on the part of their opponents.[6] Such research seems naive because we have seen it demonstrated so often. Yet it does illustrate that a proposition of fact ("Team A committed more rule infractions than did team B") may be settled on the basis of the respondents' values.

The confusion responsible for Terris' statement may be due to a confounding of "propositions" with "judgments." The "proposition" is the verbal expression of a "judgment" previously made by the speaker; this statement of a "proposition" calls, in turn, for a "judgment" (a response of agreement or disagreement) on the part of the listener. As already illustrated, a proposition of fact may produce a judgment based on the listener's values. On the other hand, it is almost inevitable that the listener's judgment in response to a proposition of value will be to some extent determined by facts, or at least by beliefs he has about facts. Confronted with the value proposition "Premarital intercourse is immoral," an individual will immediately begin converting it to a proposition of fact by defining the value term "immoral." If he believes "that is immoral which my church condemns," then his response to the proposition of value will be based on the fact that his church condemns premarital intercourse. If he believes "that is immoral which harms an innocent person," then his judgment will be based on the fact that innocent illegitimate children are sometimes harmed by premarital intercourse.

Actually, any judgment involves two components: an objective component, attributable to present sensory stimulation, and a subjective component, attributable to the residue of previous experience on the part of the judge. That there are two such components need not rest merely upon speculation. We might set a group of judges to the task of judging the darkness of skin of a number of different persons. We could then statistically compute the proportion of the variance in the judgments due to differences among the persons judged (the objective component), the proportion of the variance due to differences between the judges (the subjective component), the proportion of the variance caused by the interaction of objective differences with subjective differences, and the proportion of the variance due to unknown causes, or random error. Such studies are, in fact, quite numerous in the field of attitude measurement.[7]

What has been termed the "subjective" component seems to be further divisible into what Stevenson has termed "beliefs" and "attitudes. " He wrote, "Questions about the nature of light-transmission, the voyages of Leif Ericsson, and the date on which Jones was last in to tea, are all similar in that they may involve an opposition that is primarily of beliefs. " Other questions "involve an opposition . . . which is not of beliefs, but rather of attitudes-- that is to say, an opposition of purposes, aspirations, wants, preferences, desires, and so on. "[8] To rephrase Wagner's definitions of propositions of fact and value, a "belief" is a feeling about "existence or relationships of objects or events, " while an "attitude" is a feeling regarding the value of an object or an event.

An experiment by Rosenberg makes this relationship clear. He tested subjects regarding their liking for (attitudes toward) such concepts as increased foreign aid, increased U.S. prestige, and increased taxation. He also tested their beliefs about such questions as the extent to which increased foreign aid would cause increased U.S. prestige and increased taxation. Typically, the person who liked increased foreign aid believed it would increase U.S. prestige and would cause little increased taxation. These subjects were then hypnotized and told that they would later feel nauseated at the mention of increased foreign aid. As would be expected, when next tested their attitudes toward foreign aid were less favorable, but they were also less inclined to believe that increased foreign aid would increase U.S. prestige and more inclined to believe it would increase taxes. The subjects, unaware of the posthypnotic suggestion, invented very imaginative rationalizations for their new beliefs.[9] Fishbein and Raven, incidentally, have proposed a means of conveniently measuring beliefs as well as attitudes using scales of the semantic differential type.[10] The present writer has tried to apply this analysis to the criticism of argumentative discourse.[11]

It is not for purposes of analysis that we distinguish between propositions of fact and those of value, nor is it because their proofs necessarily demand different types of evidence. The choice

of a given type of proposition is a rhetorical device designed to prepare the audience for a particular type of argument.

Consider a situation in which the purpose of the speaker is to
make the audience less favorable toward premarital intercourse. If
he is certain his audience will be unfavorable toward an act which
harms an innocent person, he may state his thesis as a proposition
of fact: "Premarital intercourse causes suffering for innocent persons." The audience is led to expect evidence that such is indeed
the case. On the other hand, suppose the speaker has in mind a
number of reasons why the act is immoral, and feels that their
truth is so obvious that the audience will accept them without proof,
or (less ethically) wishes to avoid demonstrating the reality of the
relationship. Suppose, for example, the audience knows that the
Catholic Church condemns the act, will agree without evidence that
it harms innocent persons, and will agree without evidence that it
prejudices marital success. The speaker would then be well advised to use a proposition of value: "Premarital intercourse is immoral." The audience is then led to expect only definitions of the
term "immoral."

In either case the rhetorical device may be unsuccessful. The
proposition of fact may still yield a judgment based on audience
values, or the audience hearing the definitions of "immoral" may
demand evidence that the act fits the definitions. The process of
analysis is the same in either case, but the proposition of value is
designed to focus audience attention on the choice of the criteria,
while the proposition of fact is designed to focus audience attention
on the demonstration that the object of judgment matches the criteria.

To leave the analysis here, however, would leave the impression that the speaker always has the choice of defending either a
proposition of fact or one of value. That certainly is not true. If
it is the purpose of the speaker to change attitudes of the audience
(for example, if he wishes to change attitudes toward premarital intercourse, as in the preceding illustration), then he has the option
of restating the proposition of value as a more narrow proposition
of fact. Even if his formal proposition is one of value, he will

proceed to "prove" it by proving the propositions of fact upon which it rests. Our attitudes toward a given concept (premarital inter-course) depend upon our beliefs about its relationships with other concepts (church approval or harm to innocent persons). Festinger and numerous others have considerably enhanced their reputations by investigating the cognitive gymnastics we use to keep our atti-tudes and beliefs consistent, and our beliefs consistent with reality. More basically, if one is to achieve pleasure and avoid pain, then he must keep his attitudes consistent with relationships in the real world. One's attitude toward "touching a hot stove" had best be consistent with his attitude toward the real and predictable effect of touching a hot stove (which, as we all know, is only a sudden ac-celeration of the molecular activity of the flesh).

On the other hand, proof of propositions of fact does not "rest upon" proof of subsidiary propositions of value in the same sense. Consider the illustrations again. The speaker in the previous ex-ample, attempting to prove that a given contraceptive device is 99.9 percent effective, a proposition of fact, might find Catholics especially hard to convince because of their unfavorable attitudes to-ward contraceptives. Yet Catholics, Protestants, and atheists would agree that attitudes toward contraceptives have no bearing upon the question of their effectiveness.

Propositions of fact and value are related, then, in that the proposition of value may be validly (and effectively) supported by proof of the propositions of fact upon which it rests. A proposition of fact, however, may not be given valid support by proof of prop-ositions of value, although a speaker may be forced to deal with audience values which prevent its acceptance.

Now what of propositions of policy? Their analysis does not seem to differ from that of propositions of value as much as Hult-zén and Terris seem to believe. Certainly a proposition of value may assign a value label to a policy as well as to an object or an event. Consider how little difference there is between the following propositions: (1) the present system of immigration quotas is good, and (2) the present system of immigration quotas should be contin-ued. In both cases we proceed to establish criteria and then match

the policy to the criteria. In the first case, that of the proposition
of value, we ask as criteria, "Is it meeting an existing need, is it
working, is it creating any problems, are there any better alternatives?" In the second case, a proposition of policy, we ask, "Will
it meet an existing need, will it work, will it create new problems,
are there any better alternatives?" The only difference is that we
have moved from judgment of a past and present policy to judgment
of a future policy. Thus it appears that a proposition of policy is
merely a proposition of value extended into the future. To our analysis of a proposition of past value we must add the assumption that
a need demonstrated to exist at present will continue to exist in the
future, and the assumption that a proposal (or its analogue, or its
constituents) demonstrated to be satisfactory in the past will continue to be satisfactory in the future. These assumptions, however,
do not add much to the analysis of the proposition of past value,
since they are both inherently incapable of proof.

There seems to be one type of proposition which does not fit
any classification thus far proposed. Mills has taken note of it and
has termed it a "proposition of prediction."[12] "Recognition of Communist China will cause the U.S. to lose prestige" is an example of
this fourth type. Obviously these are close kin to propositions of
fact, since they predict existence or relationships of objects, events,
or policies. We will refer to them as propositions of future fact.

Thus a two-way breakdown of propositions has been proposed.
The first distinction to be made is between propositions which deal
with the existence or relationships of objects, events, or policies
and those which assign a value label to such objects, events, or policies. The second distinction to be made is between propositions
which concern the past or present and those which concern the future.

Of the four types of propositions which result from such a
breakdown, the proposition of future value ("The U.S. should extend
diplomatic recognition to Red China") is the most complex and the
most difficult to prove, since it assigns or implies[13] a value term
and necessitates the unprovable assumption that the future will resemble the past. Its proof depends upon propositions of future fact

(U.S. recognition of Red China will cause increased U.S. prestige) which in turn depend upon propositions of past fact (U.S. recognition in similar cases has caused increased U.S. prestige), and it requires, in addition, careful choice of audience values (increased U.S. prestige). The proposition of past fact is least complex and easiest to prove, since it does not require such careful choice of audience values and does not necessitate the assumption that the future will resemble the past.

This analysis suggests that the speaker preparing to state an argumentative thesis should forge a careful compromise based on his knowledge of what he has time to prove and what his audience will be willing to accept without proof or supply for themselves. If his purpose is to cause his audience to change their beliefs about past existence or relationships of objects, he has no logically acceptable alternative but to state a proposition of past fact, although he may have to deal with audience value (or attitudes) as obstacles to belief.   However, if his purpose is to change audience attitudes toward a proposed policy, such as a constitutional amendment outlawing the death penalty, he has a number of alternatives.   Depending on how much time he has and how much his audience will supply for themselves, he may state a proposition of future fact, such as "Outlawing the death penalty on a national scale will cause no increase in the rate of capital crimes, " or a proposition of past (or present) value, such as "Outlawing the death penalty is good. " He may even feel justified in limiting his thesis to a simple proposition of past fact, such as "Nations which have abolished the death penalty have observed no increase in the rate of capital crimes, " and may still accomplish his full purpose.   This provides the speaker with two clear dimensions upon which to narrow the scope of his argument, and seems to allow the speaker greater freedom to move from one type of proposition to another as the occasion may demand.

Reprinted from the Journal of the American Forensic Association, 3:11-16, January, 1966.   Gary Cronkhite is Assistant Professor of Speech, University of Illinois.

Notes

1. Numerous other types of propositions have been suggested, but
   these seem to be the most hardy. The "proposition of definition" suggested by Ehninger and Brockriede (see Douglas
   Ehninger and Wayne Brockriede, Decision by Debate, New
   York, 1963, pp. 219-220) has not been considered by the
   writer because it can be resolved into either a proposition
   of fact or a proposition of policy. When one says "Rhetoric means the art of persuasion," he is arguing either that
   a given group of people agree on that meaning, which is a
   proposition of fact, or that rhetoric should mean the art of
   persuasion, which is a proposition of policy.

2. Russell H. Wagner, Handbook of Argumentation, New York,
   1938, pp. 15-16.

3. Walter F. Terris, "The Classification of the Argumentative
   Proposition," Quarterly Journal of Speech, XLIX, October,
   1963, pp. 266-273.

4. Ibid., p. 273.

5. Ibid.

6. A. Hasdorf and H. Cantril, "They Saw a Game: A Case Study,"
   Journal of Abnormal and Social Psychology, XLIX, February
   1954, pp. 129-134.

7. See Carl I. Hovland and Muzafer Sherif, Social Judgment, New
   Haven, 1961; Muzafer Sherif, Carolyn Sherif, and Roger
   Nebergall, Attitude and Attitude Change, Philadelphia, 1965;
   and M.H. Segall, "Effect of Attitude and Experience on
   Judgments of Controversial Statements," Journal of Abnormal and Social Psychology, LVIII, January, 1959, pp. 61-
   68.

8. Charles L. Stevenson, Ethics and Language. New Haven, 1944,
   p. 3.

9. Milton J. Rosenberg, "An Analysis of Affective-Cognitive Consistency," in Carl I. Hovland and Milton J. Rosenberg, ed.,
   Attitude, Organization and Change, New Haven, 1960; and
   Milton J. Rosenberg, "A Structural Theory of Attitude Dynamics," Public Opinion Quarterly, XXIV, Summer, 1960,
   pp. 319-340.

10. M. Fishbein and B.H. Raven, "The AB Scales: An Operational
    Definition of Belief and Attitude," Human Relations, XV,
    February, 1962, pp. 35-44.

11. Gary Cronkhite, "Logic, Emotion, and the Paradigm of Persua-
    sion," Quarterly Journal of Speech, L, February, 1964, pp.
    13-18.

12. Glen E. Mills, Reason in Controversy. Boston, 1964, p. 63.

13. To say "The U.S. should extend diplomatic recognition to Red
    China" seems to be the practical equivalent of saying "For
    the U.S. to extend diplomatic recognition to Red China is
    good."

Issue E: Should Experts from Special Areas Be Solicited to Submit
Debate Resolutions?

> In his article "Questions on Questions," Walter F.
> Stromer voices the frequently heard complaint that the
> national debate topic, chosen annually by debate coaches
> throughout the country, is often unsuitable. He there-
> fore recommends, "Rather than waiting until December
> to call in experts from other fields to tell us about the
> ins and outs of a question, why not call in the experts
> in the spring and let them suggest some topics?" In re-
> ply, Austin J. Freeley, in "The Right Expert--At the
> Right Time," points out that the Committee on Intercol-
> legiate Debate and Discussion has followed this practice
> for several years, with dubious results, which he cites.
> Freeley concludes that the Committee could use more
> expert advice, but "from the experts in the field of ar-
> gumentation and debate."

9. Questions on Questions
Walter F. Stromer

Time and again my students have groaned, I have grumbled,
and other forensics directors have muttered imprecations about the
current debate topic, whatever the year or the topic. Articles have
appeared in the speech journals which point out that the affirmative
team hasn't a chance, either because of the lopsidedness of the
judges or of the question. If the reactions of debaters and debate
coaches are worth noting, we might conclude that our national debate questions frequently leave something to be desired. Is there
any way to improve them?

Perhaps we should admit at the outset that sometimes our debate questions are not quite realistic in that we force students to
take positions which are absolute and extreme, whereas in Congress
the sharpest debate comes not on a yes-no issue, but on the question of degree. For example, on the question of discontinuing direct

economic aid to foreign countries, we asked students to debate a
black and white issue, while in the Congress the issue is how much
aid or how little, and of what kind, and to whom, not a question of
stopping it all together. Some debate questions in the past few
years have resembled closely the debates in the nation or the world,
as when we debated the recognition of Red China or the right-to-
work laws. Perhaps we cannot always choose a question which di-
vides neatly into opposing sides, but we might try for it.

What we need, I think, is not a bigger and better committee
to tabulate our responses and do the final wording of the question,
but a different approach to the method of selecting the debate question. It occurs to me that our present system expresses an unjustified faith in the wisdom of a numerical majority of all speech teachers present.

We can probably agree that we speech teachers are well educated; we may even feel that we are more broadly educated than
some of our colleagues in education. But if we claim to be experts
on nuclear warfare, foreign aid, labor relations, and similar complicated problems, our fellow faculty members may well ask how we
have time to be expert in speech. To be sure, at the end of a year
of directing research and judging debates on a particular topic, we
may have acquired some expertness; but, by then, it is time to select the next topic. Our lack of thorough understanding of political
and economic problems may explain why some of the topics we submit for debate resolutions turn out to be not very debatable come
October and November. Even the best of wording committees cannot tabulate a thousand ambiguous and inadequate suggestions into one
valid debate resolution.

At the Chicago convention at Christmas, a professor of history
said he thought our current debate topic was a poor one because the
information on which the ultimate decision would be based was secret
and not available to the debaters whom we are asking to resolve the
problem. Granted this is one man's opinion, but personally I might
have voted for a different topic if that thought had occurred to me in
April, instead of December. Rather than waiting until December to
call in experts from other fields to tell us about the ins and outs of

a question, why not call in the experts in the spring and let them suggest some topics? From their more complete understanding of special areas they should be able to suggest topics which would be truly debatable. We would still vote on their suggestions, and we could still reserve the right to add new questions. The questions suggested by the experts could be published in the speech journals in time for us to consider them before we cast our first ballot.

It is probably safe to say that even the aid of the experts would not guarantee a perfect debate question delighted in by all students and teachers. But at least we would be putting into effect one of the principles we teach our students; i. e., make use of the best available sources of information. That could mean calling in the experts.

Reprinted from the Quarterly Journal of Speech, 45:321-322, October, 1959. At the time this essay was written, Mr. Stromer was teaching at Cornell College.

10. The Right Expert--At the Right Time
Austin J. Freeley

In a Forum letter in the October 1959 QJS, Walter F. Stromer makes the suggestion that we should call in the experts in an effort to provide our students with better balanced national intercollegiate debate propositions. I would like to agree with the idea of calling in the experts, but suggest a different sort of expert from the ones proposed.

Professor Stromer wrote, "Why not call in the experts [from other fields] in the spring and let them suggest some topics?" This has been done for the past several years. In the opinion of this writer it is of limited value. As a member of the Committee on Intercollegiate Debate and Discussion, I regularly invited a number of persons prominent in public life to suggest debate propositions. This was done in the hope that various editors, publishers, presidents of major universities, government officials, and others prom-

inent in public affairs would be "experts" on what problems would
be the subject of Congressional and public debate in the coming academic year and thus could suggest timely and significant propositions. A number replied. The following samples are representative of suggestions received over the years:

> Should not American political parties be realigned to
> provide a clear-cut differentiation between conservative
> and liberal points of view? (President of a Midwestern
> university.)

> Resolved: That science is more important than the hu-
> manities in education for the nation's service. (Presi-
> dent of a large foundation.)

> That citizens of the District of Columbia should be grant-
> ed self-government and allowed to vote in federal elec-
> tions. (Congressman.)

> That the present postal rate structure is inimical to the
> best interests of the American people (with special ref-
> erence to second-class mail). (Publisher.)

> That the European coal and steel community should be
> expanded to a broader program of economic and political
> integration. (Government official.)

> That Indians be integrated into full American citizenship
> and that the segregated reservation system be abolished
> within five years. (Government official.)

What expert in the field of argumentation and educational debate would propose any of these for a national debate proposition?
These suggestions shouldn't surprise us, however. They are, after
all, what we reasonably could expect from persons not familiar with
academic debating.

These samples suggest that the subject matter experts are not
the best source for propositions; there is still another problem.
Many subject matter experts cannot recognize a debatable proposition when they see one. Professor Stromer tells of a history professor who maintained the proposition, "Resolved: That the further
development of nuclear weapons should be prohibited by international
agreement," was a poor one because the ultimate decision would be
based on secret information not available to the debaters. This is
an excellent case in point. The fact is that if this matter does

come up for ultimate decision it would be settled by debate in the Senate and in the public forums. A good deal of secret information would probably be made public at that time, just as much previously secret information was made public at the Geneva negotiations. In this country we regularly debate matters on which there is relevant secret information. If we didn't, the history professor would have to terminate his course at some time prior to the Civil War; new information on the problems of that period is still being uncovered. Would the history professor want to suspend debate on all matters involved with secret information? Such a limitation would most seriously circumscribe the area of public debate and hamper democracy.

A subject matter expert, a well-known economist, once assured me that a proposition about agricultural price supports was undebatable. He informed me that there was no rational case for price supports; they were simply political pap for farm state senators. I'll let my friends from the farm states answer that one. Although subject matter experts have definite limitations in the suggesting or phrasing of propositions, their advice, if taken judiciously, can be of real value. In phrasing propositions on labor a few years ago the Committee profitably consulted a member of a Wall Street law firm. In another year consultations with physicists, military officials, and research men at the M.I.T. Radiation Laboratories proved of value in phrasing a proposition on nuclear weapons.

It is not my purpose to decry experts; we need more expert advice from the right sort of experts. We teach our students that an expert is an expert in a certain area only. The problem here is one of argumentation and educational debate. The experts in this field are to be found among those who direct forensic programs and teach argumentation courses. Let us adhere to our own teachings and call in the experts from the appropriate subject field.

To be sure, these experts are consulted now in the annual spring poll by the Committee. Some give most valuable replies. Many, however, limit their reply to a word or two. Such curt suggestions as "labor," "something on education," or "Supreme Court" do not reflect the judgments needed. If all those seriously con-

cerned with educational debate would take a few hours each spring
to work out well phrased, carefully considered propositions in three
or four timely and significant areas they would be making a real
contribution. Expert advice would help. Let's have more of it--
and at the right time--from the experts in the field of argumentation and debate.

There is one final problem raised by Professor Stromer's letter, the suggestion that on some propositions the "affirmative hasn't
a chance." If one studies the tournament results of certain years
it is undeniable that the affirmative--or the negative--certainly has
an advantage. Is this, however, a problem, even granted that we
want a fairly evenly balanced proposition? Will the student, or any
advocate, in a non-academic debate be guaranteed that the evidence
and reasoning is balanced exactly fifty percent on his side? Are
not the greatest advocates those who won with the odds seemingly
against them? If the concern be with the short-term goal of winning a certain tournament, there would still seem to be no problem.
Most tournaments are either unit (one affirmative and one negative
team) or team (two speakers alternating as affirmative and negative)
events. Thus any slight advantage to one side is cancelled out in
the college's total record.

Reprinted from the Quarterly Journal of Speech, 46:81-82, February,
1960. Dr. Freeley is Professor of Speech at John Carroll University.

Issue F: Are Simpler Debate Topics Desirable?

> Although high school debate topics were the subject of
> the debate which appears here, the pro's and con's also
> apply to college debate topics, which are often the same.
> Those who favor simpler topics usually argue that the
> national topics are beyond the capacity of most students
> and also that simpler topics would permit more topics
> to be debated during the year--which in turn would pro-
> duce some variety and perhaps more interest in the de-
> bate program.   On the other hand, those who defend the
> status quo usually point out, as does Christobel Cordell,
> that the student should be challenged "to meet and solve
> actual problems of government and economics," for such
> experience will be far more valuable to him than that of
> discussing trivial subjects which are within his experi-
> ence, like school athletics.

11. Are Simpler Debate Topics Desirable?   Yes!
John T. Miller

I am accepting an invitation, extended in the November issue
of Platform News, to write about a matter which should claim the
attention and careful consideration of all those interested in foster-
ing a program of constructive debate in the high school.

For some time it has seemed to me that the topics announced
periodically for high school debate have been highly inappropriate.
Their analysis has frequently required a type of thinking and an element of research too complicated for the experience represented by
the adolescent mind.   The problem becomes, therefore, largely one
of adjustment of factors involved.   There is no disposition here to
criticize the topics as such; but rather to question seriously their
propriety for purposes of effective debate on the high school level.

Most of these topics, both state and national, remind me of
an incident which is said to have happened in a small town community.   A group of well-known artists were appearing for an evening's

81

entertainment.   In presenting the visiting artists, the chairman said:
"Ladies and Gentlemen, we are greatly honored this evening by the
presence of a group of distinguished guests.   Their program will
consist only of high-class selections.   Much of it, therefore, may
be over your heads; but may I remind you that it will not be over
where your heads ought to be."

From my rather extended experience in judging high school debates, and from my own attempts to coach debate teams on the college level, I am persuaded that the debate topics employed, for the
past few years at least, have been clearly over the heads, not only
of those participating, but of the audience as well.   Just how far
"above where their heads ought to be" constitutes a problem for the
statistician.   The above conclusion, if questioned, can readily be
validated by a cross-examination of any typical high school debating
team.

The point of departure in selecting a debate topic, it seems
to me, should center around the personal experience and general
fitness of the prospective debaters.   Every other consideration
should be given secondary ranking.   An examination and comparison
of high school and college debate topics will reveal an almost total
disregard of this criterion of relative values.   If the point of view
taken here is sound, there is misplacement of emphasis somewhere
along the way.   There seems to be a lack of co-ordination of the
personal and impersonal factors involved.   There is very little dis-
cernible difference in the difficulty of topics used on the high school
and college levels.   Obviously, we are either expecting too much of
our high school pupils, or we are discounting the abilities of those
appearing on the college level.   May it not be entirely possible that
modern debate topics dealing with such subjects as: "Resolved:
That the Power of Federal Government Should be Increased" and
"Resolved: That the Nations of the Western Hemisphere Should Enter Into a Permanent Union," are too complicated for the best results, either on the high school or college level?

When a boy comes to grips with a debate topic such as the
above, he is forced to resort to the employment of agencies outside
of his own resources.   The frequent result is that he engages some-

one else to write his speech outright, or he himself may roughly
assemble the parts from whatever sources are found available, without an adequate sense of values, or perspective, to guide him in the
process. The finished product, naturally, will represent an unas-
similated mass of data, juxtaposed without regard to the principles
of Unity, Coherence and Emphasis. Debating, conducted in such
fashion, becomes a parrot-like procedure, and consequently defeats
its own purpose.

The point that I am endeavoring to make is that we need to
recast our present type of debate topic--to bring it within reach of
the high school pupil, where he can use his own resources successfully in attacking it. Furthermore, we need to be reminded constantly that debating is not an end in itself, but at best only a means
to an end. Unmistakable danger lurks here. The final product or
result must be reckoned in terms of the growth of the individual in
clear thinking and accurate expression. The topics presented should
be such as to enable the pupil, with a minimum of guidance, to
think through intelligently with a reasonable amount of individual
study and preparation. Such a change in the subject matter of debate, it seems to me, will register much more effective results and
will revitalize the whole program of high school debating.

Reprinted from Platform News, 7:4, 6, March-April, 1941. At the
time this article was written, the author was Professor of Education and Psychology, Brenau College, Gainesville, Georgia.

12. Are Simpler Debate Topics Desirable? No!
Christobel M. Cordell

It is extremely doubtful whether the moot question of the suitability of debate topics will ever be settled to the satisfaction of
everyone, because it is an argument between two completely differing points of view. Before we can answer the question "Are current debate topics suitable?" we must ask and answer another question, "Suitable for what?" Their suitability depends entirely on

whether we regard debating as an end itself, or as a means to a
greater end.

On the one hand we have a faction that persists in the belief
that the sole purpose of debating is to enable a student to discuss
a controversial question glibly and convincingly. Obviously, the
simpler the topic the more glib and convincing a speaker can be.
Those who have only this end in view are entirely justified in insisting that debate topics should be wholly within the realm of the debater's personal experience.

There is another faction, however, that views debating as a
means to broaden the scope of a student's knowledge and understanding by research, logical thinking, and competent coaching. Those
who share this view are entirely justified in their belief that debate
topics should be based on questions of national and international importance.

While I share the latter view, I will agree that not all high
school, or even college, students have the mental capacity to discuss intelligently questions that carry them beyond their own limited
experience.

This brings up another question. Should the standards of debating be lowered to come within the easy reach of the slower-
thinking student, or should they be kept at their present high level
to serve as a stimulus to the more alert student?

If the former course were pursued it would inevitably mean
the complete collapse of our present system of competitive debate,
for the less alert students would never have an overpowering interest
in debate however simple the topic; while the more advanced student
would quickly lose interest in a form of debating which did not serve
as a constant challenge to his acquisitive mental skills.

There are certain individuals, however, who persist in the belief that the current type of debate topic is beyond the comprehension
of even the more advanced student. If this were true it would certainly indicate that a change in the trend of questions was in order.

But is it true? Anyone who has attended a national, or even
a state debate tournament recently, and heard high school debaters
deliver completely extemporaneous arguments with assurance and

conviction would answer "No!" without hesitation.

Those who have not had that opportunity should analyze the current topic--"Resolved: That the Power of the Federal Government Should Be Increased."

What are the requisites for an adequate comprehension of this topic? 1st: The student must have a knowledge and understanding of the general framework of our government. Is this possible? Surely, any student who has the mental capacity to absorb Latin and geometry will not find this beyond his scope of comprehension. If he cannot now grasp the fundamentals of our government it may safely be assumed that it will be forever beyond his understanding. 2nd: He must become familiar with certain problems now facing the United States government, such as labor regulations, control of utilities, etc. Admittedly, such problems cannot be fully comprehended without a certain amount of background study, clear thinking and guidance, but the same can be said for problems of science and biology that form a part of the average high school curricula.

We will not pretend that the average high school debater may not flounder about a bit awkwardly in his first few debates on Federal Power, just as the novice swimmer flounders about the first time he finds himself in deep water. But no one ever learned to swim by flapping his arms about on a parlor table, however gracefully he may flap. Nor would his parlor table experience do him much good if he fell overboard a couple of hundred yards from shore.

In the same sense, the debater who has had to meet and solve actual problems of government and economics on the debating rostrum, will be much better fitted to deal with those problems when they become personal to him, than will the debater whose experience was confined to discussing the relative merits of homework or interscholastic athletics.

Reprinted from Platform News, 7:5-7, March-April, 1941. Miss Cordell was a former editor of Platform News.

Suggestions for Further Reading

Gregg, Richard. "The Case for Two Propositions," Gavel, 41:15-
16, November, 1958.

Holm, James N. "Debating, 1958: A Re-Examination," AFA Register, 7:12-19, Spring, 1959.

Howe, Jack. "Report on Procedures for Selecting the National Debate Proposition," AFA Register, 8:21-25, Convention Issue,
1960.

Kruger, Arthur N. "The Debate Proposition," Section V, A Classified Bibliography of Argumentation and Debate. Metuchen,
N.J., Scarecrow Press, 1964, pp. 79-86.

Markgraf, Bruce. "The Selection of the National Debate Topic,"
AFA Register, 10:24-25, Winter, 1962.

Miller, Gerald R. "Questions of Fact and Value: Another Look,"
Southern Speech Journal, 28:116-122, Winter, 1962.

Miller, N., ed. "The Status of Debating: 1958," AFA Register,
7:5-11, Spring, 1959.

Murphy, Roy D. "Selecting Topics for Debate and Discussion,"
Forensic, 48:13-14, January, 1963.

Rahskopf, Horace G. "Questions of Fact Vs. Questions of Policy,"
Quarterly Journal of Speech, 17:60-70, February, 1932.

Ross, Raymond S., and Margaret Davis. "Choosing Controversial
Speech Subjects," Speech Teacher, 5:109-110, March, 1956.

Shepard, David W. "Logical Propositions and Debate Resolutions,"
Central States Speech Journal, 11:186-190, Spring, 1960.

Taylor, Carl, and Raymond H. Barnard. "Questioning the Debate
Question; How Should a Debate Proposition Be Phrased?"
Quarterly Journal of Speech, 16:355-360, June, 1930.

Thompson, Wayne N. "Criteria for Choosing a National Debate
Topic," Forensic, 47:14-16, October, 1962.

III. Analysis

Issue G: Are Affirmative Debaters Required to Show a Compelling and Inherent Need?

A long and heated controversy seems to have been generated by my article "The Meaning of Inherency," first published in November, 1962. In response, Patrick O. Marsh wrote a long article titled "Is Debate Merely a Game for Conservative Players?" (Speaker and Gavel, 1:46-53, January, 1964), which in turn elicited a series of four articles by me under the general title "The Underlying Assumptions of Policy Questions" (see bibliography). In answer to the first of these, "Presumption and Burden of Proof," Marsh wrote "Terminological Tangle: A Reply to Professor Kruger" (see bibliography), and after the last article of the series had appeared, he wrote "The Terminal Tangle: A Final Reply to Professor Kruger" (see bibliography). I in turn wrote "The Underlying Assumptions of Policy Questions: A Postscript" (see bibliography). Meanwhile, Robert Newman also took issue with "The Meaning of Inherency" and published the article (reprinted here) "The Inherent and Compelling Need." This prompted me to write "The Inherent Need: Further Clarification" (see bibliography). To sum up the issue, the traditional position, which I support, is that affirmative debaters advocating the adoption of a new policy are obliged to show the existence of a significant problem stemming from the status quo. Newman argues that affirmative debaters are not always obliged to do so.*

*At the 1965 Speech Association of America Convention (December 27-30), Todd G. Willy spoke on the "Concepts of Inherency" and, in reviewing the controversy, seemed to disagree with all parties. Also, Thomas Mader wrote an article, "The Inherent Need to Analyze Stasis" (JAFA, 4:13-20, Winter, 1967), "to throw some clearer light on a number of arguments" introduced by the three disputants.

13. The Meaning of Inherency
Arthur N. Kruger

Apparently there is still confusion among debaters and debate coaches on the meaning and significance of inherency in relation to the development of the affirmative case, particularly the issue concerning the need for changing the status quo. Only recently one writer on the subject remarked, "If the proposed plan has significant advantages even where 'serious weaknesses' are not 'inherent in the system,' could not one logically demonstrate that the plan should be adopted?" And he goes on to state, "The 'comparative advantages' affirmative attempts to do just this."[1] Such comments reveal a lack of understanding of the underlying logic of the affirmative position that advocates the adoption of a new policy or program.

Since this whole matter is tied up with the affirmative's burden of proof, let's consider briefly what that burden is. In advocating a change or rejection of the status quo, the affirmative is asking us to abandon a program which is in existence and presumably has worked, however imperfectly, for some time. And this is to be discarded for a program whose workability can only be speculated about; that is, the affirmative in advocating the new policy can only argue what will probably happen, not what has happened, which is usually much more convincing. Since the status quo is almost never a total failure and since the affirmative policy can hardly be presented in such a way as to eliminate all doubt that it will be successful, there is an initial presumption for retaining the status quo, which operates in the negative's favor, or, from the affirmative's standpoint, presents a burden to be overcome. Now, to overcome this burden, the affirmative must try to prove that there is a compelling need to change the status quo. And in doing so, it must prove that the status quo is not only inferior to the proposed policy but is so inferior that minor changes would not put it on a par with the new policy. For if it could be demonstrated that minor changes would put it on a par, the advantage would lie with a status quo requiring only minor changes as against a new policy requiring major changes with its attendant complications and doubts. Thus, in ad-

vocating the need to change the status quo, which the affirmative is
doing by advocating a new policy, the affirmative must prove that
the status quo is inherently defective or seriously defective beyond
practical repair.

Before considering what is meant by "inherently defective, "
let us consider briefly the logic underlying the so-called "comparative advantages" case and how this approach evades the affirmative
burden, or obligation, and muddles a debate on policy questions.
To quote from Modern Debate: "In effect, the approach here is that
no serious problem exists--the status quo is working well--but the
affirmative program would be more advantageous than the existing
one. As one debater once put it, 'Although we didn't know what we
were missing when there were no electric lights, the world was a
much better place to live in when Edison finally invented the incandescent bulb. '"2 Actually, this is an indirect and somewhat confusing attempt to show that there really is a need for changing the
status quo; for if the affirmative program would result in some important gain, the absence of that gain is really a defect of the status
quo. For example, to take this year's question, if a non-commu-
nist economic community would accelerate economic growth within
the member nations, and such acceleration were extremely desirable
or very advantageous to the nations, the present rate of economic
growth would hardly be something that we could afford to be com-
placent about; for even without a communist threat, the present
growth rate (assuming that it could be substantially increased) is apparently not achieving the maximization of consumer satisfaction,
i. e. , providing goods and services at the lowest possible prices,
and it may be considered defective or "evil" to the degree that it is
failing to achieve this goal. Now if the affirmative were to argue
that the present growth rate is good but that it would be a little better under the affirmative plan, the "little better" would hardly justify our risking the abandonment of a system known to be working in
favor of a completely new system that we can only predict will be
a little better. No prudent individual, I dare say, would be willing
to take such a chance. On the other hand, if the affirmative were
to argue that the present growth rate is good but that it would be

much better under the affirmative plan, the affirmative would actually be contradicting itself; for if the growth rate would be much
better under its plan, the present growth rate can't be considered
very good.   Indeed, it must be pretty poor if there is so much
room for improvement.   So, in effect, the affirmative claim that
the status quo is working well is contradicted by its subsequent
claim for the affirmative plan.   This indirect and confusing (confused, really) approach to the need may well be lost on both the opposition and the judge, with the opposition contending that, if the
present program is wholly adequate as the affirmative claims, why
institute a completely new program on such tenuous grounds that it
might be better than what we have; why chance something untried
and unproved for something that is known to be working?   And the
judge will probably agree and vote accordingly.

Thus, it seems clear that the affirmative must first of all
show that a serious problem exists.   (To suggest that no problem
exists, as in the "comparative advantages" approach, is even worse
than contending that a minor problem exists.)   Second, to avoid the
fallacy of post hoc reasoning, it must demonstrate that the problem
inheres in, or is caused by, the existing policy.   In other words,
to demonstrate inherency is simply--though actually it isn't always
very simple--to demonstrate a causal relationship, in this instance
between the evil and the present system.   Let's consider a hypothetical case.   Although an affirmative might adduce evidence to show
that Burma resents U.S. economic aid, it would not be justified in
concluding that the U.S. should stop giving Burma aid; it would first
have to consider the specific cause of the resentment.   For resentment could be due to many things.   It might be due, for example,
to the fact that the wrong type of products was being sent to Burma,
or that the U.S. administrators of aid in Burma didn't speak Burmese, or that, being unacquainted with Burmese customs, they unwittingly offended the Burmese.   Now, if such were the case, the
resentment would not be an inherent evil; that is, it would not inhere
in, or be caused by, the essential character of the economic aid
program but by extraneous factors, which could be modified without
eliminating the program.   We could send different commodities and

change or educate the administrators of the program. No need to
stop giving economic aid in order to eliminate the resentment. But
if it could be shown that the aid was resented because it was given
bilaterally, that the bilateral character of the aid made the Burmese feel like poor relations vis a vis the United States or made
them suspicious that we were using the aid as a means of meddling
in their internal affairs, then we could conclude that if we wished
to eliminate this evil, we would have to stop giving aid, at least bilaterally. For in the latter instance we demonstrated that the evil
was directly caused by the bilateralness of economic aid, that is,
by the essential characteristic of the program that we wish to eliminate.

In most debates the key point of the need should be that of
equating the cause of existing evils with the essential characteristic
of the status quo.[3] Only thus can a real need for a change be
shown. If other than the essential characteristic of the present policy is identified or implied as the cause, the negative, as we have
seen, can claim that this characteristic can be removed without basically altering the present policy.

The failure to explore and grasp the causal relationships between the various components of the need issue not only results in
weak cases but often leads debaters to make statements which prejudice their position. A notable example was the final round of the
1958 National Debate Tournament at West Point. Here the affirmative, by not understanding inherency, indicated that they did not
truly understand the implications of their own arguments. During
the course of the debate they made such damaging statements as,
"Now, Dave and I do not contend that there is any causal relationship between corruption and the union shop"[4] and "Maybe we haven't
indicted compulsory unionism per se. "[5] (Yet compulsory unionism,
or the union shop, was the policy they were asking us to reject.)
If what they were saying was true, they might just as well have
said that they were conceding the debate. Actually, an analysis of
the affirmative's arguments would reveal that these statements were
not true, that they were indeed trying to show that compulsory
unionism was at the root of the evils cited, but what is a judge to

think when a team voluntarily obscures its true position by making such statements? The negative team, of course, was completely right and very effective in repeatedly focusing attention on such statements. [6]

In passing, it may be noted that although inherency is most often considered in connection with the affirmative need, it may also be considered in the area of impracticability. When a debater argues, for example, that there are insurmountable obstacles which would block the affirmative plan, the affirmative should endeavor to show that such obstacles are not inherently insurmountable and can thus be overcome. The negative in turn would be well advised to anticipate and to be prepared for such a rejoinder.

Summing up, inherency in a policy debate is synonymous with causality, and since both cases are basically a chain of causal relationships, it is a concept that must be understood and continually used.

Reprinted from The Gavel, 45:46-47; 54, March, 1963.

Notes

1. Patrick O. Marsh, "Prima Facie Case: The Perennial Debate
    Topic," The Gavel, XLV, November, 1962, p. 15.
2. A.N. Kruger, Modern Debate: Its Logic and Strategy. New
    York: McGraw-Hill Book Co., Inc., 1960, p. 42.
3. Occasionally, the two steps, existing evils and their cause, can
    be telescoped into one, as was possible with the 1958-59
    national topic, "The Further Development of Nuclear Weap-
    ons Should Be Prohibited by International Agreement." In
    speaking of the evil of radiation, it was hardly necessary
    for affirmatives to prove that the radiation was caused by
    nuclear weapons tests.
4. R.R. Windes and A.N. Kruger, Championship Debating. Port-
    land, Maine: J. Weston Walch, Publisher, 1961, p. 110.
5. Ibid., p. 115.
6. The affirmative blunder, as stated above, was undoubtedly due
    to their incomplete understanding of inherency and causation.
    Apparently, the affirmative only vaguely realized that the
    first of their so-called evils was not corruption by union of-
    ficials but that compulsory unionism forced workers to sup-
    port such corruption. In developing this and their other
    evils, the affirmative actually were "indicting the status quo"
    and attempting to show that these evils were inherent in or

caused directly by compulsion.

14. The Inherent and Compelling Need
Robert P. Newman

In the early 1960's it was proposed to the good burghers of
Zermatt, Switzerland, that the town water supply system should be
overhauled.   The chlorinator was ancient, the distribution pipes
were old, but the system was constantly working at rated capacity.
Nothing had yet gone wrong, and there was no cause for alarm.
When a pipe broke, it was replaced.   There was, in short, no inherent and compelling problem; and a new water system would cost
a big pile of francs.   The Town Council voted down the proposed
overhauling.

Then a main broke, undetected, letting sewage into the system.
After 300 guests came down with typhoid in the spring of 1963, and
the town was wiped out (temporarily, of course) as a tourist resort,
the Town Council decided to install a new water system.[1]

The Town Council of Zermatt behaved as American academic
debaters are expected to behave.   Before an advocate of a change
from the status quo is conceded to have made his case, he is required to show an inherent and compelling need for a change.   Such
a requirement is artificial and unreasonable.   In the real world, we
do not demand that a proposal meet such stringent conditions before
we are willing to adopt it, unless we are extremely reactionary; and
there is no reason why debaters, whose time limitations impose
enough of a straitjacket on them, should be required in addition to
carry an unrealistic burden of proof.

The concept of inherency has only recently come to be discussed in the literature on argument.   The only full-length treatment is
that by Arthur N. Kruger in The Gavel of March, 1963.   This article I will quote extensively, in order not to misrepresent the position I am attacking:

> Thus, it seems clear that the affirmative must first of
> all show that a serious problem exists. . . . Second, to
> avoid the fallacy of post hoc reasoning, it must demon-

strate that the problem inheres in, or is caused by, the
existing policy. . . . Let's consider a hypothetical case.
Although an affirmative might adduce evidence to show
that Burma resents U. S. economic aid, it would not be
justified in concluding that the U. S. should stop giving
Burma aid; it would first have to consider the specific
cause of the resentment. For resentment could be due
to many things. It might be due, for example, to the
fact that the wrong type of products was being sent to
Burma, or that the U. S. administrators of aid in Burma
didn't speak Burmese, or that, being unacquainted with
Burmese customs, they unwittingly offended the Burmese.
Now, if such were the case, the resentment would not be
an inherent evil; that is, it would not inhere in, or be
caused by, the essential character of the economic aid
program but by extraneous factors which could be modified without eliminating the program. We could send
different commodities and change or educate the administrators of the program. No need to stop giving economic aid in order to eliminate the resentment. [2]

We can at once agree that Burmese resentment of American
aid did have many causes, some of which were isolatable. We can
also agree that the giving of aid in itself might not be "the specific"
cause of resentment. We can agree that the U. S. "could send different commodities" and that various offensive acts of American administrators were "extraneous factors which could be modified. "
But what does all this mean in terms of the real world? Have the
affirmative here failed to make a prima facie case? Have they
failed to give a good reason why aid should be stopped?

Now the kinds of commodities we send to underdeveloped countries, and the kinds of projects we initiate with our aid money, are
determined by political pressures at home as well as by the needs
of the recipients. There is nothing inherent in the foreign aid program which dictates that we will send wheat to Burma, a rice-eating
nation; but if the U. S. had a wheat surplus (which we did), and there
were enough Congressmen from wheat-producing states (which there
were), you could accurately predict what sort of economic aid was
going to Burma. Nothing inherent, mind you, just probabilities.

And of course we could train a flock of Burmese-speaking administrators, given time and incentive, and teach them enough Burmese history and sociology so they wouldn't insult anybody's grand-
mother in unmentionable ways. We might even induce them to get

out of the Embassy compound often enough to meet some run-of-the-
mill Burmese, rather than the English-speaking sycophants; we
might induce them to give up their parochialism and accept or at
least tolerate Burmese values (providing McCarthy isn't around and
the House Un-American Activities Committee has gone to sleep); we
might persuade them to scale down their standard of living to something less odious in an underdeveloped nation; and to behave themselves as if they were in a community where they expected to live
the rest of their lives, and where the thousand little indiscretions
beckoning tourists and soldiers on foreign duty would not tempt
them. We might even weed out the white supremacists. We could
do all this, and if we did, our foreign aid might be acceptable.

But what is the meaning of "could" in this context? Are these
realistic possibilities? In real life, the resentment caused by the
wrong kind of aid administered by inept people is a perfectly valid
reason for scuttling the whole program. While the status quo could
change to remedy the defects cited by the affirmative, it won't; the
defect is functional (contingent) rather than organic (inherent). We
are dealing with a syndrome of causes of resentment.[3] Certainly
foreign aid in itself is not the sole cause; but in the absence of data
which it is up to the negative to produce, showing that it is practi-
cable to reform the system in such a fashion as to make the aid
palatable, the affirmative have made a prima facie case.

Nor is the foreign aid proposition, selected by Kruger, the
only topic on which a perfectly adequate affirmative case can be
built without invoking inherency. Pennsylvania has an antedeluvian
constitution. It is archaic, full of anachronisms, obscure, and confusing. It perpetrates numerous injustices on the residents of this
commonwealth (and it will probably never be changed, since the
rural sections control the legislature, and they are as conservative
as Swiss burghers). But none of its defects are inherent; theoretically, at least, it can be amended to cure them. Even the obscur-
ity can, with sufficient care, be handled by Philadelphia lawyers.
The defect is functional, not organic. As I interpret Kruger's inherency doctrine, no affirmative could ever make a case for calling
a constitutional convention and giving Pennsylvania a new constitution;

but there is not a political scientist--nor an intelligent layman--in
the state who does not believe that we would be better off with a
new constitution, that in fact we should call a constitutional convention.

Again, a perfectly valid case for recognition of Communist
China can be made on the basis of four significant but non-inherent
issues. (1) We should recognize Peking to eliminate the Asian impression that we stand ready to support Chiang Kai-shek in his projected invasion of the mainland. This impression is held by Asians
for several reasons; it is not caused by our policy of nonrecogni-
tion, but a change in that policy would help eradicate the impression. (2) We should recognize Peking to improve the channels of
communication and negotiation. Our lack of same is not caused by
non-recognition; France, for instance, communicated and negotiated
extensively with China before de Gaulle's recent coup. But recognition would ease the hostile climate, and improve communicative
channels. (3) We should recognize China to establish trade with
her. West Coast industries are hurting because all the other nations in the world have taken over our former China trade. Once
again, the lack of trade is not caused by non-recognition; but trade
would almost certainly come with recognition. (4) We should recognize China to increase the prospects for peace. The danger of war
in the Far East is not caused by our non-recognition policy; yet re-
versing that policy would contribute to the cause of peace. No inherency, no organic defect--just a complicated real-life situation
where a policy decision can be justified without recourse to one of
the recent but mistaken conventions of academic debate. A negative
can, of course, establish disadvantages to recognition which would
counter-balance this prima facie case; but the requirement that the
affirmative case be based on precise causation and inherent factors
in the status quo is wrong.

There is another phrase which one hears applied to affirmative proof requirements: they must produce a "universal" need.
Nothing in the literature bears on this; it seems to be an invention
of over-zealous negatives. Apparently they mean that whatever
problem is established must be true of the whole area of the status

quo, or must be true all the time rather than just part of the time.
If, for instance, one were arguing for federal aid to education, and
cited a number of states where per pupil expenditure on education
was below the acceptable minimum, the negative might attack the
need because it was not universal. California and New York do not
need federal aid. Therefore, the affirmative should be arguing for
specific aid to specific depressed areas, not for a uniform policy
of federal aid to all states. This is simply a variation of the inherency argument. The affirmative would need to show that there
were good reasons why there should be a blanket policy of federal
aid, rather than ad hoc measures; but it seems clear that in the
real world we justify policy because many or most or even some of
the units to which the policy is applicable would benefit from it.
Civil rights legislation can be justified at the federal level even
though some of the states may not practice discrimination.

If, then, we reject the inherency requirement, what standards
of proof should we require of an affirmative? Obviously he must
offer one or more good reasons for adopting his policy. But what
is a good reason? Logically, it normally consists of these things:

(1) An objective or goal which any policy of the sort
proposed should achieve.
(2) A measurement of the status quo against that goal.
This yields, for an affirmative, a need or problem;
the status quo does not reach the goal.
(3) A prediction that the proposed policy will help reach
the goal and hence solve the problem.

To return to Kruger's original illustration, the argument he
considers would be logically structured as follows:

(1) The U.S. should seek the good will of the Burmese
(and, presumably, of all nations).
(2) The U.S. program of economic aid produces resentment, thus frustrating this goal.
(3) Discontinuance of the economic aid program will remove this resentment and further the goal of good
will.

The first stage of the argument is not stated explicitly by
Kruger, but his ready acceptance of resentment as an evil implies
the opposite of resentment, or good will, as the implicit goal. Nor
does he discuss the third stage, the prediction that discontinuance
of the program will improve U.S.-Burmese relations. His sole con-

cern is with the measurement or problem stage. He wants to distinguish the "essential character of the economic aid program" from
the "extraneous factors," namely the products which we send, the
linguistic competence of the administrators, and the sociological insight of the administrators. And if it cannot be shown that it is
the "essential character" of the aid program which causes resentment, if it is possible that the products sent or the administrators
who distribute them are contributing to resentment, he claims the
aid program has not been sufficiently indicted and there is no adequate reason for discontinuance. He is thus demanding an organic
defect before any therapeutic action can be taken, and rejecting
functional ills. This is silly.

The truth of the matter is that we may not be able to find out
the causes of resentment of aid. We may only know that something
about the program malfunctions. And if the affirmatives have shown
a malfunction, if they have shown that adopting their proposal will
enable us to achieve a desired goal which the program frustrates,
they have a prima facie case, and the burden of rebuttal is on the
negative. The causes of the malfunction may not be known; they
may not be isolatable; or they may be myriad.

Talk about the "essential character" of any human phenomenon
should alert us to the vestige of Platonism which still hangs over
occidental culture. Kruger is as unlikely to nail down the "essential character" of the U.S. economic aid program as Robert May-
nard Hutchins is to isolate the essential nature of democracy. Essences are chimeras. Sophisticated scholars in these times do not
worry themselves about essences; functional analysis and operational
codes are the disciplines with which they work. Debaters may ap-
propriately pursue essences when they are arguing whether one
should prefer death to dishonor, but on propositions of policy the
question "How does this thing work?" is generally more fruitful than
"What is its essential nature?" And even if one could isolate the
essential nature of the foreign aid program, an attempt to dissociate
that essence from the people and products which implement it would
be hazardous.

There is a second adjective which Kruger and others insist

must apply to an affirmative need case: compelling. A minor problem which would be solved by the affirmative plan, or even a number of minor problems, will not justify it; there must be a compelling problem. On the face of it, this requirement is even more unrealistic than inherency. If the need for a policy were really compelling, chances are it would have been adopted already. Heaven help us if society makes only those changes which it is compelled to make. The insistence on compellingness, as Kruger views it, is based upon the superior predictability of the status quo, and hence on the relative uncertainty of operation of a new policy:

> In advocating a change or rejection of the status quo, the affirmative is asking us to abandon a program which is in existence and presumably has worked, however imperfectly, for some time. And this is to be discarded for a program whose workability can only be speculated about; that is, the affirmative in advocating the new policy can only argue about what will probably happen, not what has happened, which is usually much more convincing. Since the status quo is almost never a total failure and since the affirmative policy can hardly be presented in such a way as to eliminate all doubt that it will be successful, there is an initial presumption for retaining the status quo, which operates in the negative's favor, or, from the affirmative standpoint, presents a burden to be overcome. Now, to overcome this burden, the affirmative must try to prove that there is a compelling need to change the status quo.[4]

I would first like to examine the assumptions underlying this position. Since the status quo exists, we can inspect it. What we find can be projected into the future. This projection is more reliable than speculation about the operation of a new policy.

Now in general, this position has much to commend it. But it is not always the case that the system we have today will function tomorrow in the same fashion, and hence what has happened under the status quo is not always convincing as to what will happen in the future under that system. The U.S., for instance, has been successful for fifteen years in keeping Communist China out of the United Nations. I will lay Kruger a considerable sum, ten to one odds, that past performance here is not going to predict the course of the next two years. This is a changing world. Policies which have been successful under one set of conditions will not necessarily continue to be as successful when conditions change.

A new and untried policy may be just as predictable as the status quo; in fact, it may be just the advantage of predictability that commends a new policy to us, as in the arguments for city planning, family planning, and industrial planning. Sometimes the debility of the status quo is precisely its unpredictability.

But there is a more fundamental matter than predictability which is at stake here. We conventionally assume that the status quo, following a legal analogy, has a presumption in its favor. What is, occupies the ground, and to upset it one must indict the status quo. But what kind of indictment must one make, and what degree of indictment? I contend that this depends upon the specific topic under discussion; as Toulmin puts it, this is a field-dependent matter. Insofar as the legal analogy leads us to demand of affirmatives in academic debate that they indict the status quo by producing a positive evil, or a compelling need, the doctrine is false and misleading, and the legal analogy should be discarded. [5]

Society is honeycombed with policies designed to accomplish certain specific purposes. Capital punishment, for instance, is specifically designed to insure a low homicide rate. If it could be established that capital punishment deters homicide, there would be strong justification for the policy; hence the presumption in favor of the status quo would be substantial, the burden of proof of an abolitionist would be great, and the degree of indictment of the status quo would have to be correspondingly great. But suppose the statistics show (as they do) that capital punishment does not achieve its specific purpose, that states retaining it have a homicide rate as high as comparable and neighboring states which have abolished it? If, in this case, the policy which is the status quo fails to achieve its primary purpose, it is senseless to hold that one opposing it must carry the same burden of proof that would be necessary if it were basically successful, and had to be indicted on grounds other than inefficacy. The mere fact that capital punishment occupies the ground means little if it occupies that ground in vain. Status quo or not, capital punishment is justifiable primarily if it reduces the homicide rate; failing this, it has little claim on our approbation.

I am aware that other justifications have been offered for capital
punishment, such as retribution, expiation, and economy; but these
appeal to unworthy goals and play a minor role in rational discussions of the death penalty.

Kruger's chosen example, foreign aid, offers much the same
picture. Realistically, aid was instituted to raise the economic
level of various countries, thus keeping them out of the clutches of
the communists and inclining them toward the United States. But if
an affirmative can demonstrate that the policy is not achieving any
of these goals, what "ground" does the policy have to occupy?
What more need an affirmative do than to show that the presumption for foreign aid is hollow; is this not good reason for abolishing
the policy? I am not here claiming that an affirmative would content itself with exposing the inefficacy of present policy. What I
am claiming is that where an advocate seeks to have a certain policy eliminated, it is sufficient to show that that policy accomplishes
nothing. It is not necessary to establish a "need," much less a
compelling need, in Kruger's sense. Society can operate with legal
presumptions, such as that of innocence until proven guilty; but it
cannot operate with a policy presumption which requires compelling
problems before a change is made. Like inherency, compellingness
should be expunged from our already over-jargonized debate vocabulary.

The true burden of proof carried by every affirmative, whether
arguing for adoption of a new constructive policy, or merely advocating rejection of a policy presently in force, is this: he who asserts
must prove. His proof may be causal reasoning or it may not.
He may show a substantial evil in the status quo, or he may merely show that the status quo fails to meet its designated goal. He
may show a really significant problem to be solved if the policy he
is combating is deeply entrenched and partially successful, or he
may merely show that the status quo is useless. His prima facie
case can consist of any good reason why his proposition should be
adopted, and then he must defend that case.

But he should not be required to show that the world is going
to hell in a wheelbarrow before he can earn a debate judge's vote.

We have not, I hope, cast off the shackles of Aristotelian entailment after much struggle merely to be ensnared in the traps of inherency and compellingness.

Reprinted from the Journal of the American Forensic Association,
2:66-71, May, 1965. Robert P. Newman is Professor of Speech,
University of Pittsburgh.

Notes

1. "Epidemic in the Alps," Newsweek, April 8, 1963, p. 86.
2. "The Meaning of Inherency," XLV, p. 46.
3. For a more thorough theoretical discussion of the problems of
    causality in debate, and one with which I generally agree,
    see Patrick O. Marsh, 'Is Debate Merely a Game for Con-
    servative Players?" Speaker and Gavel, I, January, 1964,
    pp. 46-53.
4. Kruger, p. 46.
5. The article referred to in note (3) above also rejects the legal
    analogy, but for different reasons than those given here.
    And an excellent paper by King Broadrick, presented at the
    Illinois Speech Association, covers the matter thoroughly,
    with a similar rejection of a legal model for policy debate.

Issue H: Is the Comparative Advantage Case Logical?

This issue is closely related to the preceding one, for
the position which holds that affirmative debaters must
show a compelling and inherent need rules out the comparative advantage case, except under very special circumstances. This is the gist of my article "The 'Comparative Advantage' Case: A Disadvantage," which was
prompted, incidentally, not only by the previous ex-
changes but also by two speeches delivered at the 1965
Speech Association of America Convention: "Theoretical
Justification and the Advantage Case" by William Reynolds
and "Comparative Advantage Cases: Their Place in Affirmative Strategy" by Georgia Bowman. The article by
Dean Fadely, "The Validity of the Comparative Advantage
Case," which presents the opposing view, was apparently
written before my article appeared and is therefore addressed to some of my earlier remarks on the comparative advantage case. *

*A more recent article sympathetic to Fadely's position
is that by Bernard L. Brock, "The Comparative Advantages Case," The Speech Teacher, 16:118-123, March,
1967.

15. The "Comparative Advantage" Case: A Disadvantage
Arthur N. Kruger

I don't know whether the "comparative advantage" approach to

debate propositions of policy is gaining adherents, though I hope not,

or whether we are simply hearing more about it because of the re-

cent controversy among Marsh, Newman, and myself;[1] but I do

know that there has been more talk about this approach in recent

months than I have heard in a long time. Indeed, I was disturbed

to find that two speakers at the recent S.A.A. Convention presented

papers in which they advocated this approach as a "refreshing"

change from the traditional analysis of need-plan.[2] Although I have

touched upon this subject on several occasions,[3] I feel that recent

developments call for a fuller analysis of the comparative advantage
case. Many of those who espouse this type of case are, it seems,
either unaware of the objections to it or have no answers to them.
In any event, it is disconcerting to hear a proponent of "comparative advantage" explain what he means by it, or try to justify it,
without considering the views of those who oppose it as being confused and illogical. These opposing views, I believe, are sound,
and until we hear counter-arguments which are equally cogent, we
cannot accept the oversimplified accounts which condone the use of
a comparative advantage type of analysis. I should like at this time
to analyze some of these accounts, explore their underlying logic or
lack of it, and demonstrate the misconceptions and confusion which
characterize them. [4]

Before considering the usual arguments for a comparative advantage case, let us review briefly just what such a case is or is
supposed to be. As I understand it, the affirmative need not show
any compelling and inherent need, that is, the existence of a significant problem stemming in whole or in part from the present policy
whose removal is being advocated. It may contend simply that, although there is no real problem at present, the affirmative proposal
would be slightly more advantageous in achieving certain goals than
the existing policy and that its adoption, therefore, would be warranted. As one debater once summed it up, "Although we didn't
know what we were missing when there were no electric lights, the
world was a much better place to live in when Edison finally invented the incandescent bulb. "

The chief contentions of the comparative advantage advocates
seem to be these:

1. Some propositions lend themselves to this type of analysis,
which is to say they can be more effectively developed by it.

2. The element of surprise is good strategy.

3. It is a refreshing change from the traditional need-plan
analysis.

Unfortunately, as with many specious arguments, there is a
certain element of truth, or half-truth, here to beguile the unwary.
Let us consider these claims individually.

The first claim, that certain policy questions lend themselves more effectively to comparative advantage than to traditional analysis, is really the central issue; for if this claim could be established with any validity, the other two, which are in the nature of bonuses, or additional advantages, would seem to follow. It behooves us, therefore, to analyze this claim in detail and the reasons most commonly advanced to support it. Usually the claim is developed by the citation of examples drawn from everyday life. The following five are typical:

1. "Suppose your wife has a perfectly good cloth coat with which she is quite content. One day you happen to see a mink stole and decide to buy it for her because you know it will make her happier. No problem or compelling need here. You embark upon a course of action simply because you want to make your wife happier. She's not unhappy without the mink stole, mind you, but buying her the stole will make her happier. A clear case of comparative advantage. "[5]

2. "There's a vacant lot on the edge of town to which the townspeople have been indifferent for some time. Then a councilman gets a bright idea. 'We have some money that we're not doing anything with. Let's beautify the lot or build a playground on it. ' There's no especial need felt here. The course of action recommended is simply more desirable than the status quo. In other words, it would be comparatively advantageous. "[6]

3. "Every two years I buy a new car. Not that I need one especially, but I've been doing it for years. My choice narrows down to, say, two cars. I compare their merits--body style, interior, cost, etc.--and make a choice. No compelling need here; just a question of comparative merits or disadvantages. "[7]

4. "You're at a political convention and three candidates have been nominated for senator. How do you pick one, or more specifically, how do you argue for one? Do you show a compelling need or an inherent defect? No, you compare the qualifications or merits of the various candidates and on the basis of this comparison you pick one or urge your audience to do so. Clearly a case of comparative qualifications or advantages. "[8]

5. "You are a member of a deliberative body which is in the process of establishing a constitution. As the various planks or proposals are introduced, they are debated on the basis of their relative merits. Again, where must you show a compelling need or inherent defect? The various provisions are considered on the basis of comparative advantage."[9]

I believe these five examples represent all of the chief variations of the comparative advantage case and contain all the main arguments in support of the contention that such a case lends itself realistically and effectively to certain propositions of policy. However, a little analysis will reveal either the inappropriateness of these examples or the misleading nature of the claims made on their behalf.

Consider the first one, buying a mink stole to make your wife happier. First of all, what debatable proposition of policy could we phrase here? Perhaps something like this: "Resolved, That the Husband Should Buy His Wife a Mink Stole." Is such a policy debatable; in other words, are there good arguments supporting both sides? To answer this question, we must know something of the circumstances surrounding the proposition. A few of these are suggested in the example: one, the wife is quite happy with her cloth coat; and two, the husband apparently can afford to buy her a mink stole. Now the pertinent question is, where is the dispute? Are there valid arguments supporting each side of the proposition? Why shouldn't the husband buy his wife the mink stole if he can afford it and if the purchase will make her happier? There are really no significant issues so far as the husband or wife is concerned; there is simply nothing to debate.

This brings us to the point, apparently overlooked, that not every proposition which advocates a change is debatable. As we know, the change must be a significant change, and there must be good reasons both for and against it. Now in this particular case, if the husband has been accustomed to buying his wife gifts within his means in order to make her happy, the resolution would not be calling for any significant change at all, but would be advocating a modification or extension of the status quo, a basically negative

position. Though minor changes may be worth discussing, they are
hardly worth debating, let alone for an entire year. The fact that
college debaters were forced to debate such changes during the
1964-65 season (public works for the unemployed) and during the
1965-66 season (by misinterpreting "greater freedom" as "slightly
more freedom") is what may have given impetus to all this talk
about comparative advantage; for we may concede that the comparative advantage approach is suitable for a proposition not worth debating, or not debatable in the sense that a significant change is at
issue and that there are good arguments on both sides. When an
affirmative has to support what is basically a negative position
(minor changes of the status quo), of course it has no cause to demonstrate a compelling need for a change; it is not being asked to do
so in the first place. It is being asked to justify only a minor
change, not a major one, and it would be inconsistent to claim that
a serious problem existed and at the same time to urge the retention of the status quo with a slight change. Thus, to be consistent,
it could only resort to a comparative advantage approach by claiming a minor advantage for its proposal to correspond with the minor
change being advocated. We may conclude, therefore, that the comparative advantage case, far from being desirable, is sometimes
necessitated by, or is the unfortunate consequence of, a poor debate
proposition. In other words, a well-chosen, truly debatable proposition does not lend itself to comparative advantage analysis.

Now let us consider for a moment, in connection with this example, some possible conditions that would make such a proposition
truly debatable, or worth debating. Suppose the wife were very unhappy with her cloth coat, that she was becoming morose and constantly nagged her husband to buy her a mink stole, and suppose
the husband earned just about enough to make ends meet and that
buying a mink stole would create a real financial hardship for him.
Under such circumstances, I think we may grant the topic would be
debatable. The change advocated would be a significant one, an important one, insofar as the husband was concerned. If he were debating the issue with himself, he would have to (or should) weigh
carefully the need for a change, or the problem, and the benefits

and corresponding disadvantages which would accrue from making
the change. "But," replies our exponent of comparative advantage,
"Isn't this a comparative case? Isn't the man really comparing the
advantages of two courses of action, to buy or not to buy the stole?"
Yes, we must answer, in this sense most debates on policy involve
a comparison between two policies, the status quo and the proposed
policy. But, we must also point out, it is not in this sense that
"comparative advantage" is used by its advocates. By their interpretation we are told that a significant problem doesn't have to exist or be demonstrated. However, in our modified version of the
resolution, a version required to make the resolution debatable, a
significant problem does exist, the proposed course of action is significant for the husband, and he would be justified, rationally, in
pursuing this course of action only if it gave promise of solving a
significant problem. For him to act, in view of the possible consequences, without good cause would be imprudent.

Summing up to this point, we see that when a minor change,
or modification of the status quo, is proposed as the topic for debate, a comparative advantage case must be used. But such a
proposition, we have seen, is not debatable, or worth debating for
any length of time, for both alternatives come within the purview of
the negative position. On the other hand, when a significant change
from the status quo is proposed, such a change is prudent only
when it seems likely to solve a significant problem and when the
advantage thus gained would outweigh the disadvantage which would
result from changing a status quo presumably possessed of certain
advantages that make the proposed change debatable in the first
place. (We shall consider in a moment what happens when the
status quo is conceded not to be working at all, that is, conceded
to be devoid of advantages.)

The second example can be dealt with by much the same analysis which has been brought to bear on the first one. If the issue
of whether or not to beautify the lot is truly debatable, or worth
debating, a significant reason must be given to justify the expenditure of city funds for that lot, particularly if such funds are needed
for some other worthwhile project like building a garbage disposal

plant. If there is no real need for beautification, why spend the money? Thus again we see that if it were a truly debatable proposition, the need-plan analysis is used. But if it is a question of merely modifying current policy, that is, extending or slightly amplifying the current policy, which is to make periodic improvements without creating any financial hardships, then a proposition advocating beautification would not represent a new policy, but would be advocating the retention of the status quo with some amplification, a basically negative position. And such a resolution, as we have seen, would not be suitable for any prolonged debate.

Consider now the third example, that of the individual who is accustomed to buying a new car every two years and who makes his choice by comparing the relative merits of two cars. The debate resolution in this instance might be "Resolved, That I Should Buy Car A Rather Than Car B." Now, if, as this individual claims, he really has no need for a new car at all but buys one every two years as a matter of habit, he is conceding that his decision to buy any car is not entirely rational, or at least is not motivated by rational considerations but rather by habit. Now if we are willing to concede his need for a change on such grounds--which very few debate judges would, of course--then the issue of which of the two new cars is more desirable can be settled by comparing their relative merits. But, actually, what type of proposition have we here? It is a proposition which tacitly concedes a need for a change (on however dubious grounds) and which offers two alternatives or counterplans. So we may conclude from this example, if anything, that the comparative advantage analysis lends itself to a discussion of counterplans, which, it must be remembered, come in for consideration only when the need for a change has been conceded.

In both the fourth and fifth examples, debating the merits of competing candidates for political office or debating the various planks of a constitution, a need for a change has been tacitly recognized. In the first, it is assumed or taken for granted that a new candidate needs to be nominated; the issue is not, do we need a candidate or don't we? Apparently, all have agreed that we do need one. With this concession made, it is now a matter of what change

to make, what course of action to take, what candidate to choose,
what counterplan to effectuate. Similarly, in the second situation,
it has been conceded, or tacitly recognized, that the absence of a
constitution is not desirable, that changes must be made to remedy
this lack, and so now it becomes a question of which of the competing proposals, or counterproposals, should we adopt. Again, in
both of these examples there is no issue concerning a need for a
change, no requirement to show that a serious problem exists, because such a need, or problem, has already been assumed to exist.

At this point the reader may wonder why propositions offering
a choice of counterplans are not chosen for intercollegiate debate.
The reason is that only in unusual circumstances is a presumption
for change warranted. In the early Thirties, for example, when
our economic system was severely disordered, such a presumption
would very probably have been warranted and a proposition like
"Resolved, That the States Rather Than the Federal Government
Should Undertake Programs to Combat the Depression" justified.
Normally, however, the presumption favors retaining the existing
policy.

Another question which may occur at this time is, why can't
a truly debatable proposition, that is, one calling for a major change
of the status quo, be dealt with directly or exclusively in terms of
comparative advantage, especially since we have admitted that most
debates on policy ultimately come down to a comparison of two policies, the policy advocated and the status quo? If this is so, why
couldn't we dispense with the requirement of showing a significant
need for a change? To answer this question, let's take a debatable
proposition and see what happens when we try to treat it solely in
terms of advantage arguments. Suppose, for example, one were to
advocate the recognition of Communist China on the grounds that (1)
recognition would enable the United States and Communist China to
negotiate directly and possibly settle the issue of Viet Nam; (2) recognition would lead to increased trade with Communist China; and
(3) recognition would increase the effectiveness of the United Nations.
Now, wouldn't three such possible advantages, the reader may ask,
make a reasonably good case for recognition (assuming of course

that they could be supported by evidence)? Though I would have to
answer yes to this question, this answer would in no way conflict
with the position which I have taken throughout, namely, that an affirmative debater predicating a case on such advantages would still
not be relieved of the logical necessity to show a significant need
for a change. Let us see why. If he were to deal directly with
each presumed advantage, either he would be guilty of begging the
question, that is, assuming the existence of a problem with regard
to each, or he would be forced to deal with the problem in order to
substantiate the advantage. To illustrate, to contend that recognition would enable the United States and China to negotiate directly
and possibly to settle the issue of Viet Nam implies that the two
countries at present do not, or cannot, negotiate directly and that
conditions stemming from non-recognition make negotiation unprofitable. Now in a debate such an implication would have to be supported. Not to support it would be question-begging, assuming the
implications, and to support it would be to show the existence of a
significant problem, or need for a change. (The same thing applies
to the other two advantages.) Thus, it is clear that all "advantage"
arguments are either undeveloped or assumed need arguments--
"need arguments stood on their head, " as one debate coach has expressed it--or, if properly developed, they are solutions of demonstrated needs. In the interest of clarity (as well as to guard
against the fallacy of question-begging), all significant advantages
should be developed as the latter, particularly the chief advantage
of the affirmative plan, which is that it would solve the significant
problem which the affirmative has endeavored to delineate.

Summing up again, an advantage is an effect, and a significant
advantage is an effect which comes about as the result of solving a
significant problem. To contend that a significant advantage (or effect) is absent is tantamount to admitting the existence of a significant problem. Thus the inability to negotiate directly, or satisfac-
torily, and possibly to settle the Viet Nam question not only indicates the absence of a significant advantage but also points to the
presence of a significant problem.

To underscore some of the foregoing conclusions, consider the case of a teacher working in New York and fairly content who is offered a position in California. Now for such a person to make a change would require an important reason; normally one doesn't uproot himself and move three thousand miles without good cause. If salary were his prime motivation, he would hardly move for an increase of two hundred dollars a year. But suppose he were offered two thousand dollars a year more. One might say, if the teacher is presently satisfied, where is the need-problem here? Wouldn't two thousand dollars more a year represent an additional advantage --a comparative advantage case? Not at all. Although the teacher may have been satisfied before he received the offer, he definitely has a problem now, the problem being that he can earn two thousand dollars a year more but isn't earning it. And the reason he isn't earning it is that his present position isn't paying it to him. Thus, though the additional two thousand dollars would be a significant advantage, his present inability to obtain it and the knowledge that he can obtain it would constitute a need-problem, the solution to which would be to take the new position, provided this action did not create other problems that would offset this advantage.

In general, then, we may say that a remedy should correspond to the ailment, and that extreme remedies, such as those called for in debatable propositions of policy, can be justified only by extreme ailments. Minor problems, on the other hand, require minor remedies; to employ major remedies for such problems would be like using a sledge hammer to crack a peanut. When intercollegiate debaters are confronted with a proposition that calls for a minor change of the status quo, as they were in 1964-65 (public works for the unemployed), the affirmative can hardly be blamed for considering a comparative advantage approach (minor change, minor problem and corresponding minor advantage), nor the negative for focusing on the contention that the affirmative hasn't presented a significant change from the status quo. Such debates, as we know from sad experience, tend to be pretty fruitless, but the fault, I repeat, lies not with the debaters, who are practically compelled to resort to such arguments, but with those who choose topics which compel both teams to defend minor variations of the negative position.

As an aside, it is interesting to note that throughout the 1951-52 season most affirmative debaters chose to misinterpret the national topic ("Resolved, That the Federal Government Should Adopt a Permanent Program of Price and Wage Controls") so flagrantly that they were in fact defending the status quo. This stratagem led to some interesting ramifications. First of all, the affirmative was left without a significant need for a change, that is, it could not develop any significant problem since it was not indeed proposing any real change. Not lacking imagination, however, affirmatives managed to concoct a few minor problems and concomitant advantages, the chief one being, as I recall, that their plan would go into effect about a month sooner than the one in existence. [10] Secondly, many negative teams were somewhat bewildered by having the ground thus cut out from under them and were confronted by a dilemma. If they debated the affirmative's interpretation of terms, they were fearful of being accused of quibbling (ironical as it seems); and if they accepted the interpretation, they were hard put to find any real issues to debate and, indeed, were forced into the untenable position that the status quo could not be improved by slight modifications. This is the so-called element of surprise which the proponents of comparative advantage speak of. It is surprising, indeed, for a negative to hear an affirmative defend the status quo, or a modification of it, either by misinterpreting the resolution or by debating a resolution (chosen by the coaches) which is framed to uphold the status quo, as was the 1964-65 question. To use the comparative advantage approach on a truly debatable topic, however, may be momentarily surprising to a negative team but extremely vulnerable. For if the advantages are minor, the negative may legitimately argue, why make a drastic change, why eliminate a system which is conceded to be working so well? (If it is not producing any real problems, as the affirmative says, it must be working well.) And, if the advantages are major, what logical right does the affirmative have to assume that they are lacking, or in other words, to assume that a major problem exists? And, even if the affirmative now tries to show that significant advantages are lacking, this "upside down" approach to the need may well be lost on

the judge, particularly since the affirmative is contending in one
breath that there is no serious problem at present and in the next
contradicting itself by claiming that significant advantages would result from the adoption of the affirmative plan, significant advantages which, as we have seen, can only be effected by solving significant problems.

As for the argument that such an approach is a "refreshing
change" from the traditional, logical one, we need only point out
that change for the sake of change has little to recommend it. A
change needs to be something more than merely different. Where
debate analysis is concerned, a change must have a logical under-
pinning, a rational justification, and, as we have seen, the comparative advantage approach, except for special circumstances--debat-
ing counterplans or minor changes of the status quo--is completely
illogical and confused (not to say confusing) when applied to debatable propositions of policy which advocate a major or significant
change from the status quo. For such propositions there can be no
question of using a "comparative advantage" case as defined by its
proponents. Personally, I think it is time we expunged this term
from our debate vocabulary so that well-meaning but misinformed
coaches will not be tempted to encourage unwary debaters to try
this "refreshingly new" but confused and illogical approach to debate. [11]

Reprinted from Journal of the American Forensic Association, 3:
104-111, September, 1966.

Notes

1.   Cf. Patrick O. Marsh, "Is Debate Merely a Game for Conserva-
      tive Players?" Speaker and Gavel, I:46-53, January, 1964;
      " 'Terminological Tangle': A Reply to Professor Kruger,"
      II:54-59, January, 1965; "The Terminal Tangle: A Final Re-
      ply to Professor Kruger," II:137-139, May, 1965; Robert P.
      Newman, "The Inherent and Compelling Need," Journal of
      the American Forensic Association, II:66-71, May, 1965;
      Arthur N. Kruger, "The Underlying Assumptions of Policy
      Questions. I. Presumption and Burden of Proof," Speaker
      and Gavel, II:2-17, November, 1964; "II. Indictment of the

Status Quo, " II:60-62, January, 1965; 'III. Inherent Evil, " II:79-82, March, 1965; 'IV. Major Change of the Status Quo, " May, 1965, pp. 134-136; "The Inherent Need: Further Clarification, " Journal of the American Forensic Association, II:109-119, September, 1965.

2. William Reynolds, "Theoretical Justification and the Advantage Case"; Georgia Bowman, "Comparative Advantage Cases: Their Place in Affirmative Strategy. "

3. Modern Debate: Its Logic and Strategy, New York, 1960, p. 42; "The Meaning of Inherency, " The Gavel, 45:46-47, 54, March, 1963.

4. It is interesting to note that the Convention speakers I heard did admit that most debate coaches "won't buy"--to use their term--a comparative advantage case. But instead of considering why most coaches consider such a case illogical, the speakers contented themselves with suggesting that the coaches are stubborn or perverse, or, to use Marsh's term, reactionary, that is, unreasonably opposed to change, or simply, as one speaker suggested, uncritical adherents of some dogmatic authority: "Just because some authority says it's wrong doesn't make it wrong. "

5. Paraphrased from the speech by Georgia Bowman, loc. cit.

6. Ibid.

7. Example cited by Robert Huber in a personal conversation.

8. Suggested by Patrick Marsh, "Is Debate Merely a Game for Conservative Players?" Speaker and Gavel, I:50, January, 1964.

9. Ibid., p. 49.

10. Concerning this and another minor change, appointing a board as a substitute for a Congressional Committee, Holt Spicer, debating for Redlands in the final round of the West Point Tournament, was prompted to remark: "There is practically no difference between the plan envisaged by the gentlemen of the opposition and the status quo. It leaves us wondering if we traveled about three thousand miles by plane to debate whether we should have a board that would sit around to wait to do the same things that Congress does now. "

11. It is interesting to note that in the final round of this year's West Point Tournament, the affirmative (Northwestern) alluded to the "comparative advantage" of its proposal. However, a careful reading of this case reveals that the three advantages claimed for the affirmative proposal are linked to three problems which the affirmative team first tried to establish--jurisdictional barriers, political barriers, and penal barriers to effective law enforcement. Thus, this case was not a comparative advantage case in the usual sense of this term, and to use the term to designate the traditional need case, as was done here, could only have been confusing and damaging.

16. The Validity of the Comparative Advantages Case
L. Dean Fadely

Alfred North Whitehead once wrote: "It takes a very unusual
mind to undertake the analysis of the obvious. " This statement
seems to be the perfect embodiment of the philosophy underlying the
comparative advantages debate case. By its very definition this type
of approach lends itself to an analysis of the obvious.

A comparative advantages debate case is one which collates
the status quo with the affirmative team's plan on the basis of results and expected results. In other words, the affirmative team
contends that the adoption of their proposal would result in a significant improvement over the present system. In short, it would be
advantageous. This type of case usually places less emphasis on
the "need" arguments and the problems of inherency than does the
traditional "need for a change" approach used by many affirmative
teams. Glen E. Mills defines and characterizes the comparative advantages approach:

> Another deviation from the traditional affirmative case
> for a proposition of policy is the "comparative advan-
> tages" case. In the first part of the case the cause-for-
> action point may be played down, developed indirectly,
> or developed as fully as in the traditional case. In any
> event the general idea of this approach is the comparison
> of the status quo with the affirmative plan on the basis
> of results for the purpose of predicting improvements.
> This comparative testing is intended to arrive at greater
> probability of desirability on the side of the proposed
> change. The standard of desirability is, of course, the
> goal which the affirmative should announce early in the
> proceedings. That goal might be greater justice, ef-
> ficiency, economy, or some other ideal. [1]

In recent years forensic circles have witnessed a great deal
of dispute concerning this type of debate case. The foremost objections to the comparative advantages approach have been raised by
Arthur N. Kruger. In his book Modern Debate: Its Logic and
Strategy and in a series of recent articles, [2] Kruger takes the position that a comparative advantages case cannot be effectively utilized
in a debate. He directly, or by the strongest of implications, refers
to this type of case as confusing, indirect, negative in its approach,

strategically weak,[3] ineffective, and imprudent.[4]

Kruger seemingly has two main objections to the comparative advantages approach: (1) it cannot fulfill the assumptions underlying propositions of policy, and (2) "No prudent man would accept the affirmative proposal on such tenuous grounds that it might be slightly better than something he already knows or is conceded to be good."[5]

The purpose of this paper is to show that (1) the comparative advantages case can fulfill the assumptions underlying propositions of policy, and (2) Kruger's rejection of the comparative advantages approach on the grounds that no prudent man would accept it represents not only a misstatement, but a misinterpretation of the properties and purpose of the comparative advantages case.

To substantiate these points it will be necessary to examine the basic assumptions underlying propositions of policy. As many writers,[6] including Marsh[7] and Kruger,[8] have pointed out, these are (1) presumption rests with the status quo; (2) in order to overcome this presumption, evils must be demonstrated in the status quo; (3) these evils must be inherent, and (4) the removal of the evils must constitute a fundamental change from the status quo.

The concept of presumption in debate is largely, if not entirely, borrowed from the courtroom. However, it has existed for thousands of years and permeates our Judeo-Christian tradition and ethic. Archaeological evidence reveals that the concept of presumption is present in the first codified set of laws,[9] the Code of Hammurabi. These are thought to have been fully established by 1800 B.C.[10] They indicate that a person is innocent until proven guilty. For example, clause one of the code states:

> If a man has accused another of having practised sorcery upon him and he has not established the accusation, the accuser shall be put to death.[11]

Robert W. Smith points out that the concept of presumption ". . . is at least as old as the Mosaic Code which required that at the mouth of two or three witnesses should a point be established."[12] At the trial of Jesus of Nazareth, Pontius Pilate held a position virtually identical to that espoused by the Mosaic Code when he said:

> You brought this man before me on a charge of subver-
> sion. But, as you see, I myself examined him in your
> presence and found nothing in him to support your
> charges. No more did Herod, for he has referred him
> back to us. Clearly he has done nothing to deserve
> death. [13]

It was this concept of presumption which Richard Whately pop-
ularized and transferred to the area of "argumentative discourse."
In 1846 Bishop Whately stated the concept of presumption and its
relationships when he wrote:

> According to the most correct use of the term, a "Pre-
> sumption" in favor of any supposition means not (as has
> been sometimes erroneously imagined) a preponderance
> of probability in its favor, but, such a pre-occupation of
> the ground, as implies that it must stand good till some
> sufficient reason is adduced against it; in short, that the
> Burden of Proof lies on the side of him who would dis-
> pute it.
>
> There is a Presumption in favor of every existing insti-
> tution. Many of these (we will suppose, the majority)
> may be susceptible of alteration for the better; but still
> the "Burden of Proof" lies with him who proposes an al-
> teration; simply on the ground that since a change is not
> good in itself, he who demands a change should show
> cause for it. No one is called on (though he may find
> it advisable) to defend an existing institution, till some
> argument is adduced against it; and that argument ought
> in fairness to prove, not merely an actual inconvenience,
> but the possibility of a change for the better. [14]

Modern debate theorists, such as Auer, Baird, Brockriede,
Capp, Ehninger, Foster, McBath, McBurney, Mills, O'Neill, Potter, et cetera, expound, for the most part, Whately's views with
little or no significant changes. [15] Therefore, since Whately's writ-
ings form the basis for our modern concept of presumption, it is
especially important for us to understand exactly what he is saying,
and how it relates to the comparative advantages case.

In the preceding quotation, Bishop Whately established three
main points. In order to better understand these, let us examine
each one.

First, Whately defines presumption. The status quo exists.
It occupies ground. This occupation by its very nature implies that
". . . it (the status quo) must stand good till some sufficient reason is adduced against it." In other words, presumption favors an

existing institution simply because it is there. As people do not
change an institution without reason, it will remain there ". . . till
some sufficient reason is adduced against it. "

In his second and third points, Whately suggests ways in which
this sufficient reason may be adduced. One way is to argue for an
". . . alteration for the better. " However, this argument should
prove ". . . not merely an actual inconvenience but the possibility
of a change for the better. "

These suggestions are fully carried out within the framework
of a strong comparative advantages case. The affirmative team
proposes a change in the status quo because such a change will produce an ". . . alteration for the better. " Furthermore, a good affirmative team will endeavor to prove not only ". . . the possibility of a change for the better, " but the probability that their proposal will bring about this improvement. In fact, if they wish to
get the judge's decision, the latter course of action is almost mandatory.

Based on the foregoing analysis of the concept of presumption,
it would appear that the comparative advantages approach can overcome the burden of presumption. Therefore, it fulfills the first
basic assumption underlying a proposition of policy.

The second basic premise of a policy resolution is that evils
must be demonstrated in the status quo. This assumption follows
logically from the concept of presumption. In normal circumstances,
when one calls for the institution of a new policy one is, either directly or indirectly, indicting the existing policy. One is saying:
"We need my proposal. " The idea being, we need my proposal because the present system has problems (evils), or we need my proposal because the status quo is lacking such a program (and this
shortcoming constitutes an evil), or we need my proposal because
it would be more satisfactory than the present system.

These first two ideas may be thought of as paths which lead
to the development of a traditional affirmative case. The third (we
need my proposal because it would be more satisfactory than the
present system) is the path to the comparative advantages case.

The question now arises: Is saying that one proposal is better

than another equivalent to saying that the latter contains evils?
Based on the reasoning behind the comparative advantages approach,
the answer to this question would be yes.   This reasoning takes
two basic forms: The affirmative team contends that the adoption
of their plan would result in an important gain or gains.   Therefore, the absence of this gain is a defect (or at least a potential defect, and therefore a legitimate need argument), in the status quo.
This line of reasoning is a truncated mixed hypothetical syllogism.
When placed in proper form, the categorical premise affirms the
antecedent of the hypothetical premise, and the conclusion affirms
its consequent.   Therefore, the argument is in the affirmative mood
or modus ponens and is valid.

The second basic argument underlying the comparative advantages approach is that the present system is unable to reach an established or a desired goal which could be met, or met more effectively and efficiently, by the affirmative team's proposal.   This
inability to reach the goal constitutes a weakness (or evil) in the
status quo.

Paradoxically enough, Kruger points out the validity of such
an approach when he writes:

> . . . the criterion for evaluating a policy is the goals
> sought.   In evaluating the status quo, therefore, the af-
> firmative must first consider the question, "Is the pres-
> ent policy achieving certain desired goals, or are the
> established goals being met under the status quo?"   The
> answer must be no (for if it were yes, there would be
> no point to the debate) and must be supported with evi-
> dence, i. e., facts and expert testimony.   Since the
> goals in question are by mutual consent desirable, any
> failure to reach them must be considered undesirable,
> or "evil."[16]

In addition to Kruger's statement, the validity of the second
basic line of reasoning supporting the comparative advantages case
may be established by placing the argument in proper form.   This
reveals that it also is a mixed hypothetical syllogism in the valid
form of modus ponens.

In light of the validity of the two basic lines of reasoning underlying the comparative advantages case, it becomes obvious that
one should answer affirmatively the question: Is saying that one

proposal is better than another equivalent to saying that the latter
contains evils?

Even without considering the validity of the two supporting
lines of argument, a strong case can be adduced to show that a
comparative advantages approach can demonstrate evils in the status
quo.

Once again, paradoxically enough, support for such a case
comes from Arthur N. Kruger when he states:

> . . . to say that one proposal is better than another is
> equivalent to saying that the latter does not measure up
> to the former, that it fails to achieve the desired goals
> to the same degree that the other achieves them. Wheth-
> er the failure or differences in the ability of the two to
> achieve desired goals is significant or not, it is still
> failure. [17]

In summary, we have seen that the comparative advantages
case can overcome the burden of presumption and that it can demonstrate evils in the status quo.

We are now ready to consider the third basic assumption underlying propositions of policy. The evils in the present system
must be shown to be inherent within the status quo. The problem
of determining inherency is not a simple one. Ronald F. Reid indicates this when he defines and characterizes the essential facets
of the term:

> The task of analyzing inherency is not too easy; the basic
> process is one of (1) determining precisely which phase(s)
> of the status quo the debate proposition proposes to
> change and (2) determining whether the existing problems
> are caused by, or at least related to, those specific
> changes of the status quo. Only if the problems are in
> some way a result of the basic features of the status
> quo which the resolution will change can the problems be
> considered inherent. If the problems are not inherent,
> there are good grounds for rejecting the proposition. [18]

Before considering whether a comparative advantages approach
can demonstrate the existence of inherent evils, it should be noted
that some modern debate theorists do not feel that it has to. Recently, an increasingly great number of debate coaches have contended that the affirmative team does not have to show an inherent
evil in the status quo. This reduced burden holds true for any type
of debate case--traditional need or comparative advantages. Ac-

cording to these authors, an affirmative team need only demonstrate
the existence of a problem which can best be solved by a new (and
presumably fundamentally different) policy or program.   Robert P.
Newman sets forth the basic philosophy of these theorists in the following statement:

> The true burden of proof carried by every affirmative,
> whether arguing for adoption of a new constructive pol-
> icy, or merely advocating rejection of a policy presently
> in force, is this: he who asserts must prove.   His
> proof may be causal reasoning or it may not.   He may
> show a substantial evil in the status quo, or he may
> merely show that the status quo fails to meet its desig-
> nated goal.   He may show a really significant problem
> to be solved if the policy he is combating is deeply en-
> trenched and partially successful, or he may merely
> show that the status quo is useless.   His prima facie
> case can consist of any good reason why his proposition
> should be adopted, and then he must defend that case.
>
> But he should not be required to show that the world is
> going to hell in a wheelbarrow before he can earn a de-
> bate judge's vote.   We have not, I hope, cast off the
> shackles of Aristotelian entailment after much struggle
> merely to be ensnared in the traps of inherency and
> compellingness. [19]

The practical objections to this concept would seem to be that
failure to show inherency might result in either of two things: (1)
failure to propose a plan which represents a real change from the
present system, or (2) failure to propose a plan which solves the
problems presented by the affirmative. If, however, the proposal
put forth by the affirmative team does call for a fundamental change
in the status quo and that proposal alleviates the demonstrated evils,
then there would appear to be little reason for rejecting the idea
that an affirmative team need not present an inherent harm.   If this
concept is accepted it would immediately increase the theoretical
tenability of the comparative advantages case.   However, for the
sake of argument, let us assume that no one accepts the validity of
the foregoing proposal (an admittedly invalid assumption).   The question now arises: Can the comparative advantages approach demonstrate inherency? Once again, based on the reasoning supporting
the comparative advantages case, the answer would be yes.

     You will remember that in the comparative advantages approach the affirmative team contends that the adoption of their plan would result in (1) an important gain or gains, (2) the attaining of an established or desired goal, or (3) the reaching of this goal more effectively and efficiently than is possible within the present system. During the course of the debate a good negative team will point out the potentialities of the status quo for dealing with any problem. If the negative team can prove that the present system can make the gains, can reach the goals, [20] then the affirmative team has not established and maintained an inherent need. Conversely, if the negative team can prove that the absence of the affirmative team's proposal cannot be held responsible for the failure to make the gains or reach the goals, then, once again, the affirmative team has not established and maintained an inherent need. [21] However, if the negative team's response does not overcome the indictments leveled by the affirmative team, then it may be safely judged that the affirmative team has shown an inherent harm. This is true because the negative team would have failed to fulfill their burden of rebuttal or their burden of going forward with the debate. [22]

In relation to the third basic assumption underlying propositions of policy, the problem of inherency, we have seen two things: (1) Many debate theorists believe that it is not necessary for the affirmative team to present an inherent need for a change. (2) If it is necessary to present an inherent need for a change, the comparative advantages case can demonstrate inherent evils in the present system.

The fourth premise of policy resolutions is that the removal of any evil demonstrated by the affirmative team must constitute a fundamental change from the status quo. In other words, the affirmative team can not propose a plan which is possible within the framework of the present system. This is logically obvious for two reasons: (1) There is no reason to adopt another policy if the present one can solve the problem equally well. (2) If the present system can solve the problem, then the indictments of it can not be inherent.

It may be easily seen that the proposal accruing from a comparative advantages case can constitute a fundamental change from

the status quo by examining some of the comparative advantages approaches used in the 1965-66 debate year. For example, many universities proposed plans which would legalize wiretapping by Federal
law enforcement agencies and permit the divulgence of information
thereby obtained in Federal Courts. This constitutes a fundamental
change from the present system because Section 605 of The Federal
Communications Act of 1934, contains the following provision:

> No person not being authorized by the sender shall inter-
> cept any communication and divulge or publish the ex-
> istence, contents, substance, purport, effect, or mean-
> ing. No person not being entitled thereto shall receive
> or assist in receiving any interstate or foreign commu-
> nication by wire or radio and use the same, or any in-
> formation therein contained, for his own benefit or for
> the benefit of another not entitled thereto. [23]

Former Attorney General Robert F. Kennedy in interpreting
this law has stated: "The Department of Justice has taken the position that Section 605 forbids interception and divulgence, not interception alone."[24] Similarly, Attorney General Nicholas B. Katzen-
bach has held that "section 605 prohibits only the combination of
tapping and disclosure, not tapping itself."[25]

From this evidence, it is obvious that an affirmative plan
which allows Federal law enforcement agencies to wiretap and di-
vulge constitutes a fundamental change from the status quo.

Other comparative advantages approaches used on the question,
Resolved: That law enforcement agencies in the United States should
be given greater freedom in the investigation and prosecution of
crime, consisted of abolishing the Exclusionary Rule, establishing
immunity provisions, and changing the jurisdiction of law enforcement agencies (to name but a few).

All of these proposals can constitute a basic, fundamental
change from the present system.

Now that we have seen that a comparative advantages approach
can fulfill the basic assumptions underlying a proposition of policy,
we are ready to examine Kruger's rejection of this type of case on
the grounds that no prudent man would accept it. In relation to
Kruger's idea, two points need to be considered. First, it represents a misstatement of fact. Second, Kruger's rejection seemingly

rests on a misinterpretation of the properties and purpose of the comparative advantages case. To better understand these points, let us look at each one.

Kruger states: "No prudent man would accept the affirmative proposal on such tenuous grounds that it might be slightly better than something he already knows or is conceded to be good."[26] As will be pointed out later, the idea that the case might be slightly better than the status quo is not a true impression of the comparative advantages approach. However, Kruger's idea that no prudent man would accept a comparative advantages case is, to say the least, somewhat dubious. Either the increasing number of debate coaches who yearly vote for this type of case are all imprudent or Kruger is mistaken.

Kruger's rejection of the comparative advantages approach (and his concept that no prudent man would accept it) seems to rest on a misinterpretation of the properties and purpose of the case. A good affirmative team will not attempt to show that their proposal is ". . . slightly more advantageous than the status quo."[27] They will endeavor to show that their plan is significantly better. And, a prudent man would definitely be open to accepting the affirmative proposal on these grounds.

Kruger makes numerous other assertions concerning the comparative advantages case which indicate that he really holds a mistaken idea concerning its characteristics. For example, ". . . the 'comparative advantage' approach . . . can be used only when a negative decides to introduce a counterplan."[28] Perhaps Dr. Kruger is speaking of a comparative advantages case that is different from the types with which the rest of us are familiar. Again Kruger asserts: "The so-called 'comparative advantage' approach cannot include the status quo as one of the proposals being compared, but only counterproposals."[29] This is definitely a minority point of view as there seems to be little or no literature in the field of debate which supports this concept. While being in the minority on this point does not necessarily mean that Kruger is wrong, it does indicate that he is rather uninfluential in this area.

We have considered two main ideas. (1) The comparative ad-

vantages case can fulfill the basic assumptions underlying propositions of policy. And (2) Kruger's rejection of the comparative advantages approach represents a misconception of the properties and
purpose of the case. From our examination of these ideas, we can
conclude that the comparative advantages case is valid.

Centuries ago the poet Ovid wrote:

> There is nothing constant in the Universe,
> All ebb and flow, and every shape that's born
> Bears in its womb the seeds of change.

Intercollegiate debate is changing. Each year more and more
comparative advantages cases are being successfully employed. To
those who are familiar with the area of forensics, this change represents a more realistic appraisal of the debate situation. It is,
therefore, a change for the better.

We live in a world of modern technology, a world which is
similar to the comparative advantages case in that both place a
premium on effectiveness and efficiency. If it is desirable that debaters learn the criteria by which decisions are frequently made in
the "real" world, the comparative advantages case is not only valid,
but it has a definite raison d' etre.

Reprinted from The Journal of the American Forensic Association,
4:28-35, Winter, 1967. Mr. Fadely is Assistant Director of the
William Pitt Debating Union, University of Pittsburgh.

Notes

1. Glen E. Mills, Reason in Controversy: An Introduction to Gen-
    eral Argumentation. Boston: Allyn and Bacon, Inc., 1964,
    p. 175. Reprinted by permission of Allyn and Bacon, Inc.
2. Arthur N. Kruger, "The Meaning of Inherency," The Gavel,
    XIV, March, 1963.
    _____ "The Underlying Assumptions of Policy Questions.
    I. Presumption and Burden of Proof," Speaker and Gavel,
    II, November, 1964.
    _____ "The Underlying Assumptions of Policy Questions.
    II. Indictment of the Status Quo," Speaker and Gavel, II,
    January, 1965.
    _____ "The Underlying Assumptions of Policy Questions.
    III. Inherent Evil," Speaker and Gavel, II, March, 1965.
    _____ "The Underlying Assumptions of Policy Questions.

IV. Major Change of the Status Quo," Speaker and Gavel,
II, May, 1965.
3. Arthur N. Kruger. Modern Debate: Its Logic and Strategy.
New York: McGraw-Hill Book Company, 1960, p. 42. Reprinted by permission of McGraw-Hill Book Company.
4. Kruger, "The Underlying Assumptions of Policy Questions. II.
Indictment of the Status Quo," II, p. 62.
5. Ibid.
6. For example see: A. Craig Baird, Argumentation Discussion
and Debate, New York: McGraw-Hill Book Company, 1950.
David Potter, (ed.) Argumentation and Debate Principles and
Practices, New York: The Dryden Press, 1954. James Mc-
Bath, (ed.) Argumentation and Debate Principles and Practices, New York: Holt, Rinehart and Winston, Inc., 1963.
Douglas Ehninger and Wayne Brockriede, Decision by Debate,
New York: Dodd, Mead and Company, 1963.
7. Patrick O. Marsh, "Is Debate Merely a Game for Conservative
Players?" Speaker and Gavel, I, January, 1964, p. 46.
8. Kruger, "The Underlying Assumptions of Policy Questions. I.
Presumption and Burden of Proof," II, p. 2.
9. Crane Brinton, John B. Christopher, and Robert Lee Wolff, A
History of Civilization, New Jersey: Prentice-Hall, Inc.,
1960, p. 23.
10. Ibid., p. 36.
11. Hubert Grimme, The Law of Hammurabi and Moses, trans.
W. T. Pilter, London: Society for Promoting Christian Knowledge, 1907, p. 132.
12. Robert W. Smith, "The Law in Debate: II Burden of Proof,"
The Gavel, XLII, May, 1960, p. 59.
13. Lk. 23: 14.
14. Richard Whately, Elements of Rhetoric. Carbondale: Southern
Illinois University Press, 1963, pp. 112-114.
15. Ehninger and Brockriede, for example, while using Whately as
a source for their discussion of presumption, do add,
". . . presumption may be either natural or artificial,"
pp. 83-84.
16. Kruger, Modern Debate: Its Logic and Strategy, p. 44. Reprinted by permission of McGraw-Hill Book Company.
17. Kruger, "The Underlying Assumptions of Policy Questions, II.
Indictment of the Status Quo," II, pp. 61-62.
18. McBath, p. 61. Reprinted by permission of Holt, Rinehart and
Winston, Inc.
19. Robert P. Newman, "The Inherent and Compelling Need," The
Journal of the American Forensic Association, II, May,
1965, p. 71.
20. Ehninger and Brockriede, pp. 224-225.
21. McBath, p. 61, and Ehninger and Brockriede, p. 225.
22. Ehninger and Brockriede, pp. 85-87.
23. The Federal Communications Act of 1934, Section 605.
24. New York Times Magazine, June 3, 1962, p. 21.
25. U.S., Federal Rules Decisions, XXXII, March, 1963, p. 107.
26. Kruger, "The Underlying Assumptions of Policy Questions, II.
Indictment of the Status Quo," II, p. 62.

27. Ibid.
28. Ibid., p. 61.
29. Ibid., p. 62.

Suggestions for Further Reading

Brock, Bernard L., "The Comparative Advantages Case," Speech
    Teacher, 16:118-123, March, 1967.
Cannon, Martin A., "The 1950 Debate Question and the Burden of
    Proof," Rostrum, 25:8, 13, February, 1951.
Chenoweth, Eugene C. "Bearing the Affirmative Burden," Speech
    Activities, 6:51-52, 85, Summer, 1950.
Cleary, James W. "Debating Technique," Forensic, 35:47-49, Jan-
    uary, 1950.
Garn, Harvey A. "A Further Look," AFA Register, 10:25-27,
    Winter, 1962.
Hope, B. W. "Nothing But Need-Remedy?" AFA Register, 9:15-16,
    Convention Issue, 1961.
Huber, Robert B. "Affirmative--Kiss of Death?" Speaker, 40:11-
    14, January, 1958.
Knoll, P. X. "Presumption in the Introduction to the Argumentative
    Speech," Quarterly Journal of Speech, 18:637-642, November,
    1932.
Kruger, Arthur N. "The Case," Section VI, A Classified Bibliogra-
    phy of Argumentation and Debate. Metuchen, N. J., Scare-
    crow Press, 1964, pp. 87-98.
_____. "Logic and Strategy in Developing the Debate Case,"
    Speech Teacher, 3:89-106, March, 1954.
_____. "Teaching Analysis to a Debate Squad," Gavel, 39:9-
    11, November, 1956.
_____. "The Underlying Assumptions of Policy Questions. I.
    Presumption and Burden of Proof," Speaker and Gavel, 2:2-17,
    November, 1964; "II. Indictment of the Status Quo," Ibid.,
    January, 1965, pp. 60-62;"III. Inherent Evil," Ibid., March,
    1965, pp. 79-82; "IV. Major Change of the Status Quo," Ibid.,
    May, 1965, pp. 134-136; "A Postscript," Ibid., March, 1966,
    pp. 71-72.
_____. "The Inherent Need: Further Clarification," Journal
    of the American Forensic Association, 2:109-119, September,
    1965.
Mader, Thomas. "The Inherent Need to Analyze Stasis," Journal
    of the American Forensic Association, 4:13-20, Winter, 1967.
Marsh, Patrick O. "Prima Facie Case: The Perennial Debate
    Topic," Gavel, 45:13-15, November, 1962.
_____. "Is Debate Merely a Game for Conservative Players?"
    Speaker and Gavel, 1:46-53, January, 1964.
_____. "Terminological Tangle: A Reply to Professor
    Kruger," Speaker and Gavel, 2:54-59, January, 1965.
_____. "The Terminal Tangle: A Final Reply to Professor
    Kruger," Speaker and Gavel, 2:137-139, May, 1965.

Moore, Wilbur E. "Assumptions Underlying Analysis in Debate, "
    Forensic, 33:45-46, 51, March, 1948.
Newman, Robert P. "Analysis and Issues: A Study of Doctrine, "
    Central States Speech Journal, 13:43-54, 1961.
Scott, Robert L. "On the Meaning of the Term Prima Facie in
    Argumentation, " Central States Speech Journal, 12:33-37,
    Autumn, 1960.
Smith, Robert W. "The Law in Debate. II. Burden of Proof, "
    Gavel, 42:59-60, May, 1960.
Wick, Robert. "Burden of Proof, " Speaker, 34:16-17, March, 1952.

Editor's Note: For a direct rejoinder to Dr. Kruger's article on
    the comparative advantages case, see Bernard L. Brock, "The
    'Comparative Advantages' Case: A Disadvantage--A Rejoinder, "
    Speaker and Gavel, 5:3-7, November, 1967.

IV. Evidence

Issue I: <u>Should Debaters Be Discouraged from Using Handbooks?</u>

> A fairly common complaint of debate coaches has been about the widespread use of handbooks--publications prepared annually on the national debate topic (both college and high school) and containing background material, definitions, outlines of both cases and (the real bone of contention) hundreds of pieces of evidence. The article "Why Spend Your Time..." by James A. Robinson contains the usual arguments against the use of such handbooks, whereas "What About Debate Handbooks?" by J. Weston Walch defends them, which will not surprise debaters, who have been using his handbooks for more than twenty years.

17. Why Spend Your Time...
James A. Robinson

Early every debating season high schools and colleges are inundated with form letters announcing publication of handbooks on the national debate proposition. The first sentence of one such recent announcement caught the attention and stirred the indignation of the writer:

> Dear Debate Coach:
>   Why spend your valuable time looking for debate materials when you can get a Complete Debate Handbook at a very low cost?

Evidently there is a considerable market for these publications. In several years of both high school and college debating, I have seen many teams that seemed to regard such handbooks as prophecy lately and definitely revealed. More than once I have had negative opponents offer an "official" definition of terms from one of these handbooks, and once I faced a judge who sustained such a claim!

130

There is one publisher who manages to supplement his fall volume
with still another during the winter.   Apparently these books are
both popular and profitable.

This indictment does not extend to such sources as The Annals
of the American Academy of Political and Social Science, The Reference Shelf, the NUEA Committee publications or similar efforts,
but to handbooks which presume to pre-gather, pre-digest, and pre-
think a question and offer themselves as easy substitutes to individual research.

How do most debate handbooks square with the accepted purposes of debating?   Without entering on a philosophical disquisition,
I do suggest that most handbooks are not compatible with the values
which coaches and debaters profess to see in debating.

Besides the more ephemeral compensations of trips and trophies, one of the more enduring rewards which comes from debate
is that of analyzing a vital contemporary problem.   With the possible exception of the ad-writer who asked the question I have referred to, who will dispute the value of thoroughly investigating fair
employment practices, price controls, international policies, presi-
dential elections, and labor legislation?   But analysis is highly indi-
vidualistic.   After the politicians and the scholars have had their
word, analysis implies some personal stock-taking and sizing-up.
Whatever such effort may involve, certainly it is something far more
than finding everything in a "Complete Debate Handbook."

To rely constantly on a second-hand authority is to deny the
value that comes from learning and using the techniques of research.
The importance of learning research methods is perhaps so elemen-
tary that its value diminishes once they are mastered.   But such
techniques will hardly be mastered by indulging in the mere act of
copying quotations from a handbook or tearing out the pages and
pasting them on cards or paper.

If a university is a community of academic interests, a university debate program can not only provide social science students
and speech majors with the opportunity to practice their trades, but
it can serve to introduce scientists and students of the humanities to
the literature and scholarship of other fields of knowledge.   But such

efforts will be little rewarded if debaters are encouraged or allowed
to confine themselves to handbooks.

The values and compensations of debate are many. But it is
hard to believe that they are fully appreciated by debaters and
coaches who rely on second-hand materials. Professor Brooks
Quimby of Bates recently reported in The Gavel on the attitude toward debate of DSR alumni who had spent many years in professional or public service. Prof. Quimby summed up their reaction:
"It's not the championships, but the education that counts."[1] It is
highly doubtful if many championships are won with handbooks, and
it is incredible that education is enhanced by this method of perver-
sion.

Guest speakers at tournament banquets delight in proclaiming
that today's debaters are tomorrow's statesmen, and that they therefore must prepare for such destiny. Why tell this to the debaters?
Such sentiments had best be expressed to the compilers of the handbooks who offer to do the work in the first place.

There are countless reasons for spending valuable time looking
for materials instead of finding them in a "Complete Debate Handbook," as all debaters who bother to do their own research know.
But too many of them do not know because they have been corrupted
by handbooks. These debaters ought to shift the burden of proof and
demand of the publisher: "Why not spend valuable time looking for
materials?"

William Ellery Channing wrote that "the true sovereigns of a
country are those who determine its mind, its modes of thinking, its
tastes, its principles." Are we to lodge the sovereignty of our debating minds in the writers of "Complete Debate Handbooks at a
very low cost?" Indeed, this would be a cheap and easy education,
an inexpensive first step to intellectual sterility.

Reprinted from The Gavel, 35:58, 66; March, 1953. Mr. Robinson
was an outstanding intercollegiate debater at George Washington University, 1948-1952, and now teaches political science at Northwestern
University.

Notes

1. Brooks Quimby, <u>The Gavel</u>, 34: No. 3, March 1952, p. 4.

18. What About Debate Handbooks?
J. Weston Walch

The new N.U.E.A. program for the selection of a 1942-43 high school debate topic seems to me to be admirable. The selection of a general topic this spring and the postponement of the selection of an actual proposition until sometime in the fall, I believe, is an excellent strategic move. In the first place, it insures as well as is humanly possible, that the proposition finally selected will not become outdated before the season is over--a pretty important consideration in a war year. In the second place, it promotes a lifelike approach to the forensic problem of the year. When we as individuals think our way through problems we don't start with a possible solution. We start with a felt problem. From there we explore a variety of possible solutions. One of these finally comes to the front as worthy of the most careful consideration. Then and only then, as a usual thing, the question arises: should this possible solution be adopted? Now that is the logical approach to the 1942-43 high school debate question which debaters in 1942-43 will have to follow.

I repeat my conclusion, that the method to be followed in regard to the 1942-43 debate proposition is a most excellent one. However, there are a few of the supporters of the new plan who have made an additional argument in its favor that I cannot allow to go unchallenged. That is the argument that the new method is advisable as a means of discouraging debaters from making use of debate handbooks.

In the first place, it would seem that the argument is rather ridiculous on the face of it. Postponing the time when high school students can go to work on the actual proposition isn't going to give them more time for independent reading. Rather, during the winter, when all the other high school clubs and organizations are going full blast, debaters will have less time for individual research!

In the second place, the supposition that debate handbooks are in themselves disadvantageous to debaters is untenable for many reasons.

As a matter of fact, I do not believe that this particular thought is or was in the minds of any appreciable number at the N. U. E. A. meeting. The N. U. E. A. itself issues an annual debate handbook and a supplement to the same. Furthermore, through co-operative purchase plans, it sometimes makes the handbooks of certain other publishers available to members of its supporting leagues.

Nor do debate coaches in the country generally disapprove of the use by debaters of handbooks on the topic under discussion. Our own handbooks alone are used by over 1, 500 high schools each year, and by nearly 200 college debate groups. Interestingly, our customers include the great majority of league winners, practically all the high schools customarily represented at national tournaments, and, I might add, quite a few of that small fringe who like to speak so disparagingly of debate handbooks at the speech conventions!

Those who usually complain about debate handbooks allege that these handbooks do all the research work for the debaters, depriving the debaters of a valuable learning opportunity, and that debaters and coaches who buy handbooks simply lift ideas from them and do not go to the trouble of doing original work in thinking and organization.

Now of course, a debate handbook is nothing more or less than a textbook in the subject which is under debate. Any one of the objections commonly advanced against debate handbooks can be advanced equally logically against textbooks in general--against all textbooks! The mere fact that textbooks continue to be used by most teachers signifies that there are, in the opinions of teachers generally, valid reasons why textbooks should continue to have a place in the high school classroom.

Why are textbooks so generally used? I would not presume to give a complete answer to this question in so limited a space. However, here are some of the reasons: first, the subjects we teach in high school are too involved for most pupils unless they have at their disposal basic volumes giving them in simplified, organized fashions the elements of these subjects; second, the reference materials available in the average school or town library wouldn't begin to meet the complete needs of our ordinary high school classes; third, the ordinary high school teacher is too over-loaded with work to have the time and energy to arrange and put over his own complete course; and fourth, many high school teachers are not expert enough in their subjects, or rather the subjects assigned to them to teach, to do a first-class job without textbooks.

There, we were talking about textbooks generally, but don't all of these factors apply to our special kind of textbooks, the debate handbook?

World peace, price control, labor relations, economic reconstruction after the war--these are tremendous problems! They are problems which puzzle our leading thinkers, let alone our high school adolescents! And yet they are the kind of problems we have to have if a whole debate season is to be given over to the discussion of a single problem. And they are the kind of matters that these young citizens will have to think about, vote about, settle, when they reach maturity. Isn't it a little too much to ask of these young high schoolers that they plunge right into these topics without the aid of debate handbooks to give them something of a background?

Those who object to debate handbooks are usually instructors in large universities or teachers in our large metropolitan high schools. I would like to see one of them actually show a high school boy or girl how to do research with the facilities available in a small country high school! But like textbooks generally, debate handbooks should not mean the end of research. Properly handled they should stimulate debaters to want to learn even more about their topics. The bibliographies included, the tantalizing short excerpts from valuable sources should, under proper coaching, excite debaters to go on to read to the limit on the questions up for debate.

And then there is the viewpoint of the coach. The objectors, generally, are college and high school men well trained in argumentation and with teaching schedules limited to one, or at the most,

two preparations. The average small school debate coach is not so
well trained, and generally has four or more preparations to make
daily for ordinary classroom teaching. Quite often he is coaching
the debate teams, not because he has particular ability in that regard, but because no one else is available who will do the job. Under these circumstances, just as in similar teaching circumstances,
the debate handbook is the textbook which helps him to do a pass-
able piece of work. From the handbook the high school students
can get something of the same help and stimulation that they would
be expected to get from a well-trained coach with plenty of coaching
time.

        True, sometimes debate handbooks are misused. So are text-
books. But for that reason we don't throw away all textbooks.
There is a right way and a wrong way to use almost anything that
civilization has given us. Debate handbooks can and should be a
means of showing high school debaters that the topics they have under discussion are far wider in range and are much more exciting
and educational than they would, of their own efforts alone, have
discovered. And debate handbooks should, properly written and
properly used, lead high school boys and girls to better debating
methods than they would otherwise naturally follow.

        This by no means exhausts all that may be said in favor of
the high school debate handbook. From time to time, during the
next school year, I shall bring to you further ideas on this highly
important matter.

Reprinted from Platform News, 8:5-7, March-April, 1942. Mr.
Walch, a former debate coach, is now a well-known publisher of
debate handbooks.

                    Suggestions for Further Reading

Howe, Jack.   "Disappearing Research," Forensic, 45:5-6, March,
        1960.
"Of All the Nerve!..or, Was There Really Rottenness in Denmark?"
        Gavel, 15:17, March, 1933.

Scott, Robert L. "Discourage Handbooks?" <u>AFA Register</u>, 9:14, Convention Issue, 1961.

Soper, Paul. "The Debaters' Handbook Evil," <u>Speaker</u>, 25:4, November, 1940.

Tarver, Jerry L. "Reflections on a New Debate Handbook," <u>Journal of the American Forensic Association</u>, 21:25-27, January, 1965.

Issue J: Is Toulmin's Analysis of Argument Useful for Debaters?

As Peter T. Manicas points out in the introduction of his article "On Toulmin's Contribution to Logic and Argumentation, " it has become fashionable during the past six years for books and articles on argumentation and debate to adopt the analysis of argument Stephen E. Toulmin, a British philosopher, introduces in his book The Uses of Argument. Toulmin, who is primarily a philosopher of science interested in certain epistemological problems, would undoubtedly be very much surprised to see the influence he has had on certain members of the speech profession in America and the way in which his ideas have been adapted by those interested in debating. Among the earliest and staunchest of his supporters have been Wayne Brockriede and Douglas Ehninger, co-authors of the article "Toulmin on Argument: An Interpretation and Application. " Although admitting that Toulmin's analysis is "open to serious criticism at several points, " Brockriede and Ehninger contend that it is on the whole "a new, contemporary, dynamic, and usable logic for argument. " On the other hand, Manicas, a professional logician, argues that Toulmin's model fails "both for whatever purposes he may have had in mind and for those special purposes to which debaters have put his model. "

19. Toulmin on Argument:
An Interpretation and Application
Wayne Brockriede and Douglas Ehninger

During the period 1917-1932 several books, a series of articles, and many Letters to the Editor of QJS gave serious attention to exploring the nature of argument as it is characteristically employed in rhetorical proofs.[1] Since that time, however, students of public address have shown comparatively little interest in the sub-

ject, leaving to philosophers, psychologists, and sociologists the
principal contributions which have more recently been made toward
an improved understanding of argument. [2]

Among the contributions offered by "outsiders" to our field,
one in particular deserves more attention than it has so far received
from rhetoricians. We refer to some of the formulations of the
English logician Stephen Toulmin in his The Uses of Argument, published in 1958. [3]

Toulmin's analysis and terminology are important to the rhetorician for two different but related reasons. First, they provide
an appropriate structural model by means of which rhetorical arguments may be laid out for analysis and criticism; and, second, they
suggest a system for classifying artistic proofs which employs argument as a central and unifying construct. Let us consider these
propositions in order.

1.

As described by Toulmin, an argument is movement from accepted data, through a warrant, to a claim.

Data (D) answer the question, "What have you got to go on?"
Thus data correspond to materials of fact or opinion which in our
textbooks are commonly called evidence. Data may report historical
or contemporary events, take the form of a statistical compilation or
of citations from authority, or they may consist of one or more general declarative sentences established by a prior proof of an artistic
nature. Without data clearly present or strongly implied, an argument has no informative or substantive component, no factual point
of departure.

Claim (C) is the term Toulmin applies to what we normally
speak of as a conclusion. It is the explicit appeal produced by the
argument, and is always of a potentially controversial nature. A
claim may stand as the final proposition in an argument, or it may
be an intermediate statement which serves as data for a subsequent
inference.

Data and claim taken together represent the specific contention
advanced by an argument, and therefore constitute what may be re-

garded as its main proof line. The usual order is data first, and
then claim. In this sequence the claim contains or implies "therefore." When the order is reversed, the claim contains or implies
"because."

Warrant (W) is the operational name Toulmin gives to that
part of an argument which authorizes the mental "leap" involved in
advancing from data to claim. As distinguished from data which
answer the question "What have you got to go on, " the warrant answers the question "How do you get there?" Its function is to carry
the accepted data to the doubted or disbelieved proposition which constitutes the claim, thereby certifying this claim as true or acceptable.

The relations existing among these three basic components of
an argument, Toulmin suggests, may be represented diagramatically:

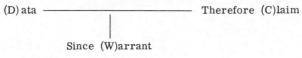

(D)ata ——————————————— Therefore (C)laim

Since (W)arrant

Here is an application of the method:

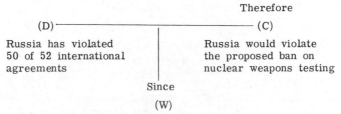

Therefore

(D) —————————————————— (C)

Russia has violated   Russia would violate
50 of 52 international   the proposed ban on
agreements   nuclear weapons testing

Since

(W)

Past violations are symptomatic of
probable future violations

In addition to the three indispensable elements of data, claim,
and warrant, Toulmin recognizes a second triad of components, any
or all of which may, but need not necessarily, be present in an argument. These he calls (1) backing, (2) rebuttal, and (3) qualifier.

Backing (B) consists of credentials designed to certify the assumption expressed in the warrant. Such credentials may consist
of a single item, or of an entire argument in itself complete with
data and claim. Backing must be introduced when readers or listeners are not willing to accept a warrant at its face value.

The rebuttal (R) performs the function of a safety valve or escape hatch, and is, as a rule, appended to the claim statement. It recognizes certain conditions under which the claim will not hold good or will hold good only in a qualified and restricted way. By limiting the area to which the claim may legitimately be applied, the rebuttal anticipates certain objections which might otherwise be advanced against the argument.

The function of the qualifier (Q) is to register the degree of force which the maker believes his claim to possess. The qualification may be expressed by a quantifying term such as "possibly," "probably," "to the five percent level of confidence," etc., or it may make specific reference to an anticipated refutation. When the author of a claim regards it as incontrovertible no qualifier is appended.

These additional elements may be superimposed on the first diagram:

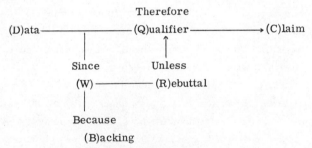

Therefore
(D)ata ——————— (Q)ualifier ——————→ (C)laim

Since   Unless
(W) ——————— (R)ebuttal

Because
(B)acking

We may illustrate the model as follows:

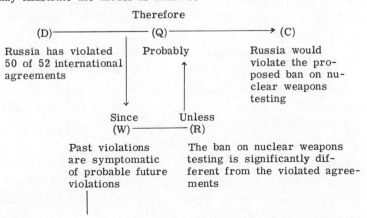

Therefore
(D) ——————— (Q) ——————————→ (C)

Russia has violated   Probably   Russia would
50 of 52 international   violate the pro-
agreements   posed ban on nu-
                                            clear weapons
                                            testing

Since   Unless
(W) ——————— (R)

Past violations   The ban on nuclear weapons
are symptomatic   testing is significantly dif-
of probable future   ferent from the violated agree-
violations   ments

|
Because
(B)

Other nations which had such a record of violations continued
such action/Expert X states that nations which have been
chronic violators nearly always continued such acts/etc.

2.

With Toulmin's structural model now set forth, let us inquire
into its suitability as a means of describing and testing arguments.
Let us compare Toulmin's method with the analysis offered in traditional logic, the logic commonly used as a basic theory of argumentation in current textbooks. We conceive of arguments in the customary fashion as (1) deriving from probable causes and signs, (2)
proceeding more often by relational than implicative principles, (3)
emphasizing material as well as formal validity, (4) employing
premises which are often contestable, and (5) eventuating in claims
which are by nature contingent and variable.

The superiority of the Toulmin model in describing and testing
arguments may be claimed for seven reasons:

1. Whereas traditional logic is characteristically concerned
with warrant-using arguments (i.e., arguments in which the validity
of the assumption underlying the inference "leap" is uncontested),
Toulmin's model specifically provides for warrant-establishing arguments (i.e., arguments in which the validity of the assumption underlying the inference must be established--through backing--as part
of the proof pattern itself). [4]

2. Whereas traditional logic, based as it is upon the general
principle of implication, always treats proof more or less as a matter of classification or compartmentalization, Toulmin's analysis
stresses the inferential and relational nature of argument, providing
a context within which all factors--both formal and material--bearing
upon a disputed claim may be organized into a series of discrete
steps.

3. Whereas in traditional logic arguments are specifically designed to produce universal propositions, Toulmin's second triad of
backing, rebuttal, and qualifier provide, within the framework of his

basic structural model, for the establishment of claims which are
no more than probable. The model directs attention to the ways in
which each of these additional elements may operate to limit or condition a claim.

4. Whereas traditional logic, with its governing principle of
implication, necessarily results in an essentially static conception
of argument, Toulmin by emphasizing movement from data, through
warrant, to claim produces a conception of argument as dynamic.
From his structural model we derive a picture of arguments "working" to establish and certify claims, and as a result of his functional terminology we are able to understand the role each part of an
argument plays in this process.

5. Whereas the modes based on the traditional analysis--en-
thymeme, example, and the like--often suppress a step in proof,
Toulmin's model lays an argument out in such a way that each step
may be examined critically.

6. Whereas in the traditional analysis the division of arguments into premises and conclusions (as in the syllogism, for example) often tends to obscure deficiencies in proof, Toulmin's model
assigns each part of an argument a specific geographical or spatial
position in relation to the others, thus rendering it more likely that
weak points will be detected.

7. Whereas traditional logic is imperfectly equipped to deal
with the problem of material validity, Toulmin makes such validity
an integral part of his system, indicating clearly the role which
factual elements play in producing acceptable claims.

In short, without denying that Toulmin's formulations are open
to serious criticism at several points[5]--and allowing for any peculi-
arities in our interpretations of the character of traditional logic--
one conclusion emerges. Toulmin has provided a structural model
which promises to be of greater use in laying out rhetorical arguments for dissection and testing than the methods of traditional
logic. For although most teachers and writers in the field of argumentation have discussed the syllogism in general terms, they have
made no serious attempt to explore the complexities of the moods
and figures of the syllogism, nor have they been very successful in

applying the terms and principles of traditional logic to the arguments of real controversies.   Toulmin's model provides a practical
replacement.

3.

Our second proposition is that Toulmin's structural model and
the vocabulary he has developed to describe it are suggestive of a
system for classifying artistic proofs, using argument (defined as
movement from data, through warrant, to claim) as a unifying construct. 6

In extending Toulmin's analysis to develop a simplified classification of arguments, we may begin by restating in Toulmin's
terms the traditional difference between inartistic and artistic proof.
Thus, conceiving of an argument as a movement by means of which
accepted data are carried through a certifying warrant to a controversial claim, we may say that in some cases the data themselves
are conclusive.   They approach the claim without aid from a war-
rant--are tantamount to the claim in the sense that to accept them
is automatically to endorse the claim they are designed to support.
In such cases the proof may be regarded as inartistic.   In another
class of arguments, however, the situation is quite different.   Here
the data are not immediately conclusive, so that the role of the warrant in carrying them to the claim becomes of crucial importance.
In this sort of argument the proof is directly dependent upon the in-
ventive powers of the arguer and may be regarded as artistic.

If, then, the warrant is the crucial element in an artistic
proof, and if its function is to carry the data to the claim, we may
classify artistic arguments by recognizing the possible routes which
the warrant may travel in performing its function.

So far as rhetorical proofs are concerned, as men have for
centuries recognized, these routes are three in number: (1) an arguer may carry data to claim by means of an assumption concerning
the relationship existing among phenomena in the external world; (2)
by means of an assumption concerning the quality of the source
from which the data are derived; and (3) by means of an assumption
concerning the inner drives, values, or aspirations which impel the

behavior of those persons to whom the argument is addressed.

Arguments of the first sort (traditionally called logical) may be called substantive; those of the second sort (traditionally called ethical) may be described as authoritative; and those of the third sort (traditionally called pathetic) as motivational.

Substantive Arguments

The warrant of a substantive argument reflects an assumption concerning the way in which things are related in the world about us. Although other orderings are possible, one commonly recognized, and the one used here, is six-fold. Phenomena may be related as cause to effect (or as effect to cause), as attribute to substance, as some to more, as intrinsically similar, as bearing common relations, or as more to some. Upon the first of these relationships is based what is commonly called argument from cause; on the second, argument from sign; on the third, argument from generalization; on the fourth, argument from parallel case; on the fifth, argument from analogy; and on the sixth, argument from classification.

Cause. In argument from cause the data consist of one or more accepted facts about a person, object, event, or condition. The warrant attributes to these facts a creative or generative power and specifies the nature of the effect they will produce. The claim relates these results to the person, object, event, or condition named in the data. When the reasoning process is reversed and the argument is from effect to cause, the data again consist of one or more facts about a person, object, event, or condition; the warrant asserts that a particular causal force is sufficient to have accounted for these facts; and the claim relates this cause to the person, object, event, or condition named in the data. The following is an illustration, from cause to effect:

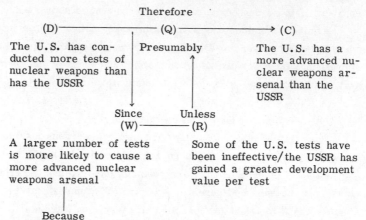

Therefore

(D) ——————————— (Q) ——————————→ (C)

The U.S. has con-   Presumably   The U.S. has a
ducted more tests of   more advanced nu-
nuclear weapons than   clear weapons ar-
has the USSR   senal than the
                                           USSR

            Since   Unless
            (W) ——————— (R)

A larger number of tests   Some of the U.S. tests have
is more likely to cause a   been ineffective/the USSR has
more advanced nuclear   gained a greater development
weapons arsenal   value per test

      Because
      (B)

Our experience with parallel testing programs indicates this/
Expert X testifies that many tests are more likely than fewer
tests to create advanced nuclear weapons arsenals

Sign.   In argument from sign the data consist of clues or
symptoms.   The warrant interprets the meaning or significance of
these symptoms.   The claim affirms that some person, object,
event, or condition possesses the attributes of which the clues have
been declared symptomatic.   Our first example concerning Russia's
violation of international agreements illustrates the argument from
sign.

Generalization.   In argument from generalization the data consist of information about a number of persons, objects, events, or
conditions, taken as constituting a representative and adequate example of a given class of phenomena.   The warrant assumes that
what is true of the items constituting the sample will also be true
of additional members of the class not represented in the sample.
The claim makes explicit the assumption embodied in the warrant.
The form can be diagrammed as follows:

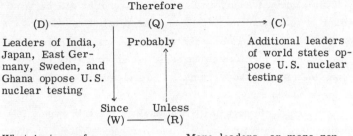

Therefore

(D) ——————————— (Q) ———————————→ (C)

| Leaders of India, Japan, East Germany, Sweden, and Ghana oppose U.S. nuclear testing | Probably | Additional leaders of world states oppose U.S. nuclear testing |

Since   Unless
(W) ——————— (R)

| What is true of a representative and adequate sample will also be true of additional members of the same class to which the items in the sample belong | More leaders, or more representative leaders do not oppose such testing |

Because
(B)

The sample is sufficiently representative/large enough/etc.

Parallel Case. In argument from parallel case the data consist of one or more statements about a single object, event, or condition. The warrant asserts that the instance reported in the data bears an essential similarity to a second instance in the same category. The claim affirms about the new instance what has already been accepted concerning the first. Here is an illustration:

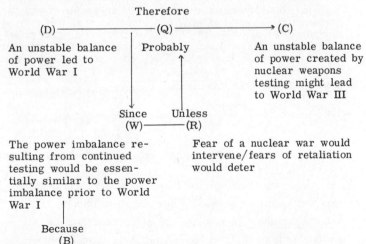

Therefore

(D) ——————————— (Q) ———————————→ (C)

| An unstable balance of power led to World War I | Probably | An unstable balance of power created by nuclear weapons testing might lead to World War III |

Since   Unless
(W) ——————— (R)

| The power imbalance resulting from continued testing would be essentially similar to the power imbalance prior to World War I | Fear of a nuclear war would intervene/fears of retaliation would deter |

Because
(B)

Both situations are characterized by an arms race, dynamic power blocs, etc.

In argument from parallel cases a rebuttal will be required in either of two situations: (1) if another parallel case bears a stronger similarity to the case under consideration; or (2) if in spite of some essential similarities an essential dissimilarity negates or reduces the force of the warrant. The example illustrates the second of these possibilities.

Analogy. In argument from analogy the data report that a relationship of a certain nature exists between two items. The warrant assumes that a similar relationship exists between a second pair of items. The claim makes explicit the relationship assumed in the warrant. Whereas the argument from parallel case assumes a resemblance between two cases, the analogy assumes only a similarity of relationship. Analogy may be illustrated so:

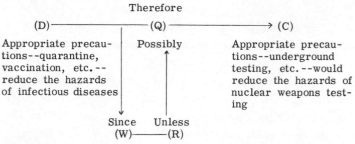

                              Therefore
      (D) ─────────────── (Q) ───────────────→ (C)

Appropriate precau-   Possibly   Appropriate precau-
tions--quarantine,   tions--underground
vaccination, etc.--   testing, etc.--would
reduce the hazards   reduce the hazards of
of infectious diseases   nuclear weapons test-
                                                ing

              Since   Unless
            (W)────────(R)

Appropriate precautions   Nuclear weapons tests have
against the hazards of in-   some peculiar property which
fectious diseases are re-   negates the general principle
lated to infectious diseases   of the relationship between
in the same way that appro-   precautions and the reduction
priate precautions against   of hazards
the hazards of nuclear weap-
ons testing are related to
nuclear weapons tests

     Because
      (B)
Both participate in the general relationship between precautions
and the reduction of hazards

In most cases the analogical relation expressed in an argument from analogy will require a strongly qualifying "possibly."

Classification. In argument from classification the statement of the data is a generalized conclusion about known members of a class of persons, objects, events, or conditions. The warrant as-

sumes that what is true of the items reported in the data will also
be true of a hitherto unexamined item which is known (or thought)
to fall within the class there described. The claim then transfers
the general statement which has been made in the data to the particular item under consideration. As illustrated, the form would
appear:

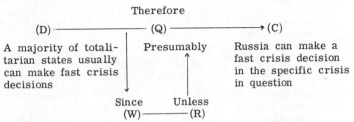

                                   Therefore
(D) ——————————— (Q) ————————————→ (C)
A majority of totali-   Presumably   Russia can make a
tarian states usually   fast crisis decision
can make fast crisis   in the specific crisis
decisions   in question

                        Since   Unless
                        (W) ———————— (R)

What is true of a majority   Russia does not share this
of totalitarian states will   characteristic of most totali-
probably be true of a par-   tarian states/special circum-
ticular totalitarian state,   stances intervene
viz. Russia
        |
     Because
       (B)
The class "totalitarian states" is reasonably homogeneous,
stable, etc./Russia generally shares the attributes of the totalitarian states class

Two kinds of reservations may be applicable in an argument
from classification: (1) a class member may not share the particular attribute cited in the data, although it does share enough other
attributes to deserve delineation as a member of the class; and (2)
special circumstances may prevent a specific class member from
sharing at some particular time or place the attributes general to
the class.

Authoritative Arguments

In authoritative arguments the data consist of one or more
factual reports or statements of opinion. The warrant affirms the
reliability of the source from which these are derived. The claim
reiterates the statement which appeared in the data, as now certified
by the warrant. An illustration follows:

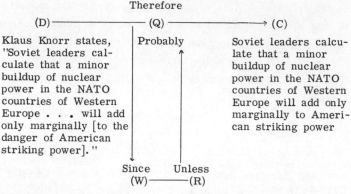

Therefore

(D) ———————— (Q) ——————————→ (C)

	Probably	
Klaus Knorr states, "Soviet leaders calculate that a minor buildup of nuclear power in the NATO countries of Western Europe . . . will add only marginally [to the danger of American striking power]. "		Soviet leaders calculate that a minor buildup of nuclear power in the NATO countries of Western Europe will add only marginally to American striking power

Since   Unless
(W)————(R)

What Knorr says about the power of nuclear weapons is reliable	Other authorities more qualified than Knorr say otherwise/ special circumstances negate or reduce Knorr's usual reliability as a witness

Because
(B)

Knorr is a professor at Princeton's Center of International Studies/is unbiased/has made reliable statements on similar matters in the past/etc.

The structure and function of an authoritative argument remain basically the same when the source of the data is the speaker or writer himself. The data is carried to claim status by the same sort of assumption embodied in the warrant. We may infer a claim from what Knorr says about nuclear weapons whether he is himself the speaker, or whether another speaker is quoting what Knorr has said. Thus the ethos of a speaker may be studied by means of the Toulmin structure under the heading of authoritative argument.

Motivational Arguments

In motivational arguments the data consist of one or more statements which may have been established as claims in a previous argument or series of arguments. The warrant provides a motive for accepting the claim by associating it with some inner drive, value, desire, emotion, or aspiration, or with a combination of such forces. The claim as so warranted is that the person, object, event, or condition referred to in the data should be accepted as valuable or rejected as worthless, or that the policy there described

should or should not be adopted, or the action there named should
or should not be performed. Illustrated the form would appear:

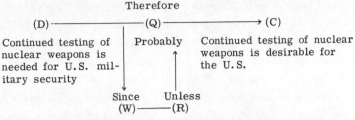

Therefore

(D) ———————————(Q) ———————————→ (C)

| Continued testing of nuclear weapons is needed for U.S. military security | Probably | Continued testing of nuclear weapons is desirable for the U.S. |

Since   Unless
(W)————(R)

| The U.S. is motivated by the desire to achieve the value of military security | The prevention of a nuclear war or some other value which is inconsistent with continued testing is desired to a greater extent |

Because
(B)
Military security is related to self-preservation, the maintenance of our high standard of living, patriotism, the preservation of democracy, etc.

4.

We have exhibited the structural unity of the three modes of
artistic proof by showing how they may be reduced to a single in-
variant pattern using argument as a unifying construct. Let us, as
a final step, explore this unity further by inquiring how artistic
proofs, so reduced, may conveniently be correlated with the various
types of disputable questions and the claims appropriate to each.

Let us begin by recognizing the four categories into which disputable questions have customarily been classified: (1) Whether
something is? (2) What it is? (3) Of what worth it is? (4) What
course of action should be pursued? The first of these queries
gives rise to a question of fact, and is to be answered by what can
be called a designative claim; the second, to a question of definition,
to be answered by a definitive claim; the third, to a question of
value, to be answered by an evaluative claim; and the fourth, to a
question of policy, to be answered by an advocative claim.

Supposing, then, that an arguer is confronted with a question
of fact, calling for a designative claim; or a question of policy,
calling for an advocative claim, etc., what types of argument would

be available to him as means of substantiating his claim statement?
Upon the basis of the formulations developed in earlier sections of
this paper, it is possible to supply rather precise answers.

Designative Claims. A designative claim, appropriate to answering a question of fact, will be found supportable by any of the
six forms of substantive argument, or by authoritative argument,
but not by motivational argument. That is, whether something exists or is so may be determined: (1) by isolating its cause or its
effect (argument from cause); (2) by reasoning from the presence of
symptoms to the claim that a substance exists or is so (argument
from sign); (3) by inferring that because some members of a given
class exist or are so, more members of the same class also exist
or are so (argument from generalization); (4) by inferring because
one item exists or is so, that a closely similar item exists or is
so (argument from parallel case); (5) by reasoning that D exists or
is so because it stands in the same relation to C that B does to A,
when C, B, and A are known to exist or to be so (argument from
analogy); and (6) by concluding that an unexamined item known or
thought to fall within a given class exists or is so because all
known members of the class exist or are so (argument from classification). Moreover, we may argue that something exists or is so
because a reputable authority declares this to be the case. Motivational argument, on the other hand, may not be critically employed
in designative claims, because values, desires, and feelings are irrelevant where questions of fact are concerned.

Definitive Claims. The possibilities for establishing definitive
claims are more limited. Only two of the forms of substantive argument and authoritative argument are applicable. We may support
a claim as to what something is: (1) by comparing it with a closely
similar phenomenon (argument from parallel case); or (2) by reasoning that because it stands in the same relation to C as B does to A
it will be analogous to C, where the nature of C, B, and A are
known (argument from analogy). In addition, we may support a definition or interpretation by citing an acceptable authority. Among
the substantive arguments, cause, sign, generalization, and classification are inapplicable; and once again motivational argument is ir-

relevant since emotions, wishes, and values cannot legitimately determine the nature of phenomena.

Evaluative Claims. Evaluative claims may be supported by generalization, parallel case, analogy, and classification, and by authoritative and motivational arguments. By generalization a class of phenomena may be declared valuable or worthless on the ground that a typical and adequate sample of the members of that class is so. By classification, in contrast, we infer from the worth of known members of a class the probable worth of some previously unexamined item known or thought to belong to that class. By parallel case, we infer goodness or badness from the quality of an item closely similar. By analogy, however, we infer value on the basis of a ratio of resemblances rather than a direct parallel. In authoritative argument our qualitative judgment is authorized by a recognized expert. In motivational argument, however, an item is assigned a value in accordance with its usefulness in satisfying human drives, needs, and aspirations. Arguments from cause and sign, on the other hand, are inapplicable.

Advocative Claims. Advocative claims may legitimately be established in only four ways. We may argue that some policy should be adopted or some action undertaken because a closely similar policy or action has brought desirable results in the past (argument from parallel case). We may support a proposed policy or action because it bears the same relation to C that B does to A, where B is known to have brought desirable results (argument from analogy). Or, of course, we may support our claim by testimony (authoritative argument), or by associating it with men's wishes, values, and aspirations (motivational argument).

This analysis concerning the types of arguments applicable to various sorts of claims may be summarized in tabular form:

	Designa- tive	Defini- tive	Evalua- tive	Advo- cative
Substantive				
A. Cause	x			
B. Sign	x			
C. Generalization	x		x	
D. Parallel Case	x	x	x	x
E. Analogy	x	x	x	x
F. Classification	x		x	
Authoritative	x	x	x	x
Motivational			x	x

The world of argument is vast, one seemingly without end. Arguments arise in one realm, are resolved, and appear and reappear in others; and new arguments appear. If one assumes some rationality among men, a system of logical treatment of argument is imperative. The traditional logical system of syllogisms, of enthymemes of middles distributed and undistributed, may have had its attraction in medieval times. The inadequacies of such a logic, however, have been described by experts; for example, see J. S. Mill on the syllogism and petitio principii.[7] The modern search has been for a method which would have some application in the dynamics of contemporary affairs.

Toulmin has supplied us with a contemporary methodology, which in many respects makes the traditional unnecessary. The basic theory has herein been amplified, some extensions have been made, and illustrations of workability have been supplied. All this is not meant to be the end, but rather the beginning of an inquiry into a new, contemporary, dynamic, and usable logic for argument.

Reprinted from the Quarterly Journal of Speech, 46:44-53, February, 1960. Mr. Brockriede is Associate Professor of Speech at the University of Oklahoma. Mr. Ehninger is Professor of Speech at the University of Iowa.

Logic 155

Notes

1. E.g., such books as James M. O'Neill, Craven Laycock, and
   Robert L. Scales, Argumentation and Debate, New York,
   1917; William T. Foster, Argumentation and Debating, Boston, 1917; and A. Craig Baird, Public Discussion and Debate, Boston, 1928; such articles as Mary Yost, "Argument
   from the Point of View of Sociology," QJS, III (1917), pp.
   109-24; Charles H. Woolbert, "The Place of Logic in a System of Persuasion," QJS, IV, (1918), pp. 19-39; Gladys
   Murphy Graham, "Logic and Argumentation," QJS, X (1924),
   pp. 350-363; William E. Utterback, "Aristotle's Contribution
   to the Psychology of Argument," QJS, XI (1925), pp. 218-
   225; Herbert A. Wichelns, "Analysis and Synthesis in Argumentation," QJS, XI (1925), pp. 266-272; and Edward Z.
   Rowell, "Prolegomena to Argumentation," QJS, XVIII (1932),
   pp. 1-13, 224-248, 381-405, 585-606; such Letters to the
   Editor as those by Utterback, XI (1925), pp. 175-177;
   Wichelns, XI (1925), pp. 286-288; Ralph C. Ringwalt, XII
   (1926), pp. 66-68; and Graham, XII (1925), pp. 196-197.
2. See, for example, Mortimer Adler, Dialectic, New York, 1927;
   Paul Edwards, The Logic of Moral Discourse, Glencoe, Ill.,
   1955; Carl I. Hovland, Irving L. Janis, and Harold W. Kel-
   ley, Communication and Persuasion, New Haven, Conn.,
   1953; Charles Perelman, Traité de l'argumentation, 2 vols.,
   Paris, 1958, and La nouvelle rhétorique, Paris, 1952; and
   John Cohen, "Subjective Probability," Scientific American,
   MCMVII, 1957, pp. 128-38.
3. (Cambridge, Cambridge University Press.) See especially the
   third of the five essays in the book. Cf. J.C. Cooley,
   "On Mr. Toulmin's Revolution in Logic," The Journal of
   Philosophy, LVI, 1959, pp. 297-319.
4. In traditional logic only the epicheirema provides comparable
   backing for premises.
5. It may be charged that his structural model is merely "a syllogism lying on its side," that it makes little or no provision to insure the formal validity of claims, etc.
6. Our suggestion as to the structural unity of artistic proofs is
   by no means novel. The ancients regularly spoke of pathetic and ethical enthymemes, and envisioned the topoi as applicable beyond the pistis. (See in this connection James
   H. McBurney, "The Place of the Enthymeme in Rhetorical
   Theory," SM, III [1936], p. 63.) At the same time, however, it must be recognized that especially since the advent
   of the faculty psychology of the seventeenth and eighteenth
   centuries, rhetorical thought has been profoundly and per-
   sistently influenced by the doctrine of a dichotomy between
   pathetic and logical appeals. (For significant efforts to combat this doctrine see Charles H. Woolbert, "Conviction and
   Persuasion: Some Considerations of Theory," QJS, III
   [1917], pp. 249-264; Mary Yost, "Argument from the Point
   of View of Sociology," QJS, III [1917], pp. 109-124; and W.
   Norwood Brigance, "Can We Redefine the James-Winans
   Theory of Persuasion?" QJS, XXI [1935], pp. 19-26.)

7. <u>A System of Logic</u>, I, Chap. 3, Sec. 2.

20. On Toulmin's Contribution to Logic and Argumentation
Peter T. Manicas

It is lately becoming fashionable for books and articles on argumentation and debate to adopt the analysis of argument which was
presented by Stephen E. Toulmin in his book, <u>The Uses of Argu-
ment</u>.[1] In what follows, the merits of this fashion will be examined
with special reference to the particular utility of the Toulmin model
for debaters. But insofar as debaters, like logicians and philosophers, are interested in what Toulmin calls "the rational process"--
the setting out and clarification of argument--it will be necessary
first to see to what extent Toulmin's discussion does shed light on
argument. If, indeed, his layout is not illuminating, as I shall argue, then the utility of his model for debaters is already cast into
doubt. Section I of this essay, then, discusses Toulmin's analysis
of argument; Section II examines the special question: Is his analysis useful for debaters?

It may be noted, however, that Toulmin's book has some
large philosophical goals. With his particular layout, he hopes to
show that many of the traditional chestnuts of epistemology--those
problems which involve justification of knowledge claims--dissolve
into thin air. Though I am sympathetic with Toulmin's feelings toward (say) the "problem of induction" or the "problem of other
minds" (and many of the others which he talks about), and though,
to a large measure, I would agree with his overall conclusion, that,
namely, we should demand of claims to knowledge standards com-
mensurate with the inquiry (rather than strictly analytic, mathematical standards), I fail to see how his innovations help to show this.
But this last point I shall not try to argue.[2]

I

It will be necessary first to sketch fairly clearly the main
features of Toulmin's analysis of argument, to see what is distinc-

tive about it and how it compares to the conventional analysis.[3]

We begin with his distinction between the claim or conclusion (C) which an argument seeks to establish and the "facts" which provide the "foundation" for the claim. The "facts" he calls the data (D). This much causes no difficulties. Even on the conventional analysis, we would distinguish conclusions from the evidence (premisses) used in support of the conclusion.

It is then argued, however, that to make the move from (D) to (C) a third sort of statement is necessary, namely, "rules, principles, inference-licences, " or what he decides to call "warrants. " "What are needed, " he says, "are general, hypothetical statements, which can act as bridges, and authorize the sort of step to which our particular argument commits us" (p. 98). It is very important to see that for Toulmin, warrants are to be sharply distinguished from data. On the conventional analysis, of course, "warrants" would simply be additional premisses necessary for the correctness of the argument.

This much provides the "first skeleton. " Every argument, to be an argument, must contain these three functional units. Warrants, however, confer different degrees of force upon the conclusions they justify. Modal qualifiers (Q), e.g., "probably, " "presumably, " "necessarily, " etc., may then be attached to the conclusions. This presents no special innovations over the conventional analysis. In deductions, the conclusion may always be written: "So, necessarily so-and-so. " In inductions, we would have: "So, probably so-and-so, " etc.[4] Next, conditions of exception or rebuttal (R) may be included into the schema. These "unless clauses" serve to indicate the circumstances in which the general authority of the warrant would have to be set aside. The notion of "rebuttal" would not have a special place in the conventional analysis, but its usefulness in Toulmin's layout may be doubted. Consider his example:

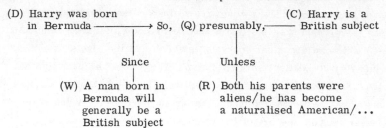

(D) Harry was born in Bermuda ———→ So, (Q) presumably,——— (C) Harry is a British subject

Since

Unless

(W) A man born in Bermuda will generally be a British subject

(R) Both his parents were aliens/he has become a naturalised American/...

It will be noted that the rebuttal (R) attaches to the modal qualifier (Q), and that the qualifier indicates the force of the warrant. But the conclusion of the argument quoted above has exactly the same force with or without the rebuttal. This is so because the warrant itself implies that there are exceptions to the rule. If the warrant were stated as a categorical (A man born in Bermuda will be a British subject), no rebuttal would have been in order; the qualifier Q would have been "necessarily," and we would have had an old-fashioned deduction.

But isn't it more useful to think of a rebuttal in terms of the distinction between truth and correctness (validity being a special case of correctness)?[5] That is, an argument is rebuttable if the premisses do not support the conclusion as stated or because the premisses themselves are challengable. Thus the valid deduction, "(Some man) Harry was born in Bermuda; a man born in Bermuda will be a British subject; so, Harry is a British subject," is rebuttable by showing that Harry was born (say) in Jamaica or by showing that there are exceptions to the rule (by showing that being born in Bermuda is not sufficient for British citizenship). Either of these rebuttals, it must be noted, would involve a new argument and for reasons which will be stated later, nothing is gained by making arguments used to support premisses a part of the original argument.

On the other hand, consider this probable argument: "(Some man) Harry was born in Bermuda; A man born in Bermuda will generally be a British subject; so presumably, Harry is a British subject." When might we use such an argument? We might if we knew that being born in Bermuda was not sufficient for British citi-

zenship, but were unclear as to precisely what were the appropriate
provisos. But in this case we could not make explicit the rebuttal
in Toulmin's sense. Were the appropriate provisos made available
to us, they could then be included as part of the premisses. Then
given additional premisses to the effect that neither of Harry's parents were alien/ he has not become an American citizen, etc., the
argument could be made considerably more cogent (if not deductive-
ly sound).[6] The point is, while the notion of rebuttal is a useful
concept, Toulmin's special use of it is more restricting than the
conventional analysis would allow.

The final distinction is that of the "backing" (B) of the warrants. These are "assurances, without which the warrants themselves would possess neither authority, nor currency . . ." (p.
103). Thus the warrant, "A man born in Bermuda will generally
be a British subject," may be backed by statutes and other legal
provisions. Again, it is important for Toulmin that we not confuse
warrants with their backings. But as with the distinction between
data and warrant (to which we shall return) the distinction between
warrant and backing is not one which grammatical tests can usually
resolve, though, says Toulmin, grammar "hints at" the distinction
(cf. p. 99). Before proceeding we should observe that it would not
be cricket to insist that a meaningful distinction must have a grammatical reflection, though to be sure, to the extent that grammatical
clues are lacking, to that extent making the distinction will be difficult. In any case, for Toulmin, his distinctions are functional; that
is, data have a different function in argument than warrants, and
warrants function differently than backings.

Before pressing the difficulties which do arise in making these
distinctions, note first that backings are not essential to the argument and need not be made explicit. Warrants may be conceded
without challenge; indeed, "if we demanded the credentials [backing]
of all warrants at sight and never let one pass unchallenged, argument could scarcely begin" (p. 196). This is obviously true, but
then isn't it arbitrary to say that the backing is part of the argument from data to conclusion? Why draw the line there? We
might as well say that an argument to any conclusion necessarily

involves us with an infinite regress.   Moreover, aren't data chal-
lengeable?   What are they supported with?   Nothing, more data, or
a different kind of backing?   It seems more plausible to me to say
that Toulmin's analysis of an argument consists of data, warrant
and conclusion (period).   If the warrant or the data are challenged,
then a new argument can be given which supports the challenged
statement.   To be sure, the sort of argument used to justify a singular statement (Harry was born in Bermuda) and the sort of argument used to justify the warrant (A man born in Bermuda will generally be a British subject) will usually be different, but recognition
of this did not await Toulmin and is not incompatible with any conventional analysis of argument. [7]

     What then of the functional differences between data and war-
rant?   Data (and backings) are descriptive, or reportive, statements
of "categorical statements of fact, " while warrants are permissive
or entitling.   Thus, in the argument quoted earlier, the statement
"Harry was born in Bermuda" simply reports some fact.   The warrant "A man born in Bermuda will be a British subject" tells you
that given the data, one may take it that Harry is a British subject.
Note that both functional units, data and warrants, are essential to
all argument.   This distinction seems to work tolerably well with
syllogisms in which (in the old analysis) one premiss is singular,
one is universal and the conclusion is singular, although the reader
may legitimately be puzzled as to how the warrant is any less a report of a "categorical statement of fact. "   The linguistic clues mentioned above are of no help since, to bring out the functional differences, grammatical transformations must sometimes be employed.
For example, the warrant with which we have been dealing, "A man
born in Bermuda will generally be a British citizen, " may be expressed, says Toulmin, in either of these two ways: (1) "A man
born in Bermuda may be taken to be a British subject" or (2) "A
man born in Bermuda will be found to be a British subject. "   (1) is
entitling, so it must be a warrant.   (2), however, is apparently re-
portative, so it can't be a warrant.   And Toulmin points out that it
isn't.   It is a backing for the warrant, the original statement of the
warrant being ambiguous.   Now this is very subtle and interesting,

but note that the same line of argument works with the singular
statement. "Harry was born in Bermuda" may be taken as (1)
"(It has been found that) Harry was born in Bermuda" or as (2)
"(It may be taken that) Harry was born in Bermuda." (1) is reportive; (2) surely seems to me to be permissive. Put this together
now: (D) a man born in Bermuda will be found to be a British subject, so, presumably, (C) Harry is a British subject, since (W) it
may be taken that Harry was born in Bermuda!

Now Toulmin himself calls our attention to what he calls the
ambiguities of the syllogism. On pages 107-113, he shows how a
statement of the form "All A's are B's" may be construed as either
warrant or backing. (For reasons which are not clear to me, he
doesn't suggest that it might be construed as a datum.) He observes
that often enough the universal statement functions as both warrant
and backing. But, however economical this telescoping may be,
says Toulmin, "it leaves the effective structure or our arguments
insufficiently candid" (p. 112). Thus, the syllogism, because of the
"over-simple" form words, "All A's are B's" leaves room for ambiguity while his analysis does not. Two observations may here be
made. (1) The (supposed) ambiguity was created by Toulmin's analysis. There need be no ambiguity in the argument: "All A's are
B's; x is an A; so, x is a B," unless, of course, we accept Toulmin's distinctions. But why should we? Could the structure of
this argument be any more candid than it now is? (2) The conventional analysis of argument need not be saddled with the oversimple
"All A's are B's."[8] If we wish to distinguish taxonomic universals
from statutes, from predictions, we can easily do so--without trying to make difficult, if not impossible, distinctions between data,
warrants and backings.

Consider next this simple form of argument: "All M's are
P's; All S's are M's; so, All S's are P's." This syllogism has no
singular premiss and the conclusion is universal. What can Toulmin
make of it? I suppose that there are several alternatives, but on
pp. 127ff., Toulmin himself suggests what might be involved. Unfortunately, he is content throughout his book to discuss only syllogisms with a singular premiss; and, if only in passing, this in it-

self should cause the reader to wonder how much of an advance has
been made.

In any case, Toulmin proceeds to note that in "analytic arguments" the distinction between data and warrant-backing is much
less sharp than it usually is (p. 127). Presumably, our Barbara[9]
is an analytic argument, though we can't be positive. And we can't
be positive since Toulmin defines analytic and substantial arguments
in terms of the sort of information conveyed by the backing of the
warrant authorizing the move from (D) to (C). Specifically, if the
backing "includes, explicitly or implicitly, the information conveyed
in the conclusion itself," the argument is analytic; otherwise it is
substantial.

But consideration of the case in point raises this question:
what is the warrant? If we can't locate the warrant, we can't locate the backing. Indeed, this is a problem. We are told that in
analytic arguments the distinction between data and backing is anything but clear, but we can't even be sure if we have an analytic
argument since we can't find the warrant.[10]

On the old (stick-in-the-mud) analysis of a deductive argument
no such problem arises. If the premisses entail (necessarily imply)
the conclusion, the argument is deductive, valid, necessary, etc.
Something approximating Toulmin's definition of an analytic argument
might be given: If the premisses "contain" explicitly or implicitly,
the conclusion itself, the argument is deductive; otherwise, it is not.
But I take it that one of the main points of Toulmin's analysis is to
show that the conventional analysis mistakenly conflates four different
distinctions into the deduction-induction distinction. But more on
this later.

Let us assume, however, that Barbara is an analytic syllogism.
Toulmin gives two alternative explications of analytic arguments with
a singular premiss which we might apply to our case. We might,
he says, be tempted to construe both premisses as data (Cf. p.
128). But then surely we need some warrant, for, insists Toulmin,
we can't move from data to a conclusion without some warrant. He
asks: "What warrant, then, are we to say does authorize this particular step?" (p. 128). He notes that several different principles

(in the checkered history of formal logic) have been put forward--
the "principle of the syllogism, " the dictum de omni et nullo, and
others.

But this is simply nonsense. No one so far as I can see considered these principles as functioning as warrants in Toulmin's
sense. It is by now generally agreed that for Aristotle, the principle of the "perfect" syllogism (called by medieval logicians the dictum de omni et nullo), was an attempt to bring the three figures of
the syllogism (Aristotle did not recognize the fourth) under one principle; that is, the principle was not employed to justify moves from
premisses to conclusions, but rather was thought of as a generalization of all syllogistic argument. Construed in any other way, Aristotle's doctrine of reduction makes little sense. The perfect syllogism (Barbara) needs no justification. As Aristotle said: "I call
that a perfect syllogism which needs nothing other than what has
been stated to make plain what necessarily follows" (Prior Analytics,
24b, 24, Jenkinson translation). Toulmin gives an argument (on p.
130) which is very nearly summarized by Aristotle's remark and
then concludes: "The suggestion that the principle really does a
job for us, by serving as a warrant for all syllogistic arguments,
is therefore implausible" (p. 130). Of course, it is; but whoever
said that it did that job?

Toulmin then tries the alternative course. "Let us reject the
request for a warrant to lend authority to all analytic syllogisms,
instead insisting that one premiss of every such syllogism provides
all the warrant we need" (ibid.). Now this maneuver is plausible
when we restrict ourselves to arguments of the form "All A's are
B's; x is an A; so, x is a B;" but how does it work when both
premisses are universals? Which premiss provides "all the warrant we need?" Nor does it seem that it will do to say that both
premisses are warrants, for then we have no data, and, on Toulmin's analysis, the data are the facts to which we must appeal if
we are to have an argument at all.

I have not shown that Toulmin's analysis could not be rescued
to "clarify the ambiguities of the syllogism."[11] Perhaps, it can.
But enough may have been said to show that his version does beset

us with gratuitous problems. Even if these problems are soluble, one may legitimately wonder how much light has been shed.

Before moving to the second section of this essay, a few comments on the conventional deduction-induction distinction may be in order.

One of Toulmin's main points was to show that the deduction-induction distinction illicitly conflates four or five different distinctions (Cf. p. 158). He does this, of course, by means of his particular layout of argument. Thus, it immediately follows that to the extent to which his distinctions between data, warrant, etc., cannot be made, then to that extent any new distinctions resting on them cannot be made. So there is a prima facie case (at least) that the distinction between (1) analytic and substantial arguments (see p. 8) and (2) warrant-using and warrant-establishing arguments (if we can't find the warrant, then what?) will be made with difficulty, if at all. The other distinctions which he wishes to enforce and separate from the deduction-induction distinction are (3) the distinction between necessary arguments and probable arguments and (4) the distinction between arguments which are formally valid and those which are not.

(3), like (1) and (2), is defined in terms of Toulmin's apparatus. In a necessary argument the "warrant entitles us to argue unequivocally to the conclusion . . ." (p. 148). So again, in many cases we have here a problem. I think, however, that a great deal of the force of his critique of the deduction-induction dichotomy stems from his criticism of formal validity. So in addition to the brief remarks entered against distinctions (1) through (3) above, the discussion of validity seems to me to be most revealing.

There are several lines which might be taken against Toulmin on this issue: (A) He attacks a straw-man conception of validity, (B) he fails to utilize his own useful distinction between the features of arguments which are field-invariant and those which are field-dependent, and (C) he relies too heavily on ordinary language.

To take these up in order: (A) Toulmin notes that "it is sometimes argued . . . that the validity of syllogistic arguments is a consequence of the fact that the conclusions of these arguments

are simply 'formal transformations' of their premisses" (p. 118).
There should be no problem sustaining this remark since if one
logician discussed syllogisms in this way, it is true.   But does
this entitle Toulmin to treat all discussions of validity (in traditional and modern formal logic) in this cavalier way?   I would acknowledge that there is some truth in saying that validity might be
construed as resulting, as he puts it, "simply from shuffling the
parts of the premisses and rearranging them in a new pattern"
(ibid.); but even if construed in this way, the picture which emerges
is a parody.   He gives this example:

> x is an A;
>
> An A is certainly a B;
>
> So, x is certainly a B.

He then asserts: "When the argument is put in this way, the parts
of the conclusion are manifestly the same as the parts of the premisses, and the conclusion can be obtained simply by shuffling the
parts of the premisses and rearranging them" (p. 119).   He concludes: "If this is what is meant by saying that the argument has
the appropriate 'logical form' and that it is valid on account of this
fact, then this may be said to be a 'formally valid' argument"
(ibid.). [12]

But is this what is meant by formal validity?   Indeed, if this
is what is meant, then it is an easy matter to show that many un-
exceptional, necessary, deductive arguments are not "formally
valid."   Toulmin gives this clinching counter-example:

> Petersen is a Swede;
> The recorded proportion of Roman Catholic Swedes is
>   zero;
> So, certainly, Petersen is not a Roman Catholic.

Now Toulmin is correct in saying that conventional discussions
do not distinguish deductions from valid arguments (note here that I
do not say "formally valid arguments."   See below).   That is, Q is
deducible from P, if P entails (necessarily implies) Q, or if it is
self-contradictory to assert P and deny Q or if the argument 'P,
hence, Q' is valid.   Each of these formulations amounts to the same
thing since, to speak very roughly, in all deductions the conclusion

Q is "contained" in the premisses P. The expression "contained
in" is, of course, a metaphor and is philosophically very troubling.
In some cases it may be understood quite literally, as in this example: "Johnson is President and Humphrey is Vice-President, so,
necessarily Johnson is President." This sort of thing is, apparently, what Toulmin has in mind. Other sorts of deductions, however,
simply do not fit this picture as, for example, "This rose is red,
so necessarily, it is colored."

To be sure, anything which is red is colored; indeed, one
might be tempted to add this as a suppressed premiss, but obviously one can always find a universal premiss to make any argument
into a deduction. (Toulmin correctly observes this on p. 119).
But in this particular argument the one stated premiss entails the
conclusion, since from the very "meaning" of the word "red" in
English, that it is a "color-word," it necessarily follows that the
rose is colored. To anyone who asserted the premiss and denied
the conclusion, we would probably say: "My good man, you simply
do not know the English language." Here validity involves semantic
considerations, considerations about meanings and their entailments.

Still other arguments can be shown to be valid which fit neither simple picture. For example, "If today is Monday, then tomorrow is Tuesday, so, either today is Monday and tomorrow is
Tuesday or today is not Monday and tomorrow is not Tuesday or
today is not Monday and tomorrow is Tuesday." No "shuffling"
will show this to be valid, nor is its validity a function of semantic
considerations; yet the argument is indeed a deduction and is valid.[13]

With respect, then, to formal validity, the test of entailment
(validity) is independent of any semantic considerations or considerations of "meaning," content and the like; that is, one can decide if
an argument is valid or invalid solely on the basis of its logical
form.[14] The reason why logicians (since Aristotle) have concentrated on the formal aspects of argument is not hard to find; but
this takes us to our second line of criticism. (B) As Strawson (Introduction to Logical Theory, Methuen, London 1962, p. 40) has
noted, the (formal) logician is not a lexicographer. He is not interested in listing all the "warrants" (Toulmin's sense) which could

be used in the fantastically diversified contexts in which arguments
appear. Indeed, he is interested primarily in those inference possibilities which are "field-invariant" and not "field-dependent."
But if this is so, he looks for the widest possible generality and
attempts to arrive at an analysis which serves that end. Thus the
argument: "Petersen is a Swede; A Swede is certainly not a Roman
Catholic, so, Petersen is certainly not a Roman Catholic," is of no
particular interest to him; but the form of that argument is.

Toulmin would seem to be aware of this.[15] What then does
he have against formal logic?[16] Though several reasons might be
given, I suspect that his distaste stems from his absolutely correct
observation that the larger class of arguments with which we are
concerned in ordinary life are simply not deductions subject to the
standards of formal validity. But indeed, if this is his main objection, then the solution is not to rename validity to cover correct
non-deductive arguments, but to look more carefully into those field-
dependent features of correct non-deductive arguments which make
them correct.

(C) Finally, Toulmin is convinced that if ordinary people say
that they are making deductions when logicians insist that they are
not and if astronomers and physicists continue to maintain that their
conclusions must be so-and-so, when logicians point out that at best
their conclusions are highly probable, then obviously, the logicians
must be wrong!

It may well be that ordinary language preserves, reflects and
reveals important distinctions, but is there any reason to believe
that only those distinctions are worth making? With respect to
those arguments which are named substantial and conclusive by
Toulmin, they are indeed deductions. But though their conclusions
follow necessarily, the conclusions are not necessarily true. Applying Newtonian mechanics to a problem of stellar mechanics does
of course yield "one single, unambiguous and unequivocal solution"
(p. 137). But this solution must be so-and-so only if we are willing to accept the sum total of assumptions and presuppositions involved in Newtonian mechanics.[17]

II

Books and articles on argumentation and debate are not, it
may be maintained, particularly interested in the questions of logical theory raised by Toulmin and discussed in section I above, nor
are they interested in probability theory, the foundations of science,
or the theory of knowledge. So that even if Toulmin's analysis is
of little help in these areas, one may counter that it still may be
useful for graphically displaying the features of "real-life" argument.

To say this would, I think, be a mistake, for insofar as debaters, like everyone else, require a clear and consistent picture
of argument, their interests are coincident with the interests of
philosophers, logicians and scientists. This is not to say that debaters have no special requirements, but these, after all, cannot be
satisfied at the expense of those demands which are held in common. If, then, Toulmin's attempt to substitute for the deduction-
induction distinction a new set of distinctions fails, and if his attempt to distinguish different "functions" of the statements used in
arguments breaks down, then his model fails both for whatever purposes he may have had in mind and for those special purposes to
which debaters have put his model.

In this context, it is worth noticing a chapter from R.R.
Windes's and A. Hastings's recent book, Argumentation and Advocacy (Random House, N.Y. 1965). These writers assert that the
traditional definition of an argument as consisting of "a statement
(conclusion) which follows from other statements (premisses) . . .
is not precise enough," since, following Toulmin, "there are three
functional elements in an argument" (p. 157). Enough has been
said about these functional elements, but it is interesting to note
that Windes and Hastings fail to see the problems located above because, like Toulmin, they all but chain their discussion to the simple quasi-syllogism. Secondly, their conception of the "traditional
definition of argument" suggests that they have exclusively in mind
deduction. At least conventionally, the expression "the conclusion
follows from the premisses" has been so employed. But why should
we restrict ourselves in this way? This observation leads me to

what I think is the main confusion underlying the ready acceptance
of the Toulmin model.

     D. Brockriede and W. Ehninger in their essay in the Quarter-
ly Journal of Speech (see above) and in their book, Decision by Debate, are strong advocates of the Toulmin layout. In both places
they give several reasons why his analysis "seems more useful for
debaters" (Decision by Debate, p. 98). But to say "Toulmin's analysis is more useful for debaters" raises this question: it is
more useful than what?

     The answer to this question is not hard to find. Brockriede
and Ehninger compare Toulmin's analysis to, in the first place,
"the apparatus derived from formal logic," and then they unpack
this to refer to Aristotle's discussion of the rules, moods and figures of the syllogism. (See Decision by Debate, p. 98 and their
article in Quarterly Journal of Speech, p. 46.) But, I submit, this
is very much like arguing that a modern physicist should employ
Nicholas Orcsme's laws of motion because they are "more useful"
than those of Aristotle![18] It is a little surprising to see that
Brockriede and Ehninger make absolutely no mention of what has
gone on in logic since Aristotle's day. Indeed, the textbooks of today[19] would have indicated that formal logic has taken vast strides
forward since the 4th century B.C. Even the simple schema, "If
p, then q; p; therefore q," which doesn't fit their understanding of
"traditional logic" was understood and well worked out by the Me-
garic philosopher Philo, who lived around 320 B.C.!

     But this is only half of the problem. As has been recognized
for several centuries, most of the arguments which we encounter in
everyday life must be judged for their correctness not on the basis
of their logical form, but on the basis of extra-formal-logical considerations. As was suggested above, perhaps this is Toulmin's
main concern and I suspect that this is properly the main concern
of debaters. But here again, the solution is not to dismiss as
totally irrelevant the highly illuminating machinery of formal logic
(traditional and modern), to abandon the useful and important distinction between deduction and induction and to obfuscate argument
analysis with fuzzy distinctions, but rather to seek more sophisti-

cated treatments of the features of non-deductive arguments.[20]

This essay is not the place to get into such a possible treatment, but the following list of items would constitute at least a partial list of the problems and areas which such a discussion would include:

1. A discussion of the limits and strengths of modern formal logic with special emphasis on the use of the methods of analysis of formal logic in non-deductive argument.[21]

2. A treatment of the criteria of relevance regarding the premisses of non-deductive arguments.

3. An attempt to delineate the special features of various types of non-deductive arguments including (a) analogical arguments (b) generalizations (c) causal arguments (d) arguments to conclusions about individuals and (e) arguments with value premisses and conclusions.[22]

4. A consideration of the questions which arise over the acceptability of the premisses which may be used to support conclusions.

5. A discussion of the typical informal fallacies, e.g., false cause, ad hominem, equivocation, etc.[23]

This essay may be concluded with the following statement: Toulmin seems to me to be mistaken in the way in which he wishes to bring logic into practice, but he is clearly right in insisting that logic must be brought into practice.

Reprinted from Journal of the American Forensic Association, 3: 83-94, September, 1966. Peter T. Manicas is Assistant Professor of Philosophy at Queens College, City University of New York.

Notes

1.   Cambridge University Press, Cambridge, 1958. All references to this book in this essay will be to the paperback edition of 1964.
      For some recent discussions which use the Toulmin model, see Wayne Brockriede and Douglas Ehninger, "Toulmin on Argument: An Interpretation and Application," Quarterly Journal of Speech, 46:44-53, February, 1960; Ehninger and

Brockriede, Decision by Debate, Dodd, Mead and Co.,
N.Y., 1963; Glen E. Mills, Reason in Controversy, Allyn
and Bacon, Inc., Boston, 1964; R. Windes, and A. Hastings,
Argumentation and Advocacy, Random House, N.Y., 1965;
James C. McCroskey, "Toulmin and the Basic Course,"
The Speech Teacher, 14:91-100, March, 1965; Austin J.
Freeley, Argumentation and Debate, Wadsworth Publishing
Co., San Francisco, 1966.
By contrast, there have been two highly critical appraisals of
Toulmin's book by professional philosophers, namely, J.C.
Cooley, "On Mr. Toulmin's Revolution in Logic," The Jour-
nal of Philosophy, 56:297-319, March 26, 1959; and J.L.
Cowan, "The Uses of Argument--An Apology for Logic,"
Mind, 73:27-45, January, 1964.

2.   In general, I fail to see how Toulmin's criticism of Strawson's
point that "inductive arguments are not deductive arguments"
stands up.   Once we take seriously this distinction, the
quest for certainty and for "wholesale justification" of knowledge claims evaporates as surely as it does on Toulmin's
grounds.   (For the skeptics, the same philosophical difficulties emerge on either view.)

3.   I shall use the expression "the conventional analysis" to refer
to (1) the definition of argument, as containing premisses
and a conclusion, (2) the distinction between deduction and
induction, and (3) the distinction between truth, and validity
and correctness.

4.   Toulmin devotes a full chapter to the discussion of probability
and makes some innovations over what probability means.
Since this is peripheral to our present problem we here
ignore it.   For a full criticism of Toulmin's ideas on this
subject, see Cooley, op. cit., pp. 297-319.

5.   By a "correct argument" I mean an argument in which the
premisses provide good grounds for the conclusion.

6.   This argument could be put into form and proven: "If Harry
was born in Bermuda (p), then he is a British subject (q)
unless his parents were aliens (r) or he has become a nat-
uralized American citizen (s).   Harry was born in Bermuda
and his parents are not aliens and he has not become a nat-
uralized American citizen; so, Harry is a British subject."
which becomes:

$$\sim r.\sim s \supset (p \supset q)$$
$$p.\sim r.\sim s$$
$$\therefore q$$

(For simplicity, I have instantiated the universal premiss
"A man born in Bermuda will be a British citizen.").

7.   On the conventional analysis, an argument could never get
started if each premiss were challenged.   As I note, Toulmin suggests that data require no backing though warrants
do.   What is the ground for this?

8.   As Cooley notes (op. cit., p. 310), "the identity of the individuals who restrict themselves in this way remains obscure."
As part II of the present essay suggests, Toulmin's analysis

of argument gains stature through bad comparison.
9. First figure syllogism, AAA (or three universal affirmative
   statements).
10. The three "tests" for an analytic argument stated on p. 131 are
    of no help either for the same reasons. Each is stated in
    terms of data, backing and conclusion. Note that if instead
    of these distinctions, we substitute "premisses" for "data"
    and "backing," then on all three tests, Barbara is analytic.
11. I chose the syllogism for discussion because Toulmin did. The
    going would have been rougher if his distinctions were
    brought to bear upon more complicated species of argument.
    Consider these few examples:
    (a) If Robinson went to New York, then he took his wife, and
        if he went on business then he took his secretary. So if he
        went to New York on business, he took his wife and his
        secretary.
    In this impeccable deduction the conclusion is hypothetical as
    are both premisses. Are both premisses warrants? Data?
    What?
    (b) If I go to my first class tomorrow, I must get up very
        early, and if I go to the party tonight, I will stay up very
        late. If I stay up very late and get up very early, I will
        have to get along on very little sleep. I can't get along on
        very little sleep; so, I must either miss my first class to-
        morrow or stay away from the party tonight.
    In chain reasoning of this sort (which presumably is so impor-
    tant for debaters) nothing whatever is gained by trying to
    mark off warrants from data. Indeed, try it.
    (These two examples are from I. Copi, Symbolic Logic,
    Macmillan and Co., N.Y. 1954.)
    (c) The cigarette butts in the ashtray had no lipstick on them,
        and were Pall Mall filters. The partner of the murdered
        man smoked Pall Mall filters and he knew that the murdered
        man knew that he was having an affair with his wife. So if
        we can show that the partner has no alibi, we have our man.
    This textbook type Sherlock Holmes induction is a plausible
    argument with nothing but data. One might insist that the
    argument is telescoped and contains many suppressed prem-
    isses. No doubt a warrant authorizing the move from the
    data to the conclusion could be formulated. But how reveal-
    ing would formulating it make the argument? It might go
    like this: We may take it that if unlipsticked Pall Mall fil-
    ters are found at the scene of the crime and if someone with
    a motive has no alibi, but smokes Pall Mall filters, then we
    may suppose that he is the guilty party. It is always possi-
    ble to frame a hypothetical which would make any argument
    deductive. (see below p. 17).
12. What is left out in this parody is that even in this simple case
    not any "shuffling" will do. What entitles one to replace the
    x, A and B in that particular way? Why not: "x is an A;
    an A is certainly a B; so, A is certainly an x?" This
    "shuffling" leads to an invalid argument.
13. Not only is it valid, but it is formally valid, as a truth-function-

al analysis will show. There is an important--indeed, fun-
damental--difference between a conclusion being one of the
premises (a petitio principii) and a conclusion being implied by the premises. In all valid arguments the latter
is true--only in some is the former true.
Consider this example:
If the U.S. Air Force bombs North Vietnam, then the Red
Chinese have not entered the war; so, either the U.S. Air
Force has not bombed North Vietnam or the North Vietna-
mese do not want Chinese assistance.
This argument, too, is formally valid though no amount of
shuffling will produce that part of the conclusion which does
not appear, even implicitly, in the premises.

14. The Aristotelian analysis of form (which analyzes arguments by
analysis of categorical statements) is perhaps misleading if
taken as the paradigm. In the first place, it does suggest
Toulmin's shuffling parody; but even then, the Aristotelian
system must (and does) generate a kind of decision procedure for determining validity. Secondly, not any and all
analyses of "form" will do. Aristotle's, of course, is successful for but a limited range of cases. Modern logic has
been able to offer analyses which greatly enlarge the range
of arguments which are formally provable. In addition to
this greater power, it has been able to bring considerably
more rigor to analysis.
    It might be here mentioned that Toulmin's Roman Catholic
    Swede example is formally provable, though we cannot here
    develop it.

15. But see his remarks, pp. 39-40, where he asks: ". . . can
one hope, even as a matter of theory alone, to set out and
criticize arguments in such a way that the form in which
one sets out the arguments and the standards by appeal to
which one criticizes them are both field-invariant?" The
answer to this question is an emphatic "yes" though of
course there will be a large class of arguments which will
not be provable by these means.
    It may be observed that the way Toulmin puts his question is
    ambiguous. Does he mean all arguments or some? If he
    means can we set out and criticize all arguments by field-
    invariant formal standards, the answer is still yes, but
    now many correct non-deductive arguments will be shown to
    be formally invalid. But so what? The predicate "valid"
    is not honorific. Obviously, if he means, can we set out
    and criticize some arguments in this way, the answer is
    positively yes, namely, the class of formally valid deduc-
    tive arguments.

16. Except his inordinate fear that university chairs in logic will
be given to no one but mathematical logicians!

17. Toulmin says: "If told that the wall is 6 ft. high and the sun
at an angle of 30 degrees, a physicist will happily say that
the shadow must have a depth of ten and a half feet" (p.
137).
    But this is perfectly consistent with the conventional distinc-

tion between deduction and induction. The conclusion fails if there was a mistake in the calculation; or, if the wall is not exactly 6 feet, the sun is not exactly 30 degrees, the wall is not at right angles to the earth, the wall is not straight, the earth not level, light is not propagated rectilinearly, etc., etc.

18. Brockriede and Ehninger conclude their Quarterly Journal of Speech piece with these remarks: "The world of argument is vast, one seemingly without end. . . . The traditional logical system of syllogisms, of enthymemes, of middles distributed and undistributed, may have had its attraction in medieval times. The inadequacies of such a logic, however, have been described by experts; for example, see J.S. Mill on the syllogism and petitio principii" (p. 53). This paragraph shows that my comparison is no exaggeration. Bringing Mill in as an "expert" is in itself remarkable. Mill's confusions on this point have by now been so thoroughly demonstrated that I can only refer the interested reader to one of several good discussions. See for example, R.M. Eaton, General Logic, Scribner's, N.Y., 1931 and 1959, pp. 140-150; M.R. Cohen and E. Nagel, An Introduction to Logic and Scientific Method, Harcourt, Brace and Co., N.Y., 1934, pp. 177-181. Just incidentally, Mill's objections were stated at least as early as 200 A.D. by Sextus Empiricus, and involve a confusion similar to the one discussed above on pp. 90ff.

    Paradoxically, when Aristotle came to discuss the "logic" of rhetoric, he did not restrict himself to syllogistic forms. See his Rhetoric, Book 1, Chapter II.

19. In their bibliography in Decision by Debate, Brockriede and Ehninger refer to Alburey Castell's seldom used text of 1935 and to F.S.C. Schiller's confused and horribly dated discussion in his Formal Logic (1912). In addition to the works already cited they might have looked at W.V.O. Quine, Methods of Logic, Holt, Rinehart and Winston, N.Y., 1950; P. Suppes, Introduction to Logic, Van Nostrand & Co., Princeton, N.J., 1957; R.B. Angell, Reasoning and Logic, Appleton-Century-Crofts, N.Y., 1964.

20. Incidentally, of recently published texts on argumentation and debate, the only one which shows any real sophistication in its grasp of logic and its application to debate is Arthur N. Kruger's Modern Debate: Its Logic and Strategy, McGraw-Hill Book Co., Inc., N.Y., 1960.

21. The reader may be recommended especially to R.B. Angell's excellent book, Reasoning and Logic. The items here listed were in a large way inspired by his illuminating discussion of many of these problems. In addition, Professor Angell has a special large section of his book devoted to "reasoning" which would be of great interest to debaters.

22. This list is not intended to be either exhaustive or exclusive.

23. By far the best treatment of such problems and areas in a debate text is that found in Kruger's Modern Debate (op. cit.).

Suggestions for Further Reading

Cooley, J.C.   "On Mr. Toulmin's Revolution in Logic," The Jour-
    nal of Philosophy, 56:297-319, March 26, 1959.
Cowan, J.L.   "The Uses of Argument--An Apology for Logic,"
    Mind, 73:27-49, January, 1964.
Hill, Forbes I.   "Discussion: Analysis of Proof in Decision by De-
    bate," Journal of the American Forensic Association, 1:36-38,
    January, 1964.
Kruger, Arthur N.   "Argumentation and Logic," Section VIII, A
    Classified Bibliography of Argumentation and Debate, Metuchen,
    N.J., Scarecrow Press, 1964, pp. 106-122.
McCroskey, James C.   "Toulmin and the Basic Course," The
    Speech Teacher, 14:91-100, March, 1965.

VI. Persuasion

Issue K: Do Emotional Appeals Have a Place in Debate?

This issue also appears in connection with several others,
namely those concerning the British style of debate, decisionless debate with the open forum, tournament debating, and debate judging. The views expressed by Walter
Murrish in the article "Training the Debater in Persuasion," with its emphasis on style, ethos, and pathos,
are fairly typical of those trained in classical rhetoric.
Although Franklyn S. Haiman's article "Democratic
Ethics and the Hidden Persuaders" appeared several
years before Murrish's and apparently was not written
as a rejoinder of any kind, it does object to some of
Murrish's views, particularly his approval of the pathetic emotional appeals, and raises doubts about others,
such as those pertaining to ethos and audience adaptation.

21. Training the Debater in Persuasion
Walter H. Murrish

A few years ago a feature writer for a metropolitan newspaper
attended his first college debate tournament as a spectator. In his
subsequent article, he described college debate as "a polite form of
mental mayhem characterized by yards of yakety-yak." Before taking offense at this accusation consider the more frequently heard
comment, "Now you're sounding like a debater." It is unfortunate
that "sounding like a debater" is usually a condemnation rather than
a commendation. We who devote time and energy to directing high
school or college debating should re-evaluate our methods if the
product we are producing is stereotyped in this fashion.

It is my thesis that we have become so engrossed in teaching
debate that we have sometimes failed to teach debaters. If debate

training is to be a functional tool in a democratic society, it must
provide effective training in oral communication--in short, a successful debate program provides instruction in persuasion as an instrument of social control. Too many debate directors look askance
at those debaters who are skilled in the art of persuasion. Perhaps
some of this animosity exists because we do not have a common denominator. Therefore, for purpose of clarification, as a debater
would express it, let us define our terms. Minnick describes persuasion as "discourse, written or oral, that is designed to win belief or stimulate action by employing all the factors that determine
human behavior. "[1]

It is within this frame of reference that we are examining persuasion as an integral part of debate training. When the debater
has learned to use the "available means of persuasion"--both logical
and psychological--he has a better chance of securing the desired
response from the audience. And yet in some circles it is considered degrading to include pathos as a unit in a debate course. Is
it any wonder, then, that we who coach debate are not always en-
thusiastic in accepting our judging assignments at debate tournaments? If debate coaches are bored by their own product--high
school and college debaters--there is some reason to believe that
we do not teach persuasion as effectively as we should. It is quite
possible that our concentration upon research, analysis, cogent reasoning, and systematic case construction has caused us to neglect
those factors of persuasion that enable the debater to arrest attention and arouse interest. It is axiomatic that if the debater cannot
maintain the interest of his auditor he has little chance of securing
the desired response. The conclusion is self-evident: We who
train debaters are at fault if it is indeed an insult to sound like a
debater.

At no time am I suggesting that logical training should be ignored. Those of us who direct debate recognize that a debater
must be capable of formulating and defending valid judgments. Without critical thinking, debate, as we know it, would not exist. But
valid arguments, per se, are not enough. Unless these ideas can
be communicated effectively, no change in audience belief and/or

action can be accomplished. It is unrealistic to assume that mere
cogency of argument can suffice without the embellishments of style
and delivery to impel audience acceptance. If a debate coach is
bored with his own debaters, it is not surprising that we sometimes
have difficulty in securing audiences for our protégés.

Instead of chastising the debater when we are subjected to a
boisterous harangue delivered at a three-hundred-word-a-minute
clip uttered with machine-like regularity, we must accept our share
of the blame. Our refusal to recognize the significance of persuasion in its broader ramifications has helped to stereotype the high
school or college debater as an automatic fact-regurgitator.

For those who contend that debating would be degraded by insistence upon high standards of oral communication, I would submit
this answer. Persuasive speaking, including emphasis upon all
three modes of proof--ethos, pathos, and logos--is not only legitimate, it is mandatory if we are to sell debating to the American
public. Only when we have accepted this challenge can we begin to
train speakers rather than talkers.

I believe in debate just as you do. We all accept the fact that
debate is necessary as a decision-making technique in a democracy.
As Joubert, the French humanist, expressed it more than two centuries ago, "It is better to debate a question without settling it than
to settle a question without debate." This is the framework within
which debate must be taught. Unfortunately, however, much of our
tournament debating takes place in a vacuum. Our debaters seemingly ignore basic principles of effective communication as they un-
leash their attacks upon the opposition. Little attempt is made to
appeal to those human factors of motivation as the debaters seek to
extract a decision from the so-called "critic-judge." Many debaters
apparently assume that a debate coach judges the contest much as
Univac interprets statistical data. But the analogy is not perfect--
Univac doesn't become drowsy from a boring recital of statistics
and jargon.

This brings us to a consideration of what must be done if
tournament debating is to have a functional application. When the
debater transfers his skills from the interscholastic or intercollegi-

ate tournaments to the normal activities of life, he discovers that methods of argumentation which may suffice for a debate coach will not help him to convert his congregation, win the election, inspire the graduating class, sell the refrigerator, or sway the jury. We should be teaching the debater to use techniques of debate and argumentation which will win decisions at the tournament and will also win the important decisions necessary for success in life.

Is it possible to debate in such a way that the critic-judge as well as the laymen can be persuaded? I am convinced that this can be done. With the expansion of mass media of communication, our audiences are becoming less and less selective. No longer can a politician use different arguments for various socio-economic sectors of our population. By a judicious blending of all the available means of persuasion we can help to make high school and college debating that functional tool of democratic processes.

The blending of these elements has been well phrased by Tau Kappa Alpha in specifying the criteria for a "Speaker of the Year Award." These criteria are as follows: (1) Intelligence. The speaker must be an informed person. He must be able to interpret the signs of his time clearly and correctly. (2) Effectiveness. He must have definite results which he hopes to achieve. His information will not only reach the ears of his auditors in an understandable fashion, but the auditors will be affected by the information in accordance with the speaker's goals. (3) Responsibility. This is the criterion which eliminates from the list of good speakers the shysters, demagogues, and charlatans. The responsible speaker is aware of the moral and social consequences of his utterances and acts accordingly.

These three criteria provide an effective safety valve as we seek to develop debaters who are skilled in the art of persuasion. This art is far more than glibness of tongue and the capacity of spellbinding. The proper emphasis upon responsibility is necessary in order that persuasion in debating can conform to the proper ethical values.

To me, the focus upon responsibility is the initial step in training the debater in the art of persuasion. Oliver states, "Per-

suasion is more than a system; it is a way of life. The truly persuasive individuals are those who represent in their own characters
and personalities the best traits of the society in which they live."[2]
This view is much the same as that expressed by Aristotle more
than 2,000 years ago when he stated, "We might also affirm that
[the speaker's] character is the most potent of all the means of persuasion."[3] I think it would be well for us to spend more time in
developing this total speech personality so that the debater sells
himself before he attempts to sell his arguments. Persuasive speaking would be enhanced if we would remind the debater that, in the
words of Emerson, "What you are stands over you the while, and
thunders so that I cannot hear what you say to the contrary."

We who coach debate should guard against insincerity on the
part of our debaters. The debater who does not have faith in his
argument is obviously weak in ethical proof. Training debaters to
become responsible speakers presupposes that the debater does have
faith in his case. I am not suggesting that the debater must believe
in both the affirmative and negative positions. I am concerned, however, with the awareness that there is some truth in both positions.
The debater who has made an assiduous investigation of all the available arguments should have faith in the validity of those which he
has selected. This faith must be communicated when he debates if
he is to be considered a persuasive speaker. Faith seems rather
nebulous to many debaters. This term can be made more meaningful by reference to a story told by Peter Marshall. A minister explained faith to his congregation in this manner: "If I were to tie
one end of a rope to the top of this church steeple and fasten the
other end to the top of that office building across the street, do you
believe an aerial artist could walk that rope? To that extent you
have faith. Now, do you believe that the same aerial artist could
push a wheelbarrow along that same rope? To that extent you have
faith. Finally, would you be willing to ride the wheelbarrow? Unless you would willingly do so, you do not have faith." That is the
type of faith we must develop in our debaters. Before the debater
can ask the auditor to "ride the wheelbarrow," the debater must
demonstrate his willingness to do so himself. A salesman cannot

expect a client to buy a product which he himself does not endorse.

Faith alone is not sufficient for persuasive speaking. This faith must be accompanied by a sincere desire to communicate the "truth." This communication is predicated upon the speaker's ability to establish "good will" with his audience. The audience is not inclined to accept the debater's argument unless the debater demonstrates that he is one that the audience can like, trust, and respect. Many debaters lose decisions because they offend or ignore the audience. It is axiomatic that "the irritated speaker irritates his audience." The debater who seeks to obtain the decision by sheer force is likely to gain the opposite reaction. The futility of coercive harangue as contrasted with the subtlety of persuasion has been satirized in this ditty: "A man convinced against his will is of the same opinion still; a woman convinced against her will is of the same opinion but is seldom still." This truism is further advanced by the philosopher's advice that, "The wise man persuades me with my reasons--the fool convinces me with his own." In short, debate arguments like all good oral communication should be audience centered. Rapport with the audience should be emphasized in tournament debating as well as in the life-situations the debater must face. Let us remind our debaters that they have an obligation to their audience. This facet of persuasion in debating can be summarized in the recommendation of the contest committee of the North Central Association submitted in March, 1951, "Successful communication depends upon the understanding, respect, tolerance, and sympathy which speaker and hearer have for each other."

I suspect that most of us agree that the debater becomes more persuasive as he becomes more responsible, as he gains faith in himself and in his arguments, and as he enhances his capacity to establish rapport with his audience. The big question is how.

I do not pretend to have a solution to these problems. I shall only outline three methods which I have found helpful in training my debaters. The first recommended therapy is the increased utilization of "lay" judges. The debater can become more cognizant of the importance of persuasion if he realizes that from time to time he will be judged by non-debate coaches. This may not mean that

training in the techniques of argumentation should be minimized. I
am inclined to agree with Samuel Butler when he observed, "The
public may not know enough to be experts, but they know enough to
judge between them. " Studies made at the West Point National Debate Tournament have suggested that non-debate coaches used as
judges at the tournament have been in the majority more than half
of the time.   Much of the stereotyped debating that many of us ab-
hor could be ameliorated if more non-debate coaches were assigned
to judge our high school and college tournaments.   If this type of
training is to be functional after graduation, it seems logical that
the debater should learn to sell his arguments to judges who are
not specifically trained in argumentation and debate.   I do not feel
that the quality of debating has suffered at those tournaments which
rely partially on non-debate coaches for judging assignments.   I do
feel that the quality of persuasive speaking improves in such instances.

My second recommendation is the use of the "terminal" ballot,
a kind of ballot in which the judge records a tentative decision after
each constructive and rebuttal speech.   I feel that audience adaptation is improved if the debater, in his post-debate analysis, can
evaluate the progression (or retrogression) of his argument.   The
final decision does not always reflect the changes in the judge's
opinion as the four debaters present their arguments.   The terminal
ballot provides a more effective "feedback" which is consistent with
modern theories of interpersonal communication.   While generally
it would not be advisable to announce the terminal decision during
the course of the debate, such a procedure is valuable for practice
debate sessions.   During the current year I have invited several
persons (some laymen, some former debaters) to audit and judge
our practice debates.   When multiple judging is used, I announce
the composite decisions at the end of each speech.   The judges are
instructed that they may vote affirmative, negative, or undecided.
I have discovered that my debaters become more sensitive to the
need for audience adaptation when they learn that their arguments
have missed the mark.   Skill in persuasion has increased but not
at the expense of cogent reasoning and evidence.

A third recommendation is the use of ballots cast by the participating debaters. A study which I made in 1953 at the University of Denver has convinced me of the merit of this method in order to improve the responsibility of the debaters and to enhance audience adaptation. This procedure is quite simple. At the end of each tournament debate, each team assigns a quality rating to the team it opposed and indicates how it feels the decision should be awarded. At the end of the last round, the debaters rank all teams which they have opposed in the tournament.

The teams which receive the highest rankings from their opponents have apparently demonstrated their ability as well as their fairness toward the opposition. If we agree that a competent speaker must have those qualities which cause the audience to like, trust, and respect him, then this technique would shed some light on the matter. Comments registered by debaters who were included in the study reflected this concept. As one debater wrote, "There is no point in misrepresenting arguments if the opposition is going to judge you." This procedure should be utilized from time to time in order to give the debater greater insight into his persuasive skill. When the debater is asked to judge the debate in which he participates, we are coming closer to the goal of self-evaluation. No real improvement in persuasive speaking can take place until the debater is aware of his own deficiencies. Self-reflexiveness, as George Meade described it in Mind, Self, and Society, should be an essential methodology in our program of training debaters in the art of persuasion.

In summary, I have suggested that persuasion must be taught as an integral part of our debate and argumentation program if we are to make that training functional in a democratic society. Principal areas in which persuasion must be stressed are (1) responsibility of the debater, (2) the demonstration of faith in himself and in his arguments, and (3) audience adaptation. Recommendations for the improvement of our debate program in relationship to the three areas of persuasion include: (1) the occasional assignment of laymen as judges in order to increase the debater's awareness of all three areas of persuasion, (2) the use of terminal ballots to pro-

184   Counterpoint: Debates about Debate

vide better audience feed-back as a means of improving responsible speaking and audience adaptation.

In exploring this problem of persuasion as a part of debate training, we recognize that the ultimate goal is difficult to achieve. Perhaps we, as debate coaches, would do well to accept the advice of the poet:

> You say the little efforts that I make will do no good;
> They never will prevail to tip the hovering scale where
> justice hangs in balance.
> Well, I'm not sure I ever thought they would.
> But I'm prejudiced beyond debate to choose
> Which side shall feel the stubborn ounces of my weight.

Our efforts to strengthen persuasive speaking as a fundamental of debate training can help us to justify high school and college debate training to the general public. Our goal is to train debaters who can function effectively and responsibly in a democratic society. Free speech requires speakers who can think clearly and speak persuasively. The cohesive bonds of argumentation and persuasion must be drawn together if we are to fulfill our mission epitomized in the slogan, "Free Speech is promoted by the kind of speech that makes men free."[4]

Reprinted from the Journal of the American Forensic Association, 1:7-12, January, 1964. Mr. Murrish is director of forensics at the University of Kansas City.

Notes

1. Wayne C. Minnick, The Art of Persuasion. Boston, Houghton Mifflin, 1957, p. 33.
2. Robert T. Oliver, Persuasive Speaking. New York, Longmans, 1950, p. 3.
3. Lane Cooper, The Rhetoric of Aristotle. New York, Appleton-Century-Crofts, 1932, p. 9.
4. Max Ascoli, The Power of Freedom. New York, 1949, p. 67.

22. Democratic Ethics and the Hidden Persuaders
Franklyn S. Haiman

1

Dramatic new developments in science and technology have become so commonplace in recent years that the American public
seems to have grown largely indifferent to them. Yet we are still
not completely immune to excitement in the face of extraordinary
advances on the frontiers of knowledge. Russia's first Sputniks
captured our imagination and set the whole country talking about
science and satellites. Meanwhile another technological event of
considerable importance has set tongues furiously wagging among
those who have heard about it. This is the experimentation which
has taken place with subliminal cues in advertising--the process
whereby the name or picture of a product is flashed on a motion
picture or television screen so rapidly that it cannot be seen by the
conscious eye. The message is registered in the fringes of the
viewer's attention and, it is claimed, may thus motivate him to buy.

Subliminal cues, for whatever they may be worth, are but the
latest weapon in the arsenal of the psychological manipulator, the
creature so vividly exposed in Vance Packard's best-selling The Hidden Persuaders. The fact that this book, originally marketed by a
relatively small publishing house, has attained such widespread
prominence is itself convincing evidence that the public is concerned.
After many years of exposure to various methods of hidden persuasion people are beginning to take notice. They are becoming aware
of the extent and efficiency of the manipulator of the psyche in our
society--in advertising, in politics, and in religion--and are beginning to examine the legitimacy of his activities.

Who is the hidden persuader and how does he differ from the
ordinary advocate? He can best be defined by describing the common denominator of his techniques. Whether they be subliminal
cues, mass hypnosis, constant repetition, loaded language, the subtle use of social pressures, or the appeal to irrelevant loves, hates,
and fears, they all seek the same kind of response from the listener
or viewer. They attempt to make him buy, vote, or believe in a

certain way by short-circuiting his conscious thought processes and
planting suggestions or exerting pressures on the periphery of his
consciousness which are intended to produce automatic, non-reflective behavior.   The methods are similar to those of Pavlov's famous conditioned-reflex experiments with dogs.   Ring a bell and the
dog salivates.   No thought processes intervene here.   Non-critical
reflex action--this is the goal of the hidden persuader.

                                    2

        The average American appears to feel considerable ambivalence
in regard to hidden persuasion.   He vaguely senses there may be
something wrong about it, but, when asked to say why, is usually
unable to present cogent arguments.   He frequently resorts to the
proposition that it is not the methods of persuasion in themselves
which pose a danger but rather that they may be used in the promo-
tion of evil causes.   In other words, the techniques are evaluated in
terms of the goals which they serve, and if the ends are good, the
means are justified.
        Hence the typical American is horrified when he hears about
the success with which the Communist Chinese use psychological devices to accomplish their indoctrination programs, but he is quite
ready to embrace the notion that we must fight fire with fire and do
a more thorough job of brain-washing our own people (although he
would not call it that) in the "American Way of Life."   A British
psychiatrist, Dr. William Sargent, author of a chilling Pavlovian
book entitled Battle for the Mind, exemplifies this viewpoint when he
states: "The Chinese Communists had the sense to avoid a purely
intellectual approach," and proceeds to suggest that we, in the West,
must ourselves become more proficient manipulators of the psyche.
        Americans deplore the mass conformity of the Brave New
World behind the Iron Curtain, yet raise hardly a voice in objection
to the social pressures and exploitation of man's conforming tendencies that are involved in such "good causes" as Tag Days and passing the plate in church.   They condemn the oversimplification of issues in Russian propaganda, yet crowd, 92,000 strong, into Yankee
Stadium on July 20, 1957, to listen attentively as Billy Graham, ac-

cording to the New York Times, "reviewed the ills of the world
from economics to moral deterioration and declared that Christ is
the only answer to our problems and dilemmas."

Nor is it an insignificant sign of public acceptance that the
Vice-President of the United States was seated on the platform at
that rally and exchanged words of mutual praise with the evangelist.
"A young man with vision, integrity and courage," said Billy of
Dick. "A sincere, humble man," said Dick of Billy. Their appreciation of one another is understandable. Mr. Nixon undoubtedly
gained admission to the guild of hidden persuaders by his noted television performance of September 23, 1952, when he sought to clear
himself of campaign charges that he had accepted financial support
in questionable ways:

> I don't believe that I ought to quit, because I am not a
> quitter and incidentally Pat is not a quitter. After all,
> her name was Patricia Ryan and she was born on St.
> Patrick's Day. And you know the Irish never quit.

Although there may have been a sizable minority who were not favorably influenced by this speech, few have questioned the morality
of its techniques.

This philosophy that the methods of persuasion a man uses are
in themselves amoral; that one who is sincere, right thinking, and
working in behalf of good causes or sound products is justified in
using whatever skills he may possess to win acceptance of his ends;
that social pressures and the like are contemptible only when used
by those whom we think are evil--this philosophy, which is held by
great numbers of our people, is what causes their dilemma as they
face the newly publicized subliminal cue technique. Little wonder
that there is no basis for condemning it out of hand. After all, it
might be used by sincere, right-thinking people who are working in
behalf of good causes. And is it really so different from the other
methods we have known before? True, it may succeed in refining
the art of manipulation to a higher perfection than has heretofore
been attained, but the intent is essentially the same. In order to
condemn subliminal cues alone, some distinguishing feature must be
found. The truth is that the difference is only one of degree. The
method of subliminal cues is but a further step along the same road

that the hidden persuaders have been traveling for centuries--the
road which circumvents man's mind and reason in order to elicit
non-reflective, semi-conscious or unconscious responses.   Those
who have at last been shocked, by the discovery of the subliminal
cue technique or by Mr. Packard's book, into facing the problem of
the ethics of persuasion may now join hands with those who since
the time of Plato's argument with the Sophists have been seeking to
find a satisfactory answer to this dilemma.   Although the problem
has been with us for centuries it may be that, as in the case of
warfare, the weapons have now become so potent that the question
can no longer be left to the idle musings of the philosophers.

3

How, then, can our people be convinced that not only the use
of the subliminal cue technique should be fought, but that along with
it they must declare war on an entire battery of practices which
they have grown accustomed to accept, and in some cases even to
admire?   What logic can be advanced for their consideration?

They must first be brought to recognize that the difficulty in
comprehending what is wrong about psychological manipulation stems
from an even more basic failure to understand one of the tenets upon which a democratic society is built--the principle that the end
does not justify the means.   We all know, at least verbally, that
democracy is based upon the dignity of the individual human being.
What we may not fully appreciate is that this concept involves the
premise, now well established both historically and psychologically,
that man is different from lower animals in that he is less governed
by automatic instinct and more aware of himself and, as a result of
these two qualities, capable of making conscious choices.   Theolo-
gians call this difference the soul, humanists call it the power of
reason--but whatever it be labelled it postulates a capacity of man
to govern, within certain limits, his own behavior.   Democracy rejects the premise that the "people is a beast," that the individual is
an instinctual creature who can only be moved by the manipulation of
his emotions and reflexes.

The realist recognizes, of course, that man's capacity rational-

ly to govern himself varies tremendously from one person or society to another, depending on the degree of intelligence, education,
maturity, and experience in self-government that is involved. But
the democratic realist is also aware that growth is the first law of
life and that man's potentialities are, and must be, constantly developing. Democracy is, in fact, primarily dedicated to the proposition that anything which helps in the development of the strength,
productiveness, and happiness of the individual is good, and that anything which blocks or hinders his growth in these directions is immoral.

   The hidden persuader, whether he is aware of it or not, is
engaging in a non-democratic practice. He takes advantage of the
fact that although men may have the latent capacity for making rational, conscious choices, they are also part animal and as such
can be exploited. They can, within limits, be made to respond reflexively. They can be moved to action by suggestions and pressure
in the fringes of their consciousness. But because they can be so
moved does not mean that they should be so moved, and anyone who
so moves them only intensifies their tendencies to respond immature-
ly and thwarts their growth toward the more dignified humanity which
democracy presumes.

4

   Lest there be some misunderstanding, it should be emphasized
that not all persuasion is undemocratic, nor is it immoral for people to try to influence one another. There are many methods of
persuasion, even of appeal to the emotions, which are perfectly in
keeping with democratic standards. A film designed to raise funds
for cerebral palsy which shows crippled children being helped as a
result of donations that have been made to their cause is employing
emotional appeal but is not necessarily attempting to short-circuit
the viewer's thought processes. As a matter of fact, it may even
stimulate his thinking by bringing him into vivid contact with a problem he has not thought about before. If the purpose of dramatiza-
tion is to help people face reality--as has been done so effectively
by so-called problem movies like The Men, Gentleman's Agreement,

Home of the Brave, and A Hatful of Rain--this can hardly be construed, even though it may have tremendous emotional impact, as
an attempt to get around their good judgment. On the other hand,
an emotional appeal may be designed to stir the listener or viewer
to set reason aside and respond before he thinks, in which case it
falls into the category of hidden persuasion and violates democratic
ethics. As Clyde Miller says of propaganda techniques: "They
make us believe and do something we would not believe or do if we
thought about it calmly, dispassionately." Democratic persuasion,
in contrast, leaves the man on the receiving end with a choice.
One does not choose freely if he is unaware of what he is doing.

It may be argued that most of the techniques of hidden persuasion referred to in this article, with the possible exception of subliminal cues and hypnosis, do leave man with a choice. He does
not have to string a tag through his lapel on Tag Day, and if he
does, it is because he has chosen to do so. To be sure, with techniques like social pressure and loaded language it is theoretically
possible for a man to become discriminating enough to detect them
and then to make a choice as to whether or not he will respond to
their influence. At least he has the sensory equipment for so doing,
which might not be the case with subliminal cues and hypnosis. If
one is to be realistic, however, he must admit that in most instances, for most people, the social, economic, and emotional pressures are so great and the degree of awareness of them so slight
that any freedom of choice that may exist is quite negligible. It is
interesting to note in an article on the Billy Graham campaign which
appeared in the Christian Century last year the author, Mr. Harold
Fey, was repulsed not by the techniques of evangelistic persuasion
in themselves (the inherent dangers of which he seems not to recognize) but by the fact that Mr. Graham's organization has perfected
them to such a high degree that their success is almost infallible.
He was horrified by the machine-like precision of the tactics used
and seems to prefer the cruder good-old-days when the listener had
at least a fighting chance of being unaffected. In short, we may
conclude that consciousness, and the freedom of choice which it
makes possible, is a matter of degree; that some advocates evade

more of it than others; and that each of us may want to draw the
line of objection at a slightly different point on the continuum. But
the basic principle must remain unclouded--that to the extent that a
persuader seeks to gain uncritical acceptance of his views, whatever that extent may be, he is in violation of democratic ideals.

5

Another matter which sometimes fogs the ethical issue is the
question of audience adaptation. If one rules out hidden persuasion,
it is argued, does it not follow logically that a speaker must ignore
the Aristotelian wisdom that he dress in a manner which will be acceptable to his audience, that he avoid using language which will offend them, and that if his views are diametrically opposed to theirs
he make some adaptation in order to avoid incurring their hostility?
Are these not attempts to influence the listener in the fringes of his
consciousness?

It must be admitted that such factors do influence an audience
and that they are responded to in a semi-conscious way. The speaker, however, by observing these amenities, is not necessarily attempting to gain uncritical acceptance of his ideas. He may simply
be trying to avoid uncritical rejection. It must be recognized that
people can respond reflexively against something as well as for
something. If a speaker comes before them who sharply violates
their norms in dress, language, or viewpoint, they might automatically close their minds to him and absorb nothing of what he says.
There is no real chance for his cause to gain a fair, objective hearing. If, therefore, in the interests of rationality, he seeks to avoid
being blocked by their prejudices, he is in no wise attempting to
circumscribe the listeners' freedom of choice. He is, in fact, attempting to broaden it. If, however, he goes so far in his adaptation to the audience that he never reveals in any way his differences
with them, and attempts to use his prestige and fluency, if he has
them, to gain acceptance of an idea or product they would not accept if they examined it carefully, he has then misused this particular method of persuasion. "Getting by on one's good looks" is a
practice most of us condemn among our friends and yet strangely

tolerate on the public platform.

6

But, it will be argued, is it not unrealistic for us to believe
that human beings, even in a democratic society, can be brought to
refrain from all of these practices of hidden persuasion? Can we
truly expect the television advertiser not to hire the most attractive
young men and women he can find for his commercials, and not ex-
ploit their sex appeal to the fullest extent possible? What difference does it make if we buy our soap because the color of the wrap-
per revives pleasant childhood memories? How are our great char-
ity-supported institutions to survive if we do not use a little psychological coercion to raise funds? How can good people get elected to
office without engaging in some oversimplification along the way?

This is the familiar "you've got to be realistic" philosophy
that idealists in all fields have been fighting for ages. Perhaps
where the idealists have gone wrong is in failing to realize, in the
first place, that an absolutist attitude toward a problem wins few
converts. Even the best of men, moralists included, will "sin" occasionally. Hidden persuasion, like any other "evil," is dangerous
only when it becomes the chronic or predominant pattern of behavior of an individual or group. We can forgive a Harry Truman or
a Richard Nixon his occasional blows below the belt if we are convinced that these are not typical of most of his behavior, but if
these men are chronic and severe offenders, they become a menace
to a democratic society. So long as hidden persuasion is largely
confined to the sale of soap and cereal we need not become greatly
exercised, but when it becomes the all-pervading mode of appeal in
a society--the rule rather than the exception--it is time to sound
the alarm. When we examine current practices in American business, politics, and religion, we may well conclude that this time is
fast approaching.

A second error commonly made by idealists is the failure to
realize that a moral appeal, in and of itself, is rarely sufficient to
overcome the "you've got to be realistic" philosophy. Before people will give up, or at least try to limit, a mode of behavior, they

must be convinced that it is in their interests to do so. Can the
hidden persuader be so convinced? Can he be shown that his methods not only are unnecessary but ultimately ineffective in achieving
his ends? Let us explore some possibilities.

7

In the first place, it can be pointed out to him that most people possess some degree of immunity against hidden persuasion.
Particularly with regard to those questions which are important to
them, and about which they possess some knowledge, their capacity
to resist suggestion and to maintain their autonomy of thought and
action is sometimes surprising.

Furthermore, psychology is far from an exact science, and so
long as man is an autonomous being, at least theoretically capable
of conscious choice, he will be somewhat unpredictable to his fellow
men. To gamble millions of dollars, on the basis of "motivation
research, " that the Edsel car can be given a "personality" that will
successfully appeal to the "young executive" is risky business indeed.

But, argues the advocate of hidden persuasion, have not psychology and psychoanalysis proved that human beings do not operate
on a rational basis? Is it not true that their behavior and beliefs
are motivated and governed by the unconscious? If so, does it not
follow that we must direct our persuasion to the unconscious if we
are to get results?

There is no question that Freud and those who followed him
have revealed the potency of unconscious motivation and have demonstrated that man does not operate in a rational vacuum. But they
have also demonstrated something else which the hidden persuader
seems not to understand. Psychoanalysis, at its very core, is
based upon the premise that under the proper conditions man is capable of bringing to light the unconscious factors which affect him,
of subjecting them to the critical scrutiny of his conscious mind,
and of thus learning to live with them and use them productively
rather than being blindly driven by them. Freud, in his relentless
searching after truth, may have uncovered the beast in man, but
his whole life was dedicated to the proposition that man, through

his unique capacity for self-awareness, can and often does rise
above the level of the beast. To the hidden persuader who justifies
his methods on the grounds that "you cannot move men by reason, "
it should be pointed out that so long as an advocate is aware of his
listener's emotional needs, and takes them into account, there is no
more effective way in the long run to move him than to help make
him conscious of these motives and to show him, clearly and rationally, how he can best fulfill them. This is the appeal to enlightened
self-interest--a process which provides a more solid and lasting
basis for conviction and action than the fickle responses of the unconscious.

8

For the hit-and-run category of hidden persuaders, those interested in the short haul and the fast buck, these arguments may
not be convincing. They know that men do respond impulsively
much of the time and that this tendency can be exploited to considerable personal advantage. What they may not know is that in the
process they do serious harm to themselves. When one talks with
individuals who are committed to the philosophy of manipulating people, one finds that they do not themselves like to be manipulated by
others. The fallacy of their position is that the two sides of the
coin cannot be split apart. As T. V. Smith and Eduard Lindeman
point out in The Democratic Way of Life: "The doctrine that the
end justifies the means is not merely immoral but unscientific. A
person's character finally takes on the pattern of his acts, not his
wishes . . . we become what we do. " Just as a good cause can be
sullied by the means used to achieve it--"the end pre-exists in the
means, " said Emerson--so a man can become contaminated by his
actions. To manipulate others he must become an actor, and to be
an effective actor of this sort requires that he manipulate his own
emotions. He must learn to appear sincere when he is not, to be
friendly when he is hostile, to seem angry when he feels no anger.
Several years of such acting and he no longer knows who he really
is or what he really feels. He is nothing but a set of masks, and
even he does not know which mask he prefers. The hidden persuad-

er must be brought to realize that he is a slave of the same game
to which he subjects others.

9

Does all this apply, it may be asked, to individuals who manipulate others unconsciously--men who believe so devoutly or fana-
tically in the causes they advocate that they engage in hidden persuasion without knowing it? Here, of course, we have the problem
of determining that elusive thing called sincerity so that we may
know whether the attempts at manipulation were truly unconscious.
Was Mark Antony simply thinking out loud and communicating his
own true feelings about Caesar's assassination to the friends, Ro-
mans, and countrymen who lent him their ears, or did he deliberately plan the masterful hidden persuasion which roused them to riot?
Did Adolf Hitler really believe that the Jews were a menace to the
"Aryan race," or did he coldly calculate and promote this scape-
goat mechanism as a device to unify the German people behind him?
These questions may be impossible to answer. But for the sake of
argument, let us assume that these men were completely sincere
and entirely unaware of the techniques they were employing. Are
they then any less guilty of unethical practices than the deliberate
hidden persuader?
Perhaps we can make the same kind of distinction here that
we do in the field of jurisprudence between premeditated crimes and
crimes of passion. Although we tend to be less harsh in our punish-
ments and to feel less moral condemnation toward those who know
not what they do, we are no less on guard against their actions and
take similar measures to protect society from them. If we are
clear in our thinking about the ethics of their behavior, it is not
particularly relevant how we feel about them as people.

10

Finally, let us consider the extremely forceful and attractive
individual who has no manipulative intentions, either conscious or unconscious, but is nevertheless blindly followed by others. He simply presents his ideas as best he can and hopes that his listeners

will decide for themselves, but his personal magnetism (ethos) is
so strong or his emotional zeal (pathos) so contagious that they respond positively to him without reflection. Certainly the speaker,
in such a case, can in no way be held to account for what has happened. We must now look to the responsibility of the audience.
They too have an obligation to aid in the preservation of human dig-
nity--first and foremost their own! It is easy enough to score
others for practicing manipulation, but those who succumb to it under little or no pressure are even more to be questioned.

In fact, it would seem that the ultimate solution to the problem of hidden persuasion lies not in attempting to outlaw the man-
ipulator--for such a law would be practically impossible to define
much less enforce--but in teaching listeners to become more sensitive to the techniques of psychological manipulation so that they can
protect themselves at least from those that are not completely subliminal. As for the latter, if they eventually prove effective, perhaps some legal action will be required to curb their use. In the
meanwhile, we must somehow develop every individual to a fuller
awareness of what he himself really thinks, feels, and wants; for
the personal magnetism and emotional zeal of even the most heroic
leader cannot by themselves succeed in influencing another human
being who is truly conscious of his own unique needs and interests.

Here, to be sure, is a great inadequacy in our society. Even
the experts on human behavior know relatively little about how to
promote the autonomy and uniqueness of the individual. Psychoanalysis has helped some, but only an infinitesimal fraction of our population has been able to benefit from such an experience. Perhaps
the arts--music, painting, writing--hold some of the secrets, but
the processes of developing creativity in those as well as other
areas are still largely a mystery to us.

The Soviet Sputniks have challenged America to re-examine its
efforts in the physical sciences and to undertake a crash program
for exploring the wonders of outer space. Let us hope that the hidden persuaders will serve as an equal challenge for us to explore
more fully the wonders of man.

Reprinted from Quarterly Journal of Speech, 64:385-392, December, 1958. Dr. Haiman is Professor of Speech at Northwestern University.

Suggestions for Further Reading

Baker, Eldon E. "The Immediate Effects of Perceived Speaker Disorganization on Speaker Credibility and Audience Attitude Change in Persuasive Speaking," Western Speech, 29:148-161, Summer, 1965.

Cronkhite, Gary L. "Logic, Emotion, and the Paradigm of Persuasion," Quarterly Journal of Speech, 50:13-18, February, 1964.

Diggs, B.J. "Persuasion and Ethics," Quarterly Journal of Speech, 50:359-373, December, 1964.

Dresser, William R. "The Impact of Evidence on Decision Making," Journal of the American Forensic Association, 3:43-47, May, 1966.

Fisher, Walter R. "Advisory Rhetoric: Implications for Forensic Debate," Western Speech, 29:114-119, Spring, 1965.

Garver, J.N. "On the Rationality of Persuading," Mind, 69:163-174, April, 1960.

Gregg, Richard B. "Some Psychological Aspects of Argument," Western Speech, 28:222-230, Fall, 1964.

Grisez, Germain G. "The Concept of Appropriateness: Ethical Considerations in Persuasive Argument," Journal of the American Forensic Association, 2:53-58, May, 1965.

Hillbruner, Anthony. "Psychological Creativity in Persuasion," Today's Speech, 12:19-21, April, 1964.

Howell, William S. "The Role of Persuasion in Debate," AFA Register, 10:20-23, Fall, 1962.

Jonas, James L. "Juries, Jargon, and Justice," Today's Speech, 12:9-11, April, 1964.

Kruger, Arthur N. "Persuasion and Rhetoric," Section IX, A Classified Bibliography of Argumentation and Debate, Metuchen, N.J., Scarecrow Press, 1964, pp. 123-164.

_____. "The Ethics of Persuasion: A Re-Examination," The Speech Teacher, 16:295-305, November, 1967.

Micken, Ralph. "A Worried Look at the New Rhetoric," Today's Speech, 12:6-7, September, 1964.

Mosier, Kenneth. "Quintilian's Implications Concerning Forensics," AFA Register, Spring, 1963, pp. 1-7.

Newman, Robert P. "The Ethics of Persuasion," Pennsylvania Speech Annual, 11 & 12:3-6, June, 1955.

Nilsen, Thomas R. Ethics of Speech Communication. Indianapolis, The Bobbs-Merrill Company, Inc., 1966.

Olson, Donald O., and John L. Petelle. "A New Look at Ethos and Ethical Proof," Speaker and Gavel, 1:93-97, March, 1964.

Rives, Stanley G. "Ethical Argumentation," Journal of the Ameri-
    can Forensic Association, 1:79-85, September, 1964.
Scott, Robert L. "Some Implications of Existentialism for Rhetor-
    ic," Central States Speech Journal, 15:267-275, November,
    1964.
Wallace, Karl R. "An Ethical Basis of Communication," Speech
    Teacher, 4:1-9, January, 1955.
_____. "The Substance of Rhetoric: Good Reasons," Quarter-
    ly Journal of Speech, 49:239-249, October, 1963.
Wright, Warren E. "A Myth That Is Rhetoric's Adversary," To-
    day's Speech, 13:12-16, February, 1965.

Issue L: Is Audience-Analysis As Important As Subject-Analysis?

       Starting with the premise that one accepts new ideas
only when they harmonize with his previous beliefs, William Utterback, in "Aristotle's Contribution to the Psychology of Argument," concludes that to construct a convincing argument requires two kinds of knowledge: a
knowledge of the subject and a knowledge of the audience.
Furthermore, "as no two audiences are quite alike, each
speech must be made to order." He complains that
standard textbooks on argumentation, though proficient in
the area of subject matter, are "strangely silent" on the
study of the audience and that the average intercollegiate
debater consequently does not know how to adapt his arguments to an audience. He points out that Aristotle
was much concerned with analyzing the Athenian popular
audience of his time and developed long lists of topics,
or motive appeals. Finally, Utterback suggests that we
would do well today to follow Aristotle's lead.

       H.A. Wichelns, while agreeing with Utterback that audi-
ence-analysis is important, disagrees that it should be
taught on equal terms with subject-analysis or that it
should be emphasized in courses in argumentation. He
also questions Utterback's assumption that no two audiences are quite alike. He rates the study of subject
matter as much more important pedagogically and suggests that speakers, particularly undergraduates, fail
"because they have not sufficiently studied the subject."
The important function of a course in argument, as he
sees it, is "to teach students to master materials, to
organize evidence, and to evaluate an inference."

23. Aristotle's Contribution to the Psychology of Argument
William E. Utterback

    The popular dictum that "All roads lead to Rome" should be
amended by the rhetorician to read, "All roads lead through Rome
to Greece." It is perhaps not surprising that a student attempting
to apply modern psychology to rhetoric should repeatedly stumble
upon trails that lead him to Aristotle, one of the first exponents of

the psychological approach to rhetoric. The wonder is rather that
he should only stumble upon them by accident and that when found
they should prove to be unblazed trails bearing no evidence of recent use. Tracing unfrequented footpaths through an unfamiliar
country may yield only the zest of the chase; but it occasionally rewards one with a novel and illuminating approach to prospects little
appreciated by the conventional tourist, and it may possibly discover
treasures of real value to the explorer. In the hopes of such a discovery I propose to follow in this paper a trail originating in a little
traversed region of modern rhetoric, the psychology of argument.

To a student interested in the psychological approach to argumentation the most significant fact about the mind is the organization of its contents into conceptual systems. Each of these systems
comprises an elaborate complex of ideas, images, and concepts
bound together by the principle of logical consistency. In the mind
of the physicist this principle knits together into a harmonious whole
ideas of such apparent diversity as the constitution of matter, radio-
activity, the construction of barometers, and Newton's laws of grav-
itation. Every idea in this system bears a logical relation to every
other idea and to the system as a whole. For the mathematician
the axioms of geometry, the definition and properties of geometrical
figures, constitute another highly organized system. The ideas organized about the mathematician's love for his wife, children, and
home compose another, less perfectly rationalized but probably more
influential in determining his conduct. The enumeration, classification, and analysis of these conceptual systems, while a profitable
employment for the rhetorician, is not to our present purpose. It
is sufficient if we note their significance in governing the conduct
and determining the intellectual outlook of the individual.

The constitution of an individual's conceptual systems determines his acceptance or rejection of any new idea submitted to his
judgment. A native tendency of the mind towards internal harmony
brings it about that before such an idea may enter the charmed circle of an individual's beliefs it must make its peace with every member of the conceptual family. If it cannot do this it is rejected at
once. The doctrine of evolution is an unwelcome intruder in the

family circle of a fundamentalist's mind and is treated accordingly. Nor will mere absence of conflict secure an idea acceptance if it fails to relate itself to any conceptual system. The idea of a protective tariff on steel probably does no violence to the ideational structure of an illiterate farm laborer's mind, but it will not be accepted nevertheless; the laborer cannot see that it bears any relation to those complexes about which his mental life revolves. But the same idea does accord most harmoniously with the mental economy of a shareholder in the United States Steel Corporation and accordingly receives a very different reception in his mind. If a new idea promises to resolve a disturbing conflict between two contradictory conceptual systems or between two contradictory portions of the same system, it will of course be accepted with enthusiasm. Witness the almost pathetic eagerness with which those who learned orthodox theology at home and modern science in college embrace any doctrine which promises to resolve the apparent contradiction between these two systems of beliefs. The influence of conceptual systems in determining the reception accorded a new idea may be generalized as follows: A new idea will be accepted as a belief only when it bears an apparent harmonious logical relation to one or more conceptual systems.

The function of constructive argument is to secure the acceptance of an idea by logically relating it to one or more of the hearer's conceptual systems. Logic thus becomes for the rhetorician the technique of hooking an idea to a conceptual system. A Democratic stump speaker addresses an audience of illiterate farm laborers in the following vein: The abolition of protective tariff on steel would result in cheaper farm implements, and cheaper farm machinery would enable your employer to raise your wages. If the argument is successful, the speaker will have succeeded in establishing a new logical connection between the ideas free trade on steel and higher wages by connecting both with the intermediary idea cheaper machinery. High wages is a member of that very important complex of ideas built up about the notion of economic advantage. Free trade on steel is thus accepted by the hearer as an integral part of that important and well established system of beliefs. The

minor premise of this syllogism connects free trade, the minor
term of the syllogism, with the middle term, cheaper machinery;
the major premise connects the middle term with the major term,
high wages. In any unit of constructive argument the minor term
is chosen with reference to the speaker's purpose; the major term
is chosen from one of the hearer's conceptual systems; and the middle term is the central pillar of the bridge erected between the two.
It is apparent from this, or any other, syllogism, that the premises
employed in popular argument are of two kinds: the minor premise
is a statement of concrete fact drawn from the subject matter of
economics, sociology, or political science; the major premise is a
more general statement relating the subject matter of social science
to the ideational systems of a particular audience.

The conclusion of this rather long-winded discussion is this:
The construction of popular argument requires two sorts of knowledge, a knowledge of the social science with which the speaker is
dealing and a knowledge of the mental topography of the audience.
As no two audiences are quite alike each speech must be made to
order. An argument on the World Court constructed without reference to the ideational systems of the particular audience is quite
as futile as the same argument constructed without reference to the
facts of international politics. These two branches of knowledge, of
subject matter and knowledge of the audience, comprise the materials of rhetoric, the warp and woof from which the fabric of all
popular argument must be woven.

The function of rhetoric is to provide the speaker with the
tools of his trade. Whatever of method, of principles, of devices
are necessary to properly arm the speaker for his work it is the
purpose of rhetoric to supply. It should instruct him, not only in
the forms and presentation of argument, but also in the art of providing himself with the materials of argument. This art, which the
ancient rhetoricians called "invention," requires a two-fold technique. Just as the physician employs one method in his scientific
study of materia medica and another equally definite method in his
diagnosis of each case that comes under his care; just as the modern salesman employs one method in the study of life insurance and

another in the study of his prospective customer; so the rhetorician must have at his command both a method of research for the study of the problems on which he speaks and a technique for the study of the audience. Until rhetoric provides him with both methods of research it has failed properly to equip him for the practice of his art.

The equal importance of these two complementary techniques may seem too obvious to require discussion, but its obviousness is only matched by the persistence with which it is ignored in practically all of our texts on argumentation. The standard texts contain full and excellent accounts of the method to be pursued in the study of subject matter. The preparation of bibliographies, the use of periodical literature, pamphlet material, and scientific reference works, the analysis of questions, note-taking, the recording and filing of evidence are all treated with an adequacy that leaves little to be desired. But on the technique of the study of the audience the standard texts are strangely silent. Not only does no modern text on argumentation present a systematic method for the study of the audience, but very few of them even emphasize its necessity. As a result the student is thrown entirely upon his own resources in one of the most difficult and important phases of speech preparation. It can hardly be a matter of astonishment to us that the average intercollegiate debater has so little conception of adapting argument to the requirements of a particular audience.

The ancient rhetoricians saw very clearly the necessity of two separate methods of rhetorical research, one leading to knowledge of subject matter, the other to knowledge of the audience. Aristotle in particular, after emphasizing the distinction between knowledge of subject matter and knowledge of the audience, informs us that knowledge of subject matter is acquired by the use of the procedure employed by the scientist. A discussion of this procedure, in his opinion, does not lie within the province of rhetoric, and he dismisses the subject rather briefly with the advice that the student apply to the scientist for his method. But the study of the audience does, in his opinion, lie peculiarly within the province of rhetoric. He accordingly devotes a large portion of his principal treatise on rhetoric to the elaboration of a procedure for the study of the audience. Aristotle's contribution to the subject consists in a minute analysis of the Athenian popular audience of his time. Each of the important conceptual systems is analyzed into its constituent elements, and each of these elements in turn analyzed into still simpler units. The result of this analysis is a long list of the ideas commonly accepted as true by the Athenian citizen, the ideas which were observed to motivate his conduct of both public and private affairs, and which determined his acceptance or rejection of any speaker's proposal. Among these ideas, or topics as they were called, are enumerated under the head of wealth, the possession of money, the possession of agricultural land, of household furniture, of cattle, of slaves, etc; under the head of health, physical strength, fleetness of foot, ability to withstand the hardships of war, freedom from illness, athletic prowess, and the like. The use of each topic is discussed and in many cases briefly illustrated from Greek literature. Aristotle's treatment of the topics covers many pages of modern text, and, so far as we may judge, was a practically exhaustive analysis of the Athenian popular audience. . . . .

. . . [Portion omitted contains a discussion of Aristotle's topics and suggestions on how the underlying idea could be taught today.]

. . . Whether this method will serve us as well as it served the ancient rhetoricians we cannot say until we have tried it. Whether a better method could be devised we cannot say without the expenditure of more time and thought than the problem has yet received. But one thing is certain. An effective psychological approach to argumentation necessitates the perfection of some more tangible and effective method for the analysis of the audience than any we now possess.

Read at the Eastern Conference, New York University, April 13, 1925, and condensed from The Quarterly Journal of Speech Education, 11:218-25, June, 1925. Dr. Utterback was a professor of speech at Ohio State University. He died in 1964.

24. Audience-Analysis Versus Subject-Analysis
Herbert A. Wichelns

Professor Utterback's article in the June issue, on Aristotle's
contribution to the psychology of argument, moves me to submit a
few counter-considerations. Mr. Utterback takes the position, not
only that audience-analysis is important, but that it should be taught
on equal terms with the analysis and organization of material, and
that, to use his own words, "As no two audiences are quite alike,
each speech must be made to order. " Agreeing that audience-analysis is important, especially in the historical study of speeches, I
cannot agree that it needs to be emphasized in courses in argumentation, nor that no two audiences are quite alike. To take up the
last point first. Bryan delivered the same lectures all over the
country, with no marked variation so far as I have heard, and with
considerable success. Conwell's "Acres of Diamonds" is another
example. Popular lecturers are constantly doing the same thing.
I think I could dig up an article or two on the Chautauqua system
in which it is said that lecturers are watched to insure their repeating verbatim the original lectures they submitted to the manage-
ment. Even where minor changes are made, as in exordia, they
will hardly outweigh the fact that the main line of appeal is found
suitable for many audiences. One need not share Mencken's contempt for the "booboisie" to feel that the conceptual systems of the
average American are much like that of his neighbor.

Mr. Utterback may draw support for the differences among
audiences from Mr. Bauer's article (in the same issue) on Lincoln's
adaptations to the local audience in his debates with Douglas; but
that article does not tell us whether the subtle variations were minor or major, does not compare the changes with the consistent
main line of argument, and does not indicate whether Douglas also
shifted ground to meet local opinions. So we are not justified in
calling the debates of 1858 examples of adaptation to distinctly different audiences, and certainly are not justified in considering these
debates typical of audience-speaker relations.

Even though audiences do not vastly differ, it may still be

urged that the study of a general audience should be included in a
college course in argumentation, on the ground of "the equal importance of these two techniques" (the technique for the study of problems and the technique for the study of audiences). Pedagogically,
the two techniques do not seem to me to be of equal importance.
I should rate the study of subject as more fundamental than that of
audiences and reserve detailed study of audience-adaptation to advanced courses.

To say that the two techniques are of equal importance is to
say that the speaker's thinking-out of his subject is in a language
foreign to his audience and to conclude that he must translate before he can be understood. Were that true, ordinary informal discussion would scarcely be possible, for that is often so impromptu
as not to permit of adaptation. Yet we do talk, unpremeditatedly,
and are understood. Human beings have an infinite variety, of
course; but they are amazingly alike under the surface. Shakespeare
made Shylock point that out, long before Kipling announced the similarity in the conceptual systems of Judy O'Grady and the colonel's
lady. The lecturer and the lectured are sisters under the skin,
too. Perhaps they are farthest apart if we take the words literally:
the academic lecturer is often far removed from his audience; the
lingo of his specialty is a foreign language to his students. But in
the usual case, the intellectual disparity between audience and speaker is not so marked: the ideational systems of speaker and audience are not strangers to each other. And where audience and
speaker think alike--have the same major premises, the same set
of fundamental values--audience-analysis is not imperative.

Why then do speakers fail? Mr. Utterback suggests that they
fail because they have not studied the audience. I suggest that they
fail because they have not sufficiently studied the subject. Undergraduates in particular are fond of picking up a few ideas and a few
formulas without really assimilating them into their own thought and
their own language. This seems to me the most important reason
for not introducing audience-analysis into courses and texts on argument. Much of the time in such courses has to be spent helping
students to make up their own minds. Making up one's own judg-

ment on public questions is never an easy process, and it is not
much promoted for the undergraduate by the usual lecture-and-text-
book course which makes up a large part of his mental fare. Hence
it is an important function of a course in argument to teach students
to master materials, to organize evidence, and to evaluate an inference. Though they are sometimes pitted against each other in classroom debates, the real opponent of each is for a long time his own
inability to handle and judge ideas. He will attend to the audience
sufficiently if he makes an effort to be clear and interesting in his
exposition of his ideas; but first and foremost he must have ideas
in some depth and fulness and with some degree of organization.
From insistence upon thoroughness and intellectual self-consistency
will come a degree of flexibility and adaptability. By splitting attention between the needs of the subject and the supposed needs of
the audience we run the danger not only of superficiality but of insincerity.

Since this selection originally had no title, one has been provided
for the convenience of the reader. The selection is reprinted from
The Quarterly Journal of Speech Education, 11:386-388, November,
1925. Dr. Wichelns was a Professor of Speech at Cornell University.

Suggestions for Further Reading

Cathcart, Robert S. "Adapting Debate to an Audience," Speech
    Teacher, 5:113-116, March, 1956.
Kruger, Arthur N. "The Audience," Section XII, A Classified Bib-
    liography of Argumentation and Debate. Metuchen, N.J.,
    Scarecrow Press, 1964, pp. 183-194.
Nadeau, Ray. "A Philosophy of Debate for Americans or De Gusti-
    bus Non Est Disputandum," Central States Speech Journal, 1:
    40-44, March, 1950.
Phillips, David C. "But Do the Dogs Like It?" Today's Speech,
    6:5-6, January, 1958.

VII. Ethics

Issue M: Is It Unethical for a Student to Debate Both Sides of the Same Question?

Characterized by Robert M. O'Neil as "the single feature of intercollegiate debate which has probably provoked more criticism and misunderstanding from the outside than any other,"* this issue involves the question of whether academic debaters should defend a position in which they do not personally believe. Apart even from switch-sides debating, a debate coach is often faced with the problem of training debaters who favor only one side of a question. As Nicholas Cripe points out, in 1950, for example, at the University of Vermont only one member of a squad of forty-two believed in the nationalization of basic industries. Thus the question is asked: was it proper for part of the squad to uphold the affirmative for the sake of training, or should the Vermont debaters have debated only when they could find other teams sympathetic to the affirmative?

This issue was dramatically highlighted by the 1954-1955 national college debate topic ("Resolved, That the United States Should Extend Diplomatic Recognition to the Communist Government of China"), when many schools, either by choice or by pressure, decided that they could not sustain a debate program because some debaters would have to defend the affirmative position. Those schools which voluntarily suspended operations no doubt acted in accord with Richard Murphy's philosophy, which he sets forth in "The Ethics of Debating Both Sides." Switch-sides debating, he contends, is immoral, for it requires the student to speak against his own convictions. In "Debating Both Sides in Tournaments Is Ethical," Cripe argues that this practice is not unethical, that it provides good training, and that it promotes tolerance for different points of view. He also points out that those who oppose switch-sides debating confuse the goals of academic debating with those of real-life debating.

*Journal of the American Forensic Association, 1:40, January, 1964.

25. The Ethics of Debating Both Sides
Richard Murphy

"Is it not risky to ignore the ethical?" wrote Senator Albert
J. Beveridge in 1924. "The practice in high schools and colleges
of appointing debating teams to support or oppose propositions, regardless of what the debaters believe, is questionable--indeed,
bad, "[1] he declared. Senator Beveridge's comment is only one of
many that one might cull on the merits of debating in disregard of
conviction. The contemporary controversy dates from Theodore
Roosevelt's declaration in his Autobiography in 1913 that he was "exceedingly glad" that as a student at Harvard he never "practiced debating. " He had "not the slightest sympathy with debating contests
in which each side is arbitrarily assigned a given proposition and
told to maintain it without the least reference to whether those maintaining it believe in it or not. "[2]

The controversy has had its worthy partisans on both sides,
and feelings run deep. Opponents of debating against conviction are
adamant in their position, and, so far as I am aware, partisans of
the debate-both-sides practice are equally one-sided in their belief.
There are, of course, variations in individual practice. Woodrow
Wilson as a senior in college refused to participate in a prize debate when drawing lots put him on the side opposite his belief. But
as a debate counsellor at Princeton, he once advised a debater not
to worry about opposing his own conviction, but to center on his opposition to Harvard. [3] And there have been vogues in the practice.
By 1917, O'Neill, Laycock, and Scales, although defending debating
against conviction, noted that since colleges then had both affirmative and negative teams, ". . . it probably very rarely happens
that a student who has ardent convictions talks against them in an
intercollegiate contest. "[4] In 1930, Dayton McKean, writing about
Woodrow Wilson's attitude on the matter, explained that "debating
both sides" is "a method now generally abandoned. "[5] As recently
as 1951, Ewbank and Auer, defending debating against conviction under certain conditions, observed, "There seems no good reason for
assuming that debaters are commonly forced to debate against their

convictions. "[6]

But with the firm establishment of the tournament system, which received its greatest impetus in the thirties, there has been a growing tendency not only to ignore conviction and side, but also to incorporate debating both sides as a part of the structure. For example, the West Point National Invitational Tournament requires that "teams debate opposite sides of question an equal number of times. "[7] Whereas in the older systems policy was largely a matter of individual schools and coaches, now one either debates both sides or he does not debate at all, or at least not in tournaments such as the West Point. An ethic has now been imposed.

In a rather objective review of what has happened to debate, a well-known political scientist, James MacGregor Burns, describes "modern debating" as primarily a system of contests. "Student debaters ordinarily do not choose their own sides. " He asks, "What would Roosevelt say today if he could see the nationally chosen debate topics, with debating teams shifting from side to side with hardly a change in pace?"[8] One answer has come from a veteran debate coach, Brooks Quimby of Bates College, who asks abandonment of the debate-both-sides policy. [9]

When there is such a sharp disagreement among worthy men, whose individual systems of ethics are presumably equally impeccable, there must be some misunderstanding, some difference in purpose, or some failure to focus on the essence of the matter. It is with the thought that a close analysis may help to clarify the dispute, rather than to add to the literature of the controversy, that I write. For years I have listened to the arguments for debating both sides, and I have read all I could find on the question. But consistent with the position I have always held, that debating both sides is of doubtful virtue, I must in all honesty set down the case against it.

The argument against debating both sides is very simple and consistent. Debate, the argument goes, is a form of public speaking. A public statement is a public commitment. Before one takes the platform, he should study the question, he should discuss it until he knows where he stands. Then he should take that stand. If, in the course of the long-term debate, one finds that he has changed

his conviction, he is free to cross the floor, to change his party,
to do what seems consistent with his honest conviction. As Beveridge put it, public speaking "means, of course, utter sincerity.
Never under any circumstances or for any reward tell an audience
what you, yourself, do not believe or are even indifferent about.
To do so is immoral and worse--it is to be a public liar."[10] Or,
as Brooks Quimby puts the matter, "our democracy" needs "men
and women of principle, who will weigh the arguments and evidence
carefully before they become advocates," rather than "men and women trained to take either side at the flip of a coin."[11] As Theodore Roosevelt stated it, "What we need is to turn out of our colleges young men with ardent convictions on the side of the right,
not young men who can make a good argument for either right or
wrong as their interest bids them."[12]

     In reply to these simple arguments, the debate-both-sides pro-
ponents have many answers. One of the sets of answers can be
classified as philosophical. The most frequent of these arguments
is the necessity of a free and open platform, with no silencing of
unpopular sides. There may be applications of John Stuart Mill's
essay, "Of the Liberty of Thought and Discussion." As Mill argued,
". . . the peculiar evil of silencing the expression of an opinion is,
that it is robbing the human race." Or the argument may be put
thus, ". . . on every subject on which difference of opinion is possible, the truth depends on a balance to be struck between two sets
of conflicting reasons." There is no contesting the usefulness of
the debate form, in which unpopular sides may be presented because
the popular side is presented to counterbalance and correct. Any
valid action to keep inquiry free, to assert the essential debatability
of disputed questions, is a contribution to our freedom of expression.
But it is not clear that one team's debating both sides has any connection with such a policy. If one follows Mill's full recommendation, it means a policy of tolerating, attempting to understand the
utterance of views one does not hold, rather than one of expressing
them oneself. Mill recommended ". . . acting . . . on conscientious conviction." The "real morality of public discussion," Mill
thought, consists in avoiding sophistic argument, or suppressing

facts or arguments, or misstating elements in the case, or misrepresenting opposite opinion. The moral discusser, on the other hand, is tolerant, frank, and fair. It is difficult to see how one can debate both sides and avoid Mill's list of malpractices or attain to his set of moral practices.

Since debate questions are purposely framed to provide a division of opinion, there should be available speakers on either side of the matter, speakers who really believe their own arguments. To do justice to arguments, Mill thought, and to bring them into real contact with our own minds, we "must be able to hear them from persons who actually believe them, who defend them in earnest, and do their very utmost for them." If for some reason a position has to be taken that no one present believes, there are devices for indicating the position taken is not of personal conviction. Socrates, when pressed to present a case he did not believe, spoke with his face covered that he might not offend the gods. But when he spoke his conviction, he spoke with head bare, no longer muffled for shame.[13] Since 1587, the Sacred Congregation of Rites has used a Devil's Advocate as a means of testing arguments in the process of canonization. The various devices of the advocatus diaboli are, of course, only a substitute for the devil himself, who, however pervasive, is not always available for a specific appearance. But these devices do permit making a case in its strongest form without the violation of any ethical principles.

A second philosophical argument is that it is necessary to understand both sides of an argument, and debating both sides helps one to understand both sides. On this point Robert Louis Stevenson is sometimes quoted:

> The best means of all towards catholicity is that wholesome rule which some folk are most inclined to condemn, --I mean the law of obliged speeches. Your senior member commands; and you must take the affirmative or the negative, just as suits his best convenience. . . . As the rule stands, you are saddled with the side you disapprove, and so you are forced . . . to argue out, to feel with, to elaborate completely the case as it stands against yourself.[14]

Such a practice, Stevenson thought, would teach cocksure young stu-

dents some humility. No doubt the practice is a useful device for
the purpose. But Stevenson was speaking of procedure in "a private club, " as opposed to speaking in "a public place, " and with
fond memories of his days in The Speculative Society at Edinburgh.
And he was not recommending a method of systematically debating
both sides. Certainly a blind, intolerant partisanship is a horrible
quality, and if there were no other way of seeing many views than
debating for them, the practice might have to be tolerated on this
count alone. But there are so many ways of seeing other views.
The debater can brief the other side. He can explore the other
side, and read about it. In actual debate, one can listen to the
other side if he will but open his ears and mind. The position of
the other side can be accurately stated for purposes of refutation
where it seems to be in error, or for purposes of admission where
it seems to be correct. To argue that the way to discover an idea
is to get up on the platform and advocate it is rather unusual pedagogy. To argue that if one does not talk against his convictions he
will be ignorant of opposing views is to ignore a basic rhetorical
principle that the speaker should read, and discuss, and inquire,
and test his position before he takes the platform to present it. As
Mill put it, "He who knows only his own side of the case, knows
little of that. " And he commended Cicero's practice, as a "means
of forensic success, " of studying "his adversary's case with as
great, if not still greater, intensity than even his own. "

A third philosophical argument is that it is never clear on
which side the truth lies; hence all positions can be maintained with
equal intensity. Addison's Sir Roger de Coverley is quoted to the
effect that "much might be said on both sides. " Sir Roger, of
course, was dodging a judgment on a personal dispute about fishing,
but even in this trivial matter he showed his usual sage judgment.
That is why we argue a matter: there is a case on each side. But
this is only the beginning. The end is to discover where the truth
lies. A variation of this argument is the definition of truth as what
can gain acceptance, regardless of what the advocates may believe.
Boswell asked Dr. Johnson ". . . whether, as a moralist, he did
not think that the practice of the law, in some degree, hurt the fine

feeling of honesty. " Pressing the point, Boswell asked, "What do
you think of supporting a cause which you know to be bad?" Johnson replied that one does "not know it to be good or bad until the
judge determines it. " Boswell asked whether "dissimulation" did
not "impair one's honesty. " Dr. Johnson was in his best form:
"Sir, a man will no more carry the artifice of the bar into the common intercourse of society, than a man who is paid for tumbling
upon his hands will continue to tumble upon his hands when he
should walk on his feet. "[15] Dr. Johnson was, of course, applying
a kind of eighteenth-century laissez-faire ethic to legal disputation,
and a method he himself seldom followed, since he rarely had difficulty discovering for himself what the universal and eternal truth
of any matter was. But to argue in contemporary times that a public speaker who has read and discussed his question shall not bring
to the deliberation any personal conviction, but shall leave it to an
audience which may never have heard the matter deliberated before,
is to resign the moral responsibility of the speaker.

A fourth philosophical argument is that debaters themselves do
not know what they believe. "My debaters, " says one coach, "did-
n't know at the end of the season what side they were on. " Their
uncertainty is understandable. If one argues at nine o'clock that he
and his colleague are firmly convinced of one side of an issue, and
at ten that he is convinced of its opposite, and keeps up this shifting of advocacy for a season, it would be remarkable indeed if he
really knew what to believe.

A fifth philosophical argument is that the debaters are too
young to take a position on questions of public affairs. "How can
an immature high school student know what our policy should be on
parity prices?" a defender of both-sides debating asks. If students
are debating questions over their heads, then the subjects should be
simplified. But if the student is incompetent to take one position,
he is certainly all the more incompetent to take two. However, we
should not underestimate the intellectual capacity of our debaters,
nor should we overlook the growing tendency to reduce the voting
age. Debaters are either voters, or about to be, and as such will
have to take positions on complex social and economic problems.

A sixth philosophical argument is that it is the function of neither the school nor the debate coach to turn out persons "with ardent convictions on the side of the right." It is sufficient to train them to think logically, and to see both sides. But the school and the teacher must have some responsibility for inducing conviction on such matters as freedom of speech, democracy, and integrity of ideas. True, we do not instruct the student how to vote for dogcatcher, but should we not give him a methodology for finding an answer in a disputed matter? The person who does nothing to determine the ballot before election day, and then enters the polling booth able only to see both sides, is not a completely useful citizen.

A seventh philosophical argument is that debating both sides, through dissociating a student from belief, teaches him the essentials of rigorous, logical thinking. It gives him skill in using facts and inferences, and in thinking accurately. If he waives belief, he may be able to think purely, his mind unclouded by prejudice and predisposition. And if he demonstrates that he is so well informed and so superior to conviction that he can debate either side on the call of a chairman, he has reached the nirvana of scientific method. Now, training in logical methods is not to be disparaged, but is not the end result the discovery of what truth the logical inferences seem to illuminate, and what position one can most validly maintain under the circumstances? Why stop the logical process before the final goal has been reached?

An eighth philosophical argument is that "lawyers do it." Even Theodore Roosevelt allowed that lawyers may have to take an assigned proposition and argue it without relation to conviction. The debaters are advocates, the explanation goes, presenting arguments now for, now against, a proposition, that an audience may see the truth. It is not quite clear, in this argument, why an audience would gain more from hearing a question debated by persons not necessarily believing their sides, than by hearing debaters of deep conviction. However, the right of a lawyer to take an unpopular case, to be permitted to make it as strongly as he can, and to suffer no social ostracism for his action, is a very precious development in social tolerance, and should not be impinged in any way.

But the connection between this virtue and debating both sides is not
very close. By "advocate" is meant ordinarily one who represents
another in his view, or pleads his own belief. There seems to be
some confusion concerning what lawyers actually do. One view is
that lawyers must argue for or against a given proposition whether
they want to or not. But Canon 31 of the Canons of Professional
Ethics of the American Bar Association specifies that the lawyer
"has the right to decline employment."[16] Canon 30 states that "the
lawyer must decline to conduct a civil case or to make a defense
when convinced that it is intended merely to harass or to injure the
opposite party."[17] In other words, the lawyer is supposed to show
personal judgment in taking a case, and he is not to take one merely for the sake of a suit or an argument. The Canon continues,
"His appearance in Court should be deemed equivalent to an assertion on his honor that in his opinion his client's case is one proper
for judicial determination."[18] By analogy one could maintain that
since debate questions are debatable, anyone could with honor uphold either side. But this contention would be a distortion of the
theory. In a debatable matter, a case may honorably be made on
both sides, but not usually by the same person. Clarence Darrow
could with honor maintain that his clients should be sentenced to
life imprisonment rather than to death. He could not, with honor,
argue on a following day that they should be electrocuted. Applying
this principle to debating, cases may honorably be made on both
sides, but not ordinarily by the same person.

Another form of the argument that debating both sides is justifiable because it conforms to legal practice is that lawyers must
represent both sides. Now, if anything is certain in the legal-for-
ensic system, it is that an advocate shall not represent conflicting
interests. "It is unprofessional," reads Canon 6, "to represent conflicting interests, except by express consent of all concerned given
after a full disclosure of the facts." The lawyer, according to the
Canon, must "represent the client with undivided fidelity."[19] Nor
may the lawyer, under the Canons, pose as an objective seeker of
truth if he represents an interest: "It is unprofessional for a lawyer so engaged [in advocacy] to conceal his attorneyship" [Canon

26].[20] These principles in the forensic system should not be confused, of course, with methods in conciliation and mediation in
which a person without interest attempts to resolve conflict. The
conflict of interest principle is a practical matter, not merely an
abstract canon. When in 1955 it was revealed in the hundred-mil-
lion-dollar Dixon-Yates contract that one person had been representing both interests without clear declaration, that element became a
major issue in the President's cancellation of the whole contract.

A ninth philosophical argument is that debating is not public
speaking, and hence not subject to the ethics of the platform, but
is "educational forensics." This terminology has led to many quips,
such as "It may be forensic, but is it educational?" But to state
the argument fairly, it goes something like this: The method of disputing a question on both sides is an old educational device, used in
ancient, medieval, and modern times. No man can say that he is
equipped to defend a position until he has demonstrated he can defend the opposite. Furthermore, in life one frequently has to present a case for, or at other times, a case against, a proposition.
So practice in disputation makes the ready man.

Exercises which train a student to analyze, study lines of argument, or to comprehend and resolve or decide disputed matters
may have their place in the educational process. Kenneth Burke
has recently suggested an exercise in which the student writes "two
debates, upholding first one position and then the other." He then
writes "a third piece" to analyze what he has done and to develop
"a distrustful admiration of all symbolism."[21] The methods used
in a closed debating society or in a classroom may be judged by
pedagogical, rather than ethical, standards. But since the development of Whately's "natural method," that one learns to talk best by
saying what one means and by meaning what one says, there has
been a decline in the use of artificial devices. The tendency has
been to make the club and classroom speaking situation an actual
one, rather than make-believe.

But modern debating is something other than a medieval exercise in dialectic. It is geared to the public platform and to rhetorical, rather than dialectical, principles. The questions are not

speculative or universal, but specific and timely, concerning practical public policy. The debater relies heavily on the use of authority and opinion, whereas in logical disputation an argument has to be taken on its merits. The debater uses ethos, a rhetorical element: "So my colleague and I ask you to agree with us." And the modern debater makes an appeal for judgment by his audience or his critic. The contemporary debater is often ill-equipped to carry on a logical disputation; he may not know one mood of the syllogism from another; but he does know certain forms of rhetoric.

Besides, much has happened since the days of medieval and Renaissance disputation. The role of the citizen in public affairs has been greatly expanded, and public discussion has become an instrument of public policy. The debater, presumably, in addition to disputing at tournaments, speaks before school assemblies, at the student council, to service clubs, and at a number of organizations of which he is a member. He is judged there, not on his ability to present both sides, but upon his honest conviction. If at such meetings it were revealed that the day before he took an opposite view, he would lose his audience.

In addition to the philosophical arguments I have considered, there are in defense of debating both sides many claims for the device in terms of administrative procedure. One argument is that if actual debates are not held until students have decided their beliefs, the program of practice will be delayed. But one may point out that many forms of speaking other than debating are available for early season work. Panels, reports, symposiums, questioning of visiting experts can be used to open a subject and to supply the motivation which comes from having to speak. A second argument is that an early debate helps to open a question, reveal the issues, and give a touch of realism to the program. If this be so, there could be little objection to an early scrub debate to feel out the question. The objection is not that on an occasion or so someone debates just for the fun of it; the objection is to systematizing debating both sides as a forensic method. A third argument is that having a two- rather than a four-man debate team means less cost in travel and wider school participation in tournaments. A fourth

argument is that a two-man both-sides arrangement permits a
school to groom its two best debaters to represent it. A fifth is
that regional and national champion debaters can be selected in the
method, rather than mere school or side champions. These and
other arguments of convenience in programming are obvious advantages in a competitive tournament system, if one cares for such a
system. Whether or not they are to be used will depend on one's
views of the philosophical and ethical matters.

Before summarizing the view I present here, it might be useful to clear away a matter which seems to cause some confusion.
That is whether or not arguing both sides is an essential element in
debating. Many people seem to feel that it is. One director of debating, in a balance sheet of good and bad in the method of debate,
lists "arguments on both sides of the proposition" as one of the
"most important aspects of debate. " He then lists on the liability
side of debate "a certain professionalism which leads students to
argue either side of any question without regard to the intrinsic
merits of the ideas. " This practice, he thinks, leads "either to
sheer hypocrisy or to a certain paralysis of decision which prevents
a person from ever making up his mind. "[22] Another writer thinks
"much good is to be derived from having students debate both sides, "
but laments that the practice causes poor public relations. She
gives the example of the debater who made such an eloquent case
for federal world government in a radio speech that he was invited
to join the movement by a local group. They were somewhat puzzled when, a week later, he made an equally moving speech on the
other side. She recommends early-season practice tournaments on
both sides with sessions "closed to all persons outside forensic circles. " After the secret sessions, the debaters come out and debate
their convictions before the public, free from reproach.[23]

Actually, the both-sides methodology is not now and never has
been an essential element in debate, although it may have been in
certain systems of disputation. The form of debate most generally
practiced, parliamentary, never has used the method. Nor has the
practice been used in debate as a form of public address. Lincoln
and Douglas did not shift from side to side as they journeyed

through Illinois. Nor has it been an essential even in debating societies. The Oxford Union and the Cambridge Union have managed
through two centuries to do without the practice. In my own experience in debating from grade school through graduate college I never
had a coach who followed, or would even tolerate, the system. To
believe that to debate one must debate both sides is to ignore what
actual practice is.

But what are the ethics of debating both sides? If one con-
ceives of debating as a closed club activity in which a rhetorical-
dialectical exercise is used for some purpose, then perhaps the
method can be judged in terms of pedagogy, rather than of ethics.
But insofar as debating is public speaking, insofar as debating is a
method of the platform, it will have to submit to the contemporary
ethic, which is that a public utterance is a public commitment. Nor,
if the view presented in this survey is correct, can the practice be
justified as realistic training for the practice of the law. Debate
would be in a stronger position if it were freed from the anachron-
istic practice of multiple positions. And those who believe in the
essential processes of democratic debate, and wish to extend them,
would no longer be held liable for a dubious practice, if the debate-
both-sides policy were abandoned.

Now, in harmony with one established practice, let one of the
men who opened, close. Said Theodore Roosevelt, "To admire the
gift of oratory without regard to the moral quality behind the gift is
to do wrong to the republic. "24

Reprinted from The Speech Teacher, 6:2-9, January, 1957. Richard
Murphy is Professor of Speech at the University of Illinois.

Notes

1. The Art of Public Speaking. Boston, Houghton Mifflin Company,
        1924, pp. 23-24.
2. Theodore Roosevelt: An Autobiography. New York, The Mac-
        millan Company, 1913, p. 28.
3. Dayton D. McKean, "Woodrow Wilson As a Debate Coach, " The
        Quarterly Journal of Speech, XVI, November, 1930, p. 460.
4. James Milton O'Neill, Craven Laycock, and Robert Leighton

Scales, <u>Argumentation and Debate</u>. New York: The Macmillan Company, 1917, p. 376.
5. Loc. cit.
6. Henry Lee Ewbank and J. Jeffery Auer, <u>Discussion and Debate:</u>
<u>Tools of a Democracy</u>. New York: Appleton-Century-Crofts,
Inc., 1951, p. 389.
7. Tenth West Point National Invitational Debate Tournament.
West Point, United States Military Academy, 1956, p. 20.
8. "Debate Over Collegiate Debate," <u>The New York Times Maga-</u>
<u>zine</u>, December 5, 1954, p. 30.
9. "But Is It Educational?" <u>Speech Activities</u>, 9:30-31, Summer,
1953.
10. Op. cit., p. 20.
11. Loc. cit.
12. Loc. cit.
13. Phaedrus, pp. 237, 243.
14. "Debating Societies," in <u>College Papers</u>.
15. James Boswell, <u>The Life of Samuel Johnson</u>, Chap. XIX.
16. <u>Canons of Professional Ethics</u>.   Chicago: American Bar Association, 1948, p. 18.
17. Loc. cit.
18. Loc. cit.
19. Loc. cit., p. 9.
20. Loc. cit., p. 12.
21. "The Linguistic Approach to Problems of Education," <u>Fifty-</u>
<u>Fourth Yearbook of the National Society for the Study of Ed-</u>
<u>ucation</u>. Chicago: The University of Chicago Press, 1955,
I, p. 287.
22. Wilder W. Crane, Jr., "The Function of Debate," <u>The Central</u>
<u>States Speech Journal</u>, 5:16-17, Fall, 1953.
23. Evelyn Kenesson de Voros, "The Purpose of College Debate,"
<u>Western Speech</u>, 18:191, 194, May, 1954.
24. Address at the Sorbonne, 23 April, 1910.

26. Debating Both Sides in Tournaments Is Ethical
Nicholas M. Cripe

Richard Murphy, writing in <u>The Speech Teacher</u> for January,
1957,[1] has pointed a finger at a considerable segment of the debate
coaches of America and said, "Shame on you!" Oh, he did not use
those exact words, but the implication was there for every coach
who allows a debater to speak publicly on both sides of a debate
topic. Mr. Murphy's contention is that it is not ethical. In fact,
to cite his approving quotation of Albert J. Beveridge in the article,
"To do so is immoral and worse--it is to be a public liar."[2] This
is a serious charge to bring against any debater or his coach. Yet

Counterpoint: Debates about Debate

this is the conclusion I draw from the contents of the Murphy article.

Any writer attempting to reply to Murphy would have to answer certain questions, such as, is it of "doubtful virtue"[3] to debate both sides in a tournament? Is it "questionable--indeed bad"?[4] It will be my purpose in this article to try to answer those questions, and, in doing so, to contend that it is ethical to debate both sides.

The whole problem seems to be one of definition, of defining what "debate" is, and what "ethical" means. "Debate," writes Professor Murphy, "is a form of public speaking. A public statement is a public commitment. Before one takes the platform, he should study the question, he should discuss it until he knows where he stands. Then he should take that stand."[5] Such a definition applies to argument in the pulpit, in the legislative halls, in the courtroom, and in the market place, when the speaker is trying to convince an audience of the "rightness" of his stand, but does it apply to the type of tournament debating practiced today? Professor Murphy seems to imply that it does. It is my contention that such a definition is too narrow, and cannot be so applied unless one favors the discontinuance of interscholastic debate of a national proposition. In fact, if the proponents of "ethical" debate are correct, and it is immoral for a team to debate both sides, then many schools would have to discontinue debate as we practice it today. This is because there seem to be frequent recurrences of the situation where for one reason or another a predominant number of members of a debate squad favor strongly one side of the proposition. This usually results from the wording of the proposition, but, whatever the cause, debate squads are all too often most unevenly divided on their attitude toward a question. For instance, the University of Vermont could not have had a debate team in 1950 when it won the West Point Tournament if the Murphy suggestion of debating only the side believed to be right had been followed. This would have resulted from the fact that at the beginning of the year only one member of a squad of forty-two believed in the nationalization of basic industries, and he changed his mind about halfway through the season.

Likewise, Grinnell College would have been unable to have a team in 1953 because every member of the squad believed that Congress should pass an FEPC law. For that matter, how many debaters this year are really against the principle of direct economic aid to foreign countries?

When the real implication of this contention against debating both sides of a proposition is considered, it becomes evident that this question involves more than some philosophical hairsplitting; it involves the future of intercollegiate debating. For if it is not ethical, then so-called "two-man debating" should be stopped, and when the topic is one such as was used this past year, a great many schools could not debate unless some means could be found so that the few ethical affirmative or negative teams in the country would not be overworked. It seems to me that Murphy never attempts to solve this problem in his article. Rather, he confines himself to supporting the argument that it is not ethical for any debater to speak on the side of the proposition he believes to be the "wrong" side. Nor is any distinction made between school debaters and those in public life.

And that is probably the basic error in the reasoning of those who condemn speaking on both sides in school debate tournaments, that is, their failure to make a distinction between tournament debating and other forms of public argumentative speaking. It is my contention that interscholastic debating is a different form of public speaking from debate that we hear the legislator or the lawyer use. Various authors of textbooks in debate support this contention. For instance, McBurney, O'Neill, and Mills write, "The student should keep in mind the differences between actual life situations, such as legislature, court, or campaign, and the situations in school or contest debates."[6] W. Charles Redding writes in "Presentation of the Debate Speech," "The form of debate may be used for both expository and persuasive speaking." Later in the same essay he writes that in a debate tournament the purpose of the debating would probably be classified as educational, rather than persuasive, and that the ". . . educational type of debate, therefore, can be considered a special case of exposition."[7] Ewbank and Auer seem to be aware of a difference in the forms of debate when they write, "The critics often seem not to understand the purposes and procedures in school debates."[8] If we assume that when a debater at the West Point Tournament stands up to speak he has the same purposes in mind as a speaker in a public meeting or a Senator in the halls of Congress speaking on the same subject, then we would have to agree that the same code of ethics should apply. But the aim is not the same. The public speaker and the Senator want to win converts to their beliefs, probably win such strong belief that their listeners will do something about it. This is not the purpose of our debater at West Point or at any other tournament. He is not trying to convince the judges, or his opponents, or any of the debate "buffs" in his audience that his side of the proposition is the "right" side, or the only side; rather, his purpose is to convince the judges that he and his partner are the better debaters. (This should not be construed to mean that the purpose of any school debate program is only the winning of debates. It is merely that winning debates is just one of the best methods yet devised to get busy students to do the research of material, the analysis, the mastering of the modes of reasoning, and the principles of refutation, the developing of good speaking styles and delivery necessary to make them into effective, intelligent, and responsible debaters.)

However, the fact that interschool debating (and thus debating both sides of a proposition) differs in purpose from other forms of debate does not by itself mean that it is more or less ethical than these other types. To determine that it would seem we must define what "ethical" means. This Professor Murphy does only by implication. His implication is that debating both sides is bad and of doubtful virtue, therefore immoral, not ethical. That such a definition of the non-ethical is correct is pointed out in a college textbook:

> . . . The term "moral" is essentially equivalent to the
> term "ethical." Etymologically, these terms are identi-
> cal, the former being derived from the Latin word
> "mores," the latter from the Greek word "ethos," both
> words referring to customary behavior. . . . Ordinarily,
> the opposite of "moral" is taken to be "immoral," so
> that we mean by a "moral man" one who is good and

does what is right, and by an "immoral man" one who is bad and does what is wrong. . . .[9]

So now we come to the heart of the controversy. Is it "immoral" for a school debater to debate both sides? Richard Murphy, supported by testimony from Theodore Roosevelt, Brooks Quimby, and Albert J. Beveridge, says that it is. On the other hand, men who have been long connected with college debaters and debating say it is not. For instance, O'Neill, Laycock, and Scales, speaking directly to this subject of a student's debating both sides, say ". . . it would not undermine his moral character if he did."[10] Ewbank and Auer write, "Even if debaters are assigned to the side of the question in which they do not believe, it does not necessarily follow that the experience is harmful; . . ."[11] This point of view is also taken by Wayne N. Thompson, a long-time coach of debate, now Director of Forensics at the Chicago Undergraduate Division of the University of Illinois, who writes,

> Debating both sides of a proposition is neither morally wrong nor hypocritical. Some writers have charged that debating both sides results in various evils, such as insincerity, shallowness, and the presentation of arguments known to be poorly founded or fallacious. These malpractices, which also occur among speakers who debate only one side, are the result of other causes--weakness in the character of the offender or a misunderstanding of the proper function of debate.[12]

It would seem for every authority quoted by the opposition, proponents of debating both sides can also quote somebody of equal merit to uphold their contention. This being the case, who is right? There are many who feel that McBurney, O'Neill, and Mills stated clearly the moral responsibility of a debater when they wrote,

> Once a cause has been undertaken, the advocate has a responsibility to present the best possible case for his proposition within the limits of the facts as he knows them or believes them to be. He should not deliberately do less nor does he have any moral right to attempt more. No man has a moral right to lie, cheat, or intentionally distort, much less a responsibility to do so. . . .[13]

Therefore, they believe, if a debater at any tournament presents the arguments he honestly believes to be the best possible arguments that can be presented in behalf of his side of the proposition, it would seem to be ethical debating, and that to condemn him is either to misunderstand or to misconstrue his purpose in speaking. Where only honesty and sincerity are present, where any intent to betray or deceive is absent, it is hard to find reason to condemn such public speaking as unethical.

Upon this argument, then, rests the case for debating both sides of a proposition, that the purpose of the speaker determines the ethics by which he is to be judged, that the school debater cannot correctly be judged unethical by the same rule of thumb that might be used to evaluate the ethics of the pulpit or campaign speaker. The purpose in speaking differs; therefore, what might be "right" for the one may very well be "wrong" for the other, though they both say the same words. It seems impossible to most debate coaches that anyone should condemn as a "public liar" the school debater who presents the best possible case for his proposition within the limits of the facts as he knows or believes them to be. Yet those who condemn college debaters' speaking on both sides of a proposition do just that. They are wrong.

Reprinted from The Speech Teacher, 6:209-212, September, 1957. Nicholas Cripe is Professor of Speech, Butler University.

Notes

1. "The Ethics of Debating Both Sides," VI, pp. 1-9.
2. Ibid., p. 2.
3. Ibid.
4. Ibid., p. 1.
5. Ibid., p. 2.
6. James H. McBurney, James M. O'Neill, and Glen E. Mills, Argumentation and Debate: Techniques of a Free Society. New York: The Macmillan Company, 1951, p. 4.
7. In David Potter (ed.), Argumentation and Debate: Principles and Practices. New York: The Dryden Press, 1951, pp. 220-221.
8. Henry Lee Ewbank and J. Jeffery Auer, Discussion and Debate: Tools of a Democracy 2d ed. New York: Appleton-Century-Crofts, Inc., 1951, p. 388.
9. Ethel M. Albert, Theodore C. Denise, and Sheldon P. Peterfreund, Great Traditions in Ethics: An Introduction. New York: American Book Company, 1953, p. 7, footnote 1.

10. James Milton O'Neill, Craven Laycock, and Robert Leighton
    Scales, Argumentation and Debate. New York: The Mac-
    millan Company, 1917, p. 376.
11. Op. cit., p. 389.
12. "Discussion and Debate: A Re-Examination," The Quarterly
    Journal of Speech, 30:296, October, 1944.
13. Op. cit., p. 9.

Suggestions for Further Reading

Bowra, D. "From Sydney, Australia," ETC, 13:153, Winter, 1955-
    56.
Burns, James M. "Debate over Collegiate Debate," New York
    Times Magazine, December 5, 1954, pp. 12, 30.
Dell, George W. "In Defense of Debating Both Sides," Speech
    Teacher, 7:31-34, January, 1958.
Ehninger, Douglas. "The Debate about Debating," Quarterly Journal
    of Speech, 44:127-136, April, 1958.
Eisenberg, Meyer. "To Debate or Remain Silent," Gavel, 37:38-40,
    January, 1955.
French, Warren G. "On Debates and Debating: Reply to Mr.
    Grant," ETC, 13:148-151, Winter, 1955-56.
Geiger, Don. "The Humanistic Disection of Debate," Speech Teach-
    er, 14:101-106, March, 1965.
Grant, W. B. "Debate on Debates," ETC, 12:238-239, Spring, 1955.
Huber, Walter G. "Should College Students Be Allowed to Debate
    the Question of the Recognition of Red China by the United
    States?" Gavel, 37:28, 30, January, 1955.
Klopf, Donald W., and James C. McCroskey. "Debating Both Sides
    Ethical? Controversy Pau!" Central States Speech Journal,
    15:36-39, February, 1964.
_____. "Ethical Practices in Debate," Journal of the Ameri-
    can Forensic Association, 1:13-16, January, 1964.
Kruger, Arthur N. "Ethics," Section X, A Classified Bibliography
    of Argumentation and Debate. Metuchen, N.J., Scarecrow
    Press, 1964, pp. 162-170.
_____. "Censorship on the Campus," Today's Speech, 3:5-6,
    January, 1955.
_____. "Is It Educational? Yes," Bul. Deb. Assn. Pa. Cols.,
    22:4-9, December, 1956.
Larson, Carl E., and Kim Giffin. "Ethical Considerations in the
    Attitudes and Practices of College Debaters," Journal of the
    American Forensic Association, 1:86-90, September, 1964.
McCroskey, James C. "Still More Debate over Debate," Forensic,
    47:7-9, October, 1962.
Murphy, Richard. "The Ethics of Debating Both Sides, II," Speech
    Teacher, 12:242-247, September, 1963.
_____. "Debating Both Sides," Speech Teacher, 6:255-256,
    September, 1957.
Shepard, David W. "The Debate on Debating: A Rebuttal," ETC,

14:70-72, Autumn, 1956.
Sikkink, Donald. "Evidence on the Both Sides Controversy," Speech
    Teacher, 11:51-54, January, 1962.
Thomas, J.D. "Cor Cordium: More of the Debate over Debate,"
    Forensic, 47:3-5, March, 1962.

VIII.   Contests and Tournaments

Issue N: Should Speech Contests Be Abolished?

On March 22, 1950, the Contest Committee of the North
Central Association of Colleges and Secondary Schools,
the chairman of which was Lowell B. Fisher, submitted
a report to the Commission on Secondary Schools of the
N.C.A. containing "specific recommendations with respect to the various fields commonly involved in contests." The recommendations concerning speech appear
below. Since the Committee had recommended that
speech contests be discontinued, their recommendation
understandably provoked a strong reaction not only from
those engaged in directing forensic programs but also
from the Speech Association of America. Consequently,
the then President of the S.A.A., Horace G. Rahskopf,
appointed a Special Contest Committee, composed of distinguished members of the speech profession, and asked
it to work with the Contest Committee of the N.C.A.
"in an effort to provide a report on speech contests mutually satisfactory to both committees." The resulting
report was eventually voted on and adopted at a meeting
of the Commission on Secondary Schools of the N.C.A.
in Chicago on March 29, 1951. Under the title "A Program of Speech Education; Recommendations of the Contest Committee of the North Central Association with Respect to Speech As Submitted by the Speech Association
of America," it was later published in the Quarterly
Journal of Speech.* Although the worth of speech contests was acknowledged in the new report, some of the
recommendations were still highly critical of the way in
which contests were conducted. The specific recommendations concerning debate also appear below.

The article, "A Look at the Contest Committee's Speech
Recommendations," by William M. Staerkel is directed
at the original report of the N.C.A. Contest Committee.
Deploring the Committee's ignorance of debate, Staerkel
points out that winning, though it may be an immediate
objective of the student, motivates him to acquire "certain skills which constitute the real purpose of debate."

*37:347-358, October, 1951.

27. Excerpts from "Recommendations of the
Contest Committee of the North Central Association"

It is rather commonly felt that the success of our democratic
form of life is dependent to a great extent upon the intelligent study
and exchange of ideas of persons within groups. It is further recognized that the solution of common problems in the democracy is
not best arrived at through dramatic, eloquent, emotional speeches.
On the contrary, deliberations on a highly intellectual plane should
be more prevalent than they are in the solution of community, national and international problems. Very little place in our democratic life is left for the long-overused dramatics and emotions in
speech making. Nor is there much purpose in a democracy for
formalized debates wherein parties resolve to win through eloquent
presentations of a side, with little if any regard to examination of
the facts involved in a problem. The purpose of debate is to win a
point, not necessarily to arrive at a solution to a problem.

The Committee can see very little real good to be derived educationally from speech contests as most of them now are organized
and conducted.

It is recommended, therefore, that the emphasis in secondary
education be placed upon the ability to conduct oneself intelligently
in group discussions. Emphasis should also be placed on teaching
pupils to be able to convey verbally their thoughts in a group or before an audience, but not to win a point or attain an emotionalized
victory. Interscholastic speech contests should be discontinued.

Reprinted from the North Central Association Quarterly, 25:254,
January, 1951.

Excerpts from "A Program of Speech Education"

The teaching of debating should be extended to include in addition to the traditional forms, other procedures, especially those of the legislative type. The moot court, the debaters' assembly, and student congress all provide useful and possibly interesting variants from standard forms, and all seem well designed to meet the essential purpose of scholastic debate, i.e., the teaching of advocacy. In all school debates greater emphasis should be placed on the speakers' talking to an audience. Possibly desirable or necessary as an exercise or as a rehearsal, tournament debating in an empty room can not be justified as an end in itself. Does not every student of debating have the right to speak before a genuine audience at least as often as he speaks in a tournament rehearsal?

The types of awards, the method of awarding them, and the manner of presenting them should be carefully examined with a view to their educational and psychological implications. To encourage the proper response, interscholastic meetings might well be called festivals or conferences rather than contests. The student's work may well be evaluated by the use of general categories such as superior, good, average. Contestants should have the opportunity to learn the bases of the judge's or critic's evaluation of their work. Interscholastic meetings will attain their greatest value when participants and teachers ask first, "How can we improve?" not "Who won?"

Extra-class occasions for speaking should be as real and as meaningful as possible. In speaking, discussion, and debate, subjects and problems can often be appropriate to the interests of the school and the community. Opportunities are afforded by the school assembly, clubs, the school council, class meetings, and the like; civic groups often welcome students who are prepared to offer them something of interest. Plays, and scenes from plays, can be chosen not only for their entertainment values but for their insight into basic human problems, character, and behavior.

Reprinted from the Quarterly Journal of Speech, V. 37, October, 1951.

28. A Look at the Contest Committee's Speech Recommendations
William M. Staerkel

Most administrators are probably familiar with the recommen-
cations of the Contest Committee of the North Central Association
as completed in March, 1950.   Among other things the recommendations covered such school activities as music, art, speech, and
athletic contests.   While much can be said in favor of many of the
suggestions advanced by the Committee, the report also reveals a
distinct lack of understanding as to the characteristics and value of
some of the activities covered.   This is especially apparent in the
recommendations regarding interscholastic speech contests.   The
specific suggestions regarding speech are as follows:

> It is rather commonly felt that the success of our demo-
> cratic form of life is dependent to a great extent upon
> the intelligent study and exchange of ideas of persons
> within groups.   It is further recognized that the solution
> of common problems in the democracy is not best ar-
> rived at through dramatic, eloquent, emotional speeches.
> On the contrary, deliberations on a highly intellectual
> plane should be more prevalent than they are in the solu-
> tion of community, national and international problems.
> Very little place in our democratic life is left for the
> long-overused dramatics and emotions in speech making.
> Nor is there much purpose in a democracy for formal-
> ized debates wherein parties resolve to win through elo-
> quent presentations of a side with little if any regard to
> examination of the facts involved in a problem.   The
> purpose of debate is to win a point, not necessarily to
> arrive at a solution to a problem.
>
> The Committee can see very little real good to be de-
> rived educationally from speech contests as most of them
> now are organized and conducted.
>
> It is recommended, therefore, that the emphasis in sec-
> ondary education be placed upon the ability to conduct
> oneself intelligently in group discussions.   Emphasis
> should also be placed on teaching pupils to be able to
> convey verbally their thoughts in a group or before an
> audience, but not to win a point or attain an emotional-
> ized victory.   Interscholastic speech contests should be
> discontinued.

The above paragraphs point to a clear misconception of modern
debating; a tendency to overlook the motivation of competition as a
learning device; an unrealistic attitude toward the role of emotions

in ideational activity, and finally to a disregard of the psychological fact that a knowledge of results is important to effective learning. It is apparent from the outset that the Committee is not familiar with present-day interscholastic debate. It would seem that the Committee's version of a debate is nothing more than a series of speeches wherein the participants shout, plead, cry, and do everything but consider the facts. Nothing could be further from the truth. Like all other educational activities debate has evolved into something far different from what it was in its infancy. As it exists today it is a critical analysis of facts followed by a scholarly presentation of those facts. It is certainly not the emotional outburst that the Committee pictures. Of course there is some emotion in debating--just as there is in all human activity. Debating, rather than utilizing emotional outbursts, teaches the student self-discipline in controlling his emotions.

The educational ideal might be an intellectual discussion of facts without any involvement of human emotions, but it is apparent that this ideal will never be reached. As long as human beings discuss controversial issues they will do so with emotion. Since this is so it becomes the duty of the school to teach the self-discipline so necessary in democratic citizens. Debate is an educational activity peculiarly suited to attain this objective.

The Committee's deplorable ignorance of debate is most clearly seen in the statement, "Nor is there much purpose in a democracy for formalized debates wherein parties resolve to win through eloquent presentations of a side with little if any regard to examination of the facts involved in a problem. " This statement is certainly true, but the inference that it is descriptive of modern interscholastic debating is an injustice to both the students and their coaches. Indeed debating itself comes only after a careful examination of the facts involved in a problem. Competitive debate discourages makeshift and inadequate preparation because the outcome of such activity is inevitably defeat.

Inasmuch as eloquence is concerned it is rather surprising that the Committee seems to deplore the cultivation of such a quality in our youth. Eloquence in itself is not an evil thing, and when

it follows critical thinking and rests upon democratic ideals it becomes something extremely desirable in national and international
statesmanship.

The Committee's superficial acquaintance with the objectives
of contest debating is revealed again when it claims, "The purpose
of debate is to win a point, not necessarily to arrive at a solution
to a problem."

Winning a point is only the immediate objective of the student,
not of debate, and a very excellent motivating device it is. In contest debating the student is given an immediate knowledge of results,
which stimulates him whether he has succeeded or failed. Psychological studies have shown that the superior student is motivated
quite as strongly by failure (and often more so) as by success experiences. And so the immediate objective of winning the debate
gives the student a goal to strive toward, which assures the acquisi-
tion of certain skills which constitute the real purpose of debate.

The primary purpose of debate then, is not to win a point,
but to give a few highly selected pupils thorough training in the qualities which are necessary and desirable to democratic leadership.
These skills include ability to do research, to collect and organize
data, to critically weigh and evaluate facts, to think critically, to
express oneself clearly and forcefully, to acquire poise and a broad
understanding of social truths and issues. Contest debating is an
activity designed to accomplish the above by utilizing the love of
youth for competitive activity.

The real purpose of high school football is not to win games,
but to use this immediate motivating device as a means of building
strong bodies, teaching sportsmanship and fair play, and building
good morale within the school. In this respect debate is similar to
football.

Above all the Committee should not underestimate the debater's
intelligence. He debates both sides of a question and his thinking is
not of the black and white variety. Indeed, a debater, to be successful, must carefully examine the various shades of gray involved in
an issue. It might surprise the Committee to know that many affirmative teams propose solutions to problems which differ only

slightly from the negative stand, and many negative teams accept sound affirmative arguments in shaping their case.

As a result of debating both sides of the question the pupil is well aware that high school debate is a sport, and that the prize of winning the decision is a tribute to hard work and superior skill. It demands searching self-analysis and an evaluation of human nature that no other subject in the curriculum offers. The writer has many times listened to high school debaters review a debate in which they have just participated and admit that they were defeated by superior reasoning and more logical presentation. The writer has likewise watched high school students eagerly pack the room for a championship debate and spend hours afterward critically analyzing everything that was said. These students, of course, were debaters, and they were acquiring skills and habits of interest which would some day give this country intelligent leaders in community forums and group discussions.

Invariably, when school forums and group discussions are held, debaters will assume leadership. Time and time again the writer has witnessed a group discussion wherein one or two debaters cooperated with eight or ten other outstanding students in reaching a solution concerning a school problem. Almost always the debaters assumed leadership and were instrumental in guiding the discussion to a successful and productive conclusion.

The intelligent application of competition through contest debating furnishes a means whereby superior students develop their talents to an infinitely greater degree than they otherwise would. To take the competition out of speech work would be equivalent to playing football without goal lines, or to conducting political campaigns without elections.

It is this writer's opinion that no high school should be without debate as an offering in the curriculum. It is a subject designed to intensively train a select few in the qualities of democratic leadership. It begins with the collection of all available data pertaining to the subject, and this results in the development of research techniques on the part of the student to an extent not realized in other subjects. This data is then sifted and evaluated, much of it being

236 Counterpoint: Debates about Debate

discarded, much of it retained. The soundest solution to the problem nearest the affirmative is then selected and the case is outlined and organized. At this point it is critically reevaluated and needed changes are made. After this is done on one side of the question it is repeated for the opposing side. There is continuous cooperation among the students in the exchange of information and ideas. The cases that are carried into the first tournament are not the ones that will be carried into the second, for contest debating is a dynamic procedure that draws from many sources in formulating solutions to problems.

All the while the above is taking place, the students are learning to speak before audiences with a proficiency that never ceases to amaze the citizens of the community. Not only this, but they are learning self-discipline, poise, and an ability to think on their feet that many a businessman would give a year's salary to possess.

The Contest Committee in its recommendations appears to be more of an anti-contest committee than one which seeks to formulate intelligent policies for the control of contests. The Committee can be a powerful force for good, but it can also be a force in the opposite direction. It is to be hoped that the future work of the Committee will rest more upon empirical evidence and less upon educational theorizing.

Reprinted from <u>The North Central Association Quarterly</u>, 25:254-257, January, 1951. At the time of writing this article, which reflected his personal views and not those of the Association, William Staerkel was Principal of El Dorado High School, El Dorado, Kansas.

Issue O: Should Competitive Debating Be De-Emphasized?

The following debate between N. Edd Miller and Leonard
Sommer was actually a public debate, sponsored by the
American Forensic Association and presented as part of
the program "Problems in Debate" at the 1952 Convention of the Speech Association of America, held in Cincinnati. In upholding the affirmative, Miller indicts the
status quo on several counts: restriction of activities to
tournaments, the number of students used, the number
of topics chosen, and the types of debate. It also, he
says, fosters poor public speaking, ignores the community, and stresses the wrong goals. His specific recommendations are designed to eliminate such shortcomings.
Sommer, in upholding the negative, counters that highly
competitive debate programs need not be restrictive and
that in recent years many have broadened their activities. He concludes by pointing up the advantages of debate and of competition.

29. Competitive Debating Should Be De-Emphasized
N. Edd Miller

Let us begin by defining the terms of the proposition: "Resolved: That Competitive Debating Should Be De-Emphasized. "
"Competitive debating" means those inter-school contests where a decision is a part of the debate. This would include debating in tournaments and would include also debates with awards and trophies as
the end product. "De-emphasize, " the second key word in the proposition, is a somewhat ambiguous word. It could mean only a slight
modification in current competitive debating practices, or it could
mean a major change in present practices. Let us assume here
"de-emphasize" to mean a major change in competitive debating as
it is now conducted.

Before we can talk intelligently about the nature of a forensic
program, we need to set up some objectives or goals for the pro-
gram--we need to know where we are going, what we are trying to

do. Let us, then, consider a set of criteria for a debate program.
We can then evaluate the nature of a debate program in terms of
these criteria.

First, a debate program should be broad. It should include
many types of activities and it should include many students. The
debate program of thirty years ago, where a college took part in,
at most, four or five debates a year, using, at most, eight or ten
debaters, is outmoded.

Second, a debate program should be profitable and educative
to the participant in the program. We are, after all, dealing with
a type of activity that is supposed to train and educate students.
We conduct our work in connection with other scholastic activities.

Third, a debate program should have values to the public--to
the community and to the school itself.

Now, in light of these three criteria, let us examine competitive debating--debate programs where the emphasis is placed on
winning debates. Let's ask the question, "What's wrong with competitive debating?" Several indictments might be raised.

1. Competitive debate quite often is not broad in scope. It is
not unusual to find schools with a strong competitive debate program
restricting most of their activities to debate tournaments. A diet of
half a dozen or so debate tournaments a year often constitutes the
bulk of the debate program. Necessarily, this tournament debating
restricts other aspects of the program. Few students are used,
since the better debaters are sent out to win the tournaments, and
there is little or no variety in types of debating, topics for debate,
or in audiences for debates.

2. We can indict competitive debating also for restricting itself to one or two debate topics. While the selection of a "national"
topic has some limited utility, it becomes a weak part of the national debate scene when teams debate nothing but the national topic.
Opportunities for really educating debaters on a variety of topics are
neglected, and audiences are driven away by the repeated use of a
single debate proposition.

3. There is no variety in types of debate. Debaters become
masters of the technique of formal, orthodox debating. But how

much good will this mastery of this narrow skill do them in other public speaking situations? How often, after school, will they be called on for participation in an orthodox debate, with ten-minute constructive speeches and five-minute rebuttals?

4. Too few students are used in competitive debating programs. It is natural to want to win as many debates as possible, when winning has been set as a major goal. This goal normally means that a "star" system develops, and those who can win debates take part in the debates. Others must be content to learn the intricacies of a stop watch and the delicacies of chairing and keeping time for a debate.

5. Competitive debating fosters poor public speaking training. Tournaments and most judged debates are unreal speaking situations. Usually, audiences are not present, and even when they are, the debaters aim their speeches at the judges and concentrate on the strategy and technique of the debate form, rather than on communicating with and persuading an audience.

6. Motivation in competitive debating is unreal. The wrong goals are stressed. Winning the debate becomes the only important consideration. Influencing an audience, and presenting information to an audience are, by and large, ignored. The winning of a trophy may be motivation, but it is a temporary sort of motivation and unreal in that most public speaking outside of contest activities has no such awards to offer people. Outside school, our motivation lies in the reactions we can get to our speaking. Why not train for that and use that motivation in school?

7. Competitive debating ignores the community. About the only value to the school or community in competitive debating is in recording with pride the number of wins of the debate team and rationalizing with dread the losses of the team. There is very little community contact and very little real service to the community.

The literature on debating is full of many complaints against contest and competitive debating. We are all familiar with the chronic criticism against our style of debating by visiting British debaters. Most of the "evils" they find in our system are due in large measure to competitive emphasis on debating in our forensic programs.

The following proposals are offered as a way of sensibly de-
emphasizing competitive debating.

To begin with, we need to set up new goals for our debate
programs. Our objectives, listed in the order of their importance,
can serve as goals for the de-emphasized competitive debating program:

1. Good public speaking training, in real public speaking situations.
2. Real public service to the school.
3. Real public service to the community.
4. Honor and glory to the school and the debaters and the
   coach.

The following specific measures should achieve these goals:

1. Let's have more school debates before school audiences.
Assemblies and school gatherings of different kinds should be used
as the occasions for more debates. And, most important, these
debates should be on school topics--topics in which the school audience will be interested.

2. Let's have more community appearances. Service clubs
in your city and in nearby cities are nearly always eager to have
debaters appear as a program. Here again, though, it is important
to find subjects which will be of interest to the audiences your debaters will talk to. Greater use of radio and television as outlets
for community service programs should be made.

3. It has already been implied in the first two suggestions that
there should be a greater variety of debate topics. This suggestion
can stand re-emphasis, however. A good debate program does not
restrict itself to a single topic or even two or three topics, but
uses as many as twenty or thirty topics.

4. A good debate program should provide a variety of forensic
experiences. Instead of training always for the contest debate, experiment with the use of discussion types, cross-question debates,
student congresses, and other types of speaking.

5. A good debate program should use many different speakers.
Everyone who wants to take part in the forensic program should be

allowed to. If coaches were to spend as much time on coaching the whole squad--distribute their energy a little--as they do on coaching the "stars" of the squad, three or four times the number of people currently participating could take part in a forensic program.

6. Adopt the rule: "No debate without an audience." Even where decisions are a must, always have an audience present, and give the debate to the audience first, to the judge or judges secondarily.

7. Use audience decisions instead of critic decisions. Shift-of-opinion ballots and other ways of measuring an audience reaction are legitimate ways of evaluating a debate.

8. Finally, go ahead with a competitive debate program and participation in tournaments, but do so only as long as you can remain consistent with the above seven suggestions.

The end result of such a change in the debate program will be much superior to a program centered around decisions and tournaments. The three criteria mentioned at the beginning will all be satisfied: the program will be broad; it will be profitable and educative to the participant; and it will be of community and school service. You will enjoy this program more; your community will support it more fully; and your debaters will be happier with it. Motivation, you will find, is as strong to do a good job under these conditions as under conditions where the end-result is a compilation of wins and losses. Elizabeth Rowe makes this point well when she says:

> Of course, it is fun to bring home trophies for the shelves, but is this really important? In thirty years which will be of more use to the community, state, nation, and world, those cups (tarnished by then, no doubt) or a group of citizens who can adequately express their carefully thought-out opinions?[1]

Reprinted from The Gavel, 36:95-97, May, 1954. N. Edd Miller is Professor of Speech at the University of Michigan.

Notes

1. Elizabeth W. Rowe, "Citizens or Trophies?" Speech Activities,
   5:126, Autumn, 1949.

30. Competitive Debating Should Not Be De-Emphasized
Leonard Sommer

As I pause for a few moments and introspect a bit on this
situation I find that there is a certain ironical value to it.   Not too
many years ago I was introduced to the field of debate, particularly
competitive debate, by necessity.   My teaching position called for
my stepping into this field.   And it was an almost entirely new endeavor.   In college I did my undergraduate and graduate work in
the field of dramatics; however, for the past fourteen years I have
coached and "plugged" for debate.   First I convinced myself, and
since that time I have been constantly expending energy to convince
my colleagues, students, and superiors of the value of competitive
debate.

Now I find myself in a public debate.   I am here defending
competitive debate against the onslaughts of my good friend Edd
Miller.   Of course we both agree that there are contained within
the essence of debate, as an activity, many values unsurpassed by
any other activity.   It is the problem of competition that we are
interested in today.   And before entering too deeply into the consideration I should like to pause long enough to proffer my thanks
to the following, who have, through articles I shall quote, helped
me formulate my presentation: Austin J. Freeley, Director of Debate at Boston University; Professor E. C. Buehler, Director of
Forensics at Kansas University; Lionel Crocker, Head of Denison's
Department of Speech; James N. Holm, Kent State's Director of Debate; G. E. Mills, Northwestern University, Director of Debate;
L. D. Hanks, Department of Speech, John Marshall High School in
Los Angeles; President W. H. Cawley of Hamilton; P. E. Lull, Purdue's Director of Forensics; and of course the University of Michigan's own Edd Miller for those two well-drawn articles, "The De-

bater and His Audience" and "Speech Activities at the University of Michigan. "

I should like to place the overall consideration of this topic in the words of my very good friend Austin J. Freeley: "Let us bear in mind these fundamental facts: If the public wants and demands competitive speech contests, there is no power that can stop them. We know competitive speech contests, and in fact the whole field of forensics, to be one of the most important and worthwhile phases of the entire educational program. Our task is simply to communicate this knowledge to the public. "

To this I would like to add my own rarefication: I believe that the successful team is one that can persuade people, by the strength of its convictions and the skill of its arguments, to vote for its side of the issue. Students should not be encouraged to argue for causes in which they do not believe for the sake of winning points, either for themselves or the institutions they represent; and audiences should not be told to regard the speakers' efforts as mere exercises in public delivery.

But what are the specific arguments which face us today? Simply these: competitive debate is too narrow; it utilizes too few students; it develops poor speech habits; it tends to ignore the community; it makes the winning of trophies the only end; and it tends to stereotype all speakers who participate. Now let us consider these points!

There has developed in debate over the past few years the surging tendency towards emphasizing training in the conversion of opinion, and in direct persuasion of audiences. A mode increasingly employed is that in which the audience indicates its position on the question both before and after the debate. Another tendency, now well developed, is that of holding debates off the campus; before clubs, labor locals, lodges, and the like. And in such situations open forum discussion is always a feature. Also, radio debates are gaining in popularity.

I know that we are at the present time carrying on a thirty-six week radio forensic program over three stations in the Michiana region. Also I know from experience that such schools as Alabama,

Case, Boston, Vermont, Maine, Florida, Georgetown, Purdue, and many, many others are developing a large majority of the activity I have just mentioned. It seems quite evident to me that if there is a failing to engage in such activity, one can hardly place the blame on the mantle of competitive debate, but would be far more justified in pointing to an inactive or disinterested moderator.

Lionel Crocker has this to say on competitive debate:

> Some say that debate should be shelved because it is too competitive. They say that students argue for the sake of winning an argument rather than finding the truth. They say that discussion should be substituted for debate. If debate has any faults they should be corrected. No one has any objection to discussion, but discussion precedes debate, it is no substitute for it.

What would become of our system of government which is based on debate? Where would we train the future leaders for that system? And where do we learn to defend an argument? Inter-school debate is as necessary as inter-school athletics--for the sake of competition. In any one institution there cannot be intramural competition among the most highly skilled, because there are not enough highly skilled to provide this clash.

No one condones the abuses of debate. But the abuses can be corrected without destroying the subject itself. No one condones the weaknesses of democracy because they realize that these can be corrected without destroying the system. The tools of democracy--discussion and debate--must not be obliterated simply because some occasional malpractice shows the need for a little policing.

President W.H. Cawley of Hamilton College and James Holm have both pointed out that we are in an era which likes to slip toward intellectualism--that system which believes that the mind of the student is the only concern of the educational institution. The fallacy of such a consideration is glaring. The necessity for four-square development--intellectual, moral, social, and physical--is nowhere better satisfied than in what is commonly referred to as the tournament circuit in competitive debate.

Everyone must realize that opinion dissent over the yes and no outcome of some proposal for group action is an essential concept in a free society, and that training in such concepts is an indispensable item in any system of general education.

The foregoing might be analyzed in three major divisions. (1) Debate, which is the technique of speaking to persuade in the presence of opposition which will reply, is thus inherent in all parliamentary practice, which is in turn the cornerstone upon which rests our entire democratic structure. (2) Ultimately we are always confronted as a group with the necessity of a yes or no decision. This is the essence of debating. This is given a more broad coverage by competitive debate, which enables groups more heterogeneous in nature to meet on the same issue. (3) Competition is contributive to the effective personality. To struggle, to succeed to be able to do well are experiences which build self-confidence, which in turn begets a positive approach to life.

Mr. Miller has pointed out in a number of articles that have enjoyed national circulation that he decries the emphasis on winning, the use of the same top men, and the lack of audiences as the main points which he finds inherently wrong in competitive debate. Again I maintain that all these weaknesses are not the fault of a system, but are indeed a reflection on a coach or moderator who first of all instills in his team the wrong ideals, who has a wrong concept of competition, and who does a poor job of public relations. Points which are inherent in competitive debate that are not considered by Mr. Miller, but are the very reasons I defend it, must now be brought forward.

And in the presentation of these issues I am grateful to Mr. L. D. Hanks, who so graphically delineated them in an article in "The Debaters Magazine."

These points are: (1) Competitive debate develops the student's experiences in speaking in other than classroom groups. (2) It gives the students experience in a wide variety of speaking situations, before dozens of different audiences, in company with and listening to a great many fellow speakers, in a great many different communities and buildings. (3) It develops tolerance and understanding of his fellow men in the student because he meets on a social and professional basis people from a wide variety of geographical locations and a wide differentiation of social and economic levels.

246 Counterpoint: Debates about Debate

(4) It helps to overcome provincial habits of speech and presentation, which inevitably develop unless there is contact with speakers from other schools trained by other teachers. It is for these reasons that I claim there must be more emphasis on competitive debate.

However, this emphasis must be on the right points. If there are weaknesses it is much more timely to call for a re-examination and an introspection on the part of those of us who lead students into the field of competitive debate, and it is not the time for the abolition of an entire system simply because some of us have taken a myopic view in the past. Let us then analyze ourselves, and then lead more students into this invaluable activity. Let us not in any manner consider the disintegration of one of education's greatest assets.

Reprinted from The Gavel, 37:36-37, 43; January, 1955. Leonard Sommer is Assistant Professor of Speech, University of Notre Dame.

Issue P: Should Tournament Debating Be Abolished?

During the past twenty-five years tournament debating
has grown phenomenally.   Today almost every college
with a debate program sponsors some kind of a tourna-
ment--four-man, two-man switch sides, even one-man;
varsity, novice, practice; orthodox-style, cross-examination, sweepstakes, etc.   Even among high schools, with
their comparatively limited travel budgets, the number
of tournaments has increased ten-fold.   Most directors
of debate explain this phenomenon by pointing out that
the tournament provides the greatest amount of experience at the lowest cost and that students are attracted
by the competition and the chance to win trophies.   The
advocates of tournament debating point out that as a result of tournaments more students are now debating than
ever before and that this interest in debate has in turn
encouraged the publication of textbooks, handbooks, and
articles on debate, as well as the establishment of many
summer debate institutes.   The critics of tournament debating, on the other hand, point out that it has led to
undesirable excesses, such as too much emphasis on
winning and rapid-fire delivery.   Thus, debates on this
issue usually resolve themselves to whether the disadvantages outweigh the advantages.   On the affirmative
side in the debate which follows, Lester L. McCrery's
basic contention is, "Tournament debating, as now conducted, has failed and will continue to fail to meet defensible educational objectives."   His three sub-contentions are (1) "Tournament debating fails to provide
speakers with audiences...."; (2) "Tournament debating
results in the concentration of too much dubious attention on too few students"; and (3) "Tournament debating
enhances the evils of competitive debating."

In upholding the negative position, Robert P. Newman
concedes that tournament debating is not perfect but argues that only one of McCrery's objections--the absence
of audiences--is inherent in the tournament system and
that this is insignificant.   The remaining objections, he
contends, can be countered by means other than eliminating tournaments.   If the coaches and debaters are culp-
able, there is no need to eliminate the system; improve
the educational process instead.   Newman concludes by
pointing out the values of tournament debating that would
be lost if it were abolished.

247

31. Tournament Debating Should Be Abolished
Lester L. McCrery

If a decision were being awarded in this debate today, I could not accept it for two reasons. First, it is a debate against debate, in a sense, and a victory would contradict the proposition. Second, it is not my fixed purpose to abolish debate tournaments but rather to submit to you some of the indictments against the activity in order that correction may be applied where needed.

Reaction against tournament debating has been developing over a considerable period of time. At the 1940 convention of the Speech Association of America, at a special meeting of high school and college debate directors, a resolution condemning further extension of tournaments just failed of passage.[1] In January, 1941, Professor Charles Templer authored an article in _Forensic_, the Pi Kappa Delta speech journal, highly critical of the tournament system and concluding that some sweeping changes were necessary if the activity were to be justified educationally and if it were to be a credit to the speech teaching profession.[2] In March 1941, the North Central Association of Colleges and Secondary Schools adopted a resolution critical of tournaments and recommended drastic curtailment of the activity. In March 1942, a special committee of this same organization recommended a discontinuance of interstate tournaments with but a few exceptions.[3] In March 1950, this North Central Association recommended in its quarterly journal that interscholastic speech tournaments should be discontinued because of their lack of achievement of sound educational objectives.[4] Following this, the Speech Association of America set up a committee to make a study of speech tournaments. A member of this committee was the chairman of the North Central Association which had recommended the discontinuance of tournaments. This committee came out with a report modifying the view that tournaments should be discontinued, but making this significant recommendation:

> In all school debates, greater emphasis should be placed on the speakers talking to an audience. While it is possibly desirable or necessary as an exercise or as a rehearsal, debating in an empty room cannot be justified

as an end in itself.[5]

Now, ladies and gentlemen, while this introduction doesn't cover all the objections which have been raised against tournament debating, it at least gives us enough background to seriously consider the proposition, "Resolved, That Tournament Debating Should Be Abolished." In support of this resolution, I propose as my basic contention the following: Tournament debating, as now conducted, has failed and will continue to fail to meet defensible educational objectives.

This basic contention will be developed by the three following sub-contentions:

First, tournament debating fails to provide speakers with audiences as recommended by the SAA-North Central Committee.

Second, tournament debating results in the concentration of too much dubious attention on too few students.

Third, tournament debating enhances the evils of competitive debating.

In support of the first sub-contention, that audiences are not provided, I feel that we must agree that this requirement has not been met, and very likely can not. We, of course, have come to take this as a matter of fact. As Professor Templer says, "There is no worry about audiences. (You don't have any and you don't expect any.)"[6] However, we must face up to the fact that the majority of those in the teaching profession haven't adopted this expedient complacency. Recently I asked our Humanities Department chairman, a newcomer to our school and unfamiliar with debate tournaments, to help me secure some additional room space for our annual tournament. When I told Dr. Smith we would need at least 50 rooms so there could be that many debates going on simultaneously, he exclaimed, "Dear God! Who listens?" Recalling evidences of increasing lassitude of judges as tournaments progressed, the behavior and responses of opposition debaters, and the otherwise empty rooms, I was forced to confess privately that a communications expert might justifiably conclude that nobody listened.

Before passing to the next contention, let us note a couple of attempts which have been made to answer the audience problem.

In their text, <u>Modern Debating</u>[7] Nichols and Baccus declare that,
after eliminations, the finalists actually have the best audience in
the world, i.e., the other debaters and coaches who aren't represented in the finals and who pack the galleries to hear the winners.
A number of pertinent observations would be appropriate here, but
for lack of time let me point out merely that the requirements of
audiences for debaters can hardly be regarded as met when only
the few finalists out of 50 or more teams are provided with audiences only for their final debates.   An even less satisfactory solution, it seems to me, is submitted by Professor J.N. Holm, who
declares the judge's purpose is to determine which team is more
effective in "swaying the audience" by "noting the outward reactions
manifest by those about him, and by analyzing his own reactions as
a typical member of the audience."[8]   This statement implies that the
judge is to allow himself to be swayed by the techniques of the debaters, just as a group might be.   At the same time the judge is
saddled with the schizoid responsibility of applying critical analysis
to himself.   How he can do this is not made clear.   However, I
feel that most of us will agree that such a procedure would not only do violence to psychology but also contradict our traditional view
of judge objectivity.

        If we are not able to find more conclusive evidence that audi-
ences are being provided for our debate tournaments, as recommended by the SAA-North Central committee, it seems to me that
on this count our activity fails and will continue to fail to meet defensible educational objectives.

        In support of the sub-contention that tournament debating re-
sults in the concentration of too much dubious attention on too few
students, we might note parenthetically that if the attention is dubious, the fewer students affected the better.   But it is too much
to expect that the proponents of tournament debating will make any
such concessions.   They may perhaps admit that a small percentage
of the student body takes part in tournaments, but they will usually
talk in terms of the size of their squad and in terms of the educational values of the program to the interested individuals.   The only
place I have found this issue faced squarely is in a statement by

Professor Karl Robinson, who says,

> Sound educational philosophy does not indicate the expansion of contest programs merely to give more training to more students. The logical solution for that point is to provide adequate classroom and course work for the great majority of "normal" students in speech who will need increased proficiency, and to allow those in special interest and ability groups to be the principal recipients of further instruction via contest programs. [9]

With the emphasis on winning so prominent at tournaments, the logical conclusion derived from Professor Robinson's forthright facing of facts might well be the concentration by each school on a few topflight debaters while the rest of the students, those "normal" souls, are excluded from this esoteric activity, which is supported by student body funds or other appropriations which are presumably available to all interested. It seems proper at this time to quote the following statement from Nichols and Baccus:

> The debate tournament is similar to a basketball tournament; in fact, was identical in plan at the beginning; but has since been modified as experience has dictated. [10]

The parallel grows more painfully obvious as we think it over. A little investigation discloses that there is an amazing amount of proselytizing going on among "outstanding" debate tournament winner schools who find ways and means of attracting star high school debaters to carry on in the halls of higher learning. Let me quote to you from a letter that recently fell into my hands:

May 3, 1951

Dear Mr. _____

We appreciate your interest in the college. You have asked for additional information about our Special Achievement Awards in Speech. Enclosed are the necessary forms for applying officially for such an award. I have taken the liberty of making a preliminary appraisal of your forensics record. On that basis, I think you could receive an award in speech. This is only tentative. If your official application supports my appraisal, I would be glad to see that you receive this award, and if your application reveals you are a more outstanding speaker than I have discovered, of course you would receive a higher award.

Signed_____

Debate coach,_____College

Lest it be assumed that this kind of activity goes on only in a limited section of the country, may I report that this letter was writ-

ten by a debate coach of a large college on the west coast, a college noted for its forensics tournament records, and that last night
I was informed by a coach of a much larger and more forensically
prominent college in New York that debate scholarships were an essential part of his school's tournament success.   What we have
here, in essence, is the sale of services to the highest bidder.
This smacks of professionalism, with such connotations as make
the analogy of Nichols and Baccus disturbing indeed to those who
seek to justify debate tournaments on educational grounds.   If we
accept Professor Robinson's thesis--and how can we deny it?--that
the forensic program is set up for the few, what are the results to
the individuals who are thus singled out?   Does the attention have
dubious value, as our contention holds?

It has been pointed out that some colleges attend, and even
sometimes sponsor, high school debate tournaments with the purpose of "buying up," through scholarships and other inducements,
star high school performers.   This tends to inflate the ego of high
school graduates unless they are extraordinarily unusual.   Their
opinions of themselves are further inflated when they go from tournament to tournament, successfully vanquishing less skilled debaters
from schools who are not able to afford speech scholarships, or at
least, cannot compete in the high school market for the best talent.

Result?   An inflated and faulty opinion of themselves; the development of a kind of superiority complex which doesn't know how
to deal with real adversity.   I'm sure we have all seen these spoil-
ed darlings of the tournaments, condescending to fraternize with
lesser lights occasionally, secure in the conviction that they of the
royalty will not be dethroned unless some judge makes an error.
I recall one of these scholarship boys, who had come up as a star
from the high school lists and who had already won more than his
share of college tournaments, going forward to get his customary
first-place cup at a particular tournament while another contestant
muttered to a companion, "Naturally, you expect God to take first
place."   And I remember this same boy with the dangerously inflated ego refusing in a later tournament to debate off second place
with another team because, he said, "If I can't have first, I don't

want anything. "

It is sometimes argued that the individual is benefited by being obliged to do exhaustive research on problems of current importance.   Were it not for the emphasis on winning tournaments,
this argument might hold some substance.   However, with things
as they are, the debater seeks not truth but techniques by which he
can alternately win the affirmative and negative "sides" of the question.   While Professor Craig Baird recommends having two teams
which present opposite sides of a given question, he retreats equiv-
ocally from this position when he says,

> Then, too, in regard to many issues, undergraduate
> opinion is so little developed that the question of well-
> grounded conviction is absent.   Concerning many social,
> political and economic questions, students, like many
> other human beings, have comparatively little knowledge
> and are ready to discuss either side. [11]

The prevalence of ready-made material supplied by the debate
handbook companies, the so-called "we-prove-anything" boys, hardly constitutes evidence that educational development is taking place
among debaters.   Even if coaches profess to shun these materials,
they cannot ignore them for fear of losing to unfamiliar arguments.

The educational value of having a team debate the same question dozens of times at a dozen tournaments during a given season
has been challenged.   Professor Templer says, "On what grounds
can we justify taking the same debaters into as many as five or six
tournaments in a single season?   I heard one team boasting of having debated the national question ninety times during the current
season. "[12]

I feel we can summarize the second contention support by
stating that tournament debating is detrimental educationally to a
small, select group of students, some of whom are subsidized after
the manner of athletes, by developing many of them into individuals
with false evaluations of themselves and by teaching them techniques
of contentiousness rather than democratic processes of truth-seeking
and thoughtful analysis.   This conclusion seems well summed up by
Abernathy as follows: "The debater is changed from a sincere student of speech into a 'debate bum' trained in tricks, fair or unfair,

of winning, rather than in the honest techniques of persuasive public speaking. "[13]

In support of our foregoing second contention, it was several times pointed out that the pressure to win tournaments was a significant causal factor in promoting undesirable results. This leads to consideration of our third contention, namely, that tournament debating enhances the evils of competitive debating. Nichols and Baccus declare that critics of tournaments must be prepared to admit the values of contest debating,[14] but I decline to be thus arbitrarily assigned to a position of defense. It is herewith submitted that the alleged values of contest, or competitive, debate are irrelevant to the present argument which is that the evils of competitive debate are expanded via the existing tournament system. Since certain evils of competitive debate have already been dealt with in relation to tournaments, I will confine the substance of the present argument to what may be termed the basic philosophy of competitive effort. I propose to show that this competitive philosophy, endorsed by the advocates of contest debate, can no longer be justified in such a complex and highly interdependent society as we have today, that this represents an evil which is enhanced by the tournament.

Although Nichols and Baccus declare that the tournament "maintains contest debating without overemphasizing the decision because there can be but one winner and one runner-up, and but four teams in the semi-finals--the rest are eliminated,"[15] the conclusion is, to say the least, a tenuous one. The mere fact that the final decisions and trophies go to but one or two teams can hardly be stretched to mean that these things don't matter to the hundred or more other persons who have been competing vigorously and prayerfully for them. Observation and experience require us to admit that the nature and structure of tournaments exaggerate the importance of the decision, the goal of competitive effort. There is so much more at stake. As Professor Templer says:

> First, there is the tendency to place more and more
> emphasis on victory. When you attend a tournament
> about the first thing you see in the headquarters hotel
> is the trophies. They are symbols of success. If you

take one of them home, you are a big shot. Your
school gets much more favorable publicity. The president smiles on you and you have your picture in the
paper as the "coach of champions. " Everything is a
lot pleasanter, if you come home with the hardware.
The paper publishes little if your contestants take a
beating and it is not as easy to make the school officials smile if all you have to show for your trip is an
expense account. It is true that your debaters have had
valuable experience, but you can't put experience in a
trophy case. Winning a trophy is the big thing at a
tournament, and next in importance is winning as many
contests as possible.[16]

Now, if the argument of Nichols and Baccus stands refuted--
and I think we must agree that it does--the next question we must
determine is whether or not the basic philosophy of competition is
evil, as I have asserted.

First, it is apparent that the supporters of contest debating
generally hold the opinion that competitiveness is a virtue. Nichols
and Baccus declare that "Life demands continued excellence, hence
perhaps it is wise for debaters to train for it. "[17] Holm says,
"While some have deplored the desire to win, it must be admitted
that the wish to surpass others is a natural and desirable ambition.
If it is properly guided, it will prove a strong motive in the better-
ment of humanity. "[18] While it is tempting to digress on a semantic analysis of terms here, my point can perhaps be sharpened by
recounting a controversy that arose at the 1951 Pi Kappa Delta convention at Stillwater, Oklahoma. During a general session a debate
coach proposed that, in addition to the customary inconspicuous
medals which were traditionally awarded to individuals with good
records, an impressive sweepstakes trophy, perhaps a cup of two-
gallon capacity, be henceforth awarded to the school with the "best"
record. Although the proposal was finally voted down, a girl student, arguing for the trophy, pleaded as follows: "We've got to
have something big to take home or else we may not get to take
the trip next time. "

This blithe indifference to the fate of all the other schools
which, by rules of competition, would fail to bring home the indispensable trophy is characteristic of the anti-social, predatory philosophy of the strenuous life which is openly or tacitly endorsed by

advocates of the kind of highly competitive debate found at forensic tournaments. While such a philosophy may have had a role in America's pioneer days, there is considerable evidence that today it creates more harm than good. Dr. W.R. Huston, former professor of medicine at Yale-in-China, says,

> There may be a direct relationship between our American proneness to high blood pressure, or hypertension, and our furious lust for success and prestige. The Chinese people are seemingly immune to high blood pressure. This is not due to any biological factor; for clinicians have reported cases of hypertension among Chinese living among us, and its loss among white people living in China. The pattern of life appears to be the decisive factor.[19]

The psychologist, D. B. Klein, says,

> Running through our pattern of competitive culture is the conviction that only the deserving will survive in the long economic run. This conviction is reflected in the stereotyped phrases of popular 'success' philosophy--'You can't keep a good man down,' and 'There's always room at the top,' and 'You can't beat the combination of brains, honesty and hard work.[20]

In his book, People in Quandaries, Professor Wendell Johnson describes what he terms the IFD disease. This he says follows the sequence of first setting up ideal goals; second, becoming frustrated because of the inability to achieve these goals; and third, becoming demoralized because of the frustration. He declares, "In my experience, no other ailment is so common among university students, for example, as what I have termed IFD disease."[21] He points out, as does Klein,[22] as does Huston,[23] and as does almost any serious student of contemporary life, that conditions today are such that many will fail to reach their goals, regardless of ambition, intelligence and application. For example Johnson says,

> It has been reported that approximately two out of every three students enrolled in a large mid-western university expressed themselves as wanting to become doctors, lawyers, university professors, or to achieve some other comparable status. The crucial fact is that only about one out of sixteen university students can achieve such an ideal in our society.[24]

It is not here advocated that college debaters will necessarily become victims of IFD desease because they have been indoctrinated

with the ideal goal of winning trophies. Rather, our third contention was that tournaments exaggerated the evils of contest debating
by idealizing competitive effort, fair or foul, and by overemphasizing the decision. Opinion of psychologists, sociologists and physi-
cians has been cited to show that go-getter competitive effort is
bad for society as now constituted. Since debate tournaments, with
greater emphasis on winning, contribute to that predatory philosophy and its attendant practices, they stand indicted on our third sub-
contention.

To sum up the affirmative position, then, evidence has been
submitted to show that tournament debating fails to meet defensible
educational objectives by failing to provide speakers with audiences
--the basic recommendation of the SAA-North Central Committee--,
by concentrating too much of the wrong kind of attention on too few
students, and by enhancing the evils of competitive debating. Professor Abernathy says, "If forensics are to better serve their purpose, I believe they must cease to be dominated by tournament debating." Your affirmative goes further and suggests that the activity be abolished.

Reprinted from The Gavel, 37:51-55, 67; March, 1955. Lester
McCrery was Assistant Professor of Speech at the California Institute of Technology.

Notes

1. "The Criticism Against Speech Tournaments" by Elton Abernathy, Quarterly Journal of Speech, October 1942.
2. "Is It Time to Reappraise the Tournament System?" by C.S.
   Templer, The Forensic of Pi Kappa Delta, January 1941,
   Series 26, No. 2.
3. Abernathy, op. cit.
4. Quarterly Journal, North Central Association, March 1950.
5. Quarterly Journal of Speech, October 1951.
6. Templer, op. cit.
7. Nichols, E.R., and Baccus, J.H., Modern Debating, W.W.
   Norton & Co., Inc., 1936.
8. Holm, J.N., "How to Judge Speech Contests," Platform News,
   1938.
9. Robinson, Karl, North Central Association Quarterly, 1950,

         vol. 25.
10. Nichols and Baccus, op. cit., p. 87.
11. Baird, A. Craig, Argumentation, Discussion and Debate,
         McGraw Hill, 1950, p. 322.
12. Templer, op. cit., p. 38.
13. Abernathy, op. cit., p. 356.
14. Nichols and Baccus, op. cit.
15. Ibid.
16. Templer, op. cit., p. 37-38.
17. Nichols and Baccus, op. cit.
18. Holm, op. cit., p. 103.
19. W.R. Huston, The Art of Treatment, Macmillan Company,
         1936, pp. 450-51.
20. Klein, D.B., Mental Hygiene, Holt and Company, 1944, p. 409.
21. Johnson, Wendell, People in Quandaries, Harper, 1946.
22. Klein, op. cit.
23. Huston, op. cit.
24. Johnson, Wendell, op. cit.

32. Tournament Debating Should Not Be Abolished
Robert P. Newman

It would indeed be surprising, given the remarkable growth of debate tournaments in recent years, if we could not find some faults in the system which call for correction. It would be even more surprising, however, if such a solid growth presented nothing but evils, fulfilled no useful functions, and represented only, as Mr. McCrery would seem to have it, a Frankensteinian monster corrupting debate coaches as well as their students. I, for one, and apparently in this I have a legion of supporters, find tournaments definitely valuable, and resort to them regularly. Let us examine Mr. McCrery's charges, to see if he has not overstated his case and overlooked some values of debate tournaments.

First, however, let us be clear about our objectives. I am sure that I see in my opponent's remarks a clear concern for the welfare of the student as being paramount in any consideration of tournaments. With this I heartily agree. The Negative in this case can stand wholeheartedly on the statement by Baird in Argumentation, Discussion, and Debate: "Although (debates) are often staged for sport's sake and are promoted as intercollegiate competition, their place in higher education is justified only because of their

value as education. They are good training for prospective teachers, preachers, lawyers, statesmen, businessmen, social and government workers, housewives, and other citizens."[1] We agree
with Baird that sport, entertainment, prestige, and all other similar outcomes of intercollegiate debating ought to be secondary. The
question, therefore, to which we must address ourselves is, are debate tournaments valuable for training students?

Now Mr. McCrery has given you four objections to tournaments which supposedly vitiate their values for training purposes.
But it is interesting to note that of the four, only one objection is
inherent in the tournament system, and that one--the absence of
substantial audiences--is of doubtful import. His other objections,
insofar as they are valid, constitute what might be termed evils in
practice, as contrasted with the generic difficulty of the absence of
audiences. Consequently, they can be disposed of rapidly, so that
we may concentrate upon the significant problem of how the absence
of audiences affects the educational values of tournaments.

Let us take up first the so-called "star system," the practice
of building a few high-powered debaters into winners, and spending
all the debate budget and coach's time on them to the exclusion of
other students who might be equally interested in debate but who
are less talented. It cannot be denied that some schools do follow
such a policy; but it is certainly not inherent in the system. In
fact, at present, tournaments offer debate training to more students
than do audience debates. According to a survey conducted by
Austin J. Freeley,[2] representing the answers of 70 institutions to
a questionnaire, an average of 11 students per college participated
in audience debates, whereas 23 took part in tournaments.

Now it can be argued that if all the resources of a college
were devoted to audience debating, and none of them devoted to
tournaments, the number of students participating in audience debates would be greatly increased. But this does not necessarily follow; in fact, without the training provided by tournaments, we
would probably put fewer rather than more students into our high
school demonstration series, simply because the standards of performance must be higher in the audience situation. It matters less

to me that a debater give a poor account of himself at the Temple
Novice Tournament, than that he disgrace Pittsburgh before 1,000
students at Penn High School. Hence, for Pitt at least, if there
were no tournaments, there would be fewer audience debaters, and
more of a tendency to concentrate on "stars."

Consequently, we find in this particular indictment of the tournament system little cause for worry. More debaters do in fact
take part in tournaments than in audience debates; and there is little reason to believe that, if tournaments were abolished, audience
opportunities would substantially increase. If tournaments are used
by some schools only to develop champions, that is their loss.
Such practices certainly do not diminish the values of tournaments
to me, nor need they to Mr. McCrery.

The second specific objection to tournaments is that they promote the competitive aspects of debating. Now it is not our purpose this evening to argue the extent to which competition is desirable. Debating is inherently competitive, and we are not debating
"Resolved: that debate should be abolished." Consequently, insofar as this is an argument against debate itself, it does not concern
us. Insofar as it is an argument against a specific abuse of debate tournaments, it can be dealt with best by admitting that anything can be carried to extremes, tournament competition included;
and that insofar as tournaments provide a competitive setting, they
will be used by coaches interested in competition as a vehicle for
securing it. If they are, in some cases, overused, and I think we
must all admit that they are, then that is indeed a specific evil.
But the values of tournaments are not thereby written off the books.
Certainly a balanced forensic program will include some tournament
competition; and if competition is an evil only by overindulgence,
then again we have no indictment of the tournament system as such.

It remains to be pointed out that there are opportunities in
most sections of the country to attend "non-competitive," i.e., non-
decision tournaments; that these offer most of the values cited below; and that if tournament offerings are over-weighted with competitive events, we need to restore balance. But we do not need
to throw out the baby with the bath water. Admitted, as Mr. Mc-

Crery's citation from Nichols and Baccus claims, that tournaments
were originally hailed as doing away with the competitive excesses
in the old debating leagues, which promise has not been completely
fulfilled. But the other side of the coin has yet to be examined,
to see what of positive value tournaments present.

The final specific objection to tournaments is a catch-all designed to cover a multitude of evils. Tournaments are said to defeat the educational objectives of forensics. They produce trickery,
contentiousness, are too strenuous, and introduce undesirable extraneous elements into the debating situation. This sounds dreadful.
It boils down to the following: some debaters use trick cases, and
some judges--we hope not Mr. McCrery--let them get away with it.
Some tournaments list 24 events in a single day, and some students
are fool enough to enter too many of them. Other debaters become
contentious, presumably due solely to the tournament system. And
one tournament--horrors!--advertises itself with a full-page photo
of the comely female running it.

We have only this to say: it does not strike us as proven
that tournaments are basically unsound because of these things.
Many of these alleged abuses flourish in any situation simply because people are human. Trickery, for instance, is just as prevalent in home-and-home debates, courts of law, and the U.S. Congress as it is in the tournaments I have attended. The contentious
student may gravitate towards debating; but the tournament should
be as good a place as any for an incisive critique to cut him down
to size. A tournament may list a multiplicity of events; perhaps
this is a good place for a student to learn his capacity. Certainly
the wise coach will discourage overloading; we need not be addicted
to sweepstakes-worship, even though some of us may incline in that
direction. And sex: is the Mary Washington outfit any more culp-
able for using it in their advertisements than the General Tire Company or Coca-Cola?

But when all these excrescences have been dealt with there
remains the very serious consideration of the lack of a substantial
audience. We admit that tournament debates rarely feature them,
and we are aware that this disturbs the North Central Association

no end, and even causes some concern in councils of the Speech
Association of America. We note the very positive statement of
these two groups that debate ". . . in an empty room . . . can
never be an end in itself, " and consider an analysis of this charge
the major business of the evening. Our original question, then,
might be refined as follows: are tournament debates, occurring as
they do without substantial audiences, valuable for training students?

The answer, we believe, as reflected in the number of tournaments held and their popularity with coaches, is a resounding
yes. The reasons why can be glimpsed by considering specific com-
petences we want our debaters to gain, and observing whether or
not they are promoted by debates held in a classroom with only
four debaters, a critic-judge, and possibly a chairman-timekeeper
present. The breakdown which follows is only one of a number of
possible analyses of the specific objectives of debate training; its
categories are neither exhaustive nor mutually exclusive; but it may
serve as a springboard from which to approach the values of tournament debating.

1. Techniques of research. Does preparation for tournament
debating teach a student anything about the gathering of material
and techniques of research? Mr. McCrery has certainly not denied
that it does, nor is it likely that he will. Even if his audience is
to consist only of his opponents, a coach from another school, and
his colleague, the mechanism of debate is strongly conducive to
making a student bone up on the subject. Whether listeners be one
or a thousand, the presence of an opponent, one of whose objectives
is to make an ass out of you, is an impelling motivation to know
what you are talking about. Granted, that the selection of a national debate proposition, and the publication of handbooks thereon, reduces to some degree the necessity for digging out one's own material; but no debater worthy of the name stops his research with a
handbook. Even handbooks contain bibliographies, in the pursuit of
which a debater is bound to learn something; and in most leagues,
"handbook case" is a term of opprobrium applied to those who hav-
en't gotten very far. I have known students who might well have
graduated from college without making the acquaintance of the Read-

ers' Guide to Periodical Literature had they not been constrained
to do so in preparation for a debate tournament; and at least 26
Pitt students, who never before appreciated the vast resources
available in the political realm, have been put up to writing a Pennsylvania Senator for a copy of S3368, the Humphrey-Ives Bill. Can
Mr. McCrery deny that the better debaters spend more time in the
library in preparation for tournament debating than does the average
student in preparation for his classes? And does this not occur
without audiences, and is it not a benefit?

2. Knowledge of contemporary problems. During the course
of a year's tournament debating, and the preparation necessary for
it, even the dullest of debaters is bound to acquire a modicum of
knowledge of an important contemporary issue. Whether that knowledge is useful or academic is beside the point. Whether he would
gain more knowledge in audience situations is also beside the point
if the audience appearances are not available to him. Early this
year, we entertained two members of the U.S. House of Representatives in a discussion of the FEPC question. Some of our debaters,
who up to that time had had only tournament experience, were better versed on the subject than was at least one of the Congressmen.
You know, and I know, that these boys would not have worked this
hard for purely intramural events. It was the incentive of tournament competition which motivated them; and here is at least one
value which accrued despite the absence of an audience.

3. Critical evaluation of evidence. Related to, but above and
beyond the two foregoing points, we want our debaters to acquire
the critical attitude so necessary to achieving a sound viewpoint in
an age of high-powered propaganda. We know only too well that
American lecture-courses, where the student is primarily a passive
receptacle into which is pumped material from pre-digested textbooks for later regurgitation, do not accomplish this end. In debate, we have an exceedingly promising mechanism for developing
critical thought. We have duplicated, at least for opposing debate
teams, Henry Adams' wish for ". . . a rival assistant professor
opposite him, whose business should be strictly limited to expressing opposite views. "[3] We need to challenge our prejudices and up-

set our preconceptions; and practice in debate, even without substantial audiences, provides training in critical thinking that we
sorely need. I remember vividly a debate some weeks ago in
which Southern opposition to FEPC was an issue. One piece of
analogical evidence was introduced to the effect that in New York,
where FEPC is relatively successful, there was no expressed opposition. The two teams fought vigorously over the significance of
this point; and in so doing, I am convinced, gained more than in a
week's lectures in any discipline you can name. This learning occurred without audience, even without critique--and we need more
of it.

4. Argumentation. Certainly one of the things we want our
debaters to learn is how to organize ideas and evidence in such a
manner as to present a sound argumentative case. We are training
them in advocacy. Many of us are awed by the forensic brilliance
of the British debaters, and wish our system of education produced
the gift of tongues as theirs does. But very few of us would sacrifice the ideal of a closely-reasoned, well-documented, straight-to-
the-issue argumentative case for their flowery oratory. We feel
this way, first, because we believe that more decisions should be
made as a result of cold, objective argument, and fewer as a result of heady, intoxicating oratory; and second, because we are
training students who are more likely to use their talents arguing
to a single judge in a court of law, a small committee hearing, or
a board of directors meeting, than to a vast, admiring throng.

As Wayne C. Eubank pointed out in the Quarterly Journal of
Speech, December, 1949,[4] ". . . the products of our forensic system fit into our institutional patterns . . . exceedingly well." And
one of the reasons this is so, is that the approach to argumentation
fostered by the debate tournament, with only five or six people listening to a debate that is supposed to be judged on the basis of
logical argument, is similar to the approach we demand of many
speakers in later life. Certainly there are debaters who go into
politics, and we shall consider them in a minute; but for the present we can conclude that the presentation of logical argument is
one of the skills we want our speakers to master; that the tourna-

ment is valuable apprenticeship in this skill; and that it ought therefore to be retained.

5. Broad-mindedness. We, as debate coaches, are interested in an open society, a society in which most questions of public policy are settled by discussion and debate, rather than by tradition, authority, or force. We should therefore be interested in turning out leaders with open minds on questions of public policy, in contradistinction to Teddy Roosevelt's cry for ". . . young men with ardent convictions on the side of the right . . ."[5] If we recognize a public question as truly debatable, we deny that any one individual knows what the Right is on that question. We do not want young men with ardent convictions on debatable topics; we want young men (and older men) with open minds. Does the tournament system contribute to building such open-mindedness? Evidence indicates that it does. Henry L. Eubank, reviewing research on the subject in the Quarterly Journal of Speech, April, 1951, concludes that "Debating is a poor method of producing either radicals or reactionaries. Debaters tend to see both sides, to be less extreme in their views at the end of the season."[6] (I assume that most of the debaters surveyed worked primarily in tournaments.) As an example of things that can happen in tournaments to encourage open-mindedness, I would cite a girl from a sectarian college near Pittsburgh who attended one of our intracity tournaments this year on the negative of the FEPC question. She contended, among other things, that FEP laws were wrong because Protestants, Catholics, and Jews should not work together in offices or factories since they had opposing views of the universe. Two of her judges, myself being one of them, spent considerable time with her in an attempt to broaden her viewpoint, inasmuch as her opponents apparently failed to do so. There are indications that we succeeded. We hope this girl received worthwhile training; and if she did, I should regard that particular tournament as worth the time and effort expended.

6. Persuasive speaking. Is it possible to secure training in this art in tournaments, despite the claims of the North Central Association? Is there anything corresponding to a substantial audience in the four or five people who customarily listen to a tourna-

ment debate? Sometimes there seems not to be. In some tournaments, during the last rounds, where people are tired and performance is mechanical, there seems not to be. In other tournaments I have definitely felt that there was. After all, the judge, even though he is supposed to be an impartial critic, is human, as are colleague, opponents, and timekeeper. Nichols and Baccus, in Modern Debating, consider for a whole chapter[7] the function of the audience in debate, and particularly the extent to which the tournament "audience" contributes to the psychological speaking situation: "The conclusion is that to have an audience, there must at least be an audience mind, an audience consciousness, and an audience soul. Can a few people or one person ever become an audience then? It would seem as if they cannot, and yet they do. Consider the minimum group at a debate; does it not have all the above requisites of inspiration and response, of action and reaction that a composite mind exhibits? There is just one factor of difference and that is numbers. Just how essential are numbers? That numbers are important and that they do magnify audience results is undisputed, but are numbers so absolutely essential that we must bemoan the fact that debates are not so largely attended as football games? Are numbers so essential that debate must be taken to the crowds for the real values of debate to accrue to the speaker?"[8] The intended answer, with which we agree, is that a debate group is a capsule audience, and furnishes some of the ethos of the substantial audience called for by the NCA.

But it is not necessary to win the previous point to establish the values of tournaments. We can forget our claim that a tournament debate offers some training in persuasive speech, and still justify tournaments on the other values mentioned. For Mr. Mc-Crery overlooks one important point: while tournaments are an end in themselves in that they promote training in research techniques, knowledge of contemporary problems, evaluation of evidence, etc., they are also a means to an end--they are a training ground for speakers whom we will use in audience debates, and a very effective training ground. And while we should regard as short-sighted a debate program which did not take advantage of tournaments, we

should also deplore a program which did not give debaters a chance
for experience before a substantial audience. My program is so
balanced, as, I trust, is that of my opponent. It is not a case of
either/or; it is a case of both, in the best proportion facilities allow. As McBurney, O'Neill, and Mills put it in Argumentation and
Debate, "When the debaters have achieved sufficient competence to
be worthy of an audience, a public situation adds much to a debate.
Although one campus affords only a few opportunities per season,
the program can be expanded by taking debates to civic clubs,
school assemblies, and other such groups. This is not to say that
tournament debating needs to be dropped from the schedule. "[9]

And now that all this has been said by way of refutation, let
us add some further good words for tournaments, and some recommendations. There can be no doubt that tournaments offer an inexpensive means of providing debate training. As of the first half
of 1952-53 at Pitt, our 78 tournament debates, involving 27 students,
cost $1.06 per debate; our 22 audience debates, before high school
assemblies, involving 10 speakers, cost $8.20 per debate. Eight
of the ten upperclassmen out for debate have had three or more
audience debates; and the other two, both juniors, will have faced
audiences before the year is over. But they have all faced tournament situations first--and have been the better for it.

One of the reasons why we regard tournaments as valuable is
that they provide systematic criticism, in the form of a critique
from a judge who, fortunately, in most cases is capable of sound
criticism. Furthermore, I know of no mechanism other than a
tournament of securing for my debaters the criticism of my fellow
coaches from neighboring schools, who can make up for my blind
spots and correct my deficiencies; and who, incidentally, will in-
form me if my debaters are contentious, given to trickery, or off-
base in some other fashion which I have overlooked. In so doing
they can genuinely contribute to the education of my students, many
of whom I would hesitate to impose on an audience in their present
stage of development.

Does this mean that the Negative in this debate is completely
happy with the tournament system? Certainly not. Many of the

suggestions made by H. P. Constans in the Southern Speech Journal
for September, 1949,[10] find hearty approval here.   Tournaments
should generally be more leisurely, with time for longer critiques
and revision of cases.   There should be tournaments on subjects
other than the national, such as the very excellent one conducted
by Williams College each spring.   There should be more non-decision affairs, and variations in the format of debating.   Pitt sponsors
each December a very successful non-decision, cross-examination
tournament, with opponent-ratings as the only tangible outcome.
Finally, provision should be made in training tournaments for substitute judges so that coaches can hear their own teams.   This is
much more revealing than hearing one's own debaters in an intramural practice session.

In conclusion, tournament debating is not the evil thing de-
picted by my opponent.   It is basically sound, and a useful mechanism by which to train students in many of the skills we desire
them to master.   It should be strengthened, diversified, slowed
down in some cases, perhaps run by better coaches--for many of
its faults are in reality our faults--but never abolished.

Reprinted from The Gavel, 37:56-60, 68; March, 1955.   Robert
Newman is Professor of Speech at the University of Pittsburgh.

Notes

1.   Albert Craig Baird, Argumentation, Discussion, and Debate,
        New York, McGraw Hill, 1950, p. 361.
2.   Presented at the Cincinnati Convention of the Speech Associa-
        tion of America, 1952, and obtainable from Prof. Freeley
        at Boston University.
3.   Henry Adams, The Education of Henry Adams.   New York,
        Random House (Modern Library Edition), 1931, pp. 303-
        304.
4.   Wayne C. Eubank, "American Versus British Debating," Quar-
        terly Journal of Speech, XXXV, p. 433, December, 1949.
5.   Theodore Roosevelt, "Chapters of a Possible Autobiography,"
        Outlook, February 22, 1913, p. 393.
6.   Henry L. Eubank, "What's Right with Debate?" Quarterly Jour-
        nal of Speech, XXXVII, p. 201, April, 1951.
7.   Egbert Ray Nichols and Joseph Baccus, Modern Debating.   New
        York, Norton, 1936, Ch. XVI.

8.   Ibid., pp. 284-85.
9.   James H. McBurney, J.M. O'Neill, and Glen Mills, Argumen-
     tation and Debate. New York, Macmillan, 1951, p. 277.
10. H.P. Constans, "The Role of Intercollegiate Debate Tourna-
     ments in the Post-War Period," Southern Speech Journal,
     XV, pp. 38-44, September, 1949.

Suggestions for Further Reading

Buehler, C.C., ed. "A Symposium: Debate Tournaments Ap-
     praised," Gavel, 32:75, 82-83, May, 1950.
Cable, W. Arthur. "A Decalogue of Contest Debating," Quarterly
     Journal of Speech, 15:254-256, April, 1929.
Clevenger, Theodore, Jr. "Toward a Point of View for Contest
     Debate," Central States Speech Journal, 12:21-26, Autumn,
     1960.
Erickson, Keith. "Calling a Spade a Spade," Speaker and Gavel,
     3:62-65, March, 1966.
Haston, Bruce. "Have We Forgotten Quality?" Western Speech,
     24:233-35, Autumn, 1960.
Hellman, Hugo E. "The Fallacy of the Fisher Report," Rostrum,
     25:2-4, December, 1950.
Holm, James N. "Debating, 1958: A Re-Examination," AFA Reg-
     ister, 7:12-19, Spring, 1959.
Howes, Raymond F. "Professor Cable's Decalogue: Reply,"
     Quarterly Journal of Speech, 15:413-417, June, 1929.
Karr, Harrison M. vs. Baccus, Joseph H. "Should Tournament
     Debating Be Discontinued?" Western Speech, 5:6-21, March,
     1941.
Klopf, Donald. "Practices in Intercollegiate Speech Tournaments,"
     Journal of the American Forensic Association, 1:48-58, May,
     1964.
Kruger, Arthur N. "Contests and Competitive Debate," Sec. XVI,
     A Classified Bibliography of Argumentation and Debate.
     Metuchen, N.J, Scarecrow Press, 1964, pp. 239-265.
Lawton, J.H. "Tournament Debating Controversy," Catholic Edu-
     cational Review, 60:392-401, September, 1962.
Lazzatti, John L., Jr. "An Artificial and Inadequate Substitute,"
     AFA Register, 5:11-12, Convention, 1957.
Mangun, Vernon L. "Debating: Sophism Institutionalized," Educa-
     tional Review, 74:195-200, November, 1927.
Miller, N. Edd. "The Status of Debating: 1958," AFA Register,
     7:5-11, Spring, 1959.
Newman, Robert P. "The Tournament in a Balanced Debate Pro-
     gram," AFA Register, 5:3-5, College Calendar, 1957.
Osborn, Michael M. "A Blueprint for Diversity in Forensic Pro-
     grams," Speech Teacher, 14:110-115, March, 1965.
Padrow, Ben. "Let's Stop Calling Them Educational," Speech
     Teacher, 5:205-206, September, 1956.

Peterson, Court, "Student Reaction to NCA Report...." <u>Gavel</u>, 33:
     53-54, March, 1951.
Robinson, Zon. "What Happens to Speech Values in Tournament
     Debating?" <u>Southern Speech Journal</u>, 7:122-125, March, 1942.
Stelzner, Hermann G. "Tournament Debate: Emasculated Rhetor-
     ic," <u>Southern Speech Journal</u>, 27:34-42, Fall, 1961.

IX. The Forensic Program

Issue Q: Are Forensic Programs Seriously Defective?

> In the spring of 1946 the Province of the Pacific spon-
> sored meetings to discuss ways of improving intercol-
> legiate debate, oratory, extempore speaking, and im-
> promptu speaking contests. The students taking part in
> these discussions had no faculty supervision so that they
> might be completely candid. Shortly thereafter their
> findings and recommendations appeared in the article
> "Evaluation of the Intercollegiate Forensic Program" by
> Edward S. Betz, which evoked several published com-
> ménts, one of which, "Comments on Student Evaluation
> of Intercollegiate Forensic Programs" by Glenn R. Capp,
> appears here. Although Capp agrees that forensic pro-
> grams can be improved, he does not agree with all of
> the proposed solutions and offers a few of his own, par-
> ticularly with regard to judging and tournaments.

33. Evaluation of the Intercollegiate Forensic Program
Edward S. Betz

At its spring meeting the Province of the Pacific held a unique
student evaluation discussion of the forensic program as conducted
in the western area. The discussions were completely student guided and only students participated in the sessions. The panels became more than gripe sessions, for out of them developed certain
concrete suggestions for the improvement of debate, oratory, extemp, and impromptu contests.

Four sections were set up to deal with the above contests;
each met twice during the tournament, first to consider what was
wrong (or right) with the contest in question and second to propose
certain specific methods of improving it. In order to stimulate the
thinking of the panel members, preliminary statements for each of

the above sections were prepared by the tournament director with
the assistance of Dr. Robert Clark of the University of Oregon and
Dr. Joseph Baccus of the University of Redlands. Using these
statements as "points of departure," the student panels drew up
their own critical evaluations and recommendations. These deserve
consideration by every director of forensics as well as by directors
of tournaments. When they are tested from the professional director's point of view, it must be remembered that these statements
represent what students (free from faculty supervision or direct
guidance of their discussion) think about the contests and their conduct.

The following is a summary of the findings of the panels as
written up by the chairmen and secretaries of each section. These
are the student evaluations and student recommendations.

Debate

Problem 1. What is wrong (right) with intercollegiate debate?

a. Inadequate judging is one of the major faults of intercol-
    legiate tournament debating.

b. Too many months are spent on the consideration of a
    single subject.

c. In tournament debating there is a growing tendency toward
    overuse of statistics and argument from authority, to the
    detriment of the use of logical materials.

d. Debate tends to develop, or provide the situations which
    make possible, the development of a "shyster" attitude on
    the part of some speakers.

e. Many debaters do not really "debate," but simply repeat
    superficialities with assurance.

Problem 2. What do you propose to improve intercollegiate debate?

a. Judging could be improved by the nationwide adoption of a
    uniform ballot containing adequate instructions for the use
    of the judge and a sufficient number of points on which to
    evaluate the speakers.

b. A debate proposition should be selected for each semester.

c. Something other than the traditional two-man style of debate should be used.   Debate tournaments are "in a rut."

d. More speaking before audiences should be the aim of debate squads.

e. Student evaluations leading to action should be included
in more debate tournaments; there is too much talking
and too little action in intercollegiate forensics.

f. It might be wise to eliminate the use of argument from
authority in tournament debating in order to counter its
apparent growth.

Oratory

Problem 1. What is wrong (right) with intercollegiate oratory?

a. The oratory contest gives the student an opportunity for
sincere expression of his personal feelings and ideas.

b. There is great value in the preparation of an oration, for
it allows concentration on developing a spoken style
through a combination of speaking and reading.

c. In most orations there is a lack of balance between logical and emotional appeals.

d. Artificial, mechanical delivery of orations is probably the
result of presenting them in empty rooms.

e. Judges seem to have no adequate concept of what an oration is and as a result there is too much variation in the
standards of judging.

f. Ballots by judges do not provide for a practical evaluation
of each speaker.

Problem 2. What do you propose to improve intercollegiate oratory
and the conduct of the contest?

a. There is a need for a regulation ballot containing a definition of oratory and a space for individual criticism by the
judge of each contestant, the latter to be so arranged as
to be immediately available to the contestants.

b. Judges should be adequately briefed on the mechanics of
the contest as well as on the nature of the oratory.   Three
judges should be available for each round.

c. Tournament directors should provide audiences through pub-

lic invitation and advertising as well as through the use
of college classes in speech and related fields.

d. Standardization of these procedures should come within
the entire western region for each season of participation.

Extempore Speaking

Problem 1. What is wrong (right) with the intercollegiate extemp
contest?

a. There are no clear objectives in this contest.

b. Topics drawn each round are frequently too narrow, demanding considerable factual information rather than individual analysis.

c. Judging is inadequate due to the lack of standards and the
failure of judges to give individual criticisms.

d. Extemp speaking is the best contest in the intercollegiate
tournament system. Even with its shortcomings, it comes
the closest to presenting a life situation and developing
better speech habits.

Problem 2. What do you propose to improve this contest?

a. The objectives of extemp should be to test the speaker's
ingenuity, ideas, and ability at clear presentation.

b. No general subject should be announced; topics should be
of general nature, drawn from current events and stated
broadly enough to allow for flexibility in direction of approach.

c. Clear statement of the objectives of the contest and standards of judging should be given to the judge. These
standards should be uniform throughout the country. Individual criticism blanks should be used and the results
sent to the speakers after the tournament.

Impromptu Speaking

Problem 1. What is wrong (right) with intercollegiate impromptu
speaking?

a. There is a place for impromptu speaking in contests, for
in later life this type of speaking is very common.

    b. Impromptu speaking helps the speaker to learn to organize his thoughts quickly while on his feet.

    c. Present contests in this field are almost completely lacking in objectives.

    d. There is a definite tendency for this contest to promote glibness in speech.

    e. The speaker has little opportunity to improve through criticism in this contest, for no one seems to know what constitutes good impromptu speaking.

    f. Judging in this contest is at its worst, for there seems to be a prevailing opinion that anyone can judge impromptu.

    g. In the conduct of the contest there has frequently been cheating when one contestant informs a friend what the topic is.

Problem 2. What improvements would you suggest for this contest?

    a. The specific purpose of the contest should be determined and made known to contestants.

    b. Ballots providing for critical evaluation of speakers should be used by judges and the results made known to the speakers.

    c. Impromptu topics should be drawn from general fields.

    d. Each speaker should have a different topic.

    e. Judges well trained in speech should be used in this contest.

Conclusions

It is notable that these students came to almost unanimous agreement that both the judging and the objectives of intercollegiate forensics are inadequate. In part, the criticism of judging may have been due to the inevitable conflict between debater and judge, but frequently expressed was the need for methods of judging that would make constructive criticism readily available to the contestants. Clearly also, the present generation of tournament speakers is interested in knowing why they are participating in tournaments and what they are supposed to be learning by the process of repeating the same procedures over and again for the entire year.

The implications of these discussions are clear: if student
needs are to be met then the recommendations which have been
made should be put into effect insofar as they are educationally desirable and administratively practical.   Certainly much can be done
to standardize ballots and procedures.   Pi Kappa Delta has occupied
a leading position in this area and might go even further.

Reprinted from The Forensic 31:95-98, May, 1946.   At the time of
writing, Edward Betz was teaching at the College of the Pacific.

34. Comments on Student Evaluation of
Intercollegiate Forensic Program
Glenn R. Capp

In my opinion the plan of student evaluation of forensic programs sponsored by the Province of the Pacific in its recent meeting should be encouraged for other forensic gatherings.   I have
long thought that much could be done to improve our intercollegiate
forensic programs and quite agree that in the past there has been
too much "talk" for the corresponding "action" which has resulted.
Only by constructive criticism and a willingness to experiment with
new forms of procedure will we be able to improve our status in
the educational field.

In reading the report of this student evaluation program I was
at once impressed by the fact that most of the criticisms and suggestions concerned the manner in which our forensic programs are
conducted.   They are not inherent weaknesses which would justify
a consideration of abandoning such programs.   Rather, they should
serve as a challenge to the teachers and directors of forensics to
improve the status of their work.   There is as much need now as
formerly for the training afforded by forensic work.   The manner
in which many programs are conducted leaves much to be desired,
however.

The most frequently mentioned criticism noted concerned the

matter of judging the various contests. The recommendation that a "nationwide uniform ballot" be adopted was not sufficiently explained, in my opinion. If by a "uniform ballot" is meant a standardized ballot to be used over a long period, I would question the proposed solution. Rather, we should study judges' ballots experimentally and use our various intercollegiate tournaments as proving grounds for new suggestions. Experimentation and frequent change to incorporate new findings should be our keynote rather than an attempt at uniformity and standardization. I have had the occasion recently to investigate some of the experimental studies of the past few years on student rating sheets, shift of opinion ballots, and various methods of evaluating and judging contest speaking programs. Much more needs to be done in this field, but it is my opinion that we are failing to utilize sufficiently such findings as have already been made. We are prone to utilize our tournaments too much for the purpose of "determining a champion" rather than as an educational project.

At least three causes for the criticism of poor judging are as follows: (1) the failure to experiment with ballots and utilize the experiments already available; (2) the sponsoring of tournaments which are so large as to prevent the securing of adequately trained judges; (3) too many rounds of debate in our tournaments without sufficient time for discussion and criticism following each round.

Perhaps the first difficulty could be overcome by the appointment of committees from our forensic organizations whose purpose would be to survey the field of experimentation in judges' ballots and rating sheets, provide for further experimentation, and provide for publication of findings in our various forensic magazines. While much is being done at present in this respect the program is not adequately organized and carried out so as to make the information available to all. Our tournaments should then utilize these findings in an attempt to improve the mechanics of judging.

In many sections our tournaments are so large and include so many different contests that it is almost impossible for the tournament director to secure qualified judges for all contests. It is not uncommon in the Southwest to find as many as 75 to 100 debate

teams in attendance at a single tournament. When you consider
that some of these tournaments include from six to eight rounds of
debate in addition to several other types of contests you can readily
realize the magnitude of the task of securing qualified judges for all
contests. Closely associated with this problem is a tendency to include numerous types of contests in the average tournament. Whether or not many of these new ventures have educational value the
mere number complicate the mechanics of the average tournament
and prevent the securing of qualified judges in many instances. Perhaps we have been guilty of stressing quantity rather than quality in
our meetings. A restriction of the number of contestants and the
number of contests to the qualified judges available would seem to
be a wiser course.

In this same connection many of our tournaments include too
many rounds, especially in debate. The visiting forensic directors,
in addition to being overworked, are not given sufficient time following each round to make a proper criticism and evaluation of the debate and speakers. Thus the educational possibilities at these tournaments are less than they should be. Many forensic tournaments
run into an endurance contest both for the judges and the debaters
simply because of the numerous contests and the number of rounds
in each contest. In my opinion we should restrict the number of
rounds of debate for any given day to a maximum of four and allow
at least two hours for each round so as to permit a proper evaluation, discussion, and criticism following each debate. By use of
rating scales winners can be determined if they are desired. The
above are practical suggestions which should improve the status of
judging in tournament contests.

Such suggestions as lack of an audience at tournaments, number of propositions debated during a college year, types of debates,
etc., can be combined for comment. Again these criticisms are
valid not because of any fundamental weakness in our forensic work
but because of the manner in which many programs are conducted.
While it may not be feasible for debate organizations to announce
two or more propositions in a given year, this does not prevent a
school from debating as many propositions as it desires. I recall

working with my students on six different questions one school year
and debates were held before audiences who were interested in the
questions for discussion.   On one occasion we were invited to debate the problem of municipal government before a civic organization in a large city prior to an election on the city manager plan.
The discussion was so well received that the debaters were invited
back for a radio debate just prior to the election.   The mechanics
of a tournament make it difficult to arrange for any sizeable audience for the contests.   The tournament should make up only a part
of a school's forensic program, however.   Other features should include taking debates to interested audiences and discussing problems
in which such audiences are vitally interested.   The tournament
should provide excellent practice periods under the direction of qualified critics which should better prepare the students for audience
debating.

The suggestions made by the students on the various contests
show that they are doing some constructive thinking on the matter.
While such suggestions as "eliminate the use of argument from authority" reflect immature judgment, in my opinion, the entire list
shows that the students are not unaware of many of the major shortcomings of forensic programs as now conducted.   These student
opinions should be a challenge to teachers of public speaking, debate
and related subjects to renew their efforts toward improving intercollegiate forensic programs.

Reprinted from Debaters Magazine, 2:180-185, September, 1946.
Glenn Capp is Professor of Speech, Baylor University.

Issue R: Is There Too Much Emphasis on Picking "Champion" Debate Teams?

>In arguing affirmatively, Fred Goodwin, in "This Business of Bestness," states, "In the greatest number of instances, to choose with any degree of reliability the 'champion' of the best debate teams cannot be done," for the measuring instrument is too crude. Thus, we should not take too seriously, "as some people seem to be doing," the final results of certain "super tournaments." Goodwin, however, does not advocate the abandonment of such tournaments, but he does object to the practice of certain schools "ferreting bestness by sending a few of their better students to far too many tournaments" and creating a group known as "debate bums." Richard A. Hildreth, on the other hand, argues that if students are to be trained for roles in society, the "selection of champions" is justified, for, in real life, decisions must be awarded by judges "ill equipped with 'fine' instruments." American society, he declares, is based on competition in which a few become "champions." Thus to eliminate "championship" competition would prevent forensics from being a complete "training device for the student in his post-school life." Hildreth concludes that if overemphasis on winning championships leads to unethical practices, the "answer lies in greater emphasis on ethics in forensic programs" and "greater deterrents to unethical practices . . . as . . . in the non-classroom competitive life."

35. This Business of Bestness
Fred Goodwin

I have been intending to write this article for some time, and this would seem to be the propitious time to be about it. The college at which I teach has just returned from the Pi Kappa Delta National Convention in possession of a superior certificate in men's sweepstakes. We have won the right to send a student to the Old Line Oratorical Contest at Michigan State University in a few weeks. We have compiled a squad record in debate this year of about 70

280

percent wins. I mention these achievements only because what I
am about to say might be interpreted as loser's bleat. It is not.
Rather, it is an effort to combat a delusion which periodically in-
vades forensic tourneys. I suppose, like the wild onions in my
front yard, this delusion will tend to sprout annually and with increasing frequency until somebody sprays the lawn. Herewith, I
hope, will be only the first dose of chlorate solution. Far too
many people are insisting that after we identify the superior forensic participants, we continue to apply our wandering micrometers
to decide which of the best is the best.

They suggest an impossible task. In the greatest number of
instances, to choose with any degree of reliability the "champion"
of the best debate teams cannot be done. The truth is, and all
coaches who are knowledgeable enough and honest enough must admit it, that in forensic contests the maximum differentiation by the
most competent of judges is that which separates the superiors from
the excellents from the goods from the rest.

You may have puzzled yourself while you were in grade school
with the query which goes: "Suppose you had a piece of string and
kept cutting it in half. How long would would it take you to complete the job?" The answer was that you never completed the job,
because if you cut away only half of the remaining piece of string,
half a piece would always remain. I can remember marveling at
that answer. Maybe you can too. But I hope you haven't bothered
yourself with nonsense like that recently, because the only reasonable answer to the question is: "You cut until your cutting instrument becomes too crude to cope with the size of the remaining piece
of string. Then you quit." I suggest that after we isolate the superior speakers in debate, oratory, discussion, and extemporaneous
speaking, our measuring instruments are, and always will be, too
crude to separate them further with any degree of meaning.

The last Pi Kappa Delta National Tournament which named a
national debate "champion" was in 1934. The final round pitted
Gustavus Adolphus against St. Olaf College. Named as judges in
the final round were nine people considered by the contest committee
to be capable critic judges. They heard the debate and voted a per-

fect split, 5-4. People who were upset by the divergent opinion
made the naive assumption that a judge or a group of judges reach
a decision in debate as they might solve a problem in geometry.
This naive reasoning is that judges are supposed to listen to the arguments, and carefully apply axioms and postulates of reasoning,
analysis, organization, speaking skill, etc., to see which team's
performance squares with those axioms and postulates. It sounds
very simple. But there is one big difference. Real students of
Euclidean geometry don't assess a problem and split their decision
5-4, 3-2, or 2-1. Let me say it again. After we identify the superior speakers, we have made the last reliable measurement possible in competitive public speaking no matter how competent the
judging.

I do not necessarily hold that tournaments which purport to
cleave the "superiorest" from the superior should be abandoned.
But when you realize the inherent inadequacy of the yardstick we
must use to compute the results in the super tournaments some of
us attend, and in the final rounds in the elimination tournaments
most of us attend, it's pretty hard to take them as seriously as
some people seem to be doing.

Right now I am staring at a trophy on my desk which is supposed to symbolize that an entry of Southeast Missouri State College
was "best" in one of the tournaments we attended this year. The
student is happy to get the trophy. The editor of our campus newspaper was delighted to hear about such a newsworthy item. The
college publicity director was tickled to death. The college president was reservedly pleased. My colleagues congratulated me.
After all, we have a "state champion" at our school. And let me
be the first to admit, I like the attention and the publicity. But I
know that "state champion" is a kind of fraudulent label. I know,
and thank goodness the student knows, that if the whole contest were
run again with another set of equally qualified judges, he might not
be rated on the top. And this knowledge bothers neither of us one
whit. What we aim for is the superior rating. If you consistently
earn that, then you have earned the last of the reliably meaningful
plaudits in the game of intercollegiate competitive public speaking.

You are at the top. A few others are there with you, but it's not too crowded unless you tend toward greediness. However, if you like to be alone in your bestness, if you seek the "champion" label, which admittedly is easier to explain to the local press and your campus committee on prorations, you may be opening the way for trouble. For example, at one tournament we attended this year an obviously superior debate team was not satisfied with recognition as superior. Intent upon protecting its bestness rating, the team deliberately misrepresented some evidence. The opposing team knew it, and fortunately the judge knew it. In the critique he confronted the offending team with his awareness. They openly admitted their tactics, claiming, "Everybody quotes out of context when they get in a tight spot." I hope their coach wouldn't hold their claim to be true! But it's tempting to be nefarious when seeking as fickle a sprite as bestness.

I have sometimes wondered too at the academic standards of schools ferreting bestness by sending a few of their better students to far too many tournaments. I recently heard a college director of forensics call these debaters "debate bums--as much as the athletic bums we used to condemn." And he has a point without doubt.

Then there are some institutions hoping to embrace bestness by recruiting debaters with the fervor of two Big Ten football coaches after a 250-pound high school tackle who can run 100 yards in 11 seconds in full equipment. Don't misunderstand me. There is nothing wrong with trying to get promising high school students to come to your school. If you're normal, you believe you don't have enough of the good ones as it is. But I hope you'll agree that one can go too far in this direction. Some schools have, in my opinion.

In my scale of values forensics can be justified only as an educational endeavor. It is not for the aggrandizement of an institution or its department of speech, though bestness tempts some school administrators to use forensics for those purposes. Debate does not exist for the ego inflation of the debate coach. Most of us stand in no need of that anyway. But bestness can poison a coach's previously sane forensic philosophy. Forensics exists--and I hope

your cortex is not beginning to flash the trite signal, because I feel
this sincerely--to teach straight thinking and clear talking. Tournaments, decisions, and awards help those of us who work specifically at the job of teaching better thought and speech. But it's time
to whittle away at the tournament bestness bogey. He's growing a
bit too large. I try to teach this forensic sanity to my students.
Will you join me?

Reprinted from The Forensic, 45:3-4, October, 1959. Mr. Goodwin teaches at Southeast Missouri State College.

36. Bestness Has a Place
Richard A. Hildreth

"Forensics exists . . . to teach straight thinking and clear
talking," reads the conclusion of "This Business of Bestness" in the
October, 1959, Forensic. Unfortunately the rest of this philosophic
statement was implied rather than stated. Forensics, as one part
of the total educational process, must reflect the basis of all educative endeavor. Therefore, this writer would like to submit the
above quotation in its implied context and attempt to determine what
answers the full contextual statement makes to the charges advanced
by Professor Goodwin.

> "Forensics exists . . . to teach straight thinking and
> clear talking" to better train the student to meet the de-
> mands of the sociological environment in which he will
> exist following his formal education.

If we assume that forensics has a total educational purpose of
training the student in all phases of public speaking endeavor to better fit him to take his place in his future sociological environment,
then we must combine the general benefits of forensic training for
the non-championship calibre person as well as the "stars." In such
a program the "selection of champions" would seem justified. Let
us analyze this concept in the light of Professor Goodwin's comments.

In 1934 Pi Kappa Delta selected its last national champion, as
Mr. Goodwin has pointed out. The "perfect split" decision, 5-4, by

nine competent judges is coincidentally related to the 1959-60 debate question. Supreme Court judges frequently have split their decisions, mainly because of the lack of fine enough instruments, reliable measures, or Euclidean analysis. A study of the American judicial system, a part of the sociological environment in which a debater must learn to live, reveals that in a majority of cases a single judge, ill equipped with "fine" instruments, must make a decision to determine which of two lawyers, or two teams of lawyers, who have prepared and presented arguments, is deserving of the "championship." The opposing lawyers, in this contest for the judge's decision, are subjected to pressures to win which can lead to misrepresentation or falsification of information.

Law is but one area where the element of competition exerts great pressure on the participants. Business, small and large, requires careful evaluation of the spirit as well as the letter of the law. Medicine has its Hippocratic Oath to guard against infractions and even this is not completely successful. It is certain that Professor Goodwin and this writer can agree that even teachers are subjected to severe tests of their ethics. Journalism, the military, and even various forms of creative art are subject to competition and thus to the flaws which it produces.

This is the environment into which a forensics student must step. If we accept the premise that forensics is an educative process and thus a training device for the student in his post-school life, and if we acknowledge that the American sociological environment is based on competition in which a few become "champions," then Mr. Goodwin's contention that we eliminate "championship" competition is obviated because forensics would be sterile if removed from its practical function.

This writer would like to submit that a more realistic answer lies in greater emphasis on ethics in forensic programs and that possibly greater deterrents to unethical practices might be devised-- as is done in the nonclassroom competitive life.

The American Bar Association governs practicing lawyers to the extent that attorneys found guilty of such practices are subject to disbarment. The American Medical Association acts as a similar deterrent on members of that profession, while business and education organizations govern the ethics of their members. If the problem is as serious as Professor Goodwin suggests (a position this writer is not ready to accept) then "self-policing" by forensic organizations would seem to be the answer rather than elimination of the selection of champions.

If we accept the basic educational, contextual premise that "forensics exists . . . to teach straight thinking and clear talking" to better train the student to meet the demands of the sociological environment in which he will exist following his formal education, then the arguments against championship competitive forensics, of which Professor Goodwin is one more spokesman, narrow themselves down to one of four categories involving the forensics coach and the administration of his respective institution: (1) the "sour grapes" approach, (2) lack of recognition of the practical educative goal of forensics, (3) a lack of willingness to meet the heavy demands which a broad educational as well as competitive program demands, or (4) a lack of administrative understanding and support of a total program.

Reprinted from The Forensic, 45:3, 6; January, 1960. Richard A. Hildreth is Assistant Professor of Speech at Kansas State Teachers College, Emporia, Kansas.

Issue S: Should a Strong National Organization Regulate Competitive Debate?

In "The Need for Standards," Thomas Mader recommends that the American Forensic Association become more selective and set high standards for schools conducting debate programs, for directors of debate, tournament debate judges, the use of ballots, and the running of tournaments. Under his plan schools and coaches who failed to meet these standards would be censured or excluded from officially sponsored A.F.A. events. In rejoinder, Bruce Markgraf, in "Standards and In-Service Training: A Reply to the Need for Standards," declares that, although he agrees that higher standards are needed, he disagrees "that they should be developed and enforced by a police state." His basic reason is, "I have always believed that standards which tend to emanate from within (supported by guidance from others) are more effective than those placed upon us by an outside organization which punishes us when we sin." His solution for improving the quality of "debate coaches who are not specifically trained in the debate field" is to develop "a national, systematic, and intensive in-service training program."

37. The Need for Standards
Thomas F. Mader

Despite the amount of criticism leveled at intercollegiate debate, it is obvious that this forensic activity is in a period of prosperity, if the increase in the number of colleges participating in debate is any criterion. Certainly many colleges are attracted to debate because of its prestige value, and many embryonic debaters are convinced, as a result of the recent national campaign, that anyone can be President if he is a Great Debater. My concern is not with the reasons why debate has become universally attractive, but rather with the opportunity afforded us to improve the total debate situation. We are faced with one crucial weakness. We lack stand-

287

ards, and therefore we lack genuine organization. Perhaps we need confidence in our own professional worth; we certainly need the imagination and initiative to undertake the necessary steps to equate quantitative prosperity with qualitative progress.

Concomitant with the establishment of standards, there must be a national agency responsible for enforcing these standards. The agency must have the power to certify and to censure, and its influence must be formidable.

But as long as debate associations seek members indiscriminately (certainly the ability to pay dues is no substantial criterion), then there is little chance that any association can undertake to wield a strong arm. The strength and prestige of an organization depend upon its exclusiveness, and an organization can exclude people only when it has standards.

I therefore suggest that the American Forensic Association, as a nationally recognized fraternity of debate coaches, undertake the following courses of action:

(1) The certifying of institutions that provide satisfactory working conditions for debate coaches. This would presume the previous determination of the number of hours that a debate coach should be required to teach, the amount of money he should receive for coaching, and the maximum number of debaters he should be expected to coach. There have been many interesting surveys taken to discover the different policies of numerous colleges, but to what avail? The fact that debate coaches teach from two hours a week to fifteen hours a week indicates extremes in administrative procedure and the lack of a standardized formula for compensation.

It is folly to presume that working conditions will change significantly when forensic organizations resign themselves to the whims of administrative policies. Granting that improved working conditions must to a large extent depend upon the persuasive pleadings of the overburdened coach, nevertheless there must be a substantial basis for persuasion. Administrators do make comparisons, and the fact that parallels and precedents can be found for unsatisfactory working conditions provides an argument for the status quo that often is unanswerable and final.

If standards for working conditions were established, could they be enforced? Yes; any college or university that did not adhere to these standards would be denied membership in the AFA until such time as specified requirements were met.

The AFA would also deny membership to individual coaches whose working conditions were substandard. Perhaps this denial seems harsh and unfair; it isn't. Common sense would dictate that a debate coach cannot be effective if he is faced with an impossible situation. Realizing, of course, that there are a few rare coaches capable of the "impossible," then I submit that any approval of their success stifles progress toward achieving improved working conditions. The obvious disadvantage of hurting a few people must be weighed against the probability of helping the majority.

(2) The certifying of debate coaches based on the coaches' knowledge of debate fundamentals. The fact that a college appoints a faculty member to direct debate activity is merely gratuitous sanctioning of the individual's ability to coach debaters and to judge intercollegiate contests. Too many competent and conscientious coaches have had their debaters exposed to the ignorance and inexperience of judges whose bases for decisions were at least questionable. I find it hard to be charitable when a judge gives a decision to a team that shows ingenuity in answering arguments in the last rebuttal. And I am more than impatient with those judges who think that an affirmative team is wasting time because it presents a solution to the problem under consideration. Moreover, I find it difficult to console a team that places first and second in speaker rankings when they lose to opponents who receive rankings of third and fourth. I confess that such weird judgments are rare, but exceptional stupidity should not be tolerated under any circumstances.

Once the standards for certification were established, then the regional organizations would be responsible for qualifying judges. Now I am not naive enough to contend that certification procedures would not be subject to the fallibility of human judgment; I am sure that mistakes would be made. But mistakes are unintentional; what is unforgivable is the lack of initiative in attempting to set professional requirements for an obviously specialized activity. Since col-

lege administrations do not always select debate coaches with the
loving care that they give to the appointment of athletic coaches,
some certifying agency must establish a control factor.

(3) The censuring of institutions that sponsor poorly organized
and poorly run tournaments. If "censure" seems strong, then I
suggest that the AFA give its seal of approval to worthwhile tournaments. Since I am a member of the "Have Budget, Will Travel"
fraternity, I am more than sensitive to wasting time in attending
some forensic fiasco. Of course, experience helps tremendously in
determining what tournaments to avoid, but I have noted at times
that the worth of some tournaments changes over the years. I
would suggest that every AFA-approved tournament satisfy these
minimum requirements:

a. All judges must be certified by the AFA.

b. The ballot form should have AFA approval. This is an
   oblique method to compel tournament sponsors to use one
   of the AFA ballot forms.

c. The determination of tournament winners must be uniform,
   or variations must be subject to AFA approval.

d. The tournament officials must submit results to the AFA.
   The following procedure is simply an example and therefore arbitrary: the top five units; the top five affirmative
   and negative teams; and the top five affirmative and negative debaters.

I would also have the tournament officials indicate the number
of colleges participating and the structure of the tournament, i.e.,
the number of rounds, matching system, etc. At the end of the
year, the AFA would publish tournament results in the Register.
Such publication would give effective recognition to successful teams
and would be of interest to AFA members.

(4) The censuring of institutions that display irresponsibility in
debate activity. The bases for such censure cover a wide area, so
I will cite only a few examples of debate delinquency:

a. Sending a team to a tournament without a judge or with an
   unqualified judge.

b. Sending a team that arrives late without reasonable excuse.

c. Not sending a team to a tournament when a commitment has
   been made, and when the reason for non-participation is not
   offered.

I think that it is unfair to tournament officials who make proper preparation for an efficient activity to suffer at the hands of in-
considerate guest teams. People who are indifferent to their responsibilities need a fairly good slap on the wrist.

These are the major recommendations I would offer. However, I would like to see policies adopted to exclude from AFA
membership obviously inactive colleges. I would also like to exclude coaches who never attend national or regional meetings, and
who show indifference in voting for officials of AFA. In short, I
would like to see a strong, effective national organization that merits
respect and confidence. Our policy should be not to please people,
but to impress them. We do not lack the method--I question whether we have the desire.

Reprinted from The American Forensic Association Register, 9:4-6,
Winter, 1961. Mr. Mader, formerly a debate coach at St. John's
University, now teaches at Hunter College, New York.

38. Standards and In-Service Training:
A Reply to The Need for Standards
Bruce Markgraf

Admittedly it was a frightening experience for me to read
Thomas Mader's article in the Winter, 1961, issue of The Register
in which he suggested the establishment of a Big Brother (our American Forensic Association) to provide for me in the critical years
to come. It was frightening because at first I was tempted to consider seriously his proposal of the Big Brother concept: a friend
in need who would impose his will upon our sovereign colleges, who
would certify me to be an acceptable Director of Debate if my standards of judging a debate were in agreement with his, and who would
be capable of censuring an institution of higher learning because it
was endeavoring to learn the mechanics of directing a debate tournament or because it was being somehow irresponsible concerning de-

bate activity.

I would be one of the first to advocate that we need higher
standards; that they should be developed and enforced by a policy
state seems to be a questionable proposal. I have always believed
that standards which tend to emanate from within (supported by
guidance from others) are more effective than those placed upon us
by an outside organization which punishes us when we sin.

Mader's first proposal is, "The certifying of institutions that
provide satisfactory working conditions for debate coaches." Unfortunately he does not define "satisfactory working conditions." I
would submit that debating would reach a slightly higher level if we
coaches had no teaching duties at all. Such a teaching load does
not seem imminent--but neither does a universal and uniform load.
Each school has its own administrative policies, practices, and
problems; I doubt seriously that any major alterations would be
made because of what the AFA might think is best for a debate
coach. Some schools might cherish the idea of instituting a modest
debate program for what might be considered educational reasons.
As the coach's working conditions would not be up to snuff, and as
the institution, quite respectable in most things, therefore would not
be certified by our organization, it might very readily discard the
whole program. I do not believe that this is what we want.

It would seem to me that it would be much more profitable
for the AFA and for debating in America if instead of censuring and
denying we welcomed and admitted. It is from this type of policy
that we can grow and that debate standards can rise. A small
school with modest debate activity and an untrained coach could
learn much from being affiliated with our national group. Our membership roster should be open to all. It is our task to help train
these coaches and schools once they are members, to provide them
with the benefits of our training and experience, and to stimulate
them to want to raise their own debate standards.

Mr. Mader's second proposal concerns the certifying of debate
coaches. Admittedly, debate coaches should be competent in their
field; if they are not (and often it is no fault of their own that they
are untrained) the AFA should be willing to provide them with in-

service educational programs. We desire higher standards; I am confident that we can develop these standards most effectively by working within our membership and by the in-service training of that membership, instead of by posing as a judge who denies admittance until an individual is qualified.

Mr. Mader then suggests censure of those institutions which sponsor poorly run tournaments or which display irresponsibility in debate. Again, a frightening proposal, again a proposal based upon the idea that standards are best developed when forced upon people from without, again a proposal which will tend to curb our organization's potential for instruction, and consequently, the formulation of more rigid debate standards.

A national, systematic, and intensive in-service training program should be developed for debate coaches who are not specifically trained in the debate field, and even for those who are. Such a program, the details of which I cannot discuss here, will provide us with a positive power for attaining the high standards which concern Mr. Mader and, indeed, which concern all of us.

Reprinted from the American Forensic Association Register, 9:28-29, Spring, 1961. Dr. Markgraf is an Assistant Professor of Speech at Wesleyan University.

In "A Second Reply to The Need for Standards" (AFAR, 9:29-30, Spring, 1961), Malthon M. Anapol wrote briefly:

In regard to Mader's article: I cannot agree to the universal use of the AFA ballot. We happen to have a ballot here which we like better and I am sure that many other people have ballots which they prefer.

The major problem is in the area of qualified judges. Here the AFA can do a great deal. It could develop an objective test of debate judging principles and require a certain grade on the exam in order to be certified as a qualified judge. The examination procedure could also include a tape-recorded debate which the prospective

judge would have to vote upon and for which he might be required
to write a critique. Working from this certification by examination
system, major tournaments might require a certified judge as a
condition of entry. I do not think that any other program could do
as much as such a procedure to improve the judging of debate.

Suggestions for Further Reading

Bilski, T. "Directing the Debate Program," Teachers College
    Journal, 34:95-99, December, 1962.
Bradley, Bert E., Jr. "Debate--A Practical Training for Gifted
    Students," Speech Teacher, 8:134-138, March, 1959.
Buehler, E.C. "What Should Be the Philosophy and Objective of a
    Debate Program?" Gavel, 39:31-34, January, 1957.
Cripe, Nicholas. "A Survey of Debate Programs in Two Hundred
    and Forty-Six American Colleges and Universities," Speech
    Teacher, 8:157-160, March, 1959.
Edney, Clarence W. "Forensic Activities; Strengths and Weakness-
    es," Southern Speech Journal, 19:2-13, September, 1953.
Ehninger, Douglas, "Six Earmarks of a Sound Forensic Program,"
    Speech Teacher, 1:237-241, November, 1952.
Harkness, P.J. "Comment [on Betz's article]," Debaters Magazine,
    2:148, 174; September, 1946.
Kruger, Arthur N. "Teaching and Coaching," Sec. XIII, A Classi-
    fied Bibliography of Argumentation and Debate. Metuchen,
    N.J., Scarecrow Press, 1964, pp. 195-202.
_____. "The Debate Program," Sec. XIV, op. cit., pp. 203-
    229.
Mader, Thomas, "Reply to Markgraf," American Forensic Assn.
    Register, 9:16-17, Convention Issue, 1961.
Merrill, Barbara. "Comment by a Student" (on Betz's article),
    Debater's Magazine, 2:221-222, December, 1946.
Murphy, Roy D. "Comment on Foregoing [Betz's] Article," De-
    baters Magazine, 2:148-150, September, 1946.
Osborn, Michael M. "A Blueprint for Diversity in Forensic Pro-
    grams," Speech Teacher, 14:110-115, March, 1965.
Pinkerton, Herman. "Comments on the Betz Article," Debaters
    Magazine, 2:179-180, September, 1946.
Reid, Ronald F. "What It Takes to Build a Good Forensic Program:
    The Urban University," Gavel, 4:7-8, November, 1958.
Samovar, Larry A. "A Second Attempt at a Philosophy for an Ex-
    tracurricular Forensic Program," AFA Register, 8:15-20,
    Winter, 1960.
Smith, Robert L. "Bestness Re-Visited," Forensic, 45:3-5, May,
    1960.
Thornton, Helen G. "Improving the Forensics Program: The Stu-
    dents Speak," Southern Speech Journal, 21:133-137, Winter,
    1955.

Walsh, Grace. "Nine Steps to a Good Forensic Program," <u>Central States Speech Journal</u>, 9:35-37, Spring, 1958.
Windes, Russel, Jr. "Competitive Debating: The Speech Program, the Individual, and Society," <u>Speech Teacher</u>, 9:99-108, March, 1960.

X. Forms of Debate

Issue T: Is the British Style of Debating Superior to the American?

Each year, for the past eighteen years or so, a team
representing Oxford, Cambridge, or occasionally some
other British university tours the United States and debates at various colleges, [1] usually before large audiences. Unlike their American counterparts, the British
are very informal, joke a great deal, and do not rely
on files of evidence. They seem to be more interested
in enjoying themselves while developing certain platform
skills. Their appeals are generally more emotional than
logical, and the audience usually delights in their antics.
As Jonathan Aitken and Michael Beloff, members of the
Oxford team that toured the United States in 1964, sum
up the British approach: "Faced with time trouble and
given the choice between throwing a point or a joke overboard, the British debater would always sacrifice the
point. "[2]

When the 1949 British team, consisting of four Cambridge University debaters, toured here, the editor of
the Quarterly Journal of Speech invited their leader,
Denzil K. Freeth, "to submit the team's impressions of
American debating. " The result was the article "American Versus British Debating: A British Impression" by
Freeth and Percy Cradock. Since the authors had invited a reply, the editor of the Journal solicited some
American debate coaches and intercollegiate debaters for
their views. As a result, "Some American Replies, "
written by several directors of debate, appeared in the
same issue, and two more selections, "Rebuttal Notes
on British and American Debating, " written by former
American intercollegiate debaters who had since become
well known, and "Replies from American Debaters, "
written by students who had opposed the Cambridge team,
appeared in the next issue. The articles which appear
here, by P. E. Lull and Harry B. Stults, were chosen
as being the most representative replies to the British
point of view.

1. The team is sponsored by the Speech Association of America, and, to defray expenses, schools that wish to de-

bate the British team must pay a fee.
2. A Short Walk on the Campus. New York, Atheneum,
   1966.

39. American Versus British Debating: A British Impression
    Denzil K. Freeth and Percy Cradock

For five weeks last spring four undergraduates of Cambridge
University, England, representing the Cambridge Union Society,
toured American universities and colleges. One team of two, Percy
Cradock and Duncan Macrae, went westwards from New York to
Colorado, and the other, comprising George Pattison and Denzil
Freeth, kept to the eastern states from Vermont to Florida. In all,
the teams debated thirty-eight times, at some places as a team and
at others split, each Cambridge undergraduate having an American
as a partner. Thus a fairly comprehensive view of American debating was obtained, and at the invitation of the Editor of The Quarterly Journal of Speech we have recorded our impressions.

1

The American style of debating is completely different from
ours. The British method is modelled on that of the House of Com-
mons, whence it draws its procedure and technique, and of which
the Union Societies of Cambridge and Oxford have long been considered training grounds. It is political and oratorical. It accentuates
audience appeal. The British debater, at home, is surrounded by
his audience, who consider themselves a vital and equally important
part of the debate, cheering, interrupting, barracking, asking questions. He learns how to put himself in touch with the audience and
evoke in it an immediate response. He becomes an orator, a politician, a leader, and, if a lawyer, one whose most sympathetic atmosphere is that of the criminal court, with its strange mixture of
fact and fiction cunningly compounded to sway the jury. To us, the
American debater, on the other hand, seems desirous of training
himself as a junior business executive who wishes to give to his
senior a severely factual, eminently statistical report on a given

situation, recommending a particular course of action. And thus
the audience becomes superfluous, ignored, unwanted, and departs,
alas, unmourned. Debating becomes a mental exercise for research
students, an arid game of intellectual mathematicians, cold, hard,
devoid of all emotions, a fitting forcing house for company lawyers
or departmental civil servants.

2

With that great courtesy which is so typical of Americans at
home, our hosts often tried to adopt the English style. A few jokes
were introduced into their arguments, the audiences were not merely
tolerated but even appealed to, and having come to see the mad
English, discovered with surprise, as one student put it to us, that
debates can be fun. But it must be admitted that this attempt to do
the English style was not often successful. One noticed an inability
to grip an audience and win its sympathy, a lack of oratorical and
rhetorical technique, an ignorance of how to insert humor into the
very web and woof of a speech, except by extraneous funny stories
which often impeded the flow of the argument, bringing one up short
as against a brick wall. Above all, our American friends appeared
to have no real feeling for words as living things or for their natural or emotive associations; words seemed to be regarded merely
as mathematical symbols or handy labels with which to avoid deeper, rational analysis. Perhaps it might all be summed up as a
lack of flexibility, too great a sense of logical argument and formal
speech structure, impeding a conversational style without stiffness,
humor that is genuinely unprepared, naturally witty rebuttals. To
us a 'canned rebuttal' is a sin against the very name 'debate.' An
excellent antidote for this we found in the Michigan cross-examination system, although five minutes is far too short a time to develop
an idea.

3

To be frank--and this article is frank, since among friends it
is natural and little else is much use--we see the cause of these
defects, as they appear to us, in two American institutions: the de-

bate tournament and the debate coach.

Historically, we are told, the one has brought the other. Once, we hear, there was a Golden Age, when Americans debated for the fun of it, joyous, lively, bacchic stuff, not in order to win as a team by integrated case-presentation, but for the delights of argument, of swaying and convincing an audience, of making a speech. Tournaments have dragged debating down, professionalised it, stereotyped it, turned it into an annexe of the faculty and examination syllabus. Debate coaches, faculty men, appeared to direct all debating energies, to turn debating into a speaking contest, to shear it of all but argumentative essentials so that debating victories might figure on the prospectus with scholastic successes; and the audience left unsung, and interest in debating flagged, and the careless rapture and heady joys of oratory fled. For, though as a critic he is useful, the debate coach is really superfluous, teaching in oratory what good speakers know instinctively and what bad ones will never learn, and otherwise things that should be taught in composition classes, or learned from experience by contact with other debaters and an audience alive. Semantics and phonetics are of far less use to debaters than a study of the great orators of the world. Demosthenes, Burke, Lincoln, Roosevelt, Churchill can teach far more in a week than debate coaches in a year.

4

Our message is: 'Set American debating free!' You will reduce your average level of efficiency, admittedly, but your giants will be greater far.

This article is avowedly polemical. We hope it will be roundly refuted by Americans believing their standard to be higher than ours. We hope to welcome American teams in Britain, who will prove that it is.

Free speech is the great inheritance of the English-speaking peoples; it is an inheritance of which we must prove ourselves fit.

Reprinted from the Quarterly Journal of Speech, 35:427-429, December, 1949.

40. Some American Replies
I. P. E. Lull

Considering the shortness of their visit, Messrs. Freeth and Cradock have exhibited keen powers of observation in spotting some of the major faults of American debating. If they had actually inspected a few of our tournaments they might have had cause for even greater dismay! But their recorded 'impressions' of our debating hardly constitute a fair appraisal for there is no acknowledgment of any of our positive qualities. Not all of our debating is done in tournaments, but in some of our tournaments, changes are taking place. For example, at the National Forensic Conference held at Purdue University, and at the next West Point Invitational Tournament, most of the debates will be held before student class audiences. Outside the tournaments, our British visitors might have noted the breadth and depth of preparation that is characteristic of most of our debaters, the thoroughness of their analyses, the consistency and coherence of their arguments, and their persistent zeal to find the facts in the case.

I'm not sure that our critics are correct when they state that the American and British styles are completely different! Although no one can deny that all of the faults that were mentioned do exist, not all of our American debaters are guilty of these practices. Some of our student speakers can discriminate between evidence that is valid and that which is not; many can use reasoning effectively, and do a pretty good job of convincing an audience (when they have an audience). On the other hand, I have heard British debaters who made occasional use of factual material, and even went so far sometimes as to present cases that had a semblance of logical arrangement! The truth may be that each class of debaters does some things better than the other and that both the British and the American debaters can profit by these opportunities to observe the other fellow's way of getting the job done.

But, the implication that we could 'set American debating free' from its faults by going over to the British system doesn't make sense. Debating, as the Cambridge gentlemen describe (and practice) it, is pretty frothy stuff. Speaking in the Cambridge manner, 'Fun for all and all for fun' may deserve a place on the program, but it shouldn't become the whole show. With 'its strange mixture of fact and fiction cunningly compounded' to 'evoke an immediate response' from an audience, it may well be 'joyous, lively, bacchic stuff' for the participant, and highly entertaining for the audience, but it falls far short of the solid values of training and experience that debating can provide. I like circuses, and I enjoy hearing British teams 'debate.' Both of these types of performances are entertaining. Furthermore, I hope we can continue to schedule at least one debate each year with a British team. But a good forensic diet needs variety and something substantial for the main course. The 'careless rapture and heady joys of oratory' won't sustain life for very long!

Again, it seems to me that our British critics have been too harsh on the Debate Coach, when they label the 'coach' as one of the major causes for the conditions that they found. It may be true that some coaches get over-anxious in their desire to produce 'winning teams.' But the rank and file of our coaches are good teachers, trying to inculcate in their student debaters concepts of straight thinking and effective speaking that will serve them well in their later lives. I see no more necessity for a Debate Coach, than for a Good Teacher in any academic subject area. It cannot be denied that some students, given access to a good library and opportunities for experience, might become 'self-made' persuaders, without payment of any tuition fee. But the same could be said of writers, historians, engineers, lawyers, and business men. Furthermore, I understand that at Cambridge and Oxford, there are very extensive tutorial systems, with Dons advising and counselling students on all phases of their activities. Messrs. Freeth and Cradock should realize that although we go about our teaching job a little differently in America, the basic principles are essentially the same.

Good teaching should be an essential part of debating activities in England and in America. Good debate teachers are aware of the great potential values of debating, not only as training for future

Congressional and Parliamentary debaters, but also as preparation
for the less formal, but no less important, speaking in the world
of business, industry, and the professions, and in the multitudinous
activities of community life. Such teachers can do much, on both
sides of the Atlantic, to rid debating of its faults, to develop a kind
of speaking that is effective, not only as far as the immediate results are concerned, but also aims at producing impressions and
convictions that will endure. Finally, Good Debate Teachers, shun-
ning 'argument for the sake of argument,' will seek constantly to
develop in their students, British and American, a realization that
Freedom of Speech carries with it responsibility for that which is
spoken! and that to fulfill these responsibilities, men must first
know whereof they speak--the speaking techniques come afterward.

Reprinted from the Quarterly Journal of Speech, 35:429-434, December, 1949. At the time this article was published, P. E. Lull was
teaching at Purdue University.

II. Harry B. Stults

The American style of debating is decidedly different from the
British style. Here, at least we may both agree. No American
debater who has faced, no spectator who has observed a performance by the 'mad British,' has any doubt that the Union Societies
accentuate audience appeal. In comparison, the American debater
appears as a candidate for a position of 'junior business executive.'
Trained in the methods of research and problem-solving analysis,
he is prepared to offer rational arguments for a carefully weighed
course of action. To be sure, the American debater urges the adoption of his particular course of action, but he also respects the considered judgment of his board of directors, whose privilege and desire is to adopt the best of all alternatives. In this sense, the
British debater is not so confident of the audience. He approaches
it more like a politician 'whose most sympathetic atmosphere is that
of the criminal court, with its strange mixture of fact and fiction

cunningly compounded to sway the jury.' With such a contrast, one frequently hears this typical comment about an Anglo-American clash: 'well, judging by British methods, they were superior; by American methods, we were superior.' Consequently, wisdom would suggest that we may well learn from each other.

If the debaters we have met are typical products of British debating, we would offer the following considerations:

1. You are distinguished for your excellent rhetoric and superb diction. Continue to orate for the amusement and to the amazement of your audiences.

2. The use of argumentum ad hominem against your opponent rather than against his argument may appear as spontaneous wit to the British audience. The American audience resents it as impolite, though clever, sarcasm. Control your humor.

3. The success of the democratic process depends in a large measure upon an enlightened and rational citizenry. Respect its capacity to judge the issue fairly when all the facts are presented. Raise the level of debate above a cunningly compounded mixture of fact and fiction. Give more facts! Let the people think!

For American debaters we would offer the following considerations:

1. Accept the sincerity of the British recommendations and turn the spirit of their suggestions to future advantage.

2. To do this we should not abolish the two institutions blamed for American 'defects'--the debate tournament and the debate coach. Indeed, that would be retrogression, for the debate tournament and coach have made an outstanding contribution to democracy. The British would have us return to the good old days of bacchic, heady oratory served to intoxicate the audience. Those were the days when a small, select aristocracy of debaters prepared all year for one or two popular public appearances. Today, the naturally gifted still rise to the top as leaders in debates and in civic affairs. But with what a difference! All students have an opportunity for the training necessary to achieve their individual peak of development in research, problem-solving analysis and platform delivery. The average debater could discredit many of the giants who swayed the

emotions of the audiences of yesterday. The debate tournament and
coach have helped make possible a more enlightened and articulate
participation in and leadership of today's electorate. The good ol'
days were not so good!

3. Yet today is not so good that tomorrow need not be made
better. Too often our debating has victory in a tournament as its
goal. Continuous speaking to four blank walls and a judge is not
adequate training for public speaking. The tournament should be
used as a means of testing logic and preparation. The real test of
delivery should be to an actual audience presentation.

To establish intimate and sympathetic contact with the audience,
to utilize the naturally humorous situation, to present what has been
prepared rationally and tested formally in a tournament--to do all
this with the flexibility of a showman requires repeated experiences
with audiences. Thus we need to increase the outreach of the
school and college debate work to their respective civic communities.
The increased use of speakers' bureaus and program services could
play a major role here for the convenience of the community and
for the enrichment of the speaker. The use of varied styles of debates, such as cross-examination and audience-participation, would
add interest. Our excellent training needs to be directed toward its
use before 'live' audiences.

With more experience before audiences, American teams will
be eminently prepared to accept the British invitation to prove that
American standards are fundamentally superior.

At the time of writing, the author was a student at the College of
Wooster.

Suggestions for Further Reading

Aitken, Jonathan, and Beloff, Michael. A Short Walk on the Campus.
    New York, Atheneum, 1966.
"American Debating Evaluated," Gavel, 32:78, 84; May, 1950.
Baird, Albert C. "Shall American Universities Adopt the British
    System of Debating?" Quarterly Journal of Speech, 9:215-222,

June, 1923.

Benn, Anthony W. , Edward Boyle, and Kenneth Harris. "American and British Debating, " Quarterly Journal of Speech, 34:469-72, December, 1948.

Dunn, Edward P. , and Norman J. Temple. "British Students Take Debating Seriously, " Gavel, 29:26-27, January, 1947.

Howes, Raymond F. "American and English Debating, " Quarterly Journal of Speech, 11:45-48, February, 1925.

Hunt, E. L. "English Debating Reconsidered, " Quarterly Journal of Speech, 21:98-102, February, 1925.

"Is the English Debate System Superior to That of the United States?" Forensic, 14:122, October, 1928.

Kruger, Arthur N. "Forms of Debate: British Debate, " A Classified Bibliography of Argumentation and Debate. Metuchen, N.J. , Scarecrow Press, 1964, pp. 273-276.

Norton, Aloysius. "Why We Lost (and Why We Will Probably Go On Losing), " AFA Register, 9:26-27, Spring, 1961.

Quimby, Brooks. "Can We Learn from Debating with the British?" Quarterly Journal of Speech, 33:159-161, April, 1947.

Radcliffe, Charles W. "Let's Adopt British-Style Debating, " Gavel, 34:30-31, January, 1952.

"Rebuttal Notes on British and American Debating, " Quarterly Journal of Speech, 36:10-15, February, 1950.

"Replies from American Debaters, " Quarterly Journal of Speech, 36:15-22, February, 1950.

"Some American Replies, " Quarterly Journal of Speech, 35:427-434, December, 1949.

Issue U: <u>Does Cross-Examination Debating Meet Academic Debate</u>
<u>Objectives Better Than Orthodox-Style Debating?</u>

Since this issue involves the objectives of academic debate and the role of the audience, it is related to the
previous one. Dissatisfied with the orthodox style of debate, particularly as practiced in tournaments, the proponents of cross-examination debating argue that it promotes better speaking habits and more awareness of the
audience. They also believe that the direct clash which
occurs in the cross-questioning periods is more interesting to an audience than complete speeches. The opponents of this type of debating usually argue that it is too
difficult for the student to master, that debaters are not
being trained to be public entertainers, and that the direct clashes encourage rudeness and other anti-social
attitudes.

Although the following two articles did not initially appear as a debate--in fact, the negative case appeared
twenty-five years before the affirmative--they are coup-
led here because of their opposing points of view. In
recommending that college coaches "talk up cross-examination debating" and "try using this form . . . every
fourth year for the entire year," Dwight L. Freshley, in
the article "A Case for More Cross-Examination Debating," argues that the cross-examination technique results
in advantages to the speaker, the content of the speech,
the audience, and the occasion. C.E. Grady, on the
other hand, in "Debate Must Be Realistic," defends "the
dynamic style of speech" and objects to cross-examination debate because it discourages students from entering
debate, enables "a strong affirmative speaker to win a
debate with but little help from his colleague," leads to
evasions, and is not realistic.

41. A Case for More Cross-Examination Debating
Dwight L. Freshley

When the adult American thinks of debating, he summons
schoolday memories of Webster-Hayne, Lincoln-Douglas, or Bryan-

Darrow, and at least imagines the confrontations as featuring exciting cross-examination lines of attack in a crowded hall with ardent
supporters roaring their approval.   Compare this with the image
which many conjure up of the typical academic debate: a bare classroom with a lonely sextet comprised of four hardware-hungry debaters, a sleepy judge, and disgruntled timekeeper.

To be sure the comparison is overdrawn, for all of us have
heard cross-examination debates which were less laudable than some
expertly-wrought battles in the orthodox style.   But the picture does
suggest the direction of this paper.

In 1926, Stanley Gray introduced his Oregon plan of debating
and, with variations, it has been increasing in popularity.   With the
adoption by the National Forensic League in 1952, cross-examination
ceased to be a stepchild of the debating family and is becoming a
favorite offspring.   The popularity around the Pittsburgh area, for
example, was noted in the report by Fuge and Newman in 1956.[1]
The University of Pittsburgh Cross-Exam Tournament continues to
be a season highlight for many teams.

Though the foregoing demonstrates considerable interest in
cross-examination debate, the author would like to see much more
debating of this style on the collegiate level.   Toward this end,
after a short analysis of the status quo and a delineation of advantages versus disadvantages of the cross-exam format, a suggestion
will be made for adopting this format in more collegiate debates.

The number of cross-examination tournaments has been increasing over the years but, according to Klopf's study based on the
1962-1963 season, still only eight percent employ this format exclusively, while four percent use a combination orthodox and cross-
exam, and five percent feature other styles.[2]   Related to this, a
study by the author in 1960 indicated that 58 percent of 108 respondents from 33 states thought that we should provide different types of
tournaments or different types of debates in the tournaments.[3]   This
would seem to indicate a desire for change.

In considering the advantages of the cross-examination technique, let us relate them to the four constituents of the public speech,
namely, the speaker, the speech, the audience, and occasion.   An

initial benefit to the speaker is the improvement of thinking on his
feet, with concomitant fluency.   This cannot be accomplished by
memorized speeches.   Modern debate judges are not new in their
rejection of canned passages.   In referring to this practice, Quintilian asked, ". . . how [do] such men find appropriate arguments
in the course of actual cases which continually present new and different features?   How can they answer the points that their opponents may bring up?   How deal a rapid counter-stroke in debate or
cross-examine a witness. "[4]   Though it would be ideal perhaps if
this skill were learned at home, few domestic environments are
comparable to the Reuther or Wilson homes, for example.   The
father of Walter and Victor Reuther used the Sunday mealtime for
an analysis of the sermon heard that day, with plenty of opportunity
for each son to state his point of view and to be questioned by the
other.   In trying to effect good communication habits, Woodrow Wilson's father would not permit his son to blurt out any answer but
would say, "Steady, now, Thomas.   Wait a minute.   Think.   Think
what it is you wish to say. "[5]

Another benefit which accrues to the speaker is the training
in the use of tact.   One learns how to indict ignorance or stupidity
without insult while concentrating on facts and not the person; he
learns the art of pummeling the opposition with a velvet glove.

Finally, since a premium is paid for the quick wit in the cut
and thrust of cross-exam, a debater sharpens his skill in this area.
For example, a University of Georgia debater was put to the test in
a debate with the delightful Irish debaters recently.   He observed
that his opponent had been on the rowing team and that perhaps that
accounted for his case being "all wet. "   To which the Irishman re-
torted from his seat, "Please dry up. "   Unruffled, the home team
advocate rejoined, "But you're the one who was in the water. "

The second and perhaps most important area which is improved in cross-exam is the content of the speech itself.   First of
all, facts are clarified more quickly.   The orthodox style forces the
ten or five-minute wait before clarification takes place.   For instance, in a debate on Federal aid to education heard this past season, the first negative's point on the family's ability to pay was

never clear as to whether it was based on the median income for
all families or only those who were qualified for college. Cross-
exam could have clarified this immediately. Furthermore, issues
are discovered more quickly. This avowed purpose of analysis can
be realized with more assurance when the opposition's misunder-
standings are clarified, insufficient evidence is disclosed, and un-
substantiated claims are unmasked. Another advantage to the speech
is that the amount and use of evidence are improved, since questioning forces the debater to plumb the depths of research. It does-
n't take many "Are you aware that the NDEA Act in Section 4A
states that . . . " to send the unwary scurrying for another fistful
of evidence. Finally, cross-exam bares subterfuge and uncovers
strategy (while, of course, exercising a bit of strategy of its own)
and elicits frankness. Longinus recognized very early that "people who are cross-questioned by others in the heat of the moment
reply forcibly and with utter candour."[6]

The third area in the cycle of communication affected benefi-
cially by cross-exam is the audience. There can be little doubt
about the potential of this format to engage and sustain audience attention. The reasons are quite obvious. The element of conflict is
heightened for the protagonist in carrying his cause directly to his
opposition. There is drama here but it can be more exciting than
the stage variety. In the theatre, the playwright has already decided the ending. Here one is aware that the issues are being un-
folded before you and, though less scintillating verbally, this medium nonetheless conveys a realism unmatched beyond the proscenium
arch. Let me inject a word of warning here. We have a problem
similar to that of our drama colleagues, to wit, the temptation to
sell some slick, glamorous ware in the market place. The possibility of "putting on a show," of drawing big crowds, of getting lots
of laughs, or gaining favorable publicity, etc., beckons enticingly at
times. But we must recognize that our basic purpose is to train,
not entertain; to educate the masses, not merely to titillate the
senses.

The fourth and final component in the speech process that can
gain advantage from the cross-exam technique is the occasion. This

has already been implied in the discussion of the effect on the audience, that is, cross questioning is more adaptable to audience debating. The "Great Debate" series at several universities and colleges, which attracts top debating schools in the country plus the
debaters from the United Kingdom to various campuses, lends itself
to this vivid verbal exchange. The increasing popularity of television debating both academically and politically has demonstrated
how adaptable the format is to this medium and has heightened the
need for more experienced practitioners in the art of cross-examination. Finally, used in demonstration debates before junior bar
associations, this type of debating can do much to attract pre-law
students and to provide a valuable training ground for them when
they start their professional debating careers.

The weight of the foregoing tips the scales heavily to the side

Having demonstrated some of the advantages of cross-examination debate, it behooves us to note also the shortcomings, for there
should be no pretense here that the format alone is the touchstone
to intelligent, effective, and responsible debating. The chief faults
with regard to the effect on the speaker are that the format may encourage the ad hominen appeal, that it may tend to emphasize strategy for its own sake rather than for discovering the issues, and
that it can project unsatisfactory models onto the scene, e. g., the
Perry Mason syndrome. On this last point, a judge's pointed critique from a cross-exam tournament ballot is relevant: "John, this
is not a grade B movie. "

The deleterious effects on the speech can also be seen. Poorly executed, cross-exam does not advance the case, it merely muddles it, since, without a purposeful pattern, the debate is harder to
follow. Also, using irrelevant and unimportant questions bogs down
the debate and allows precious questioning time to evaporate. Most
of these disadvantages to speaker and speech can be subsumed under
poor training.

The weight of the foregoing tips the scales heavily to the side
of advantages for cross-examination format. There are, of course,
more points on both sides and each reader analyzing the arguments
would perhaps stress different ones. I believe, however, we might
agree that, if properly taught, cross-examination is superior to the

orthodox system. It has most all the advantages of the present system plus the ones noted above.

  With the desire for a change expressed by a majority of
coaches and the benefits attending the cross-exam style which are
outlined above, it would seem worthwhile for the American Forensic
Association to recommend to its collegiate members that they try
using this form of debating every fourth year for the entire year.
This schedule would provide each generation of debaters one solid
year of participation in this style of debate.   Not just the chosen
few would gain the opportunity to try this "variation on the theme."
With many more cross-exam tournaments from which to choose, the
entire squad could receive its baptism of verbal cross-fire.   Further, the excitable temperament, easily provoked in conflict, could
find new control under repeated exposure; the canned question, hastily contrived on the way to the tournament, could become a welcome
casualty; the forensic director who has eschewed this format for
lack of experience would find considerable company at initial tournaments and would find no better training laboratory for himself; and
since so little has been done in research on comparative advantages
of the variety of time formats of the cross-exam style, here would
be fertile ground for seeking answers.

  The National Forensic League has led the way in high schools.
Still, there are many high school--and some college coaches--who
fear their students cannot handle this approach.   Let me suggest
that whether in high school or college, we should not talk down to
our students but should talk up cross-examination debating.

Reprinted from the Journal of the American Forensic Association,
2:21-24, January, 1965.   Dwight L. Freshley is Associate Professor
of Speech at the University of Georgia, Athens, Georgia.   This article is based on a paper read at the Southern Speech Association
Convention, Houston, Texas, April, 1964.

Notes

1. Lloyd H. Fuge and Robert P. Newman, "Cross-Examination in
    Academic Debating," Speech Teacher, 5:66-70, January,
    1956.
2. Donald W. Klopf, "Practice in Intercollegiate Speech Tourna-
    ment," The Journal of The American Forensic Association,
    1:50, May, 1954.
3. "Tournament Debating During a Factfinding Truce," The Regis-
    ter, 8:15-17, Winter, 1960.
4. Institutio Oratoria ii. 4. 28, trans. H. E. Butler, New York,
    1921.
5. Dayton D. McKean, "Woodrow Wilson," History and Criticism
    of American Public Address, ed. William N. Brigance.
    New York, 1943, II, p. 969.
6. On the Sublime xviii. 2, trans. W. Hamilton Fyfe, London,
    1953.

42. Debate Must Be Realistic!
C. E. Grady

For some time, many leaders have advocated changes in debate procedures. This paper seeks to defend the present method
used in the Mid and Far West. We favor the present plan, for it
is the method used in everyday life.

Not many weeks ago, I heard a United States Senator representing New England literally tear into our President's policy of handling the gold. That part of his speech certainly was not of the conversational style. He struck a telling blow at our system of buying
gold. It was a forceful, dynamic speech of the Webster type. I
was much surprised, for I had been informed that New England orators never "got het up." He hit blow after blow, but never below
the belt. The audience applauded generously. This is the system
we use in debate--the New Hampshire style--and it worked with a
Colorado audience.

I recently heard a radio address by a Republican Congressman
from Pennsylvania. He bitterly attacked the Reciprocal Trade
Treaties. He spared no words in denouncing Mr. Hull's trade agreements. He went after his man and apologized for nothing. In fact,
he was looking for a political fight. Out in the West we would be
delighted to accommodate him. We like this in debate. Don't you?

One more illustration, if you please. We who heard the Congressman at Terre Haute last spring, vividly recall his forceful, dynamic speech. Had he used the mild conversational style as advocated by many of our forensic leaders, you and I would have forgotten that address long ago.

It is indeed interesting to note the changes that come over the college professor when he enters the political arena. His old classroom methods will not work and he changes to meet the requirements of actual life. The method of appealing to the masses is the same everywhere, and this is our field. The dry dull speaker, whether he be a college professor, a preacher in the pulpit or a candidate for office, should no longer be tolerated.

Cross Examination

I do not care to answer all the arguments used against our method of debate, but I would like to tell you why I oppose the question and answer method used at our National Tournament. First I believe this method will prevent the timid little girl from entering these contests. Many of these could and would succeed if they could only get started. Today I look back over my life and note the good timber I let go by. More good timber will pass if this question method is continued, is my firm belief.

Again, I oppose the new method for I believe that it is possible for a strong affirmative speaker to win a debate with but little help from his colleague.

Let's see how this works. Teach the first speaker to deliver a well prepared address on the subject under discussion, setting forth all the arguments for the affirmative. Follow this with a method of evading the questions, frequently saying, "My colleague will take this up in his speech." Then let the second speaker write all the questions to be asked and all will be well for the affirmative. For the second affirmative speaker can do all the rest of the work! A team should be made up of two speakers, not one and a half! We saw this in operation at Terre Haute.

This is not all. I believe the question and answer system will lead to wrong methods. I watched the skillful way of evading an-

swers, the tricks used to trap the speaker or catch him off guard.
This is not all bad but it falls short of what I wish in debate.   I
oppose anything but straightforward debating.   Our arguments must
stand the attacks of the opposing team and everything must be above
the table all the time.

We attempt a solution of the question under discussion.   We
not only attempt a solution on the affirmative, but we present a case
on the negative.   And when the negative puts up a case, the present
NFL cross-examination debate rules leave the affirmative at a disadvantage.   For there is only one five-minute rebuttal on each side.
After the affirmative speakers have completed their main argument,
the negative has a complete ten-minute speech time, and a five-
minute rebuttal time, to which the affirmative has only a single five
minutes in which to reply.   The negative may leave all their strong
constructive arguments until the second speech.   In this case, the
affirmative must rebuild its own case, answer the blows dealt by
the negative, and refute the case as presented by the negative.   This
cannot be done in five minutes.

I am not through with my opposition to the Oregon plan of debate.   The pastor in the pulpit, the lawyer before the jury, and the
orator in a campaign seldom, if ever, meet the question method.
This is practiced only in legislative halls.   In class discussions, we
use the question method in our work.   The time for research is
over when the minister enters the pulpit.   The question method
denies the one half of the team the very best part of the debate--
that portion of the discussion that tests the debater's wit, wisdom
and ability, the rebuttal speech.   This is the climax, and must not
be destroyed.   For all these reasons, I strongly condemn the new
method in debate.   Go to life and use the way laid down by society.

Reprinted from Platform News, 7:18-19, October, 1940.   C.E.
Grady, who was known as "Pop," was a well-known high school debate coach, whose teams twice won the National Championship, in
1937 and 1939.

Suggestions for Further Reading

Beard, Raymond S. "A Comparison of Classical Dialectic, Legal
    Cross-Examination, and Cross-Question Debate," Journal of
    the American Forensic Association, 3:53-58, May, 1966.
Fuge, Lloyd H., and Robert P. Newman. "Cross-Examination in
    Academic Debating," Bulletin of the Debating Association of
    Pennsylvania Colleges, 21:9-15, December, 1955; Speech
    Teacher, 5:66-70, January, 1956.
Hance, Kenneth. "The Dialectical Method in Debate," Quarterly
    Journal of Speech, 25:243-48, April, 1939.
Jacob, Bruno L. "Why N.F.L. Will Retain Cross-Examination
    Style," Platform News, 7:12, 14; December, 1940.
Kruger, Arthur N. "Forms of Debate: Cross-Examination," Sec.
    XVII, A Classified Bibliography of Argumentation and Debate.
    Metuchen, N.J., Scarecrow Press, 1964, pp. 270-273.
Palzer, Edward. "Let's Examine 'Cross-Examination' . . .,"
    Gavel, 24:33-35, January, 1942.
Robie, Fred S. "Cross-Examination Achieves Debate Objectives
    Best," Bulletin of the Debating Association of Pennsylvania
    Colleges, 15:22-26, December 10, 1948.

Issue V: Are Decisionless Debates with the Open Forum Preferable
to Judged Debates?

Before the growth of tournaments, when intercollegiate
debating was usually done on a "home-and-home" basis
before local audiences and with hired judges (usually
three), the issue of whether debates should be judged
was a lively one. Much was written about the decisionless debate with the open forum as a substitute for
judged debates. In 1921, the Quarterly Journal of Speech
Education sent a questionnaire to many well-known directors of debate, asking them to respond to nine questions
concerning the decisionless debate with a half-hour's
open forum. Some of the questions were:

> Does the debate lose any interest for the audience?
> Is anything of value lost in not having a decision?
> Are there noticeable changes in the manner of
>   speaking and presenting material?
> Is this kind of discussion more in line with what
>   young men will encounter in afterlife, especially
>   outside of the courtroom?

The answers received to this questionnaire, though on
the whole favorable to the decisionless debate with the
open forum, expressed a "wait-and-see" attitude because
of the limited number of such debates which had been
held. Most of the respondents agreed that the preparation for such debates did not suffer, that the delivery
was pretty much the same, except during the forum period when it was more informal, that the audience as well
as the debaters seemed to enjoy the forum period, that
the program was more typical of a real-life situation,
but that the debaters preferred to have decisions and the
taste of victory over rival institutions.

The articles appearing here were written from seven to
nine years later, during which interval the issue of judge-
less debates became more common. They are quite
brief and deal with some of the sub-issues raised by the
earlier questionnaire.

43. Why We Favor Non-Decision Open-Forum Debates
Lida McBride

We have adopted non-decision open-forum debates because we find them far more informative, requiring a more exact knowledge of the question, calling for a far deeper and fuller research than does the decision debate.

In the decision debate it is possible for the youthful debater to make a constructive speech--polished, memorized, possibly the student's own honest effort, possibly rehabilitated through the earnest endeavors of his overzealous coach. This is followed by a rebuttal quite too often as carefully prepared and as closely censored as was the constructive speech. Then one trusts to the possible efficiency of the judge's decision; all your eggs are in one basket. The student is thru, he knows it, heaves a sigh of relief, yet awaits with tense nerves, on strain for the judge's decision.

Nothing is more of a game of chance than a judge's decision. This for various reasons. Qualified judges cannot be obtained for all the debates which are required. Several times during the year I have been frantically appealed to by telephone at the last minute to please help find some one who would, not necessarily could, judge a debate. Ministers, lawyers, teachers, business men, students have all been appealed to in vain, regardless either of training or natural aptitude in this most specialized phase of work. The problem has become a worse farce than even our jury system--than which most of us would acknowledge there is none greater. The decisions, whether fair or unfair, have too often been met with the bitterest criticism.

It was partly to escape all this both unpleasant and unprofitable state of affairs that we changed our decision to non-decision open-forum debates. In the latter our young people must be prepared to answer questions which have arisen in the minds of the listeners while the case is being presented. One sees then the need of clear, logical, presentation in forceful, understandable terms. One must not only say words but must have them fortified into real informative ideas. He must present effectively in a manner that challenges and holds attention;--for a speech which does not provoke much query we consider a "flop."

Then he must adequately defend every statement which he has advanced; he must establish authority values, and render clear, concise summarized judgments. He must see for himself in clear outline just what he is propounding, and whither his argument is leading. All this means a much broader knowledge of the subject, a more effective presentation, an absolutely clear understanding of the ramifications of the subject, a confidence which insures an exceeding poise.

Since we have met various schools in this type of debate, we find them gradually leaning much more strongly to this form. There is no chance for "coach prepared" work. There is no incentive for it.

A novel feature introduced two seasons ago, and one that is gradually growing in popularity, is the mixed team, open-forum, non-decision form of debate. This holds great interest for the teams and adds greatly to a general feeling of goodwill, which we have found the open-forum non-decision cultivates. By a mixed team debate, we mean an affirmative team composed of a debater from each school, and a negative of the same type.

Thus each school has a representative on each side. The host and visiting debater meet an hour before the debate, confer together, readjust their arguments, arrange their line of debate, and then go forth "to war" not only with the opposing school but with their own team. The sides are arranged so that the visitor refutes the host of each side. As each side knows the line of argument of his own team, having met them in conflict before, the ingenuity of attack and defense is put to a greater test. How each side strives to find something new to use is worthy of considerations. Goodwill abounds, and as a rule our greatest trouble is to give time enough for all the argument. The greatest fun is when one side asks a question which it is absolutely sure that its own people have never been able to answer. Quick wit survives, naught else.

Is it stimulating? Ask the listeners as well as the debaters. I grant we sometimes find a few who want a decision because they

are vainglorious enough to feel that maybe they may personally gain
a slight prestige, but they are in such a small minority and the
general sentiment is so strong that we joyfully cling to our non-decision open-forum debate. Please note the last half of this form
for upon it "dependeth the issue." To summarize, then; increased
research--broader and deeper knowledge--greater "rapport" with the
audience--more enthusiasm, a truer idea of values, absence of hostile criticism. These are what we summarize as the advantages to
be gained through non-decision, open-forum debates.

Reprinted from The Gavel, 12:5-6, November, 1929. At the time
this article was written, Lida McBride was Head of the Speech Department, East High School, Wichita, Kansas.

44. Non-Decision Debates
Edwin H. Paget

Much has been said during the last few years against decision
debating. The friends of the decision debate either have not felt it
worth their while to answer these criticisms, or their answers have
not been given full consideration by the profession. As proof of
this neglect, I cite the arguments advanced by those who favor the
non-decision or audience-vote types of debate. Many of these arguments can be easily refuted; yet they are continually advanced.

A notable example of this is Professor Parrish's letter in the
November issue of The Quarterly Journal. In his piercing style
Professor Parrish exposes some of the evils of contest debating.
He complains of falsification and misuse of evidence. He states
that another debate coach allowed his team to build "a case that was
purely an appeal to local prejudice, ignoring entirely the real significance of the question to the country at large." He concludes that
"surely an open debate sponsored by university professors of Public
Speaking" ought to represent an honest attempt to get at the truth
on public questions. And although Professor Parrish does not openly advocate in this particular letter the non-judge debate as the logi-

cal means of reaching this elusive truth, he and many others have
at other times taken exactly that stand. Now those of us who favor
the judge's decision in debating agree that debating should aid the
audience in approaching nearer the truth, but we are unable to see
how the non-decision debate does this.

The aim of the non-decision debate, especially if an audience
vote be taken, is to impress and to move the audience. What is to
keep the college or high school debater from falsifying the evidence
or misinterpreting statistics? Certainly an untrained audience is
more easily deceived than an expert judge. What is to prevent the
debater from "appealing to local prejudice" and ignoring entirely
"the real significance of the question to the country at large?" (The
most popular statement which I have ever heard in a college debate
occurred in an "open discussion" followed by an audience vote. The
speaker said that "the United States had beaten England twice and
could easily do it again. " The audience, largely Irish, applauded
for three minutes. This debater's side won the debate.) Further,
what is to prevent the speaker from imitating crudely the Oxford
manner, which seems to be to spend about ten minutes of the constructive speech in making what are informally known as "wise-
cracks"--witticisms which have very little to do with the actual issues, or even the question, and which have as their unexpressed object the creation of the impression that the speaker is a devil of a
clever fellow.

Nor is there less temptation to the coach. A debate coach in
a western university recently confessed to me that he had spent the
two weeks before a debate with Oxford thinking up clever lines which
his debaters could use with apparent spontaneity! No matter what
the system of debate, the coach must see to it that his team makes
a better impression than the other team. Remove the expert judge
for a few years and the debaters will be free to present as superficial a case as can be constructed--provided it offers sufficient opportunities for appeals to prejudice, waving the flag, and witticisms.
Every evil found in the decision debate can be matched by two under
any other system. If you would see how many there are, make a
list for yourself.

Reprinted from The Quarterly Journal of Speech Education, 13:53-
54, February, 1927. Edwin Paget taught at Purdue University and
later at North Carolina State University.

Suggestions for Further Reading

"Decisionless Debate with the Open Forum," Quarterly Journal of
    Speech, 7:279-291, June, 1921.
Kruger, Arthur N.   "Forms of Debate: Forums," Sec. XVII, A
    Classified Bibliography of Argumentation and Debate.   Metuchen,
    N.J., Scarecrow Press, 1964, pp. 280-292.   See also "Judg-
    ing Debate," Sec. XVIII, pp. 291-311.
Miller, Edd.   "I Believe in Decisions," Gavel, 12:16, January, 1930.
Mundt, Karl E.   "The Fallacy of No-Decision Debates," National
    Forensic League Bulletin, 3:1-3, February, 1929.
Parlette, John W.   "Overcoming Dislike for No-Decision Debates,"
    Gavel, 12:8, January, 1930.
Peterson, Owen.   "Forum Debating," Speech Teacher, 14:286-290,
    November, 1965.
Schrier, William.   "Some Objections Against Judged Debates,"
    Gavel, 10:10, November, 1927.
Smelser, J.N.   "Why Have a Decision?" Speaker, 25:5, November,
    1940.
Taylor, Carl.   "Decisionless Debating," Gavel, 12:13-14, January,
    1930.
Woodward, Howard S.   "Debating Without Judges," Quarterly Jour-
    nal of Speech, 1:229-233, October, 1915.
Woolbert, Charles H.   "On Critic Debate Decisions," Quarterly
    Journal of Speech, 11:286-288, June, 1925.

XI. Judging Debate

Issue W: <u>Should Decisions Be Based on Issues or Debating Skills</u>?

One of the most extended debates on a single issue was undoubtedly that between Hugh N. Wells and James M. O'Neill, published over a period of several years in the <u>Quarterly Journal of Speech Education</u> (as the <u>QJS</u> was then called), around the time of World War I. The debate was generated by an editorial comment in the <u>New Republic</u> that "collegiate debating . . . enables the student to espouse all sides of every question with equal conviction."[1] In answer to this criticism, O'Neill replied that a decision for a team does not mean that the team "got nearer to the truth" than the other team but rather that it was "on the whole composed of better debaters" than the other team.[2] This view evoked a dissent from William H. Davis, who wrote that "what the judges need to determine is . . . which side is more likely to convince the audience that its view is the correct one."[3] In reply, O'Neill repeated his original point, "The object of any particular team is to demonstrate its superiority over its opponent in debating."[4]

At this point Howard S. Woodward suggested that having non-decision debates would solve the problem,[5] a proposal which O'Neill rejected.[6] Davis then reentered the fray with an article that contended that debating is not merely a game "engaged in for fun" and that "when debaters are animated by a genuine desire to convert their hearers to the truth as they see it, the term 'debater's argument' will become what it ought to be, a commendatory and honorable appellation."[7] O'Neill's rejoinder was that academic debate is a valuable activity even if its object is not to convince others of the truth.[8]

Shortly thereafter Lew R. Sarett wrote an article setting forth eleven criteria (organization, proof, rebuttal, delivery, etc.) as a basis for judging debating skill,[9] the criteria which now appear on most debate ballots. In effect, he was reinforcing O'Neill's position. It was then that Wells entered the controversy, taking issue with Davis, O'Neill, and Sarett, and contending that judging is essentially a matter of determining "which team succeed-

ed in doing what the topic demands. " In attacking the
score-sheet method of judging, he wrote:

> Most instructors and coaches of debate endeavor to
> prevent percentage calculations in arriving at de-
> cisions, as it is conceded that such calculations
> lead to palpably absurd results. No one credits a
> preacher with 80 percent for argument, 10 percent
> for diction, and 10 percent for presentation. But
> how may debate be judged upon the elements of 're-
> search, reasoning, and speaking' unless the judge
> adopts some percentage method, in fact or in ef-
> fect?[10]

Thereafter, O'Neill and Wells exchanged several articles
until the final presentation, "Juryman or Critic: Three
Rebuttal Arguments and a Decision," appeared in the
October, 1918 issue of the Quarterly Journal. The two
articles appearing here were part of that "closing presentation." The two articles omitted are Wells' opening
summary "A Final Reply" and Sarett's "A Juryman-
Critic's Vote," which understandably rendered a decision
in favor of O'Neill, whom Sarett had earlier supported.

In his final comment on Wells' views, O'Neill contended
that since some debate questions are inherently stronger
on one side than on another, debaters would be penalized
if a judge's decision were based solely on the strength
of the case presented, or on the "merits of the question."
Hence, he argued, as before, that a judge, like a critic,
should vote on the basis of which team did the better debating, or demonstrated the better debating skills as indicated by Sarett's criteria: organization, evidence, refutation, teamwork, strategy, delivery, etc.

Wells, on the other hand, continued to argue that he
found it difficult to understand how O'Neill's (or Sarett's)
criteria could be applied; for superior debating skill, he
contended, can be measured only in terms of who presented the superior case, or, in legal terms, who had
"the weight of evidence" on his side. How, he asked,
"can a judge isolate the several elements of debating
from . . . the 'case,' or 'the weight of evidence'?" In
other words, for the affirmative to win it must prove the
proposition to be probably true and for the negative to
win it must either create a reasonable doubt or prove the
proposition to be probably false. Since this is how a
case is determined in a court of law, the debate judge in
effect is a juryman.

Although the difference in the two points of view may not
seem very great, the implications are quite significant;
for where an "issues" judge would vote against an affirm-

ative team for not showing any "need," a "skills" judge could vote for the same affirmative for being the better all-round debaters, as determined by their delivery, organization, use of evidence, refutation, etc.

1. April 3, 1915. This remark was not made concerning switch-sides debate, as the reader might think, but concerning the fact that on the same evening a Yale negative team beat a Princeton affirmative while a Yale affirmative beat a Harvard negative.
2. "A Disconcerted Editor and Others," Quarterly Journal of Public Speaking, 1:76, April, 1915.
3. "Debating as Related to Non-Academic Life," QJPS, 1:105, July, 1915.
4. "Able Non-Debaters," QJPS, 1:201, July, 1915.
5. "Debating Without Judges," QJPS, 1:229-233, October, 1915.
6. "Judges Again," QJPS, 1:305-307, October, 1915.
7. "Is Debating Primarily a Game?" QJPS, 2:171-179, April, 1916.
8. "Game or Counterfeit Presentment," QJPS, 2:193-197, April, 1916.
9. "The Expert Judge of Debate," QJSE, 3:135-139, April, 1917.
10. "Judging Debates," QJSE, 3:336-345, October, 1917.

45. Juryman or Critic: Comment on Judge Wells' Last Ms.
James M. O'Neill

I am not trying to "equalize matters," or to enforce fairness primarily, but to get a decision that can be of some significance, that the students can win and lose largely on the merits of their own industry and ability--not on the chances of wording and the accidental weight of evidence, and the judges' opinion as to which side is right according to a weird lot of presumptions. I think my original wording is somewhat to be preferred for the expression of this idea to Judge Wells' change of it; "comparative showing of the debaters in knowledge, etc." instead of "comparative merits of the debaters in their display of knowledge, etc."

I agree that no system should be bent to accommodate exceptional cases. We should have one that will work right all the time because fundamentally sound. The schools may not be guilty. The discussion need not at all be a farce because the question is poorly worded or (a part of my comment which Judge Wells overlooked) so worded that one side has no chance to present the stronger evidence, especially in a few minutes to men who know nothing or who assume they know nothing about the problem.

The statement that one side will have a greater opportunity to display knowledge, parade speaking, research, etc., is such that it is a bit hard to take it seriously. All you have to do is to think over the propositions you have heard debated and see if you can find any on which this will be a serious thing. Of course there may at times be questions on which the opportunity for research and knowledge is better on one side than on the other. I grant this; but I have two comments to make, either of which seems to me to be a complete answer. 1. Such an advantage when it exists does not settle the decision so completely as would the advantage of stronger evidence under the other system, because this is harder to make use of. It tests the industry and ability of the student to make much of this opportunity. To present the stronger evidence, when it exists, when it is either easily worked out, accidentally found, or given to the debater outright by his "coach," requires neither ability, industry, or much else. A decision which rewards the use of an advantage in regard to research or knowledge has some educational significance. One rewarding an advantage on "strength of evidence" has none whatever. 2. When this advantage does exist, it is one of many elements in the critic's vote; so the weight of the accidental advantage is minimized. In the juryman's vote the weight of evidence is conclusive, so the accidental advantage may determine the whole decision. That one side of a question can offer an advantage in reasoning, honesty, courtesy, good English, good speaking, etc., is simply (in my opinion) ridiculous.

In regard to the Sarett questions: I have written already that I am inclined to think that I did not even think of them when I wrote that paragraph. They will illustrate the critic's vote if you please, or other similar lists of points will, or one needn't use any list at all.

I have denied all along Judge Wells' position that a system of judging requires the specific segregation and separate appraisement

of the elements considered by the respective questions. Why should
overlapping be utterly destructive? As a matter of fact overlapping
is practically essential in questions (if you insist on having questions) which would lie at the basis of judgment in any field. Take
music, poetry, bridge building, horse breeding, dramatic writing,
or acting, composition, sculpture--anything--and draw up a list of
questions which a judge might use as the basis of his decision.
The questions are bound to overlap. And why should it not be so?
Judge Wells' whole discussion of these questions seems to me an
unsuccessful attempt to pervert the obvious intent of these questions.
Of course all that is done must have some relation to the case. In
a debate each team has presumably a case and evidence, and their
job is to present the best possible case and the strongest possible
evidence, and do it all in the best possible manner according to the
best possible standards. Questions 2, 3, and 4 in Professor Sarett's
list do overlap somewhat, are bound to in my opinion; but the main
point at the basis of each is different. To me, 2 is primarily a
question of evidence; 3 is a question of strength of case; 4, of rebuttal. But these three, of course, overlap somewhat. But what
possible difference does that make? We are not assigning definite
percents, simply looking at the work done from various angles, not
mutually exclusive angles. Suppose you were to view a statue from
different points of view in deciding a contest in sculpture, would the
points of view have to be mutually exclusive, due north and due
south? My opponent's ignoring of clearness and coherence in 1. and
his interpreting of effective to make this a question of "strength of
case" hardly meets the point. Of course, one must have material
in order to arrange it clearly and coherently. But still the weaker
case may be clearer and more coherent. Even Judge Wells' own
wording "Which team most clearly, coherently, and effectively presented its case?" is patently a question of work done, not of
strength of case. Under the "juryman" system such a question is
clearly irrelevant. One can answer that for one side and hold that
the other had the stronger case, or stronger evidence. Note that
even these two concepts overlap: "strength of case, " "weight of
evidence;" but they are not identical.

The statement that superiority in analysis, team work, etc.,
has to be superiority in working toward strengthening the case is
quite sound. But the seeming inference from this that because
these things are related to the case that they are therefore adequately judged by judging the case as a case is very weak. One team
may be superior in analysis, or team work, or strategy, or lots of
other things, and the other team have the stronger case through an
accidental weight of evidence available, through no credit of theirs.
And it is teams and their work that we should be judging and not
evidence or propositions. This seems to me to answer all of Mr.
Wells' discussion in which he shows, what any one will admit, that
all these questions have to do with the team's work in relation to
its case--in other words that they have to do with debating. But
what of it? As long as we can answer these various questions or
others like them for team A and then say that team B has the
stronger case, or the weightier evidence, or is right in its contentions, it seems to me to be necessary for him to show that these
questions are improper ones for a judge to have in mind. You will
admit that an honest and intelligent juryman will vote on the evidence regardless of how it is presented. The lawyer may be ignorant, uncouth, sly, discourteous, may use bad grammar, bad pro-
nunciation, loose thinking, etc., etc., and still the evidence in favor of his client will be strong enough to win. And all honest and
intelligent jurymen will vote for his client, for his side of the proposition, regardless of the contempt they may feel for him as a lawyer. What is the matter with this illustration? Does anyone really
want this in contest debating? Or what was the matter with my
earlier one in regard to the prizes for lawyers? Does anyone need
to be told how such a board of lawyers could tell which practitioners
before the court were better, except by deciding who won or who
ought to have won the cases tried?

Mr. Wells says on page eight that the other ten questions can
only be answered in favor of any team when it has forcefully and
clearly presented its case to the judges; that the only legitimate purpose of delivery and kindred elements is to impress the points advanced on the minds of the judges. But we certainly must admit

that if the evidence is strong, it would have to be submitted very poorly indeed to such a jury as would judge an intercollegiate debate in order to have the judges fail to get the weight of it. And if the evidence on one side is stronger and we are to have a decision on the evidence, then we must not inquire whether a team has forcefully and clearly presented its case. Delivery certainly is of use only in presenting the case; but under the circumstances governing intercollegiate debate, if you have a decision on the evidence, and the strength of the case as a case, it is difficult to see how you can reward good delivery or good English, courtesy, honesty, analysis, reasoning, etc., etc.

Judge Wells' greatest difficulty, perhaps, is that he has not received a definite and clear-cut explanation of the operation of the critic's vote. His difficulty in regard to this is honestly and sincerely hard for me to understand. In essence, the critic's vote is simply that, after listening to different people debating for two hours, the judge expresses an opinion as to which side has done the better debating. I do not yet see what further explanation of that sort of vote is needed. I can suggest a list of questions which the judge might have on a card to refresh his memory in regard to certain points, so he would not overlook phases of debating which might slip his mind for the moment; or I can suggest a table which a judge might use, such, for instance, as the one below.

The questions Mr. Sarett suggested might be used, or other sets somewhat like them. It is clear that in using such questions, or such a chart, the judge is paying attention to much besides the weight of evidence and the strength of the case. Please note that he is not supposed to leave out of consideration the weight of evidence or the strength of the case, but he is asked to pass an opinion on the debating done, and not upon the evidence presented. This is a contest in debating. It is not a matter of settling the question for all time. We haven't the circumstances under which such a question could possibly be settled; we do not even parallel the circumstances in real life in which such questions are settled, for nowhere do people try to settle in jury trials the type of question which university people discuss in intercollegiate debate. And in no

Judge's Ballot

Interscholastic Debate
March 22, 1918

Andover High School, Affirmative
vs.
Brownsville High School, Negative

Resolved, that . . . .
. . . .

Points to be considered in arriving at a decision	Affirmative			Negative		
	1	2 3	Team	1 2 3		Team
Analysis or interpretation of the proposition (plan of case).......						
Knowledge, information..........						
Strength of evidence.............						
Reasoning, inferences based on evidence presented.............						
Ability in extemporizing.........						
General conduct or deportment toward opponents, judges, audience, presiding officer........						
Ability in rebuttal..............						
Use of English.................						
Clearness of speech--easy to hear, pronunciation, enunciation, etc..						
Power or effectiveness in public speaking.....................						

Note:--The critic or judge may fill in percentages for each speaker or one for teams as a whole; or he may use + and - to indicate his general opinion on each point, either for individuals or teams.   The judge shall decide for himself the relative weight to be given to each of the points mentioned.

On the basis of the criticism as indicated by marking on the above blank, it is my decision that, on the whole, the better debating was done by the . . . . team.

(Signed) _____

Judge.

jury trials anywhere do people try to settle even jury questions under the limitations of time, etc., which govern intercollegiate contests. I have gone into this rather in detail in my first article, and shall not repeat it here. But it is utterly impossible in passing upon the weight of evidence to get safely clear of the judge's private

opinion as to the merits of the question, because evidence on such
questions supporting one's belief is pretty likely to seem stronger
than evidence which goes contrary to one's belief. This being true,
it is possible to attempt to apply the juryman's vote under only a
tremendously complex system of artificial presumptions, which seem
to remove the last vestige of reality from this public discussion
which the students are indulging in. I have difficulty in seeing what
more can be said about how this system works. As a matter of
fact, it isn't a system. It is simply a point of view in regard to
the contest. Students study and practice debating, and then engage
in a contest in debating. And why should the decision be given on
any basis except the basis of ability in debating? Why not judge debating instead of evidence? Will you demand to know how a judge
or a critic decides who is the best singer? And will you in a contest in singing ask him to refrain from judging the singing, but to
judge exclusively (assuming the truth of a dozen conditions which
everybody knows can't be true) which song he likes best? If this
seems too much like making a plea for judging on delivery only,
change to a contest in poetry. Can't one who knows poetry read or
hear read, as you choose, a list of poems, and give the prize to
the best poetry, regardless as to whether or not he likes the subjects of the best poems presented? Or suppose you have a prize
offered in carpentering, and a group of carpenters build some barns,
would anyone think of awarding the prize on any basis except the
building of the barn which shows the best workmanship? You would-
n't give it to the biggest barn, or the barn that had the best lumber
in it, or to the barn that you liked best, as a barn for certain uses.
Now the choice of good material is a part of the job; but it seems
to me ridiculous to award the prize on that basis. If you want to
settle a question, then pass upon the evidence only; but if you are
going to do that, you must have other conditions than those governing intercollegiate contests. Most assuredly the critic judge pays
attention to the weight of evidence and the strength of case; I doubt
if there is a single phrase in anything I have written to indicate that
he should ignore these conditions. His attention should not be di-
verted. He should take in all that goes to make good debating, and

then give the prize to the one who has done the best work.

Mr. Wells seems to assume constantly that the best work
must coincide with the best evidence; that the best carpenter must
build the biggest barn out of the best lumber; that the best lawyer
must necessarily be on the right side of the case before the jury;
that the best lawyer always wins; palpably an unwarranted assumption.

The defender of the "juryman's" vote is very unhappy in his
discussion of courtesy, good English, nervousness, rudeness, etc.
He says that a debate is an intellectual contest and must be judged
as such; but he declines to judge it on that basis. He is not judging the combat at all; he is judging evidence. He says that debate
is not a contest in either etiquette, grammar, or literature. To
him it seems simply a contest in evidence. In my opinion, it is an
intellectual combat. It is a contest in public discussion. Grammar
and etiquette, attitude toward audience and opponents, knowledge and
reasoning, good English, good speaking--all that goes to make intelligent discussion--are a part of it. And all that goes to make intelligent discussion ought to be taken into consideration in reaching a decision, and the decision should be given to the students who do the
best work in debating. It seems to me no answer to the statement
that rudeness ought to be deliberately counted against a debater, to
reply, "But if you mistake legitimate ardor for discourtesy for a
few times, and punish accordingly, the result is likely to be the ruin
of some young man's forensic career." Quite true, but once we
mistake evidence for twaddle, and decide accordingly, we may ruin
a young man's forensic career in another way. I don't see how we
can have a system which will be foolproof, and will work well whether the judge makes a mistake or not. I am not saying that only a
fool could mistake courtesy for ardor, but I object to explaining
away difficulties by saying that if you try to decide from a certain
point of view and make a mistake, damage will be done. Harm will
be done when mistakes are made under any system. When my opponent says that sheer nervousness is the cause of much supposed
rudeness, and it is exceedingly difficult to draw the line between legitimate agressiveness and discourtesy, my answer is that the de-

bater who is so nervous that he appears rude, and so aggressive
that he appears discourteous, is a poor debater, and that that kind
of debating should be discouraged by being penalized; and further,
that nervousness is not the only cause of rudeness, and aggressiveness not the only cause of discourtesy. His whole discussion based
upon the discussion of the mistakes the judges might make, will
work one way as well as the other. He says if the judge should
mistake discourtesy for aggressiveness and enthusiasm, he would
probably accredit it as debating skill. A sufficient answer to this
comment is that if the juryman should mistake denunciation of the
opponents for evidence and argument, he would probably accredit it
to the strength of the case.

Mr. Wells again says that nowhere is he told how the judge
is to distinguish cheapness, bombast, superficiality, dishonesty,
etc., from thorough, honest, intelligent debating. Well, how does
a man tell one of these qualities from another in private life, in
private conversation, in listening to talking anywhere? How does a
critic of poetry actually tell the difference between a silly jingle and
a great poem? How does a judge of work in manual arts tell a
piece of botchwork from a perfectly finished article? The only
thing I know of to meet this situation is to choose men in whose
taste, training, experience, and intelligence you have some faith.
You cannot enter into the minds of your judges and give them a process of thought by which they can mechanically determine bombast
from intelligent discussion any more than you can give a similar
mental mechanism to a musician by which he can tell ragtime from
good music. How under the "juryman" system does a judge determine the weight of evidence or the strength of the case? How is it
done? It seems to me that it is just as easy to comprehend how
one who understands debating can have an opinion as to which group
of two debaters has been doing the better work for the last hour or
two as it is to understand how the same board can decide which side
has presented the strongest evidence. It is simply a question of
which kind of decision you want the board to render. If you are going to have a decision rendered on the weight of evidence, of course
all you need is judges who can weigh evidence. If you want a deci-

sion on the quality of the work done in public discussion, then you
want men who are competent critics of public discussion. If a detailed and scientific analysis of all this is needed, I must at present confess my inability to give it. In all seriousness, Judge Wells'
questions on this point are simply incomprehensible to me. For
years now I have been judging debates with other men who use this
same system--that is, who give an opinion on the debating, and not
on the evidence. It never occurred to any of us that we were doing anything weird or strange. It seems to me that we are doing
precisely what judges are doing in any other field that I have been
able to think of.

Mr. Wells says that he knows what correct standards are in
research, reasoning, public speaking, etc., but that the correct
standard required in their application to the judging of skill in debating must be some system by which we can severally distinguish
and correctly and proportionately evaluate these elements. And he
wants to know what that correct standard is. I must answer that I
don't know what he is talking about. Anyone who knows what are
good standards in research, reasoning, public speaking, and everything else that makes good debating, can necessarily, it seems to
me, express an intelligent opinion, after he has listened to a debate
for two hours, as to which side on the whole was better in these
things. Now if there is any mystery about that, I must beg to have
the mystery pointed out to me before I am asked to explain.

We are told that such things as knowledge, original work, and
honesty are impossible of actual determination during the course of
the debate, and the critic judge can only accredit their exhibition.
You can tell, can't you, after you have heard people talking about
a subject for two hours, which side presumably knows most about
it? Sometimes haven't you observed traces of work which is not entirely honest? I have. It seems to me that these matters are as
easy to detect as the weight of evidence.

Would I be wrong in assuming that Judge Wells seems to think
that a cheap, bombastic, superficial, dishonest exhibition is debating skill? My point is that these things are the very opposite of debating skill. That the skillful debater is one who presents the

strongest case possible, directly, sincerely, without bombast, without superficiality, dishonesty, cheapness, etc. And again, I insist that debaters will try to avoid anything insincere, bombastic, and superficial if they know they are to be judged by critics of debating who do not believe that those qualities constitute good debating. Debating ability is, of course, directed to the development of the case. It is the ability shown in the conduct of the case which should be passed upon in the decision, and not the right or wrongness of the case itself. Again, take the analogy I suggested long ago, of the prize for lawyers. If this prize would be properly administered, wouldn't it go to the lawyer who conducted his case to the best of his ability in the courtroom? Would the lawyers try to play up to such a system of judging by being guilty of cheapness, bombast, superficiality, etc.? Of course not. They would do the best work possible under the circumstances. They would win or lose their cases before an intelligent jury according to the rights and wrongs of the proposition, and the strength of evidence they had to present. But it is manifestly absurd to say that you should look to the record, pick out the law firm that won the largest number of cases, and present them the prize for having shown the highest order of ability and conduct in the practice of their profession. Again, I insist that all these glib and tricky evils can be encouraged under a critic's vote only on one or two assumptions. There are no other possibilities. Either (1) the judge is not able to tell the difference between cheap, superficial, bombastic ranting, and honest, sincere, thoroughgoing discussion, or else, if he is able to tell the difference, (2) he deliberately chooses to reward the former. For myself, I am satisfied that I can choose in this section of the country some dozen or two competent critics who can tell the difference just as easily as a critic in another field can tell good work from poor work, men who are always glad to reward the better work. Mr. Wells says he is unable to condemn men for any attempt to display those elements upon which they are to be judged. I agree with him entirely. I should judge them upon their display, if you like that word, of the elements of good debating. Any man best exhibits his ability in good debating when he honestly, sincerely, thoroughly pre-

sents in the best possible manner the strongest case of which he is
capable under the circumstances. But my opponent must admit that
one team may do all of this, and the other team present to a given
board of judges, what that board of judges would agree was stronger evidence. If not, I wish he would take the pains to offer some
proof of the thesis that the better work and the stronger evidence
are always found in conjunction. Skill can only be legitimately employed to produce a strong case, but the more skillful worker does
not always have the stronger case to present. This fallacious assumption seems to persist through all Judge Wells' discussion.

I am perfectly willing to substitute the other expression, "The
ability of the debaters to practice the art they are supposed to be
practicing," as I used it, as it seems to me to be substantially
synonymous with the expression, "The excellence of the practice of
the art of debate which they are supposed to be practicing." I do
not know that I have proscribed the judging of the practice of the
art.

The discussion of the difference between judging the practice
of the art and judging the mere ability to practice the art leaves me
floundering. It is the practice of the art which I wish to have judged. I have had nothing else in mind in this discussion. But apparently there is objection to judging the practice of the art. Mr.
Wells wishes to take one element and judge everything on that ap-
parently--to judge the "weight of evidence." I wish to pass upon
the workmanship, if you like, shown by the students in the art of
oral discussion. Because of the nature of the contest and the subjects presented, it is obviously impossible to judge by results in the
minds of the audience. I say it is obviously impossible, and I suppose everyone will agree with me in this. Therefore we do the
next best thing we can. We get competent critics in this field, ask
them to listen to the contest and award the decision. It is as
though we should have a contest in bridge building among engineering
students. Each student is to work out a model bridge. He hasn't
the opportunity to spend a half-million dollars in building a real
bridge, but he works out a model. Competent engineering experts
are called in to examine the models and give the prize to the stu-

dent who has exhibited the greatest ability in working out his model
--not to the biggest model, nor to the model made of the best material, not the model necessarily of the kind of a bridge that this
engineer likes, or would like to have on his grounds or in his
neighborhood. But from his knowledge of engineering, he is able
to render an intelligent decision as to which student has shown the
greatest ability in the practice of the art of bridge building. And
this may be paralleled, I submit, in any field in which one can
imagine a contest.

I think the "juryman" advocate is quite inconsistent in all that
he says about wishing to judge the art of debate. I submit that this
is what I wish to judge, and not anything else, but that he is not
judging the art of debate--he is not judging any art at all when he
gives his decision in any case upon the weight of evidence or the
strength of the case. If this is not true, I wish again that he would
offer a line of reasoning to support the thesis that the strongest evidence or the strongest case is always coincident with the greatest
ability in the art of debate. It seems to me perfectly obvious that
if you enter an intercollegiate contest with the assumption that the
negative is right and that the affirmative must prove its case in the
few minutes allowed it, or else you will vote for the negative, and
then try to meet this situation by passing simply upon weight of evidence and strength of case, that your decision must necessarily be
for the negative nine times out of ten, and that your decision will
never have any necessary relation to ability in the art of debate, and
can have no educational significance.

I submit the following nine questions with the statement that it
is quite possible for a judge to answer the first eight in favor of
one team, and to answer no. 9 in favor of the other team. And
"9" covers completely the juryman's vote as it has been set forth.
And under the juryman's vote it would be necessary to award the decision to the team against whom answers questions 1-8, inclusive.
And again, I point out that questions 1-8 are not mutually exclusive,
and submit that they do not have to be mutually exclusive, and that
there is no reason in the world why we should try to frame exclusive questions, or why we should try to assign a definite percentage

to these questions.   Following is the list:

1. Which team made a better analysis of the proposition?
2. Which team apparently knew more about the question?
3. Which team used better English?
4. Which team exhibited a better attitude toward opponents, audience, judges, etc. ?
5. On which side was there better teamwork?
6. Which team showed greater ability in rebuttal?
7. Which team showed greater ability in extemporaneous adaptation of their case to the case of the other side?
8. Which team did the better speaking?
9. Which team would you vote for if the question were to be decided by you as a juryman, basing your decision upon the weight of evidence, or the strength of the case simply, under the assumption that the affirmative have a burden of proof which they must sustain or else lose the case?

Finally, may I ask Judge Wells how he chooses men in debating trials?   I have read his interesting article on coaching debates, but that is not what I refer to.   I mean, what attitude does he take? What sort of question would he put to himself if he were to listen to trial debates to pick out three debaters to make up a team? Couldn't he tell the good debaters from the poor ones by passing simply upon their ability as debaters, and isn't this precisely what he would do rather than to pick out the three men who presented the "strongest cases?"

Reprinted from The Quarterly Journal of Speech Education, October, 1918.   James M. O'Neill was a Professor of Speech at Brooklyn College.

46. Comment on Professor O'Neill's Latest Ms.
Hugh N. Wells

1. It ought not to be necessary to prove that the two sides of any debatable resolution are likely to be equal in their opportunities for the exhibition of debating skill.   To my mind these inequalities are fatal to the argument in favor of the critic vote.   Professor O'Neill's answer to this contention again develops what I am convinced is the fundamental fallacy underlying his entire argument, namely, that debatable propositions are likely to be of unequal argu-

mentative values.   It is necessary for Professor O'Neill to submit
a resolution, which is properly phrased and upon a debatable subject, which is inherently and demonstrably stronger in argumentative values upon one side than upon the other, before he can be
said to have established his major premise.   Where the subject is
debatable and properly phrased, it is almost inconceivable that either team will be able to demonstrate, in the short period of an intercollegiate debate, any inherent argumentative advantage in its
side of the resolution.   Professor O'Neill's system of judging, therefore, can only receive validity if we consent to bend a system of
judging to protect people who are careless in their selection of subjects and in the phrasing of resolutions.

   2. Professor O'Neill challenges my statement that Professor
Sarett did not offer his questionnaire as an illustration of a system
of judging.   If my statement is wrong, I nevertheless submit that I
was entitled to make it, for Professor Sarett says in his article on
page 137 of the April, 1917 Number of The Quarterly:

> Debaters and audiences frequently are at a loss concern-
> ing the devious processes by which a judge decides the
> merits of a debate.   Occasionally they are disposed to
> question the soundness of his decision and to attribute it
> to a lack of definite and sound professional standards.
> Accordingly, in order to avoid this possibility and to im-
> prove the quality of future debates by a statement of a
> few of the elements of effective debating which constitute,
> or ought to constitute in one form or another, the proxi-
> mate standard of a judge, I request that the following
> brief analysis of the debate be read: (Followed im-
> mediately by the questionnaire.)

I have insisted that the questionnaire is offered for the purposes of analysis, and I submit that that is precisely what Professor
Sarett says.   He may intend his questionnaire to be used for the
purposes of judging, but he does not say that that is its primary
purpose in his article.

   3. Overlapping is utterly destructive, for the reason that the
critic judge is attempting to adjudge the comparative merits of the
debaters.   It is necessary for them to adopt definite and sound professional standards if their decision is to receive the approval of
reasoning people.   Such standards require every element to be cred-

ited apart from other elements. Segregation is necessary, otherwise elements of skill cannot be evaluated truly and definitely. I do not understand why the elements judged in "music, poetry, bridge building, horse breeding, dramatic writing, acting composition, or sculpture" should overlap. I do not think that they do overlap. I know that there are definite standards upon which horses are judged in horse shows, and I know that any judge of horses will be able to explain precisely the system by which he arrives at his decision. So far as I am acquainted with the other arts mentioned by Professor O'Neill, the same may be said of them. In any event, I have never heard of any of these branches being judged in terms of the skill of the artist. Music is judged upon the merits of the entity which the technical elements form, and not upon the skill of the artist in these several technical elements. The same is true of poetry. The thing to determine in bridge building is the comparative merits of the bridges: Is this bridge a better bridge than the other bridge? In deciding this question the judge would not determine which builder displayed greater skill in each separate element of bridge building, but would determine which result was superior to the other. So also, in a horse show. Which is the better horse; which horse most nearly approaches the perfect standard of weight, line, etc. ? We do not judge the technical skill of the breeder in raising the horse.

Professor O'Neill asks the question: "Why not judge debating instead of evidence?" I have sometimes used the term "weight of evidence," as a synonym for the term "strength of case." If Professor O'Neill means by his question, why not judge debating instead of strength of case, then I will answer that debating consists in the development of the stronger case. The definition in Professor O'Neill's book and his own argument admit this. The objective of debating, and the purpose to which all legitimate "debating skill" is directed, is the establishment and maintenance of the stronger case. I want the debate to be judged, and I am judging the debate when I judge the result of the work done, just as I am judging bridge building when I determine which is the better bridge. I will ask Professor O'Neill: Why not judge the debate, instead of debating skill?

In Professor O'Neill's practical application of the critic's vote, in the March number of The Quarterly, he says: "Each judge listens to the discussion and at its close votes for the team which in his opinion is made up of the better debaters." Why not judge the debate, instead of debaters? It surely is not too much to say that a team may often demonstrate that it is composed of the better debaters, while its debate is obviously thin and ineffective. Why not judge the debate, instead of the idiosyncracies of the persons who are attempting to present the debate? In judging a contest in bridge building, shall we first determine which builder is most industrious, the more profound student of the subject, the more versatile in meeting emergencies? Of course not; we want to determine which has constructed the better bridge, be he ever so inferior in personal attributes. The prizewinner in a horse show may belong to a common drunkard, but we are not interested in that. The person who bred him does not concern us; we are interested in his product. So, also, in debate, we are interested solely in the argumentative product, for debate is an argumentative contest. Good deportment and good grammar are excellent attainments, but it does not happen to be a contest in these desirable qualities.

4. Professor O'Neill refers again to the hypothetical case which he suggested in his article on page 354 of the October, 1917 Quarterly; it is this: A reward is offered for "great examples of distinguished ability and high standards of conduct in Court practice." "A committee is appointed by the American Bar Association to hear the trials and award the prizes" to the lawyers deemed entitled to them. The trouble with this illustration is that it is not analogous. Moreover, it is a splendid example of the fallacy of "arguing in a circle." The main issue in our argument is whether or not superiority in debating skill is the thing to be determined by the board of judges. Professor O'Neill submits an illustration, which, by its terms, complacently assumes that debating skill is the thing to be determined, and having assumed as a premise the very point in issue, proceeds, by his illustration, to prove it. Manifestly, in a contest where prizes are given "to the law firms whose representatives show the highest order of ability in the work done in connec-

tion with trial work, " since the thing to be adjudged by the very
terms of the contest is ability in trial work, the committee of judges
would not base their decision upon the number of cases won, or upon any other element other than skill in trial work, but, if the decision were to mean anything, it would be necessary to adopt certain definite standards of professional skill, or, borrowing Professor
Sarett's phrase, "definite and sound professional standards" would be
established, upon which to admeasure the respective skill exhibited.
I do not know how such standards could be established for such a
supposititious contest, and, if it were held, I think that every practicing lawyer of sound judgment would agree that the decision would
necessarily represent the personal opinion of the judges, based very
largely upon guesswork and individual preferences.

     5. I am quite aware that no system of judging is foolproof.
But I am not willing to enlarge the opportunity for mistake as I believe is done under the critic system. Indeed, I deem that system
so complex, that I would not desire to apply such an epithet to the
judge who should make a mistake in attempting to use it. I do not
understand how he can avoid mistakes, when he assumes the omnis-
cience necessary to determine who is the author of all argument
which a debater may advance, or when he assumes to pass upon the
industry and research of a debater, practiced through many weary
hours prior to his entrance upon the platform. At any rate, I can
never consent to a system which is calculated in its every method
to award a decision to a team which has been utterly defeated in argument, by reason of a mistake made in the determination of the
question as to whether or not a debater were rude or merely over-
zealous. I do not care to turn a debate into a contest in the display
of etiquette and deportment. I hold no brief for the bully in debate
or elsewhere, and I protest against any attempt to wile me into a
false position. If we start upon this tangent, we will next have the
judge undertake to pass upon the debater's personal appearance, the
cut of his dress suit, the style of his vest, or even the color of his
hair. And, unless we confine ourself to the judging of the debate,
that is, the argumentative contest as such, why should we not undertake to pass upon the matters just mentioned? They, also, have

educational value, and our institutions of learning desire to turn out men who have good taste in dress and a realization of the value of a good presence. Moreover, the debater who has the temerity to appear upon the platform in an untidy condition should be reprimanded for his failure to observe due decorum. Of course, his ill-fitting dress suit may be due to his poverty and the necessity of renting a dress suit for the evening, but it is no more difficult for the judge to determine that fact, and give it due consideration, than it is for him to pass upon the debater's skill in research and his industry employed during the weeks or months prior to the debate.

6. Professor O'Neill has misunderstood me. I have never said, and I do not assume that "the best work must coincide with the best evidence," if he means by "the best work" superior skill in debate. On the contrary, it is because I know that the more skillful debater will frequently establish the poorer case, that I object to his system of judging. I do not want the decision in the contest in oral reasoning to be awarded to the team which has presented the weaker argument, however superior that team may be in the elements of debating skill.

Professor O'Neill is right: His first eight questions might be answered in favor of a team exhibiting superior debating skill, while the 9th might be answered in favor of its opponent. But I cannot think of anything more shocking to good sense, than to have the decision awarded to the first team. Why do we train men to analyze? Is it for analysis as an objective in itself? Isn't it in order that they may be better able to state and prove a case? It is pleasant to know much about a question, but rather useless in this practical old world, if we are unable to use our knowledge to definite purposes.

7. Professor O'Neill's eight questions do overlap. How will a team exhibit better analysis without at the same time, and by its superior analysis, showing a greater knowledge of the question. True, it may not have a greater knowledge of the question, but under the critic system we are solely concerned with what is exhibited. At least, superior analysis tends to show greater knowledge. Questions 5, 6 and 7 clearly overlap, for ability in rebuttal is very

largely a matter of teamwork. It is very important to have rebuttal offered by the right speaker and in the right place. It is mighty poor rebuttal and a very weak exhibition of rebuttal skill to use rebuttal in the wrong rebuttal period, or in constructive argument when it should be reserved for one of the rebuttal periods. Usually rebuttal will clinch the argument only when it is offered at the right time.

Professor O'Neill says it is immaterial whether or not a questionnaire be used, but he clearly indicates that the critic judge must ask and answer certain questions in order to reach his decision. For the purposes of my argument, it is immaterial whether or not he does this in substance; the result is the same if he does it in effect. Any consideration of debating skill, as such, for the purpose of deciding which team is to be declared the winner in an oral argumentative contest must, of necessity, result in double-crediting of such elements as proficiency in speech art, strategy, and research. In other words, after the argument has received added force from the aid given it by these elements, after the contest in argument has been decided in favor of the team presenting the stronger case, it may be deprived of the decision by reason of its failure to exhibit facility in extemporaneous speech, or adroitness in strategy, or diligence in research. If it be deemed advisable to have forensic contests decided in this manner, let us not travesty reason by calling them debating contests, or let us define debate as something other than an "oral argumentative contest."

8. Professor O'Neill desires to know how I select men at trials. I have really answered this question in my article on coaching, in the March number of The Quarterly. I do not select men at trials, for I deem it impossible to pass upon their respective skill in this manner. Debating skill can only be determined by association with the men and the subject they are debating. Some men are poor in one subject and excellent in others; weak on one side, but strong on the other. I hold a preliminary try-out and all who show merit are admitted to the final squad. I select the teams from the final squad after three or four weeks of work upon the subject. Even then, the teams are not finally selected. Two teams

are pitted against each other, and numerous shifts are made during
the training period. The work of these teams is adjudged each day,
in accordance with "Jurymen's" standards, and the team which, after
every combination of men has been tried, presents and maintains the
strongest case, is the team which is sent upon the platform.

Reprinted from The Quarterly Journal of Speech Education, 4:422-
427, October, 1918. Judge Wells taught in the Law School of the
University of Southern California.

Issue X: Should a Judge Take Notes During a Debate?

Viewing real-life debate as an activity which seeks to win over large numbers of people, like an electorate, Dale Drum, in "The Debate Judge As a Machine," argues that it is unrealistic to expect the judge of an academic debate to take notes since real audiences do not take notes while listening to a persuasive speech. Tournament debating, he believes, encourages students to speak as though they were addressing a court stenographer, or machine. A debate speech, he contends, should be primarily persuasive--which means adapting to an audience, using emotional and psychological appeals, memorable phrases, and not just facts and dry logic. If students were trained to be persuasive in this sense, the judge would not have to take notes. And if judges were forbidden to take notes, students might be more inclined to develop this type of speaking.

While Robert P. Friedman, in "Why Not Debate Persuasively?" agrees that tournament debaters slight audience adaptation, he disagrees with Drum's solution. He says, "To make no distinction between debate and persuasion, as Mr. Drum suggests, is to adulterate the former." His conclusion: "train . . . debaters in logical processes" but also provide them with greater opportunities for becoming "acquainted with the principles of oral discourse." In short, train students how to debate persuasively as well as logically.

47. The Debate Judge As a Machine
Dale D. Drum

A great deal is being written these days about machines that act like men, great computers that outstrip the brain in fantastic computations, automata which take the place of manual control of complex industrial processes, and many more almost unbelievable products of man's genius for replacing himself.

However, not enough has been written about those instances where, rather than machines acting like men, men act like ma-

chines. The "genius" of man, the factor which sets him off from
the lower animals, and which makes his existence something more
than animalistic, is generally considered to be the fantastic asso-
ciative, integrative, and generalizing ability of the human cortex.

Where these forces are brought to bear on complex problems,
where these activities are characteristic of behavior, and where
these manifestations of the humanness of man are present, then it
can be said with assurance, "That is a man." But what of those
many instances where the brain of man is relegated to the role of
mere computer, analyzer, or manipulator? Then, by that degree,
man is acting more like a machine than utilizing the full potentialities of his humanness.

Of course, there are many instances where such machine-like
activities are quite legitimate. There is great need for some jobs
which are not representative of man's fullest potential but which cannot be done by either animals or machines; there are also many people who do not have the intellectual endowment to realize the best in
man; and there are many activities which are designed simply for
relaxation--such as hobbies, sports, and entertainment--where the
question of man's potential has very little meaning. However, there
are many instances where persons of high intellectual potential are
employed in handling what should be highly complex situations, situations that should call forth the best in man but which, because of
the way they are structured, do not permit the fullest realization of
human attributes.

One such example, in the opinion of this writer, is the debate
judge. Here is an instance where a person of high intellectual and
human potentiality is confronted with one of the most complex functions of the developing powers of young humans: the manipulation of
verbal symbols toward an end of reasoning, conclusion-drawing, judgment, and social progress. Certainly here, if anywhere, the fullest
powers of the human brain are called for; surely it is in this situation that one should be able to say, "This is a man--a man sitting
in human judgment so that other, younger men might learn." Such
it should be, but such it generally is not.

Consider for a moment what actually happens in the usual de-

bate.   Five people enter a room: four debaters and one judge;
there may be one or two more, a relative or two, a bored "unemployed" debater, or an unhappy "draftee" for timekeeper.   But, essentially, there are four debaters all concentrating their attention
and efforts on a single person: the judge.

As his turn arrives, each debater speaks to that judge.   He
usually speaks forcefully, not so much because he feels forceful,
but because (1) he is excited, (2) he knows this is expected of "a
winning debater, " or (3) he doesn't know any other way to present
a case.   He usually speaks carefully and deliberately, making sure
as he does so that the judge has plenty of time to write down all
that is being said.   He speaks in the clearest and most easily
copied concepts, again so that the judge's pen may not miss a syl-
lable.   And, finally, he makes sure that he is well bolstered by
small white cards which give many and varied "facts" assiduously
copied from some "authority, " because he knows that it is the ac-
cumulated weight of the "authorities" cited and not his own knowledge of the subject which will weigh most heavily with the judge.

And what does the judge do during this performance?   He
sits--because he must--at the rear of the room (probably to protect
his eardrums) and busies himself for sixty minutes writing extensive
notes gleaned from the oratory of the debaters.   It is this process
of taking notes which I should like to examine in more detail.

Consider carefully the role which the judge's notes play in a
debate tournament.   Should the judge be so daring, or so utterly
bored, as to take no notes, there is often a clamor, with the debaters' coach if not with the tournament authorities.   It is contended
that he isn't listening (since everyone knows that no one can really
listen to a speech without taking notes), that he's so prejudiced nothing the speakers could say would change his verdict (since everyone
also knows that only thoroughly bigoted people are so unfair to a
speaker as not to record his every point on paper), or, perhaps,
that he is an incompetent who knows nothing of the mechanics of debate.   This last is particularly interesting, since the complaint is
so very often couched in the term "mechanics of debate, " much as
one might speak of the "mechanics of building a Ford" or the "me-

chanics of pressing pants. "

It would seem, then, that note-taking in a debate is not simply
an aid to the memory of the judge: it is a required ritual to pla-
cate the gods and fulfill the highest expectations of the authorities.
Yet, in fact, what is the result of this?

All too often, the result is that debaters do not speak like people who have any desire for or familiarity with problems of molding
the opinions of others, but disport themselves like nothing quite so
much as a business executive dictating a letter to a secretary. Ask
a debater about the problems of persuasion, swaying the actions or
beliefs of the public, or influencing large groups and you will most
likely draw a blank, a veritable morass of misinformation, or a
stubborn wall of resistance to the very suggestion. But, ask the
same debater about the problems of making sure a stenographer (in
this case called a judge) can follow the dictation, of "being logical"
and of manipulating the "mechanics of debate" and you will get
enough information to fill a full semester's course.

Yes, the debater is certainly versed in these "mechanics."
He knows how to "size up" a judge, what the odds are that any
given line of attack will be fruitful in terms of a win or loss, what
are the most favorable positions in which to speak, and the like.
One cannot deny that, in terms of debate tournaments as they are
now constituted, the college debater is slick, clever, certain, and
almost frighteningly facile. But when it comes to problems such as
he may meet in everyday life, he is woefully lacking.

One has but to attend a typical clash between the annual debating teams from the British Isles and their foes in American garb.
These debates, performed before an audience and often without the
hovering pencil of a judge in the background, usually represent a
rather obvious victory for the English. And it is not enough to say,
simply, that the English are often older; American graduate students
would do little better than undergraduates in this matter, providing
they had been thoroughly trained in current debate techniques.

The American debater is trained to look upon the debate judge
as a machine, a machine which copies down every bit of evidence
and then, much in the manner of Eniac or Univac, ticks forth a de-

cision. And be it noted that, like the mechanical computer, the judge is supposed to have no emotions, no biases, no feelings on the matter, and, in fact, no memory.

And it is perhaps this last which is the most important factor. It is true that memory, per se, is not the criterion for "human action," but it is most certainly one very important measure and aspect of it. Yet the American debater is trained to believe that memory is a characteristic to be ignored (there will always be the judge's notes or the court reporter). One should not wonder, then, that the fantastic rate of flow of information in an American debater's speech contrasts so strikingly with the slower rate evidenced by the British.[1] The human brain is a wondrous instrument, but it cannot assimilate and remember a torrent of facts such as the average debater depends upon. The average person must have simpler and more slowly presented concepts to remember, for he has no note-pad nor does he care to have one.

The taking of notes by the judge has another effect of consequence. Since every bit of evidence is ostensibly there before him, he generally feels he must "weigh" the evidence--again like a machine--ignoring all matters of emotional impact, worth of presentation, integration of materials, and the like. And it is on precisely this point that the American debater most frequently fails. He does not integrate matters logically enough, emotionally enough, or, most important, psychologically enough to be really telling with an audience.

Debate is supposed to be a part of an educational program, and as such it is indefensible unless it can be shown that it actually does fulfill educational aims. Certainly, debaters are learning, but the question is, "What?" On the positive side of the ledger, they are learning poise, fluency, arguing, and to a certain extent, the analysis of a problem, research, and reasoning. But, unfortunately, they are also learning argumentative and persuasive techniques that are artificial and unrealistic. They are learning, not how to speak to human beings, but how to speak to machines. They are learning to present materials, in many ways not so much in human terms as the way taped information is fed into an electronic computer. They

all too often learn to be cold, uninterestingly logical, and out of
touch with persuasion as it exists in normal human intercourse and
communication.

The very fact that, even among the coaches, there is often
set up a system of classes which puts "persuasion" in one generalization and "debate" in entirely another speaks volumes. If persuasion is an aim of speaking designed to change the beliefs and/or
actions of an audience, what, then, is debate? Should it not be
aimed at the world as it is, rather than a world of science fiction
that may exist in the twenty-first century, where machines make all
the decisions? Should not persuasion in its best sense be a part of
this process which is supposed to be such an integral part of training for a democratic society?

Consequently, a radical suggestion will here be made. Suppose, for instance, that judges were forbidden to take notes. Would
chaos set in? Would darkness cover the earth? Would the world
cease to spin on its axis? I suspect not. On the contrary, the debaters might, thereby, be forced to speak as one would speak in a
normal human manner rather than as to a court stenographer; the
debater might be forced to learn how to couch his arguments in
memorable phrases, how to make points interesting, and how to
communicate in the fullest sense of the word. And, at the same
time, we might also tend, to some slight degree, to get away from
the mechanical nature of present-day debate and to make it somewhat more realistic.

Of course, it must be admitted that debate can never be
thought of as real training for a real world until the really drastic--
yet ultimately necessary--step is taken of eliminating the judge and
substituting an audience. It will only be through such forthright action that our debaters can learn to be less cold and calculating in
mechanical virtues and come down to the sometimes stupid, sometimes foolish, but always real world of human beings where emotion
and vitality are not nasty words.

The debates of the Middle Ages provided valuable training by
employing artificial and unrealistic methods, because they flourished
in an artificial and unrealistic world. But we are not living in an

artificial and unrealistic age; we are living in an age where the
realities of life are terrifyingly close and their solution of overpowering importance to the very existence of mankind. In such an
atmosphere, to take the potential leaders, the best of our youth,
and to train them in artificial and unrealistic manners better suited
to the twelfth century than the twentieth is not only foolish, it is
downright dangerous. Mankind is in no position today to allow itself
the luxury of such a waste of man's brain. We must, if we are to
fulfill our much-voiced goals of improving the democratic and communicative processes of our society, tear the blinders from debate
and make it conform in some degree with the realities of our world,
so that the awful possibilities of future conflicts may become less
and less likely.

Reprinted from Today's Speech, 4:28-31, April, 1956. At the time
this article was written, Mr. Drum was an instructor of Speech at
the Pennsylvania State University.

Notes

1. It should be noted that this refers to rate of information transfer, not word-rate.

48. Why Not Debate Persuasively?
Robert P. Friedman

This response to Mr. Drum's stimulating article[1] is offered
somewhat reluctantly, for the writer applauds much that was said.
However, Mr. Drum's analysis of current debate leads him to replace one set of problems with another, equally undesirable.

Mr. Drum's attack on debate is refreshingly new. He denies
the wisdom of continuing "a system of classes which puts 'persuasion' in one generalization and 'debate' in . . . another." He asks,
"If persuasion is an aim of speaking designed to change the beliefs
and/or actions of an audience, what, then, is debate?" The answer

to that question is that debate is a discipline designed to teach its
students the need for reliable evidence, sound reasoning, and skillful argument to establish probability on significant questions. It allows the student to test his evidence, reasoning and argument in the
heat of controversy. It develops and sharpens his logical processes.

These things it can do and does; it should not be criticized for
failing to do that which it does not profess to do. I know no teacher of speech who daily does not bemoan the shortcomings of his students when he measures them against criteria. The debate course,
more than any other in our curriculum, and debate training in our
extracurricular program help remedy these deficiencies.

Let's not remove from our forensic activities this most valuable training. To make no distinction between debate and persuasion, as Mr. Drum suggests, is to adulterate the former. Gres-
ham's economic law tells us that the introduction of a cheaper currency into a monetary system in which a dearer form is already
present serves to drive the dearer from circulation. It is reasonable to believe that persuasion, the "cheaper" commodity in the
sense that it is psychological attack (based on human motivation) invented by the speaker, will drive debate, the "dearer" commodity in
the sense that it is logical attack (based on evidence) discovered by
the speaker, from circulation. Evidence is much too precious a
commodity to be dispensed with.

What is there in Mr. Drum's article, then, that the writer
would applaud? Why the reluctance to reply? Because Mr. Drum
correctly perceives that most of our debaters

> . . . are learning, not how to speak to human beings,
> but how to speak to machines. They are learning to
> present materials, in many ways not so much in human
> terms as the way taped information is fed into an elec-
> tronic computer. They all too often learn to be cold,
> uninterestingly logical, and out of touch with persuasion
> as it exists in normal human intercourse and communi-
> cation.

Two observations are in order:

1. More often than not students who participate in extracurricular Speech activities get all or almost all their Speech training
through the forensic program. Speech courses are not required of

all students; most curricula leave the student little opportunity for
elective courses; and many students prefer to fill their available
elective hours with subjects other than Speech.

2. More often than not debate serves as the focal point of our
extracurricular Speech activities.   Many of our competitive meetings
are limited to debate; where events other than debate are scheduled,
usually they are worked into the program at odd hours and serve as
little more than side shows to the main event; and many of our students participate in debate exclusively even when other events are
available.

Mr. Drum has cited the results of these two observations:
Our debaters speak almost always to the proposition, almost never
to the audience.   When an occasional debater does find himself in
an advanced public speaking class or a persuasion course he is, as
Mr. Drum suggests, "woefully lacking." His professor is gratified
with his analysis, evidence, reasoning, and fluency, but distressed
at his inability to adapt himself and his argument to an audience.
The debater adopts an antagonistic approach and defies his hearers
to disagree with him; they find disagreement all too easy.

Frequently we do a positive disservice to our extracurricular
students. We take them as freshmen, with or without previous debate experience. We put them first into novice and then varsity
tournaments. We bring them along to the point that in their junior
and senior years they bring home consistent winning records, if not
cups and plaques, that attest to their skill. And we turn them out
after four years ill-prepared to put all their fine training to work
in just causes, ripe to have their ears pinned back by anyone who
knows how to talk to people.

If it is wise to train our debaters in logical processes, to
equip them to arrive at more circumspect and reasonable points of
view, it is also wise to teach them persuasive processes, to enable
them to gain from their listeners acceptance for those points of
view.

Our forensic programs should be modified to accommodate
these ends.

In the first place our extracurricular students should become

acquainted with the basic principles of oral discourse available to
beginning students in public speaking.   If they have had this training
or can get it through the established curriculum, fine; if not, then
our forensic program must hold itself responsible to provide instruction.   Certainly novices can work with each other to their mutual benefit on such a project; more experienced members of the
squad can assist the faculty member in charge in tutoring the novices and evaluating their efforts.

Having mastered a basic understanding of the principles of
public speaking and developed a measure of proficiency in the use
of them, the novices should move ahead into a debate program.
This program should concentrate the students' attention on logical
processes.   It should enhance their respect for the complexity of
public questions and for reliable evidence, sound reasoning, and
skillful argument in proposing solutions to these questions.   Our
current programs acquit themselves well in this measure.   Our debate tournaments keep our students close to their sources and provide them with challenges to their reasoning and their conclusions.
This portion of the students' training should be concentrated and
thorough.

But, as has been indicated, if we give our students no further
training we do them and ourselves an injustice.   We fail to prepare
them to handle themselves and their arguments before popular audiences, and, consequently, we reduce the chances for their reasoned
conclusions to be instrumental in establishing public opinion.   Training our extracurricular students in persuasion should be an integral
part of our forensic program.

This is not intended to suggest that students discontinue debating at some arbitrary point in their forensic career; I do suggest,
however, that students reach a point of diminishing returns in their
debate training, and that they can profit from an altered emphasis
after that point has been reached.   The advanced students should
continue to debate, but much of their forensic time and energy should
be channelled into the study and practice of persuasion. [2]

Every effort should be made to provide persuasive opportunities for the advanced students who participate in our forensic pro-

grams.

Many of our programs already include vehicles for this kind
of practice, although the vehicles are not, employed consistently toward that end.   Speakers bureaus exist at many schools, and most
of us try to have audience debates from time to time.   All too frequently, however, we merely transfer what happens on the debate
rostrum to the new platform.

The students sense that the situation is different but they do
not know how to cope with it.   Usually their adaptation consists of
cutting out two or three pieces of evidence to shorten their speeches
by a couple of minutes and inserting in the place of the missing evidence two or three current jokes to acknowledge to the audience that
they are aware of its existence.   Other than that the audience hears
the same logical argument that we are accustomed to hear in the debate tournament.

If the debate judge is frequently confused by some of the arguments and allusions to sources he hears employed in debates, how
much more confused is that kind of audience which is perhaps hearing the term Guaranteed Annual Wage, or whatever, for the first
time?   Better uses can be made of our occasional audiences; if
better uses were made those audiences might not be so occasional.

Mr. Drum has offered us another, perhaps the most fruitful
suggestion for providing opportunities for persuasion to our extracurricular students.   Although we should not do away with our standard debate procedures, as he suggests, we can make use of his alternative proposal as a complement to the debate tournament.   We
can institute persuasion tournaments either on the ten-and-five framework used for debate or on modifications of it.[3]

These and other means can be used to put our extracurricular
students in persuasive situations which should make our forensic
program of more value to its director, its students, and ultimately
to our society as a whole.

"The Debate Judge As a Machine" rightly senses that problems
do exist in our forensic programs, but Mr. Drum's tendency to
blame the debate judge and his ever-present pencil for these problems is unjust.   Mr. Drum suggests that if debate judges put down

their pencils and ceased taking notes,

> the debaters might, thereby, be forced to speak as one
> would speak in a normal human manner rather than as
> to a court stenographer; the debater might be forced to
> learn how to couch his arguments in memorable phrases,
> how to make points interesting, and how to communicate
> in the fullest sense of the word.

What the debate judge hears is what his alter ego, the director of forensics, teaches the debater. The debater does not have
to be "forced" to change his methods, and if he did have to be
"forced" I seriously doubt that the absence of a pencil in the judge's
hand would provide sufficient coercion. The debater has to be
taught persuasive skills and their significance, just as he was taught
debate, and the person to do that is the debate judge, himself, in
his other role--that of director of forensics.

Reprinted from Today's Speech, 5:32-34, January, 1957. At the
time this article was written, Dr. Friedman was an assistant professor of speech at Purdue University.

Notes

1. Dale D. Drum, "The Debate Judge As a Machine," Today's
    Speech, Vol. IV, No. 2, April, 1956, pp. 28-31.
2. I do not feel that this is a contradiction of my previous citation
    of Gresham's economic law and its application to speech.
    It is to be hoped that having first learned the value of the
    "dearer" commodity, evidence, the student will also learn
    that it is dearer in the spending than the hoarding. Teach-
    ing him persuasion after teaching him debate will enable
    him to spend his evidence more wisely and with greater com-
    pensation.
3. See Jack W. Murphy, "A New Look for Debate," The Speaker,
    XXXVIII, No. 1, November, 1955, pp. 3ff. for another sug-
    gestion.

<u>Should Judges Be Required to Announce Their Criteria</u>
<u>Before a Tournament</u>?

> In "Decision Debating: A Judge's Point of View, " Henry
> von Moltke argues affirmatively, because students would
> then be aware of how they were going to be judged and
> would be able to adapt themselves accordingly. This
> procedure, he believes, would eliminate some of the mis-
> understanding between judges and debaters and would ob-
> viate the latter's asking, "Why did our opponents win the
> decision?" In his rejoinder to von Moltke, "Debate Judg-
> ing and Debater Adaptation: A Reply, " Bruce Markgraf
> contends that the type of adaptation advocated "favors
> winning over truth, " and he asks rhetorically, "Should
> debaters prostitute their intellectual honesty because de-
> bate judging is not uniform . . .?" He argues, further,
> that the procedure would be impracticable, because the
> debaters, preoccupied with thoughts of their forthcoming
> debates, would be inattentive and the coaches, pressed
> for time, would limit themselves to "generalities and
> banalities. "

49. Decision Debating: A Judge's Point of View
Henry von Moltke

"We appreciate your criticism of our case and respect your
decision, but why did our opponents win the debate?" This obviously inconsistent question and others similar to it are frequently asked,
even by seasoned debaters.

To the experienced critic-judge they are warning signs of an
impending period of frustration. To the inexperienced and uninitiated
judge they are invitations to some unnerving and unsettling moments.
To both they present a classic dilemma. For the judge who chooses
to restate those factors which determined his decision will inevitably
become involved in a second debate on a more personal level. Because of the circumstances he may feel compelled to debate the side
of the question to which he gave the decision. His chances of ade-

quately justifying his decision to the satisfaction of the questioning
debaters, however, are about the same as during the original critique period. The judge, on the other hand, who attempts to circum-
vent such personal involvement by refusing to comment further on
the decision must take leave from the debaters with the feeling of
having evaded rather than resolved the problem at hand. In either
case the cause for debating has hardly been advanced.

It is not uncommon for judges to attempt to seek reasonable
answers for such disturbing questions. At face value one might argue that the judge himself probably was the motivating factor. He
may simply have failed to demonstrate clearly the strengths and
significant weaknesses of the debate case in question. Or the debaters, believing their case to be the soundest under the circumstances, may have presented it with the firm conviction that an unfavorable judgment could hardly be assessed against them. Any
judge would have difficulty changing their attitude under these circumstances.

Although these may be contributing factors, the present system
of debating may be the primary factor and should be cause for concern. For it is not what is said after the debate has taken place
that is so difficult for debaters to understand, but rather it is the
lack of interaction prior to and even during the debate between critic-
judge and debaters that lies at the heart of the problem. Thus,
while the debaters have been preparing their case without the benefit
of a specific audience or judge in mind and while they have ostensibly established their rationale for the judgment of effective debating
from their point of view, the judge brings his own criteria to bear
on the situation. Hence, the first opportunity for judge and debaters
to meet is only moments before the actual contest.

The consequence of such procedure is soon apparent even to
the inexperienced judge. Almost everyone who has been active in
judging tournament debates has observed debaters struggling to adjust their case from round to round upon the conflicting advice received during each subsequent critique session. Debaters hurrying
from one round to the next can be overheard commenting upon the
diverse opinions expressed by the judges. Thus, for example, while

a debater may hear one judge criticize his failure to develop a particular argument or line of reasoning adequately because it "is of
basic consequence and obvious to the case, " he may be penalized by
another judge for spending too much time on the argument which
"is basic to the case and rather obvious. " Or while one judge, finding the affirmative and negative teams to have developed their cases
with approximately equal skill, decides that he is "entirely justified
in deciding a debate on the basis of delivery alone, "[1] another judge
might refrain from making such a decision because he agrees with
the view that after all, "delivery . . . is only the vehicle of communicating ideas; of far greater importance are the ideas themselves. "[2]

The conscientious critic-judge, bent upon establishing realistic
criteria for the evaluation of debates, realizes all too soon that even
the source books on this subject lend little structure to the development of sound debating standards.   Consulting them he may learn
that "fortunately or not, definite rules and regulations cannot be applied in debate procedures as they are in athletic events. "[3] Further,
he may discover that the critic-judge is expected to "evaluate both
students and teams in terms of some absolute standard of what he
considers effective debating. "[4] But perhaps of greatest consequence
will be the discovery that "since judgments are relative, even the
most expert of judges will frequently disagree, especially in close
debates. "[5] This contention is corroborated by a recent survey in
which 244 college teachers with coaching experience were unable to
reach complete agreement on any one of forty items listed in reference to ethical debating practices.[6] Thus, with these findings in
mind, the probability of winning a debate would seem to depend
more upon presenting the right aspects of the case to the right judge
at the right time.   What aspects of a given case are considered
right, however, is a moot question since the criteria for judgment
may vary from one judge to another.

Admittedly, sincere attempts have been made to insure greater uniformity among judges' criteria and decisions. Perhaps the
best example of such attempts is the use of a uniform debate ballot
with elaborate and sometimes intricate rating scales. But such de-

vices apparently have not succeeded as well as desired.[7] The introduction of hybrid forms of debate which permit members of opposing teams to interact with one another makes some allowance for
adaptation of material to the circumstances and the occasion. However, such devices, instituted for other reasons, also fail to provide
the critic-judge with an opportunity to indicate to the contestants
what he deems appropriate, important, and necessary to effective
debating. In comparison, most students of public speaking courses
receive detailed instructions regarding the goals and objectives of
an assignment prior to the presentation of their speeches. While
this is also true of the debating situation the analogy ends here, for
the individual who establishes the goals and objectives to be achieved
in the public speaking situation also assumes the role of critic-judge
in the classroom. Thus, the student is aware of the evaluator's
criteria for judgment even while making his initial preparations.

At present, critic-judges participating in debate tournaments
are frequently invited individually or as a group to speak on one or
more aspects of decision debating. It is at this point that such
topics as Analysis of the Case, Refutation and Rebuttal, The Role
of Evidence, and Delivery are presented. Such discussions usually
occur upon completion of the event when the results are being tabu-
lated. While such procedure undoubtedly is educationally profitable
it falls short of being of utmost value because of two basic reasons.
First, the debaters are preoccupied during this period with such
matters as their final standing in the tournament and second, the
topics which were of great importance prior to and during the event
are being discussed after the fact. Consequently, giving each participating judge a few minutes to present his interpretation of the
items listed on the debate ballot prior to the tournament, for instance, might be more desirable from the debaters' vantage point
simply because they are infinitely more attentive and receptive to
any last words of advice. Such procedure might also have a bene-
ficial effect upon the judges for it may induce them to reevaluate
their standards and most important, produce a closer proximity
among the criteria used for judgment.

The implementation of such a plan may take on many forms

limited only by the circumstances of the contest itself and the re-
sourcefulness of the sponsors involved. The practice of having to
answer the question "Why did our opponents win the decision?" after
the critique session may decrease in frequency, and the critic-judge
may experience an added degree of confidence and pleasure in the
task of judging debates.

Reprinted from The Journal of the American Forensic Association,
1:98-100, September, 1964. Mr. von Moltke is Assistant Professor
of Speech at Kent State University.

Notes

1. Dallas C. Dickey, "The Judging of Debates," in Argumentation
   and Debate, ed. David Potter, New York, 1954, p. 417.
2. Arthur N. Kruger, Modern Debate, New York, 1960, p. 370.
3. Dickey, p. 414.
4. Waldo W. Braden and Earnest Brandenburg, Oral Decision-
   Making, New York, 1955, p. 524.
5. Dickey, p. 419.
6. Donald Klopf and James McCroskey, "Ethical Practices in Debate," Journal of the American Forensic Association, 1:13-
   16, January, 1964.
7. For a series of illustrations concerning the diversity of decisions made by judges evaluating the same contests see
   Kruger, p. 363fn.

50. Debate Judging and Debater Adaptation: A Reply
Bruce Markgraf

Having studied Mr. Henry von Moltke's article entitled, "Decision Debating: A Judge's Point of View," which recently appeared
in the Journal of the American Forensic Association (September,
1964) and taking exception to what he has written, I would like to
make several observations.

Mr. von Moltke is troubled, as are many, by the absence of
uniformity of standards in debate judging, and in particular, the con-
sequential confusion and frustration felt by debaters during and after
critique sessions. Present practice, he contends, inserts judges

into uncomfortable situations whenever they orally analyze a debate
and defend, especially to the losers, their decisions. What lies at
the heart of this problem, he observes, " . . . is the lack of interaction prior to and even during the debate between critic-judge and
debaters . . . ." This lack, according to Mr. von Moltke, is detrimental because it leaves debaters unaware of the personal preferences and criteria of decision-making of the judges before debates
begin; therefore, unlike the public speaking classroom situation
wherein students are provided with judgment data prior to performances, debaters are unable to adapt cases and arguments to individual critics. The consequence of this is often revealed by debaters
at tournaments who adjust their cases and lines of attack from
round to round as each judge urges this or that for improvement.
But debaters become confused and discouraged because while Judge
A likes White, Judge B prefers Black. Mr. von Moltke seems surprised and disturbed at the fact that expert judges frequently disagree on a debate decision and concludes lamentably that: " . . .
the probability of winning a debate would seem to depend more upon
presenting the right aspects of the case to the right judge at the
right time. What aspects of a given case are considered right, however, is a moot question since the criteria for judgment may vary
from one judge to another."

I suggest that the ultimate goal of debaters is to present what
the debaters believe to be the strongest case, logic, evidence, argument, etc. which support their side of the resolution. If a judge
criticizes a certain method or argument, it does not become the
task or obligation of the debaters to automatically adapt and change;
debaters are not machines, although a number of coaches train them
as such. It is the task of debaters to evaluate for themselves criticism in terms of what they hold to be the strongest possible case
which they can deliver. Debaters should think; they should accept
and discard. Mr. von Moltke seems to assume that debaters heed
on face value any critical comment and reform accordingly.

Mr. von Moltke advocates that debaters adapt their cases to
the particular eccentricities and preferences of each judge. An attitude which urges specific adaptation at the expense of what debaters

hold to be strength is one which favors winning over truth and learning. Should debaters prostitute their intellectual honesty because debate judging is not uniform and at times based upon prejudice? If
judges legitimately weigh differently the value of Analysis, Evidence,
and Refutation, may not debaters do so also? This does not suggest that debaters do not learn and change from hearing criticism.

　　To remedy the problem of uncomfortable and often meaning-
less oral critique periods and to encourage specific adaptation to
specific judges, Mr. von Moltke advocates providing prior to any
tournament a platform for each judge to present in a few minutes'
time his interpretation of the debate ballot. He fails to realize that
for some tournaments which attract over forty schools this occasion
will consume time exceeding two hours. He predicts, because his
proposed session is to occur prior to the debates, that students
will be more attentive to matters discussed than they are during ab-
breviated judging symposia held presently at the conclusion of a
small number of tournaments because the students under the latter
circumstances are usually prepossessed by final team tabulations
and fail to comprehend the relevance of evaluation analysis after the
fact. It appears, however, that debaters would be just as inatten-
tive during the proposed early meeting because of the length of the
session, the undoubted repetition of remarks, and their own preoc-
cupation with their forthcoming debates. Coaches during such an assembly could deliver in a few minutes' time generalities and banali-
ties only. Each would present a set speech, and after several tournaments each speech by each coach would sound alike. A coach's
preparatory thinking might run: "Professor Smith considers Delivery to be important. His teams win a lot, so I'll also say that Delivery is important; certainly wouldn't want to clash publicly with
him. In fact, to be safe, I'll say that Everything's important, which
is true, I'm sure." I am convinced that the remarks of coaches
over a period of time would become more glittering and longer; I
am convinced also of the great discrepancy between professed ideals
and actual debate judging.

　　During their initial stage such meetings would prompt some debaters to prepare coach casebooks which would eventually come fitted

with photographs and minutiae and, as heirlooms and exam files, would be handed down from year to year to new debaters. Tournament hosts would soon rent at cost portable computers so that debaters could more easily reshuffle, substitute, add, and twist file cards and cases the moment any round's judge was discovered. Wise coaches would dispatch to tournaments eight or ten debaters in order to field proper teams: Judge X prefers smoothies, Judge Y likes machines, Judge Z enjoys girls in sweaters. I do not mean to appear absurd while stretching; I mean only to indicate the implausibility of the proposal.

Mr. von Moltke is convinced, upon implementation of his plan or one similar, that, "The practice of [the critic-judge] having to answer the question 'Why did our opponents win the decision?' after the critique session may decrease in frequency . . ." I submit that no amount of general discussion by coaches concerning evaluation procedures is going to dissipate the problem of determining, examining, and explaining individual decisions given within the contexts of individual debates.

Mr. von Moltke's proposal emphasizes, to debate's detriment, the goal of winning over that of truth and learning. Let debaters, knowledgeable in debate technique (including general standards of evaluation) and in the topic, strive to develop on their own, without regard for extraneous data concerning minor preferences of possible judges, the strongest possible case, and let the critic-judges be damned. The responsibility for objectiveness lies with the judges; debaters have no responsibility to cater to critic whims. Of utmost immediate concern in tournament debating is the encouragement of the highest standards for judgment; this concern is subverted when debaters are urged to stoop to hour by hour adaptation to judges. Such encouragement admits to debaters the failure of us judges. It is our responsibility to demand from debaters their strongest possible case and argument and to judge it accordingly. Are we up to it?

Reprinted from the Journal of the American Forensic Association, 3:37-39, January, 1966. Mr. Markgraf is Assistant Professor of English and Speech at Wesleyan University, Middletown, Connecticut.

Issue Z: Should Debate Judges Be Permitted to Halt a Debate at
the End of the Second Affirmative Speech?

> In "The Prima Facie Case: A Modest Proposal," Bruce
> Markgraf recommends the procedure used in criminal
> courts. After the prosecution has presented its case,
> the defense routinely asks for dismissal on the grounds
> that the former did not establish a prima facie case. If
> the judge agrees, the debate is over; and the defense
> wins without having to present its case. Markgraf con-
> tends that several significant advantages would accrue
> from a similar procedure in academic debate: it would
> alert affirmative teams to their burden of proof and re-
> sult in better affirmative cases; it would save valuable
> time if the affirmative obviously has failed in its obliga-
> tion; and it would permit "on-the-spot" critiques. In
> dissenting, Robert L. Scott, in "The Problem of the
> Prima Facie Case: A Reply to Mr. Markgraf," ques-
> tions Markgraf's assumption that academic debates should
> be judged on the basis of issues. As an advocate of the
> skills school of judging, he believes that decisions should
> be based on "which team did the better job of debating"
> and declares, "I have often voted for an affirmative team
> which did not in my opinion make a prima facie case for
> the proposition." (Shades of the Wells-O'Neill debate.)

51. The Prima Facie Case: A Modest Proposal
Bruce Markgraf

The story goes that an Indian chieftain and a representative of
the United States Department of the Interior held a debate in the late
1870's on the federal government's right to appropriate Indian terri-
tory. Supporting the affirmative, the representative spoke at length
before relinquishing the floor to the chief. The old Indian remained
cross-legged smoking a pipe. The representative, embracing silence
as an acknowledgment of surrender, promptly took to the platform
again to pound home his arguments. Finally finished, he once more
invited the chief to speak. No response. The debate had ended.

As the smiling representative mounted his horse for the return trip
to his agency, the wise chief remarked to a friend: "Need say nothing till he proves a case." The Indian had won the debate, though
of course had lost his lands.

The prima facie case has been defined as ". . . a case which
in and of itself establishes good and sufficient reason for adopting
the proposition unless it is successfully refuted or weakened."[1] It
is the minimum burden of the affirmative team. Authorities suggest,
as did our Indian friend, that the establishment of a prima facie
case is independent of any negative response, and that the negative
is not obligated to speak until the affirmative confronts it with such
a case. Marsh[2] writes in The Gavel: "My position is that regardless of what (or even whether) the negative answers [it] is immaterial to the affirmative's establishment of a prima facie case."
McBurney, O'Neill, and Mills[3] note: "Theoretically, the negative
is not called upon to reply until the affirmative has set out a prima
facie case." Freeley[4] points out that, "Unless the affirmative team
establish a prima facie case, they cannot logically win a debate.
Actually the negative need not even reply to the affirmative until the
affirmative has established a prima facie case." Rowland and Eubank[5] state: "After the affirmative has established a prima-facie
case, it is the responsibility of the negative to respond."

Occasionally debate judges hear an affirmative case which, in
their opinion, is not prima facie; often, after thirty minutes, the
judge is satisfied that the negative has gained (but hardly earned)
the decision simply because the affirmative team has failed to support its burden. As Kruger[6] states: "If, at the conclusion of the
debate, the judge feels that the affirmative did not present a prima
facie case, that is, a case believable on the face of it if there had
been no negative refutation, the judge is obliged to vote against the
affirmative." I am sure that most of us have anxiously awaited the
end of such a debate; so have negative teams. They are handicap-
ped, however, because they cannot objectively learn what the judge
is thinking. Consequently, negative teams have been forced to attack cases which by themselves, do not logically stand. And judges
have been forced to sit by idly.

I believe that we should institute a debate convention that would eliminate this problem which both judges and debaters encounter at least once each season.

The convention might be as follows: After the second affirmative constructive speech, the second negative speaker would rise and say: "I submit that the affirmative has failed to prove a prima facie case." If the judge agreed, he would respond by saying: "It has so failed." If he held the opposite, that the affirmative had presented up to this point a prima facie case (which he would probably do 95 percent of the time), he would say: "It has not failed in its obligation." If the judge's response were the latter, the negative team would continue in its usual manner. If, however, the judge supported the claim that the affirmative had failed to meet its responsibility by not advancing a prima facie case, the negative could elect one of several options. It could continue as usual. It could relinquish its second constructive speech and first rebuttal. (The affirmative would be hard pressed, within the requirements and confines of rebuttal speeches, to transform their case into a prima facie one. It might be proper to advocate here that if the affirmative has not supported a prima facie case by the end of the second affirmative speech, the judge could stop the debate and award his decision to the negative.) Thirdly, and most likely, the negative could choose to move directly into a presentation of negative constructive arguments oblivious of the affirmative case.

Such a convention would aid in making affirmative teams more conscious of the fact that the burden of proof lies on their shoulders; it is reasonable to assume that there would be fewer instances of absent prima facie cases. It would eliminate the practice of negative teams devising arguments to use against a case which by itself does not stand. It would permit judges to either stop a debate or help determine its course, thus preventing a waste of valuable time for all concerned. It would permit on-the-spot critiques concerning an important, and often neglected, part of debating.

Let us borrow the essence of a courtroom procedure, shaping it to our own ends, in order to help make debate even more realistic and practical than it is presently.

Reprinted from the Speaker and Gavel, 1:27-28, November, 1963.
Dr. Markgraf is an Assistant Professor of Speech at Wesleyan University.

Notes

1. Austin J. Freeley, Argumentation and Debate, San Francisco,
   Wadsworth Publishing Co., 1961, p. 18.
2. Patrick O. Marsh, "Letter to the Editor, " The Gavel, Vol. 45,
   No. 3, March, 1963, p. 56.
3. James H. McBurney, James M. O'Neill, and Glen E. Mills,
   Agrumentation and Debate, New York, The Macmillan Co.,
   1951, p. 161.
4. Freeley, p. 19.
5. A. Westley Rowland and Wayne C. Eubank, "Organizing the
   Case, " in Argumentation and Debate, ed. by David Potter,
   Holt-Dryden, 1954, p. 65.
6. Arthur N. Kruger, Modern Debate: Its Logic and Strategy,
   New York, McGraw-Hill Book Co., Inc., 1960, p. 369.

52. The Problem of the Prima Facie Case:
A Reply to Mr. Markgraf
Robert L. Scott

   In the November, 1963 number of the Speaker and Gavel, Professor Bruce Markgraf set before us a modest proposal, i.e., that
the second negative speaker in a traditionally patterned debate might
assert, "I submit that the affirmative has failed to prove a prima
facie case." This challenge would be sustained or overruled by the
judge. Mr. Markgraf claims two advantages for the proposal.
First, the "convention, " which he believes derivative from courtroom
procedure, would "help make debate even more realistic and practical than it is presently." The second I find implied rather than directly asserted--it would shorten and enliven some dull, pointless
debates in which negative teams are "forced to attack cases which
by themselves do not logically stand" and judges are forced "to sit
by idly. "[1]
   I find myself in nearly complete disagreement with the case
Professor Markgraf has made. But at least his proposal, if accept-

ed, would throw into bold relief the question of what prima facie means, a question which I do not find simple and to which I once addressed an article.[2] Not all argumentation texts use the term and most of those that do, I have argued in the article mentioned, give definitions which are vague and probably circular. Most debaters I have heard use the term seem to mean roughly "good case." I would contend, then, that when a judge would hear such a challenge under the Markgraf proposal he would have at best a scant notion of what the debater meant. His sustaining or overruling the challenge, at any rate, would depend on his own meaning for the term.

Let me make clear an assumption about judging intercollegiate or interscholastic debates. The only question that the judge should ask in making a decision is, "Which team did the better job of debating?" An analogous question most emphatically is not the basic query for a judge or a jury to ask when directing a court case. I have often voted for an affirmative team which did not in my opinion make a prima facie case for the proposition. One is probably seldom happy in trying to decide which is the poorer debating--failing to make a prima facie case or failing to seize upon the peculiar weakness of such a case. But ordinarily there are also other questions the judge will ask himself about the general quality of the debating he has heard in rendering a decision. However, if one disagrees with this basic point of view toward debate judging, one might very well disagree with my attitude toward prima facie questions.

In making any analogy, one must consider dissimilarities. We have already pointed to one which applies to the comparison of academic debating and courtroom debating. In reference to prima facie questions, we should recognize that the courts have in the written law and in precedent a body of rather well-defined requirements which help decide whether or not a particular set of arguments is acceptable on its face.[3] College and high school debaters do not have this advantage except insofar as the stock-issue analysis serves the purpose in regard to propositions of policy.

"The affirmative has not argued that the supposed problems are inherent in the present system." This charge, which reflects

stock-issue analysis, asserts in effect that the case is not prima
facie complete even though the negative may not realize this implication. As a matter of fact, we often hear the negative make arguments which come down to "the affirmative has not presented a
prima facie case." These instances demonstrate that attacks on
cases which are not complete and/or consistent (a phrase which I
contend can ordinarily be substituted for prima facie) may not be
artificial or "forced." If under the present practices a judge is
"forced to sit by idly" wondering why the negative doesn't say,
"This case is not acceptable on its face," he might, if Mr. Markgraf's proposal were to become conventional, be moved to ask a
negative who makes the challenge, "Just why do you believe that it
is not a prima facie case?" That is, he might be so moved if he
is interested in understanding what a particular negative speaker
means and in evaluating his argument.

Although a case which is not prima facie does not require rebuttal in a close sense of the word, it does in ordinary debate require a reply. Presumably the affirmative is unaware that the case
presented is not acceptable on its face. Should the negative debaters assume that without further explanation every listener (or at
least the judge) will also see what the affirmative debaters have
failed to see? A good debater should be able to point out the in-
completeness and/or inconsistency of the affirmative's contentions
and will probably wish to do so. (If non-prima facie becomes a
conventional challenge, should a judge assume that the debater making it understands the force of the charge against a particular case
or that he's just taking a I-have-little-to-lose-anyway risk?)

My own opinion is that every negative should form the habit of
considering each case he hears as possibly failing to be acceptable
on its face. The fact that he "cannot learn objectively what the
judge is thinking" will not necessarily keep him from doing so. If
he decides that the case is not prima facie acceptable, he should
consider replying in this manner: "Let us assume that everything
the affirmative said is true. Even so, it does not follow that we
should accept the proposition because. . . ."

Prima facie questions are fundamentally logical questions, i.e., they refer us to the form of the argument. Accepting the premises, does the conclusion follow? For example, it seems to me that a majority of the affirmative cases which I have heard this year in support of the proposition Minnesota high schools are debating (Resolved: that social security benefits be extended to provide complete medical care) are not prima facie.

Most of these cases come down to the following sequence. The cost of medical care is high and going higher. Comparatively the income of persons over 65 years of age is low. Therefore, these persons are unable to provide adequately for their own medical care. This is only the "need," to use the jargon of stock-issue analysis, but we need not go further since it is here that the problem lies. A possible negative response is, "Even if these two contentions are true, the conclusion does not necessarily follow." But a negative speaker will probably want to explain why he does not think that conclusion follows. As a judge, I would much prefer to hear his explanation than to sustain or overrule a conventional challenge as Mr. Markgraf modestly proposes be possible.

What I have tried to illustrate I call the "first level"[4] of prima facie questioning, i.e., is the case considered as a whole acceptable on its face? Each contention in turn may be taken as a unit and considered from the viewpoint, prima facie? This second level of prima facie questioning makes possible the interesting prospect of the affirmative's turning the charge against the negative. For example, a negative may contend that since the income of persons over 65, when one takes into account the fact of tax advantages and lower family size, compares very favorably per capita with the average incomes of persons under 65, therefore, older persons certainly can provide readily for their own medical care. As a matter of fact, I heard a negative make this argument on the proposition referred to above. The affirmative could reply that this argument is not prima facie. It assumes that persons under 65 can provide readily for their medical needs, which has not been argued and need not be accepted. Further the argument assumes that the medical needs of both age groups are comparable, another assumption that need not be accepted.

372   Counterpoint: Debates about Debate

This final illustration raises another point. Lawyers talk about prima facie evidence. A third level of prima facie questioning asks, "What sort of data are sufficient to establish an alleged fact as a fact?" Again legal usage has some well-established conventions which ordinary argument does not have. An attack which asserts that "the data are not sufficient to establish the fact alleged" always in my opinion needs explanation in ordinary argument.

Thus I would conclude that the term prima facie might be useful, but it points to systems of analysis which must be understood and applied. The arguer will be unwise if he assumes that everyone will see a case, contention, or a set of data as he does. Further, he will be unwise if he assumes that his listeners will necessarily share his knowledge of particular schemes of analysis. He will, therefore, not simply peg his refutation on a few technical terms.

It is the job of a debater to make cogent replies to arguments. It is the job of his teachers to help him learn to do so. The task of judges is to evaluate the quality of the debating he does.

Incidentally, although I failed to mention it earlier, I do not believe that Mr. Markgraf made a prima facie case for his modest proposal. Would I have been wise to have simply said this at the outset? Well, I chose to make my case on other grounds. But the alternative course certainly would have saved time.

Reprinted from the Speaker and Gavel, 1:81-83, March, 1964. Dr. Scott is Professor of Speech and Theatre Arts at the University of Minnesota.

Notes

1. Bruce Markgraf, "The Prima Facie Case: A Modest Proposal," Speaker and Gavel, Vol. 1, No. 1, November, 1963, pp. 27-28.
2. "On the Meaning of the Term Prima-Facie in Argumentation," Central States Speech Journal, Vol. XII, No. 1, 1960, pp. 33-37.
3. William T. Foster gives an interesting example of this fact. If a farmer should sue a railroad for damages resulting from a burned field, it would be enough for his lawyer to prove that a fire did occur and that it was kindled by the engine.

He would not be required to prove that any member of the
crew was negligent or that the engine or any equipment was
defective. The elements of the prima facie case (the fire
and its source) have been set by practice for this category
of claims (see Argumentation and Debating [New York, 1945],
pp. 247-249).
4. Scott, op. cit., p. 34.

Suggestions for Further Reading

Barker, Larr L. "An Investigation of Judging Practices in Debate,"
    Speaker and Gavel, 2:22-23, November, 1964.
Bauer, Otto F., and C. William Colburn. "The Maverick Judge,"
    Journal of the AFA, 3:22-25, January, 1966.
Covelli, Eugene F. "Debate: Won or Lost?--James M. O'Neill's
    Legacy," Speaker and Gavel, 4:60-63, March, 1967.
Harvey, P. Casper. "How Shall Debates Be Judged?" NEA Jour-
    nal, 13:108, March, 1924.
Hufford, Roger. "Toward Improved Tournament Judging," Journal
    of the AFA, 2:120-125, September, 1965.
Kruger, Arthur N. "Judging Debate," Sec. XVIII, op. cit., pp.
    299-311.
_____. "The Debate Judge as Critical Thinker," Today's
    Speech, 5:29-31, January, 1957.
McCroskey, James C. "Fifty Articles in Fifty Years: A Selected
    Annotated Bibliography on Debate Judging, 1915-1964," Journal
    of the AFA, 1:67-69, May, 1964.
McCroskey, James C., and Leon R. Camp. "Judging Criteria and
    Judges' Bias in Debate," Journal of the AFA, 3:57-62, May,
    1966.
Musgrave, George M. "The Wells-O'Neill Controversy," Debaters
    Magazine, 2:218-220, 251-254, December, 1946.
O'Neill, James M. "Judging Debates," Quarterly Journal of Speech,
    3:336-355, October, 1917; 4:76-92, January, 1918.
_____. "The Juryman's Vote in Debate," Quarterly Journal of
    Speech, 3:346-355, October, 1917.
Parker, W.W. "Why Should Debates Be Judged?" NEA Journal, 13:
    301, November, 1924.
Sarett, Lew R. "The Expert Judge of Debate," Quarterly Journal
    of Speech, 3:135-139, April, 1917.
_____. "A Juryman-Critic's Vote," Quarterly Journal of Speech,
    4:428-433, October, 1918.
Weiss, Robert O. "Judgment and Decision-Making," Journal of the
    AFA, 1:43-47, May, 1964.
Wells, Hugh N. "Judging Debates," Quarterly Journal of Speech,
    3:336-345, October, 1917.
Williams, Frederick, and Sally Ann Webb. "Factors in Debate Eval-
    uation," Central States Speech Journal, 15:126-128, May, 1964.